BY SEA AND LAND

Robin Neillands is a journalist and travel writer, with a growing reputation as a popular military and medieval historian. He is currently researching a History of Special Forces. He served in 45 Commando, Royal Marines, during the 1950s and lives in London.

By the same author

The Desert Rats:
7th Armoured Division, 1940–45

The Raiders: The Army Commandos, 1940–45

D-Day, 1944: Voices from Normandy
(with Roderick de Normann)

The Conquest of the Reich: Germany 1945

Wellington and Napoleon: Clash of Arms

The Dervish Wars: Gordon and Kitchener
in the Sudan

A Fighting Retreat:
The British Empire, 1947–1997

BY SEA AND LAND

THE STORY OF THE ROYAL MARINES COMMANDOS

ROBIN NEILLANDS

CASSELL&CO

Cassell Military Paperbacks

Cassell & Co
Wellington House, 125 Strand
London WC2R 0BB

British Library Cataloguing-in-Publication Data
A catalogue record for this book is available from the British Library

ISBN 0-304-35683-2

Printed and bound in Great Britain by
Guernsey Press, Guernsey, C.I.

They received, each for his own memory, praise
that will never die, and with it the grandest
of all sepulchres, not that in which their
mortal bones are laid, but a home in the minds
of men, where their glory remains fresh ...

Pericles

Major-General Julian Thompson, CB, OBE, retired after a long and successful career in the Royal Marines, a service spent entirely with the Commando Units, moving from second-lieutenant to command 3 Commando Brigade, Royal Marines, during the war in the South Atlantic. Since leaving the Corps, he has turned to writing and his first book on 3 Commando Brigade in the Falklands, *No Picnic*, enjoyed considerable success.

Contents

Maps

Major-General Julian Thompson, CB, OBE

Although there have been a number of books written about the Royal Marines Commandos, or books with substantial sections about them included in the text, a fuller account of their deeds both in action and in more relaxed moments has long been overdue. Rob Neillands, who served in 45 Commando, has recognized this and, perhaps more important, seen the need to collect stories from the men who served in the Commandos during the Second World War before memories fade, or the old Commando soldiers die.

The formation of the Royal Marines Commandos in 1942 came at a critical period in Royal Marines history; the Royal Marines Division was kicking its heels in England, having taken part in only one operation since its formation in 1939. It appeared that nobody wanted it and Rob Neillands explains why. The Royal Marines' role at sea, in cruisers, battleships and carriers was an anachronism and had been so since the late nineteenth century. This is no slur on their loyal and courageous service with the Fleet, but their employment in jobs that could just as well be done by others, was the result of a total lack of any amphibious doctrine in the Royal Navy, so much so that the greatest fleet the world had ever seen (until the emergence of the US Navy in the Second World War) had no amphibious capability and consequently no ability to project their power ashore, and apparently did not want to, perhaps because of strategic and tactical myopia in failing to understand that navies can lose wars but cannot win them. Wars are won by men seizing and holding ground, and if this has to be done from the sea, it is best done by men who are trained and equipped for this specialized amphibious role.

The birth of the Royal Marines Commandos was not

without its problems, with detractors both inside and outside the Corps of Royal Marines. The critics outside, the Army Commandos, jibed that the Royal Marines Commandos were not volunteers and were attempting to usurp a role created by the Army Commandos. On both counts these were pretty spurious charges. Although Royal Marines battalions were converted directly into commandos, the unfit were weeded out and the faint-hearted 'voted with their feet', requesting a transfer to a less demanding assignment. There is an interesting analogy here with the splendid parachute battalions of 6 Airborne Division in the Second World War, who were raised in the same way from infantry battalions, and were able to carry their battalion *esprit* into their new role, and were sometimes regarded disparagingly as 'non-volunteers' by the battalions of the 1st Parachute Brigade in 1 Airborne Division. As to taking over an Army Commando role, this is precisely what they, the Army, had done to the Royal Marines in the first place! However, these petty jealousies were very largely forgotten in the forge of battle where shared experience soon breeds mutual respect. Today there are over 1,000 Army Commando soldiers in the Royal Marines Commando Brigade, all much respected and fondly regarded members of the green beret family.

A more serious, and certainly more long-lasting problem, was the suspicion with which the Royal Marines Commandos were regarded within their own Corps. This persisted well into the late 1950s, and as a young officer I can remember the overweight gunnery instructors at the Royal Marines Barracks, Eastney, the last foot-hold of the blue-bereted, sea-service Marines, making disparaging remarks about the Commandos. As I suspected that their antipathy was based on a disinclination to swap the peacetime shipboard existence of three square meals a day, a tot of rum and a warm bed at night for the 'mud, sweat and tears' of Commando life, their remarks merely served to strengthen my aim of never serving at sea in a ship's detachment, and to spend the majority of my service in the Commandos – I achieved both. I am happy to state that those days of 'them' and 'us' have long since gone; many gunnery instructors re-trained in Commando skills, and acquitted themselves with distinction in our campaigns, from Aden to Borneo. Today, everyone in the Royal Marines, except recruits, wears the green beret as a symbol of having passed the Commando course, and the unfit are still weeded out and the faint-hearted still 'vote with their feet'. Everyone in the Royal Marines Commandos is a volunteer and no one is there who does not wish to be.

It is good to see that Rob Neillands has included in this book many accounts by Marines and Non-Commissioned Officers. In other activities man may propose and God dispose, but in any form of soldiering the reverse applies; commanders may propose but the soldiers dispose. Having served as a commander at every level from platoon to brigade, I was always well aware that the success of any operation rested in the hands of 30, or 100, or 750, or 5,000 men, mostly in their early twenties and late teens. It was their battlecraft, cunning, courage, humour and ability to 'stick it' which would decide the day, however brilliant my plan, and indeed, they would wrest success from the pot-mess of a bad plan. 'It will depend upon that article over there,' said the Duke of Wellington, pointing to a private soldier sight-seeing in Brussels on the eve of Waterloo. Although I would hesitate to refer to the peerless men of the Royal Marines Commandos as 'articles', the sentiment holds good to this day and always will. Like their gallant forebears of the Second World War, Korea, Suez, and many other campaigns since, the Royal Marines Commandos continue to do 'whatsoever the Queen commandeth'.

Julian Thompson

Preface

This is the story of a fighting force. It is the story of the Royal Marines Commandos during the first forty years of their existence, told in the words of the men themselves, from 1942, when the first Royal Marines Commando unit, No 40, went into the shellfire before the beaches of Dieppe during World War II, to 1982, when the three Commandos, which now make up the cutting edge of 3 Commando Brigade, Royal Marines, went ashore in the Falkland Islands during the South Atlantic campaign.

During the intervening years, the number of Commando units raised by the Corps of Royal Marines rose briefly to nine, and Corps' records recall only one year between 1942 and 1982 when the Royal Marines Commandos were not in action somewhere in the world. The story of these nine units is therefore a complex and exciting one, and so it seems wise to explain at the start, what this book is about, the problems presented in telling the tale, and how they have been tackled.

Four of these units, Nos 44, 46, 47 and 48 (Royal Marine) Commandos, knew only a brief if glorious existence during World War II. Others, like 41 and 43 Commandos saw a brief post-war revival, notably when 41 (Independent) Commando was raised for Korea. Three others, Nos 40, 42 and 45 Commandos, Royal Marines, have managed to endure to the present day, although not without certain changes, but since the continuity is not universal, I have elected to tell this story, not by unit but *by campaign*. To keep the complexity to a minimum, I have been ruthless in eliminating all but the most necessary references to other units or arms of the Corps which fall outside my main brief.

There will, therefore, be few tales here of the Army Commandos, of Force Viper, of 30 AU, of the Royal Marines Special Boat Squadron, or of the countless other units of the Corps, the Army, the Royal Navy and Royal Air Force, other than when and if they abut directly onto the exploits of my subject, the Royal Marines Commandos. It has also been necessary to leave out many personal stories and details of such activites as the Corps' participation in the Oman, to give but one example. Please note that no disrespect is intended by this or any other omission; there simply isn't the space. I found that in attempting to give due acknowledgement to everyone involved, the storyline was becoming enmeshed in a web of detail. That the Royal Marines Commandos owe and acknowledge a debt to other arms need not be doubted, and such acknowledgements are made regularly by the Marines Commandos themselves in their own words throughout this book. The stories and the amount of detail available has depended very much on the willingness of those who served in these units to tell me about them, so that the amount of coverage given to each unit does vary from time to time and place to place, but I am grateful, and record more fully elsewhere, the debt I owe to those Royal Marines Commandos who wrote to me from all over the world, and told me about their unit and their friends. It has been said that I favour 45 Commando too much in Chapter 12. Well, 45 people came forward, and I once served in 45 myself, so . . .

It should also be made clear that this is not intended as an 'authorized' or 'official' history. The story of the Commando units is told here in the words of the men who served i.. them, and by whom the traditions and reputations of these units were so well and firmly established. I have attempted to leave their stories exactly as I heard or received them, adding no more than a few commas. There may be errors implicit in this method of writing history, for memories grow dim over the years, but these tales of great deeds done are ever fresh and should not be forgotten.

This is not, therefore, one of those histories written by post-war observers or commentators, or compiled from the memories of the Commanding General – though Generals have contributed generously to the following pages – but eyewitness accounts of battles and campaigns in the words of the men who fought them, from Rifle Troop Marine to Commanding Officer. I have been at some pains to collect 'other-rank' stories, for their accounts are all too often neglected in military histories, which can lead to the impression that the role of the Marine or private soldier in battle is to stand around in watchful admiration while the officers do the work. Here again, in bringing the men downstage, no disrespect is intended. The attuition among the officers recounted by their men in the pages which follow, as well as the respect and affection which one rank holds for another, speaks for itself.

There is one other problem which needs an airing. With the end of compulsory military service, the public in general today has little contact with the serving soldier. His life, outlook, attitudes, ways of speech, are increasingly foreign to the man or woman in the street, and I have had to take this into account when selecting my words, terms or phrases. Simply for the sake of clarity, I have also had the manuscript read by a layman, Paul Reynolds, and explained more fully any term he found confusing or inexplicable. Service readers will see the need for this, and for a certain amount of background, as well as for only fleeting references to the more arcane details of Service life, calibres, words of command, ranks, jargon and so on . . . absorbing stuff perhaps, but it can clog the flow. To help those with no Service experience I have added a small glossary of terms.

Behind the exploits of the Royal Marines Commandos stands the long and distinguished history of their parent Corps, the Royal Marines which, as part of the Naval Service, established those traditions of amphibious warfare, discipline and training; and which provided, and still provides, the bedrock on which the Royal Marines Commandos stand. The Corps has also given the Royal Marines Commandos their unique style and spirit, which those who have not had the good fortune to serve in the Royal Marines tend to view with scepticism, wonder and, (one suspects) a certain amount of envy. Since I hope to attract and entertain an audience of readers rather wider than that provided by the Corps itself, a few words of explanation here may help to show why Royal Marines consider themselves to be somewhat special.

Esprit de corps is not an adequate explanation, for all good regiments make it their business to inspire the loyalty of their members. Many regiments, by so doing, have established a solid reputation in other parts of the military world and not least in the minds of the enemy. The Royal Marines have done this over several centuries, and have long realized that a lasting reputation must stand on the solid foundations of good training, strong discipline and sensible handling in the field. There is, however, something more here, something that is no less strong for being less tangible. Put simply, the Royal Marines seem to belong to that class of institution which possesses, over and above any military gifts, the power of inspiring affection.

It is a small Corps, with a strength hovering at around the 10,000 mark or less in peacetime. It is a family Corps, into which sons follow fathers for generations and, be it noted, not just among the officers. General Sir Ian Riches records that members of his family have served in

the Royal Navy or the Corps since before Trafalgar, and
he is one of many, but Marine Jake Brooks, who served
with 40 Commando in Cyprus in the 1950s, saw his son
sail off with 40 Commando, Falklands-bound, in 1982,
and there are many like these, fathers, sons, brothers,
who served or are serving in the Corps. Like all families,
the Royal Marines Commandos have their bright stars
and their black sheep, and in telling the story of this
family I have not attempted to disguise the fact that
within this family there are occasional disputes, scandals,
private jokes, intrigues, and brushes with disaster. It is
one of the many saving graces of this famous Corps, that
those who serve in it do not take themselves too
seriously, and tend to flinch at this sort of florid prose:

> The green-beret men of the British Marine Com-
> mandos, the toughest fighting men in the world,
> were led by Brigadier Rex Madoc (49) who had
> spent the last ten years on tough assault course
> training. His men are hard-bitten specialists as cliff
> climbers, parachutists, frogmen and canoeists. As
> the ramps thudded down on the sandy beaches,
> they raced inland. . . .

When I showed that gem, a report on the Suez
operation from *The Daily Sketch* of November 1956, to a
Royal Marine friend of mine, he shook his head slowly
and said, 'I wonder how we ever got in.'

Marines tend to be humorous, thank goodness, and
are great raconteurs, loyal to one another and to their
Corps, long after their full-time service in it is over.
Marines are expected to help each other and therefore do
– it's one of the rules. It has been said, with great accuracy, that there is really no such thing as an ex-Marine, a
point which can be illustrated with the following
anecdote.

Terry Brown, who served with 42 Commando in

Malaya and drew the maps for this book, has never come to terms with the 24-hour clock; 1900 hours to Terry is often 9 pm. He was therefore sitting at home when he should have been at the London Motorail terminal, loading his car onto the train for a family holiday in Scotland. When the penny finally dropped, at about 1915 hours, frantic phone calls followed. 'I'm sorry,' said the voice on the line, '. . . you've missed it. Get here early tomorrow evening and we'll try and squeeze you on then.' On the following day Terry was at the terminal when the ticket office opened. 'Hello,' said the clerk, noticing Terry's Royal Marines tie (Terry only has one tie), 'a royal, eh? Which unit were you in?' 'I was in 42,' replied Terry. 'Were you?' cried the clerk, delighted. 'Blimey, I was in 42 as well. Now, if you had only told me last night that you'd been in 42 Commando, I'd have kept the bloody train for you!'

Once a Marine, always a Marine.

This then, is the story of the Royal Marines Commandos, told in their own words, with as few interjections from me as possible. On a personal note, it is also a small way of saying thank you to the Royal Marines for giving me the best friends anyone ever had, and some very happy years.

It was not the comfort of a salary
nor the fun in the Officers' Mess, nor
the pony riding that made my time
so satisfying . . . I was in love with
my platoon. The whole of my thoughts
and affection were for the forty
Yorkshiremen with whom my life was so
unexpectedly linked. They were a rough,
tough lot, but if there are better or
braver men in this world, I have yet
to find them.

Charles Carrington

Acknowledgements

My thanks go out first to everyone who has contributed
to this book. Their names and their stories appear in the
pages which follow, but it is necessary to thank them for
their time and trouble and to apologize for the omission
of those stories which, for lack of space, could not
appear, but were still of immense assistance in providing
me with the background to other tales, and as cross-
reference material. Within that general framework, some
particular thanks are due. Firstly, to an old friend,
Brigadier Peter Young DSO, MC, of No 3 Commando
and 3 Commando Brigade, for telling me of the early
days of the Army Commandos, and the coming of the
Royal Marines. Captain Derek Oakley, Editor of *The
Globe and Laurel*, kindly offered to publish a request for
help in the Corps magazine, which brought many willing
volunteers forward. I am especially grateful to Major
General Julian Thompson, CB, OBE, who commanded 3
Commando Brigade, Royal Marines in the Falklands, for
both agreeing to write the foreword and giving me much
good advice on that campaign. My thanks also to
Lieutenant-General Sir Steuart Pringle Bt, KCB, DSc, to
Major General J. I. H. Owen OBE, and to Major General
Sir Jeremy Moore KCB, OBE, MC, for agreeing to read
the manuscript, as did Paul Reynolds, who read it from
the layman's angle and helped me reduce or explain the
jargon. Henry Brown of No 1 Commando, the Secretary
of the Commando Association was very helpful in
tracking down World War II Commandos, and Bill
Stoneman sent me full and interesting tape recordings of
his experiences in the World War II Commandos, while

another 'old ships', Joe Cartwright, rounded up Marines in South Africa, and Frank Nightingale DCM, wrote from Australia to tell me of hard times in 41 Commando at Salerno and Walcheren. Norris Peak, Secretary of the 43 Commando Association, and Bishop Ross Hook MC, were more than helpful in finding me books and explaining what life was like among the Partisans, and Fred Heyhurst, Secretary of the 41 (Independent) Commando Association told me his story of Korea and introduced me to Colonel D. B. Drysdale, Commanding Officer of that fine unit. Colonel Michael Marchant and General John Owen were also most helpful in tracing ex-Marines, and my thanks to them both for this assistance. Particular thanks must go to Lieutenant Colonel Whitehead and Captain Ian Gardiner of 45 Commando, and Lance-Corporal Tubb, Lance-Corporal Spiers and Corporal Gillingham for their accounts of the Falklands Campaign.

The Royal Marines Public Relations Office at the Ministry of Defence were unfailingly helpful, and my thanks therefore to Major Graham Langford RM, Captain R. A. Need RM, and Sergeant Peter Williams RM, who provided so much assistance and many useful contacts. My thanks must be extended to Miss Bridget Speirs and Matthew Little at the Royal Marines Museum and Library Archives, Eastney; to the staff of the Imperial War Museum, London; the Combined Operations Museum, Inverary, Scotland; and the Musée de Débarquement, Arromanches, Normandy, and to Toby Oliver of Brittany Ferries and Townsend Thoresen. P&O kindly supplied photographs of the *Canberra* in the South Atlantic, and Major Ian Uzzell provided some personal photographs from his tours in Northern Ireland.

Terry Brown, late of 42 Commando, drew the maps and criticized the text, and for this, and thirty years of friendship I am, as always, grateful. I must thank Major-General J. L. Moulton CB, DSO, for letting me borrow the background papers of *Haste to the Battle*, his own excellent history of 48 Commando, and to Major Dan Flunder MC, also of 48 Commando, for supplying so much information on their advance from D-Day into Germany. Finally, my thanks to Estelle Huxley for typing the manuscript several times and stitching this story together.

To everyone else, who provided maps or photographs, my thanks and the hope that the final result justifies their efforts and enthusiasm. To those who told me that this book would be a considerable task, I can only say they were right, but I enjoyed it anyway, and I hope the reader, layman or Royal Marine, will find these stories of the Royal Marines Commandos as fascinating as I did. These people saw hard times. Their stories ought to be remembered.

1

The Sea Soldiers, 1664–1942

If they be well ordered, and kept by
the rules of good discipline, they fear
not the face nor the force of the stoutest
foe, and have one singular virtue, beyond
any other nations, for they are always
willing to go on.

'The English Soldier',
A Warlike Treatise of the Pike 1642

On 28 October 1664, during the early months of the Second Dutch War, a new regiment was formed on the Artillery Ground by Bunhill Fields in the City of London. Drawn mostly from the Trained Bands of the City Militia, and designated The Duke of York and Albany's Maritime Regiment of Foot, but also known as the Admiral's Regiment, it was armed with flintlocks and had a parade strength of '1200 land sodjers, raysed to be in rediness to be distributed in His Mat's Fleet prepared for sea service.'

These Marines were employed on board ship in various capacities, serving as snipers in the main tops, as a handy force to board or repel boarders, and to provide the infantry content in naval landing parties or cutting out expeditions. They were also used to discourage mutiny, do guard on the hatches to stop men fleeing below in the heat of battle, and to protect the officers' quarters and the magazine. They fought in the sea fight off Lowestoft in 1665, in the Four Days Battle in 1666, and in many other naval engagements during the Second and Third Dutch Wars, but when William and Mary came to the throne of England in 1689, the Admiral's Regiment was disbanded, the men being drafted into the ranks of the Coldstream Guards.

In 1690, two fresh Marine regiments were raised at the outbreak of the War of the League of Augsberg, and served with the fleet until 1699, when at the end of these wars against the French, the Marines were simply transferred to the Army and their regiments abolished, but only briefly, for the War of the Spanish Succession broke out in 1702. New regiments had to be raised, six of them of Marines for the fleet, and two years later these Marines fought in their first memorable action at the siege and taking of Gibraltar. The Marines took Gibraltar in August 1704 and held it against the French and Spanish forces for eight months until April 1705. It is in memory of this epic defence that 'Gibraltar' is the only Battle Honour to be carried on Royal Marine colours.

By now, the basic structure of what was to become the Corps of Royal Marines was clearly established. As long as Britain was a maritime power, it would need a fleet, and the fleet would need Marines. These Marines were, in effect, the Navy's infantry, raised, trained and paid by the Board of Admiralty, as Marines are to this day. In the early days, they were assigned to act primarily as a bulwark against mutiny, or as a landing detachment, although all too often ships' captains, always hard pressed for men, would take the Marines to help work the ship, and Marines were serving the cannon on warships as early as 1694.

The War of the Spanish Succession lasted until the signing of the Treaty of Utrecht in 1713, which brought peace and incidentally ceded Gibraltar to Britain. That long struggle established the Marines as part of the Royal Navy, and their story from 1713 to the end of the Napoleonic Wars, a hundred years later, may be briefly told. Ten Marine Regiments were raised for the fleet in 1739 for the War of Jenkins' Ear, and in 1740 over two hundred Marines sailed with Lord Anson on his famous circumnavigation of the globe. Lord Anson clearly found his Marines most useful, for in 1755 he pressed Parliament and the Admiralty to establish a regular body of Marines, organized on a company or ships' detachment basis, rather than with a battalion structure, and with permanent bases while on shore. In April 1755, an Order in Council created the establishment of 50 companies of Marines, organized into three Grand Divisions, one each for the three great Naval bases of Chatham, Portsmouth and Plymouth.

Amphibious warfare had been a Marine role almost since their formation, although their fortunes had been, to say the least, mixed, but during the Seven Years War which began in 1756, Marines took up the role of coastal raiders, razing batteries on the Ile d'Aix, establishing a beach-head on the island of Guadeloupe, capturing Havana in Cuba, and making a feint to cover General Wolfe's assault on Quebec; in 1761, they took part in another famous action, capturing the island of Belle Isle off the coast of Brittany, slinging their muskets over their backs to swarm up the cliffs to the attack.

Admiral Keppel wrote to Parliament of this action, 'Major General Hodgson, by his constant approbation of the battalion of Marines landed from the ships . . . gives me pleasing satisfaction of acquainting you of it, that his Majesty may be informed of the spirited behaviour of that Corps.'

And so it went on throughout the ceaseless wars of the eighteenth century. The Marines fought at every engagement of the fleet, at Quiberon Bay, at the Saints and at the Battle of Bunkers Hill during the American War of Independence. When the Napoleonic Wars broke out in 1794, the Marines were there, at the Nile, at the Glorious

First of June, at Copenhagen, and the great Napoleon himself later remarked that 'one might do much with 10,000 soldiers such as these.'

Praise from the enemy was matched by approbation from the Navy. 'I beg to observe to their Lordships,' wrote Captain Waldegrave of *HMS Prudent*, 'that this party (the ship's Marines) behaved with the utmost steadiness, keeping up a regular fire until necessity called them to the great guns where they showed an equal share of spirit and good order.'

The Marines sailed to Australia with Captain Cook, fought the French at Cape St Vincent in 1797 and were also employed in suppressing Naval mutinies at Spithead and in Plymouth. It was during this period, under the instructions of Lord St Vincent, that the ship's Marine detachments were first quartered amidships, set between the officers and the ratings, as a bulwark against mutiny or, as the Marines usually put it, '. . . to keep the Naval Officers and men from eating each other.'

More to the taste of the Marines was their role in landing parties during those frequent shore skirmishes and cutting out parties mounted by ships of the Fleet against enemy shipping, sheltering under the delusive protection of shore batteries. The Marines were clearly seen as an integral part of the British fleet, and in 1802, Lord St Vincent, a firm friend of the Corps who was by then First Lord of the Admiralty, informed the fleet that His Majesty, King George III, had been pleased to designate the Corps as The Royal Marines, adding some words of his own that the Corps would cherish.

'I never knew an appeal made to them for honour, courage or loyalty, that they did not more than realize my highest expectations. If ever the hour of real danger should come to England, they will be found to be the country's sheet anchor.'

The Royal Marines were to need such stout friends during the difficult years which lay ahead.

At this point, with those scattered regiments and detachments, often raised and as often disbanded but at last officially established as The Royal Marines, it might be as well to look again at the role of this long-established but still fledgling regiment, and where it fitted into the naval and military establishment of the time.

The Royal Marines were part of the Naval service, raised and paid for by the Admiralty. When not in their barracks ashore, in the three great Naval bases of Chatham, Plymouth and Portsmouth, they served by detachments in the fleet. Their duties at sea were to serve as marksmen, to provide boarding or landing parties, to provide the captain with guards and a force for the supression of mutiny and, if need be, to assist the sailors in serving the main guns. These tasks continued to fall to the Royal Marines for the next hundred years, so that the Corps grew up and developed traditions which were mainly Naval, and only incidentally amphibious, with more attention being paid to the Marines' role on board ship than their possible use ashore.

The Corps took on an artillery role in 1804, although it had long been the practice for small detachments of the Royal Artillery to serve the mortars on board the bomb-ships of the fleet. These men served under the Army Act, and were not therefore subject to the more stringent Naval Discipline Act, a fact which irritated many Naval captains, so in 1804 the Admiralty authorized the formation of the Royal Marine Artillery. These men wore artillery blue rather than infantry red, and so began the division into Blue and Red Marines, which became firmly established in 1855 when the Corps was divided into the Royal Marine Artillery and the Royal Marine Light Infantry. During the Battle of Trafalgar in 1805 Admiral Nelson, wounded by a French marksman from the fighting troops of the French *Redoubtable*, was carried below by Sergeant Major Secker of the Royal Marines who, finding the Admiral's blood encrusted on his buttons, refused to clean it off. Senior NCOs also refused to clean their buttons in memory of Nelson, and their gilt buttons became both a distinguishing mark of a Royal Marine Senior NCO and another link in the Naval-Marine tradition.

In the War of 1812, against the United States, the Royal Marines fought against the United States Marine Corps at sea and marched inland as far as Washington, where they set fire to the White House before returning to the coast.

At the end of the Napoleonic Wars, the Royal Marines numbered some 30,000 men, organized in four groups (or Divisions) at Plymouth, Portsmouth, Chatham and, for the Royal Marine Artillery, Woolwich. In 1827, Colours were presented to these four Divisions, and as it was customary to carry Regimental battle honours on these flags, King George IV was asked to select some for the Corps. His Majesty was offered the choice of some 106 actions, in which the Corps had played a significant part, and found the decision difficult.

According to the Duke of Clarence, afterwards William IV, who presented the Colours to the Corps, 'His Majesty determined that the difficulty of selecting amidst so many glorious deeds such a portion as could be inserted in the space, so directed that in lieu of the usual badges and mottoes of the troops of the line, that the Globe encircled with Laurel shall be the emblem of the Corps, whose duties carried them to all parts of the globe, in every quarter of which they have earned laurels by their valour and good conduct.'

In addition, these Colours were to carry King George's own cypher as well as the Foul Anchor of the Admiralty, and the word 'Gibraltar', commemorating the capture and defence of the Rock in 1704. As a badge they were granted 'The Great Globe' itself, circled with laurel, and finally, for a motto, he gave them one which summed up their purpose and methods: '*Per Mare, Per Terram*' – By Sea, By Land.

During the Victorian era, the Corps, now divided into the infantry and artillery roles, continued to serve the nation and in particular the Navy, throughout that long period of police and colonial wars which marked the progress of the nineteenth century, in the Crimea, in India, in China, in Egypt and the Sudan, in Burma, in Crete. Wherever there was war, or a job for the fleet, the Marines were there, but by the time the Victorian era ended, in 1901, the Royal Marines' future was in serious doubt, and the need for their very existence was frequently called into question.

The problem, which had developed steadily during the nineteenth century and was to continue until well into the twentieth, was that of finding a positive role for the Corps. As the Age of Sail ended, so there was less need for landing parties or marksmen, or even for forces to suppress mutiny, so that the need for Marine detachments on ships became less obvious, and their active role increasingly ceremonial. True, Royal Marines served the guns in one or more of the turrets on board the battleships and cruisers, but they could have done so equally well as sailors. If landing parties were contemplated, these could, at a pinch, have been provided by the local garrisons of the Army. Royal Marines found themselves providing Guards of Honour, guarding gangways or the ship's keyboard, providing MOAs (batmen), or wardroom attendants for Naval and Marines officers.

Among the officers, especially at senior rank levels, there were almost equally serious problems of promotion and training. On board ship the officers had little to do, and the chances for advanced infantry training ashore were limited. Since the Corps functioned, in the main, at detachment level, in units set at about the size of an Army company, opportunities for battalion training, let alone experience in handling larger formations of Brigade strength were also limited, and this naturally restricted a Marine officer's experience and so barred the path to higher promotion and senior command. In addition, the need for a Corps of Royal Marines at all, came into question at the Admiralty. In increasingly frequent times of financial stringency, while faced with the ever-increasing cost of an ever-more-sophisticated Navy, the Naval lords could find no easy solution to this matter and debated either disbanding the Corps completely or handing it over to the Army.

The Corps gained glory, and a useful breathing space, by their stout defence of the British Legation during the Siege of Peking, when Captain Lewis Halliday won the VC. King George V, then Prince of Wales, became Colonel-in-Chief of the Corps in 1901, a practice followed by later monarchs, as Captains-General of the Royal Marines, a position held today by HRH The Duke of Edinburgh. But brief glory and Royal connections were not in themselves enough.

During the early years of the twentieth century, when Admiral Sir John Fisher was the rising power in the Royal Navy, the Royal Marines suffered still further. The practice of forming Marine battalions ashore and letting them train or exercise with larger Army formations was abandoned. Detachment training in landing operations was also deemed outdated, as the development of mines and torpedoes rendered inshore work dangerous for capital ships. The bias of training for the Corps swung to a concentration on naval gunnery, while Sir John himself came increasingly to the belief that the Corps was simply an anachronism. His solution was to transfer Marine officers over to the Navy, and this was done frequently from 1907 until the Corps found a new role, at sea and ashore, with the outbreak of World War I in 1914.

When the British fleet mobilized in August 1914, some 10,000 Marines served on board the capital ships. In the same month a Royal Marine Brigade, from the Royal Marines Light Infantry (RMLI), with battalions drawn from each Grand Division, was formed for service in Belgium and later fought in the defence of Ostend and Antwerp. This Brigade later formed part of the Royal Naval Division which served in the Western Front and did notable service at the Battle of the Somme, as did units of the Royal Marine Artillery (RMA). In April 1917, Major F. W. Lumsden, RMA, a famous name in the Corps, won the VC on the Western Front, while commanding a battalion of the Highland Light Infantry.

Royal Marines served in the Battle of Jutland, where Major F. J. W. Harvey of the RMLI won the Victoria Cross, and it is interesting to note that Major Harvey was serving in a gun turret, while Major Lumsden was commanding an Army infantry battalion – but Marines are nothing if not versatile.

The first hint of a future role for the Corps came on St George's Day 1918, when the 4th Battalion of the Royal Marines attacked the U-boat base at Zeebrugge on the Belgium coast, a raid from the sea which anticipated by some twenty-five years the great Commando operations of World War II. The basic plan for the Zeebrugge raid was to block the canals which U-boats were using to reach the sea from their shelters in the hinterland around Bruges. The Marines were to storm the protecting mole while blockships were sunk in the harbour. The storming party comprised 200 sailors and 700 Marines of the 4th Battalion under Lt-Col Elliot, carried in *HMS Vindictive*, and two Mersey ferryboats, the *Iris* and the *Daffodil*.

HMS Vindictive came under heavy fire when only 300

yards from the Zeebrugge mole. Lt-Col Elliot was killed and the storming parties suffered heavy casualties, but the ships ran alongside and the troops landed, the Marines storming the batteries and staying ashore for an hour before the riddled *Vindictive* recalled them and pulled away. The 4th Battalion lost almost half of its strength in the Zeebrugge raid and gained two VCs for the Corps, which were awarded by ballot to Captain Bamford RM and Sergeant Finch.

By the time the war ended, the combined strength of the RMLI and the RMA totalled 55,000 men. This was soon reduced to 15,000 by demobilization, and then as a step towards further reductions it was decided in 1922 that one Division must be abandoned, and that the two arms, the RMLI and RMA, be amalgamated into a single Corps. This decision was contained in an Admiralty Fleet Order of June 1923, when the ranks of Gunner and Private were replaced by that of Marine, and recruit training for the entire Corps was centralized at Deal. This amalgamation gave the Admiralty yet another chance to re-examine the role of the Corps and define its purpose into a set of Official Instructions.

> The function (of the Royal Marines) in peace and war is to provide detachments which, while fully capable of manning their share of the gun armament of ships, are especially trained to provide a striking force, drawn from the Royal Marine divisions (Chatham, Portsmouth, Plymouth) or from the Fleet, immediately available for and under the direction of the Naval Commander-in-Chief for amphibious operations such as raids on the enemy coastline and bases, or for the seizure and defence of temporary bases for the use of our own fleet.

In short, apart from the possibilities for amphibious raids shown up by the Zeebrugge operation, no real change was envisaged in the role of the Corps. This blind spot on the need for an experienced, properly equipped, amphibious force by an island nation is curious, because the problems of making opposed assault landings had been fully discussed by a joint Army and Navy committee as long ago as 1911. Their findings had been published in 1913 in a *Handbook of Combined Operations*, and most painfully illustrated at Gallipoli in 1915, when the Anzac and British forces were checked on the beach, savagely mauled, and eventually forced to withdraw.

When in doubt, the British prefer to form a committee, and the role of the Royal Marines came under examination yet again in 1924, in a committee chaired by Admiral Sir Charles Madden. This committee began, most usefully, by setting out to define the nature and purpose of the Corps, while not neglecting to consider yet again whether the Corps should be disbanded. Sir Charles Madden, who later became First Sea Lord, invited submissions from the Corps, on ways to resolve their present problems and suggest future tasks, and he received an extensive report from the then Adjutant General of the Corps, General Blumberg. (The title Adjutant General, was later replaced by that of Commandant General.)

This pointed out that while the ships' detachment Marines were proficient in infantry weapons, they generally lacked field training in infantry work, since they were, in the main, confined to their ships. A similar but more critical situation existed among the officers where '. . . few proved equal to the task of leading men in action on land, and from the age of, say, thirty, were conditioned by the system to serve without opportunities of developing their qualities of (higher) command or initiative.'

General Blumberg proposed to the Madden Committee that the Royal Marines' role should include the defence of naval bases at battalion or brigade strength during their time ashore, between serving in ships' detachments, and these suggestions and solutions were taken into account in the committee's final report.

Admiral Madden concluded that if the Navy were to be adequately equipped for all liabilities, it must be provided with an efficient Corps of Marines, and to this end he went on to define the future role of the Corps. The Royal Marines' duties were to include '. . . their share in ships' gunnery armament in capital ships and light cruisers, the landing in peacetime of specially trained detachments to protect British nationals during disturbances ashore, while in wartime they could *make use of the command of the sea in small scale operations ashore*. On mobilization for war, the Corps could provide a strike force to seize bases, attack enemy lines of communications and supply the army with units for operations where Naval experience is necessary, and take part *in landing an army on a hostile shore*.'

Translated into specifics, these proposals meant increasing the Corps' strength to around 16,000 men, of whom less than one third would serve at sea in ships' detachments in the naval gunnery role. The balance would be formed into an Infantry Brigade, equipped for rapid deployment, and to strengthen the Marine element in what was to become the Mobile Naval Base Defence Organization (MNBDO). The idea for MNBDOs had arisen in 1920, with the aim of allowing the Navy to seize advanced bases and war anchorages in any part of the world, and place them in an adequate and efficient state of defence.

The Madden Committee pointed the way to an amphibious role for the Corps but the Government declined to provide funds for an experimental amphibious infantry role, although work continued on equipping the MNBDO, whose tasks fortunately did involve the Corps in amphibious work, and they came to appreciate more than most the importance in amphibious assault of the state of the tides, the slope and texture of the beach, and the problems of landing supplies over open beaches or on hostile shores. By the time war broke out again in 1939, what little amphibious experience the British armed forces possessed, existed exclusively in the Royal Marines.

In September 1939, the strength of the Corps stood at something over 15,000 men, including reservists and pensioners under fifty years of age who could be recalled to the Colours. To these were soon added a multitude of wartime recruits.

As always, the first requirement for the Corps was to man the fleet, but orders were out to bring the MNBDO (initials later interpreted hopefully by many of its members as Men-Not-to-be-Drafted-Overseas) up to strength and to form the Royal Marine Brigade as recommended in the Madden Report of 1923. Second priority was therefore given to the MNBDO, and when the first wartime recruits or HO (Hostilities Only) men joined the Corps in October 1939, they went, in the main, to the MNBDO or the new Brigade while, significantly, the trained Marines and recalled Reservists were drafted for sea-service with the fleet. Although this is certainly where the main action was during the next year or so, it also indicates the real priorities for the Corps, at least in the eyes of the senior officers.

In May 1940, as the Wehrmacht overran Holland and began its *blitzkreig* into France, the Admiralty received authorization to raise the Brigade to a full Royal Marine Division of three brigades, each of two battalions; but before this could be established, the British Army had fallen back to Dunkirk, and been evacuated over the beaches back to England. The way back into Europe and towards the defeat of Germany now lay across the beaches; the time was right for the coming of the Commandos.

The need for Commando forces was seen by the new Prime Minister, Winston Churchill, and he summed up their composition and tasks in instructions to the Chiefs-of-Staff dated 4 and 6 June 1940.

In the first of these, he stated 'We should immediately set to work to organize small self-contained, thoroughly-equipped raiding units.' In the second, he called for 'Operational Planning: Enterprises must be prepared with specially trained troops of the hunter class who can develop a reign of terror down the enemy coast.' In spite of their long amphibious tradition, there seems to have been no pressure or thoughts towards creating these units from the men of the Royal Marines. Churchill's directives were acted upon with alacrity, but the call for volunteers for this hazardous service went out to the Army.

The task of raising and organizing the first of these units, No 3 Commando, was entrusted to an officer of the Royal Artillery, John Durnford-Slater, and it is some indication of how quickly matters worked in those difficult days that Durnford-Slater's authorization to raise his unit came through on 28 June and No 3 Commando paraded for the first time at Plymouth on 5 July. Among the officers was a young lieutenant who was to become one of the great Commando soldiers of the war, Lt Peter Young of the Bedfordshire & Hertfordshire Regiment.

Quickly raised, and composed of trained soldiers with fighting experience, No 3 Commando was quickly in action. On 11 July a small party set out to raid the enemy occupied island of Guernsey, an affair which Durnford-Slater admitted achieved very little, though they learned a great deal; Churchill referred to it in another tart memo as a 'silly fiasco', but a beginning had been made.

Fortunately, the need for Commando forces had taken firm hold in Whitehall and Churchill had already appointed Lt General Sir Alan Bourne, Adjutant General of the Royal Marines to take overall command of raiding operations, and he took up his appointment in a small suite of offices in the Admiralty, where he commanded this embryo force of enthusiasts for just over a month. On 14 July, Admiral of the Fleet Sir Roger Keyes, a veteran of the 1918 Zeebrugge Raid, replaced General Bourne and was appointed to the post of Director of Combined Operations, though his first act was to ask General Bourne to stay on as his Deputy, which General Bourne willingly agreed to do.

Meanwhile, more Army Commando units were being formed. Once established, they were formed into what were to be called Special Service Brigades, which was often abbreviated into SS Brigade, a term with unfortunate connotations at the time. They were therefore later changed to Commando Brigades. By the end of March 1941 the first contingent of no less than 4,000 men in eleven Army Commando units, Nos 1 to 11, was busy training and exercising, at points all along the coast. None of these units was from the Royal Marines, although a few Marines had joined No 8 Commando as individuals.

These men, Army or Marine, had not joined the Commandos to sit at home and simply train, but for offensive action against the enemy. Throughout 1940 and the early months of 1941, a series of proposals were put forward for the use of this new striking force, including a joint operation by Army Commandos and Royal Marines against the Azores, but the first major Commando operation went against the enemy occupied islands off Norway.

On 4 March 1941, Nos 3 and 4 Commando, each two hundred and fifty men strong, and supported by demolition parties from the Royal Engineers, were carried in two infantry landing ships, escorted by five destroyers on a successful raid against the Lofoten islands off the coast of Norway. Other raids that year included one on Spitzbergen and others against various enemy defences on the coast of France, while on Boxing Day 1941, 3 Commando, aided by detachments from 2, 4 and 6 Commando, delivered a smashing blow to enemy oil installations at the Norwegian port of Vaagso.

At the end of 1941 a change of deep significance took place at Combined Operations HQ, where on 27 October Sir Roger Keyes was replaced as Chief of Combined Operations by the charismatic figure of Captain Lord Louis Mountbatten, who was, and remained throughout his life, a staunch supporter of the Royal Marines.

Sir Roger Keyes' departure from Combined Ops was not a happy one, and his first move on stepping down was to air his many and justified grievances in the House of Commons, of which he was a member. 'After fifteen months as Chief of Combined Operations and having been frustrated at every turn in every worthwhile offensive action I have tried to undertake, I must fully endorse the Prime Minister's comments on the strength of the negative power of those who control the war machine in Whitehall.' In an attempt to muzzle him, the War Office sent him a pointed reminder in the shape of a copy of the Official Secrets Act and later tried to impound his papers.

Lord Louis was in a slightly happier position, for he possessed not only the confidence of Churchill, but also great influence and powerful connections in the military establishment. A cousin of the King, he had seen action in the North Sea and Mediterranean when commanding the destroyer *Kelly*, and in addition to his role as Chief of Combined Operations, he was soon appointed to high military rank in all three services, as a Commodore in the Royal Navy, an Air Marshal in the Royal Air Force and Lt-General in the Army. Lord Louis was a master at the power game and he soon made his influence felt at Combined Ops HQ.

Meanwhile, the Royal Marines had been active at sea, notably at the Battle of the River Plate, where Lt Ian De'ath was awarded the DSO on *HMS Ajax* for dealing with fires after his turret had been hit by a salvo from the *Graf Spee*. Marines had covered the evacuation from Norway, where Captain G. W. Wilson put himself into Corps history by telling an irate Naval Captain, anxious to sail, 'It is not the policy of the Corps to leave its equipment in the hands of the enemy.' The Corps had also expanded or raised other formations, the MNBDO, and the Royal Marine Siege Regiment, equipped with fortress guns, and a small group of Marines had taken part in the invasion of Madagascar and Marines had helped to sink the *Bismarck*, and lost most of the detachment when that ship sank *HMS Hood*; as always, gallantry and dependability were never lacking.

But the Corps, while always willing and frequently busy, had added little of great significance to the course of the war by the beginning of 1942, a fact which had not escaped the attention of Winston Churchill. 'I have heard nothing of the Royal Marine Division since the Royal Marines Brigade went on the Dakar expedition,' he wrote in a minute in June 1942. 'What are the plans for its employment?' It was a fair question. In the spring of 1941 a force from the Royal Marines Division with the Special Service (Commando) Brigade, had been assembled under Major-General R. G. Sturges RM for a proposed invasion of the Canary Islands in the event of Spain entering the war on the side of Germany. At about the same time it was proposed that the Royal Marine Division should be brought up to full establishment, but although two new battalions, the 9th and 10th, were added and the Division formed into two Brigade groups, it still lacked operational employment, and was short of artillery, transport and logistical support.

The MNBDOs were more successful; MNBDO I served in Crete and Egypt, and by the end of 1941 was in the Indian Ocean, where some ranks left to form Force Viper, which served in Burma.

Whilst Royal Marines were serving at sea, in the Royal Marine Division, and in the MNBDOs, in February 1942 they at last got a chance to get into the Commandos. Early in 1942 a signal was sent to the Corps, calling for volunteers for what was then simply described as the Royal Marine Commando. This was later redesignated the Royal Marine 'A' Commando, but it did not become designated as No 40 (Royal Marine) Commando until October 1942. At this point, with a Royal Marine Commando on the point of formation, we might pause and consider two areas of dispute which were to disturb the Royal Marines Commandos in the first years after their creation and to an extent for much of their existence.

The first and most sensitive area of friction arose between the Corps and the recently created Army Commandos. The latter felt that they had created the Commando tradition, given the Commandos a task, and created a role which the Royal Marines were now attempting to usurp. On a personal level, men in the Army Commandos, a purely volunteer force, deeply resented the name 'Commando' being applied to 'turned-over' Marine battalions, although it is both fair and necessary to point out that 40 Commando was an entirely volunteer force, and all the Marine Commandos later made great efforts to weed out from their ranks any men who were unwilling or unsuited to Commando operations. Nevertheless, the difference was there, and the argument between volunteer and 'pressed man' will never be fully resolved.

The Royal Marines were always willing to concede that 'one volunteer is worth three pressed men', but felt in their turn that the Army had 'stolen a role which rightly, by tradition and training, should have gone to the Corps', although, while claiming that, many senior Marines viewed the Commando concept with distinct scepticism.

'I have to say,' commented Peter Young, when interviewed for this book, 'that we did have considerable difficulty selling the Commando concept to many senior Colonels in the Royal Marines, who seemed to be principally interested in competitive Naval gunnery. I can also distinctly recall a Marine officer who joined us in Italy from the Mediterranean Fleet, commenting that he had not joined the Royal Marines to play soldiers. We had another one – the Concrete Gunner – who felt that Marines should be in ships' turrets or coastal forts.'

This attitude existed in the Corps until well into the 1960s, and placed the 'khaki Marines', who wanted to serve in Commando units in a difficult position. 'It was made clear by a lot of people that real Marines went to sea', says Norris Peak of 43 Commando. 'All the rest were rubbish.' The Army Commandos themselves were none too popular with the military powers-that-be. 'What are Commandos?' was a rhetorical question put by General Sturges, who then provided two replies: '"An undisciplined rabble," said a War Office General; "The famous *British* Commandos", said a high-ranking German General.' The Marine Commandos had to fight for their place in the sun, even after the war was over.

'When I joined in 1950,' says Fred Heyhurst, who served with 41 Commando in Korea, 'the Corps was divided into Them and Us. *They* were the Sea-Service ratings, who felt that the Corps' real job was firing guns or guarding the keyboard on Big Ships. I've always been one of Us.'

'In my squad, all six promotion candidates elected to go to the Commando Brigade,' says a Marine from 45 Commando in 1955, 'and the squad drill instructors and officers were amazed; even a bit annoyed at us. You see, if you became a Diamond (Marine recruits chosen for promotion wear a distinguishing red diamond on their sleeve) the big perk was a first choice of posting, and the instructors assumed that anyone, given a choice, would choose to go to sea. I only joined the Corps to serve in Commandos'.

'I think that had largely died out by the middle 1950s,' recalls Maj-Gen Jeremy Moore. 'I did three years in the Brigade, and then, as a lieutenant, went straight back to Eastney, a real bastion of the sea-Marines, where, on arrival, everyone said, "You don't want the Adjutant to see you in khaki and green beret." I was creeping up to the Mess when this resplendent figure swept out crying, "How nice to see someone from the Brigade. Come and have a drink!" That was John Taplin and he *was* the Adjutant, so that was all right.'

These first Marine Commandos, now gathering at Deal in the bleak month of February 1942, were faced with no easy task. The Army Commandos ignored them, or didn't want them, the Corps' feeling in general was against them; so, they had to fight for recognition on three fronts – with their comrades in the Army, with the traditionalists in the Corps and, not least, against the enemy.

2

Dieppe, 1942

In the heat of battle mistakes in command are
inevitable and amply excusable. The real fault
arises when attacks which are inherently vain
are ordered merely because if they could succeed
they would be useful.

Basil Liddell Hart

The concept of Combined Operations had been accepted
by the British military hierarchy by the middle of 1942,
and Combined Operations Headquarters, under the
leadership of Lord Louis Mountbatten, was seen as the
focal centre for developing the techniques and equipment
needed for the eventual invasion of German-occupied
Europe. One area that exercised the minds of the invasion planners especially was the problem of supply.

While it is a relatively simple matter to land a small
force on an enemy-occupied coast, the problems of doing
so increase dramatically with the size of the force and the
diversity of its arms, and become even more complex if
the force intends to stay ashore and develop operations
outside the initial beach-head. At this point all aspects of
military thinking become preoccupied with logistics –
with the supply of ammunition, food, petrol,
reinforcements, transport and the evacuation of
wounded and prisoners. All these problems, complex as
they must be in the face of enemy resistance, are greatly
eased if the landing force has the good fortune to seize a
working port.

The MNBDO had been one successful attempt to

develop techniques of amphibious warfare, and the
Royal Marines had been involved in another small scale
effort in Combined Operations long before the outbreak
of hostilities, in the shape of the Inter-Service Training
and Development Centre (I-STDC) which was established during the 1930s at Fort Cumberland,
Portsmouth. The chairman of this organization was a
Naval Captain, L. E. H. Maund, who later became Rear-
Admiral, and his personal staff comprised an RAF Wing
Commander, a Major in the Royal Artillery, and as
adjutant, Captain Joseph Picton-Phillips, who was later
to become the commanding officer of the first Royal
Marines Commando. Their brief was the development of
Combined Operations, which many Service officers,
notably in the Royal Navy, had deemed obsolescent or
impossible due to the development of air power.

A manual on Combined Operations had been built up
since World War I, subsequently developed on the actual
experience gained in exercises at the various Staff Col-
leges, but it was little more than a well-thumbed col-
lection of duplicated sheets of paper. On the equipment
side, progress was even slower. In 1930, the Armed
Forces of the British Empire, then the greatest military
power on earth, possessed exactly three landing craft,
which had a top speed of five knots, and drew over four
feet of water. By 1938, this total, though not technically
better, had risen to six.

Admiral Maund recalls a combined Naval-Army landing exercise at Slapton Sands in 1938. 'The landing force
sailed west, carried in ships of the Home Fleet, anchored
offshore, and the men went ashore, as in the time of
Nelson, rowed in the pulling boats, whalers and cutters
of the Royal Navy, with muffled oars.' Events like this,
and constant prodding from I-STDC did lead to work
commencing on the development of a 40-man LCA
(Landing Craft Assault) and later an LCM (Landing

Craft Mechanized) which could carry guns and transport; a number of such craft were on order in September 1939 when, on the outbreak of war, the Director of the I-STDC wrote to the War Office for instructions. The reply was brief and to the point. I-STDC was to be disbanded forthwith, and the staff returned to their various Services. There could be no Combined Operations during the coming war, as the British Expeditionary Force (BEF) was already in Europe. A year later came Dunkirk.

By early 1942, Combined Operations became a priority, and it is fair to say that the British military began planning the invasion of Europe almost as soon as the BEF withdrew from Dunkirk in 1940; for it was apparent, even as the army was evacuated, that this act of withdrawal would make an invasion necessary some time in the future, if Germany was ever to be defeated from the West. The planning for the invasion was already underway at a high level in 1942, but the practical details of carrying it out were being explored and tested by Combined Operations Headquarters, which now had eight Army Commando units as a cutting edge.

In the previous two years, these Commando units had developed useful techniques in raiding and amphibious warfare, including the development of a variety of specialized craft and equipment that would be invaluable when D-Day eventually arrived. They had also been gradually extending the size and scope of their raids, from pin-prick attacks at troop strength to all-out assaults by two units, or small brigades. The assaults on the Lofoten Islands and Vaagso had been the major events; Commandos had also been active in the Middle East, notably in Crete, and in a host of small raids along the French coast, which culminated in a major assault on the German submarine base at St Nazaire, at the mouth of the river Loire. This was carried out by selected parties from various Army Commandos with Naval and RAF support. In spite of heavy casualties, the St Nazaire raid was a resounding success, well described then and since, as the greatest raid of all. All the same, it was a raid, pure and simple; the same cannot be said of the attempted *coup de main* against Dieppe.

The first difficulty confronting anyone writing about the Dieppe raid is to discover exactly what the raid was for. This is not because the raid lacked objectives; far from it. All military orders for any attack, large or small, begin with a declaration of intent. The difficulty arises when the stated objectives are related to the forces deployed, and then weighed on the scales of previous and subsequent experience. There is also the problem of deciding how, if the force was not to stay ashore, it was to be withdrawn in the face of the not usually quiescent Wehrmacht and Luftwaffe. The available documents are strangely reticent on this point, and no capital ships were provided to cover such a withdrawal.

The idea of a raid on Dieppe was first proposed as early as April 1942, and the reasons then given were as follows; to test the possibilities of securing an enemy-held port; to test in action the handling of an assault fleet; to try out new types of assault craft and equipment. Of these three, all but the first could have been tested equally well on exercises, as indeed later developments were, before the assault landings in Italy and Normandy.

The first objective does have a certain validity, for if the invasion of Europe was to succeed, the invasion forces would require, and very quickly, the services of a working port, where men and supplies could be rushed ashore to reinforce the initial landing forces. If the attack on Dieppe did nothing else, it demonstrated beyond all possibility of doubt that if the *Overlord* (invasion of Normandy) forces wanted a port for re-supply, they would have to take one with them. This fact, rubbed in at

Dieppe, was to lead to the development and use of the Mulberry artificial harbours, which kept the Allied armies supplied in the weeks just after D-Day.

The forces employed at Dieppe were far larger than any used on previous raiding operations. The landing force included six battalions of Canadian infantry and a Canadian tank regiment, all from the 2nd Canadian Division; three British Commando units, including the newly-formed Royal Marine Commando; elements of the American Rangers; men from No 10 (Inter-Allied) Commando, and some Royal Engineers. The naval force consisted of 252 ships and landing craft plus two flotillas of mine-sweepers, and included no less than eight destroyers for convoy work and inshore supporting fire. The Royal Air Force put up no less than sixty-nine squadrons, eight of them from the Royal Canadian Air Force, so that the total strength committed to the raid was both large and well supplied. It should be added that the men were keen, well trained and well equipped.

In the beginning there were two tactical plans for the Dieppe Raid, and both were ambitious. The first involved landing seven battalions of Canadian infantry on various beaches to the east and west of the town, while the second plan developed this and included parachute landings, plus a direct assault on the town itself. This direct assault was charged with destroying the German defences within the town and capturing German invasion barges in the inner harbour, and if possible, sailing them back to England. Further objectives included the destruction of radar installations, and the airfield at St Aubin, three miles inland, and an attack on a German divisional HQ at Arques-la-Battaille, which is six miles inland. The time allotted to these tasks, from landing to withdrawal, was seven hours. What the Germans would do during this period was not seriously considered.

The German forces deployed in the Dieppe area were

certainly not numerous. They consisted of the 302nd Division, a second rank formation of which the 571st Infantry Regiment was stationed in Dieppe itself, with a battalion in reserve at Ourville-la-Rivière, five miles to the south-west. However, these forces occupied a position which offered strong natural defences which had been carefully developed and reinforced with gun positions, concrete blockhouses, mines and wire, as a bastion on Hitler's developing Atlantic Wall. These defences, particularly those around Dieppe town, should be considered in detail.

The coast of France around Dieppe is well known to holidaymakers. It consists of high chalk cliffs, which run north from Le Havre all the way eastwards to Calais, broken here and there by small coves or gaps carved by river mouths. The river Arques flows into the sea at Dieppe, with the town itself occupying a wide re-entrant on the west bank of the river. The beach before the town is completely overlooked by two headlands, the western one occupied by a late-medieval castle, while the eastern one, overlooking the harbour entrance, was secured at the time with concrete artillery emplacements and machine gun posts which enfiladed the beach.

The beach extends for the best part of a mile. The composition is stone and shingle, set fairly steeply and 50 metres wide at high tide; it is backed by a wide, flat esplanade, of lawns and flowerbeds about 150 metres deep, behind which now stands, and then stood, a long line of seafront hotels. In 1942, the western edge of this esplanade was occupied by a large building standing on the sea wall, which in pre-war years was the resort's casino.

To this natural defensive site the Germans had added wire, mines, and a number of coastal batteries, including sixteen 100 mm howitzers of the 302nd Artillery Battalion which were deployed in four positions east and west of the port. The two headlands contained French 75 mm guns, and there were other, heavier pieces in the hinterland. Apart from light artillery and anti-aircraft guns on the headlands on either side of the town, the Germans deployed a total of thirty-three large calibre artillery pieces, plus a considerable number of mortars and heavy machine guns of various calibres. The Official History concludes '. . . the defences of Dieppe were at least as strong as those assaulted by the full weight of the Allied Armies in Normandy two years later.' To overcome them, the invaders would need a good plan, surprise, and luck.

The final plan for the assault on Dieppe called for landings on eight separate beaches, with two outer-flank attacks, two inner-flank attacks and a landing in force, by Canadian infantry and tanks, directly across the beach, against the port of Dieppe itself.

The original plan, for the operation code-named Rutter, called for use of parachute troops for the two outer-flank attacks, against the coastal batteries, which would in fact be carried out by No 3 Commando, and No 4 Commando. No 3 would land to the east at Petit Berneval (Yellow Beach I) and attack a cliff defence near Belleville (Yellow Beach II). No 4 would land to the west, at Varangeville (Orange Beach I), and two miles further west at the mouth of the river Sarne (Orange Beach II) to attack a six-gun battery in the woods behind the chalk cliffs.

The inner-flank attacks would be carried out to the east, by the Royal Regiment of Canada, who would land at Puys (Blue Beach), to storm the positions on the eastern headlands, and to the west by the South Saskatchewan Regiment, who would land at Pourville, to take the village there and subsequently the western headland. This battalion would be reinforced by the Queen's

Own Cameron Highlanders of Canada, who would advance up the valley of the river Scie to the airfield at St Aubin. These landings would all take place at 4.50 am.

At 5.30 am the main force would assault the beach before Dieppe town. This force would consist of the Essex Scottish, who would land on the eastern half of the beach (Red Beach) and the Royal Hamilton Light Infantry who would land on the western half (White Beach). Once the beach had been secured, the Churchill tanks of the Calgary Regiment would come ashore, the town and port would be secured and, after linking up with the flanking attack forces at St Aubin, this force would then attack the German Command HQ at Arques-la-Bataille. The Fusiliers Mont-Royal, a French-Canadian battalion, would be the floating reserve; and while the main assault was in progress, the Royal Marine 'A' Commando would sail in, enter the harbour and capture or destroy the shipping there after the port had been secured. The total landing force consisted of 6,100 men; of these 4,963 were Canadians.

That was the plan. What followed from it depends on your point of view. The Prime Minister described it in Parliament as 'a reconnaissance in force'. The Chief of Combined Operations later claimed that '. . . the battle of D-Day was won on the beaches of Dieppe'. A Royal Marine Commando who found himself crawling about on the shingle of White Beach, among burning tanks and dead or dying Canadian infantry, described it later as 'the biggest cock-up since the Somme'. Any verdict must ultimately be a matter of subjective judgement.

The first Royal Marines Commando was formed at Deal on 14 February 1942, and was largely, but by no means exclusively, composed of 'HO' (Hostilities Only) Marines from the Royal Marine Division, having a total strength at Dieppe of 18 Officers and 352 other ranks, commanded by Lt-Col Joseph Picton-Phillips. In view of the subsequent hostility shown by some Army Commandos to the Royal Marine units, it is important to state that the Royal Marine Commando, which then became the Royal Marine 'A' Commando and, after Dieppe, No 40 (Royal Marine) Commando, was an entirely volunteer force.

'I was a corporal then,' writes Bill Hefferson, a founder member from Chatham, 'and with Jim Horsfall, another corporal, I took a party of 35 Marines to open up a part of the Deal North Barracks. The officers arrived later, led by Lt-Col Picton-Phillips, a great officer, who had been my Adjutant back in 1938. Major "Titch" Houghton was there too, and Captain Hellings, and we spent several months at Deal, training and weeding out the unfit or unwilling, who we called RTUs (Return to Units) – then we went to Scotland.'

The training and discipline soon denuded the Commando of unsuitable candidates. The unit diary records 40 RTUs on 17 February, 30 on the 21st, and 30 on the 27th – but meanwhile more volunteers were arriving.

Kenneth Richardson remembers the early days of 40 Commando. 'On the morning parades at Deal, Colonel Picton-Phillips always inspected the unit while seated on a white horse. Once, when he saw someone move, his voice bellowed out, "Sergeant, that man in the front rank moved, take his name." The Sergeant replied, "That man is a corporal, Sir," and the Colonel replied, "Well, damn it all Sergeant, then take the name of the man standing next to him." We all respected the Colonel, but God help you if you batted an eyelid on parade.' Ken Richardson was an 'HO' Marine, who joined the Corps in 1940, and volunteered for the Commandos from the MNBDO.

From Deal, the 'A' Commando, now mustering around 250 officers and men went to Scotland, first to Glen Borrodale, and later to the Commando Training

Centre at Achnacarry, the estate of that Highland chieftain, the Cameron of Locheil, at Spean Bridge near Fort William, where Lt-Col Charles Vaughan put them through their paces.

Charles McNeill joined the Commando at Glen Borrodale, and remembers their arrival later at Achnacarry. 'We got off the train at Spean Bridge, and were met by a big Highland soldier, wearing a kilt, who told us to put our kitbags in the transport, then fall in on the road. We then speed-marched seven miles to Achnacarry Camp, doing a mile every ten minutes, and believe me, that was tough in full kit and platoon weapons, and after sixteen hours on the train. Outside the gates we were halted, tightened slings and marched in at the slope, past a line of graves. I found out later these were fakes, but the remarks on the gravestones still stick in my mind. "This man ran in front of the Bren." "This man forgot to wet his toggle rope." . . . things like that.

'Reveille at Achnacarry was at six or thereabouts, when a piper marched right through the Nissen huts, leaving all the doors open. That's no joke in March in the Highlands, and most of the training was physical. You ran everywhere at Achnacarry, even when off duty, even to the sick bay to have the blisters cut off your feet. Officers had to do the same, and all exercises used live ammo. It was a very fit unit that marched out a few weeks later.'

All Commando soldiers who passed through it remembered Achnacarry, and recall how the tough training extended to every level of activity. 'All washing and shaving was done in cold water, and every morning, rain or sleet or shine began with PT, stripped to the waist. The huts were heated, if at all, by a small stove, and we each had one blanket and a groundsheet,' writes Ken Richardson. 'Most of all I remember the series of assault courses; climbing cliffs, crawling through bogs, under barbed wire, while the staff shot over us with Brens, or chucked grenades about. It rained all the time, so we were never dry, and then there were the speed marches, six or seven miles in an hour, for hour after hour, in full kit with platoon weapons. Many would have fallen out, but were helped on by their mates.'

C. E. 'Knocker' White joined the Commando at Achnacarry directly from a ship's detachment. 'Coming from a ship it proved very hard, and I remember pulling myself up some of those peaks on hands and knees. However, we soon got super-fit. The only thing was, we got so hungry – we'd eat anything. We were organized in companies at that time, not Troops like the Army. I was in "A" Coy, when we moved down to civilian billets on the Isle of Wight.'

The tactical unit of the Commando was the 'section', divided into three 'sub-sections', which usually consisted of about fourteen men, commanded by a sergeant, with a corporal in charge of the rifle or assault group, and a lance-corporal in charge of the LMG Bren group. The Support section would contain a 2-inch mortar man, and later on an anti-tank team armed with a PIAT (Projector Infantry Anti-Tank) was added to this role. The Commandos were divided into 'rifle troops' or, as they were then called, 'fighting troops', with an HQ Troop and a Support or 'S' Troop armed with 3-inch mortars and Vickers MMGs, and this Troop usually included an Assault Engineer Section.

From the start, Marine Commando units also contained an administrative element, of clerks, signallers and drivers, a useful practice which was adopted by Army Commando Units in 1943. As a link with their Naval gunnery tradition, Marine Commando troops were later listed as A,B,X,Y, and Q Troops, since these are the initials used to distinguish gun turrets on capital ships, but the 'A' Commando was organized on a company basis until after Dieppe. The strength of these wartime units varied considerably according to the situation and casualties, but the establishment in 1943 was for about 460 all ranks, although this was rarely achieved. Apart from their platoon weapons, the individual Marines were heavily, even exotically armed.

'I carried a tommy gun,' recalls Ken Richardson, 'a .45 automatic pistol, a fighting knife concealed in a sheath sewn into a seam of my trousers, a pair of knuckledusters, and a couple of grenades, plus ammunition. Each man carried his personal weapon which would be a rifle or Sten, plus the Bren, 2-inch mortar or PIAT, and each man carried a toggle rope about six feet long, with a wooden toggle at one end and a loop at the other. Linked together, these could be used to scale walls or make a bridge. In the beginning we had rope-soled boots, or ammo boots, but these were eventually discarded and we got the rubber-soled type. We never wore steel helmets, even in battle, just the green beret, or sometimes the traditional woollen cap-comforter.'

From Achnacarry, the 'A' Commando moved to the Isle of Wight for more training. Here they were in civilian billets, and spread out by troops among the citizens of Sandown, Shanklin and Ventnor. Commando soldiers much enjoyed staying in 'civvy' digs. The idea was to give the men personal responsibility and the chance to practice self-reliance, for they were responsible for getting on parade each day without the usual barracks coercion, and it also spared the Commando from carrying an administrative 'tail'. The men, more practically, enjoyed all the comforts of home while not on exercise, and the civilians received 6s 8d per day as a subsistence allowance for lodging and feeding them.

'Life on the island was pretty good,' recalls Charles McNeill, 'but the locals weren't very observant. One day the CO got some men to dress up in German uniforms and walk about the town, but nobody even noticed.

Most of the time was spent cliff-climbing, which we did nearly every day, or on tactics.'

'I was billeted at Ventnor,' says Ken Richardson, 'and we worked long and hard there to improve our ability, notably in street fighting, with lots of cliff-climbing and speed-marches to keep us fit and build up stamina. I remember we used our toggle rope to span a breach in the pier at Ventnor – it had been gapped to stop the enemy using it, had they invaded in 1940. When my section was crossing, a rope snapped and we fell about thirty feet onto rocks or into the sea, fully loaded. I managed to loosen my kit and swim free, but I was convalescent for four or five days, and then I was put on a charge for losing my kit, regardless of saving myself from drowning.' Accidents were frequent and sometimes fatal.

Through the spring and early summer of 1942, this training continued and meanwhile, the landing force and ships were assembling and training for Dieppe. The final plan for the attack was submitted to the Chiefs of Staff by the Chief of Combined Operations, Lord Mountbatten, on 11 May, and approved by them two days later, with the raid provisionally set for the night of 20/21 June. However, a rehearsal on the Dorset coast on the night of 11/12 June was such a shambles that a further period of training was deemed necessary. The landing forces were assembled for intensive training on the Isle of Wight, and a second re-hearsal at the end of June went off much better. The raid was then rescheduled for the night of 4 July. The troops embarked on 2 July, but then the weather broke, with strong gales in the Channel and these continued unabated until 8 July. It was then considered that since the operation had been underway for such a long time, its secrecy must be in serious doubt, so the plan was then cancelled, to the considerable disappointment of the Canadian battalions who had spent two years in England and seen no action.

However, during the waiting period but before

cancellation, certain modifications were made to the original plan. Since it was obvious that the weather factor would be critical, the idea of using parachute troops for the outer flanking landings was dropped, and Nos 3 and 4 Commandos substituted. It was also decided that due to the risk of heavy casualties among the French civilian population of Dieppe, there could be no preliminary bombardment from the air or by capital ships. The success of the plan would therefore rest entirely on surprise. One week after Rutter had been cancelled, the plan was revived, modified in the light of these decisions, re-named Operation Jubilee and set for the night of 18/19 August. As the sun set on the evening of 18 August, the force weighed anchor and set sail from the shelter of the Solent, from Shoreham and from the little port of Newhaven, from where, in more peaceful times, day trippers still make the crossing to Dieppe. H-Hour for the first troops to land was 04.50 on the morning of 19 August 1942.

All went well until 03.45, when the invasion fleet was only seven miles from the French coast, and still completely undetected. Then, quite without warning, a star-shell came up to illuminate the small group of landing craft carrying 3 Commando into Yellow Beach I at Berneval. Knocker White takes up the tale. 'We were on French gun boats called chasseurs, and out at sea, where we joined a lot more ships and units and were on our way. Just before dawn we could see and hear firing away to port. (This was No 3 Commando which had run into a small German convoy.) This proved very serious as what surprise we might have sprung was totally lost.'

Accidents will happen in war and this small force had the bad luck to run into a German coastal convoy, escorted by armed trawlers, which opened a heavy and accurate fire on the landing craft and their escort vessel, the steam gunboat SGB5. In a few minutes SGB5 was badly damaged and the landing force compelled to scatter. Even worse, although the enemy lost one trawler sunk and another damaged, the alarm was raised on shore. Only seven of the twenty-three craft carrying 3 Commando managed to run ashore at Berneval, and from the men of 3 Commando, who landed, no less than 120 were killed, wounded or captured.

At Yellow II beach, only one landing craft made it to the shore, but this contained the redoubtable Major Peter Young who elected to go ashore with two other officers and seventeen men and attack the German batteries. Major Young's party went ashore just before H-Hour, climbed a wire-choked gulley, attacked the German battery and its supporting infantry, a total force of 200 men, with Bren and sniper fire, and managed to prevent the battery opening fire on the shipping offshore for more than two hours, before they withdrew to the beach and their patiently waiting landing craft. Peter Young finished the war as a Brigadier, with the DSO and no less than three Military Crosses, but still says, 'If there is one action in the war that I'm proud of, it was Dieppe. I took nineteen men ashore there, did the job we had to do, and brought nineteen men back.'

Over on the Western flank, No 4 Commando had got ashore intact, and were moving in two groups, one under the CO Lord Lovat, the other under the command of the Unit Second-in-Command Major Derek Mills-Roberts. They landed within three minutes of H-Hour, 04.50, and attacked the Varangeville battery at 06.20. The enemy put up a stiff resistance, and the battery was finally taken at the point of the bayonet, although the three officers leading the attack were all wounded, one of them, Captain Peter Porteous, winning the Victoria Cross.

No 4 Commando lost five officers and forty-one men at Varangeville including twelve dead and thirteen missing, but they silenced the battery, blew up the guns and were back in their landing craft by 07.30, a classic Commando attack. So far the British Commandos were doing well.

On the other beaches, where the inner flank parties and the main force of Canadians were coming ashore, it was a different and more terrible story.

The flanking battalions were to land at Puits and Pourville, which lie about two miles on either side of Dieppe. The landing craft carrying the Royal Regiment of Canada lost formation during the run in to their beach at Puits, which was encircled by high cliffs and guarded by fortified concrete pill-boxes. This confusion caused a delay of nearly half an hour, so that when the troops touched down it was already broad daylight and the defences above Blue Beach were alerted and fully manned; what happened was therefore inevitable.

The first two waves to get ashore were machine-gunned on the beach, and decimated. Still the battalion continued to land, with the supporting companies, C and D, landing on the western side of the beach. A detachment from this group, led by their CO, Lt-Col Catto, soon cut a way through the wire and had scaled the western headland, before they were surrounded. Meanwhile, Blue Beach became a slaughterhouse.

A Royal Artillery officer who went ashore with the Canadians to control the fire of their supporting des-troyer, *HMS Garth*, records what happened.

'In five minutes the Royal Regiment of Canada was changed from an assault battalion on the offensive to less than two companies pinned down by heavy and accurate fire from positions they could not discover.'

Apart from the party that got onto the western head-land, the Royal Regiment of Canada was pinned on the beach and annihilated; attempts were made to evacuate the survivors at 07.00 and again at 09.00, but by 09.30 no troops remained alive on Blue Beach. The Royal Regiment of Canada put 26 officers and 528 men ashore on 19 August. Of these, all the officers and 496 men became casualties.

At Pourville, to the west of Dieppe, the South Saskatchewan Regiment went ashore about 04.55, and achieved almost complete surprise, getting ashore and crossing the beach without casualties. But then there was a snag; the original plan called for the battalion to put ashore astride the mouth of the river Scie but, once again, confusion among the landing craft put only one company on the east side of the river mouth. The rest landed on the west side, so that not only was the battalion divided, but the bulk of the troops were on the wrong side of the river.

Nevertheless, the South Saskatchewans did very well, disposing of enemy defences and moving up in good order towards their initial objectives. They still had to cross the river and this was soon accomplished, although the only bridge was by now under heavy machine gun and mortar fire. The CO, Lt-Col Meritt stood in the middle of the road and waved his men across, crossing himself four times to bring the companies forward. For his gallantry on the Scie, Lt-Col Meritt later received the Victoria Cross.

Back on the beach, the Queen's Own Cameron Highlanders of Canada were landing, but under heavy fire, losing their Colonel, who was killed by a sniper as he stepped ashore. The Camerons advanced two miles inland, and then stopped to await the arrival of their tanks, which should by now have landed at Dieppe and advanced to join them.

As the hours wore on, German resistance around them

stiffened, and still no tanks arrived. The two Canadian battalions made a fighting withdrawal to Pourville, only to be told that no landing craft would be available to evacuate them until eleven o'clock. The Canadians dug in and held on against increasing pressure until noon and were eventually evacuated under the covering fire of *HMS Brocklesby*. About one hundred men of the South Saskatchewan Regiment remained ashore to cover the withdrawal, and fought on under Lt-Col Meritt until their ammunition ran out at about 1.30 pm, when they were compelled to surrender. The South Saskatchewan regiment lost 19 Officers and 498 men at Pourville, and the Queen's Own Cameron Highlanders of Canada lost 24 Officers and 322 men out of a total of 32 officers and 471 men.

Down in Dieppe town the situation was even worse. The main assault on the sea front at Dieppe went in at 05.20, half an hour after the flank attacks, and was to be carried out, it will be recalled, by two Canadian battalions, the Essex Scottish on Red Beach to the east, and the Royal Hamilton Light Infantry on the western section, White Beach. When these battalions were ashore, the Churchill tanks of the Calgary Regiment would land in support, and advance with them into the town.

The supporting destroyers laid down a five-minute bombardment and Hurricane fighters swooped in to rake the seafront with fire as the two battalions came into land at 05.20. As dawn was breaking heavy fire was opened on their landing craft when they were still three hundred yards from the beach from directly ahead and from the headlands, coming from mortars, artillery pieces, light and heavy machine guns, even rifles. The defenders of Dieppe were alert and aggressive, but still the Canadians came on.

The two battalions landed exactly at H-Hour, and

splashed up onto the shelving shingle, with a hundred yards to go to the illusionary shelter of the sea wall. It was then discovered that the beach was laced with barbed wire entanglements.

'When we landed, we were confused for some time,' wrote an RHLI soldier, 'but then we began to fire back and started to cut the wire – then we found we could get across it without cutting it, but the beach was covered by light MG fire from the buildings up ahead, and heavy MGs firing down on us from the flanks.'

The Germans had established a stronghold in the Casino building which stood on the edge of the sea wall and completely overlooked the beach. The Canadians fought for the Casino for over an hour, finally taking it at 07.12, after which small groups of men began to dash across the broad esplanade and so get into the town. Very few made it.

On the eastern section, Red Beach, the Essex Scottish were having an even worse time. They came under heavy fire before they stepped ashore, and on the more exposed, eastern half of the beach, unsheltered from the western headland by the bulk of the Casino building, they were open to enfilade fire from either flank, which grew steadily in volume and accuracy. Within half an hour of landing, over forty per cent of the Essex Scottish had been hit; some estimates say seventy-five per cent, pinned down on the beach with the fire continuing to mount against them as more and more German troops came forward and took up position, engaging the Canadians with rifles and grenades.

The tanks, which should have landed in support, were delayed and the first wave of nine tanks did not beach until some twelve to fifteen minutes after the infantry. From then on however, each wave of tanks landed more or less on time, with the final wave of twelve tanks landing exactly on schedule at 06.05. The officer commanding the Calgary Regiment of Churchill tanks, Lt-Col Andrews, was killed as his tank came ashore, and the 4th Canadian Brigade Commander, Brigadier Lett, who had intended to land with the tanks, had already been wounded on board his LCT (Landing Craft Tank).

Fifteen of the twenty-seven tanks which landed managed to cross the beach, which was not mined, and made it to the esplanade, but by now strong road blocks had been established by the Germans, and barred every exit from the esplanade into the town. Out on the flat, open esplanade, the tanks were even more vulnerable to artillery fire, so eventually they rolled back to the shelter of the sea wall, and began to give what help they could to the beleaguered infantry on the beach. By 06.30, the assault on Dieppe was already stalled and turning into a shambles.

The 'fog of war' can be a very real thing. It was now clear to the Force Commander, Major-General J. H. Roberts, that all was not well, but actual details were very hard to come by, not least because the beaches were obscured by the heavy smokescreen laid to shield the offshore fleet from the coastal batteries. Nevertheless, there was a considerable amount of shell fire falling among the shipping, the German airforce was active overhead and a consistent if garbled steam of reports was reaching Force Headquarters on *HMS Calpe*.

A conference held by Major-General Roberts, Captain Hughes-Hallett and Commander R. E. D. Ryder VC, decided that since Puits had not been taken and the German positions on the east headland were still in action, any attempt to enter the port by *HMS Locust* and the Royal Marines Commando should be abandoned. The Marines on *HMS Locust* were already attempting to close the port when this decision was made.

'Things were pretty confused,' recalls one marine on

HMS Locust. 'What with the smoke and shelling, and someone near me on the bridge said, "Where's the entrance – I can't see the mole." I took hold of him and said, "The harbour mole's over there; the one with the bloody great gun on it – the one that's firing straight at us."'

HMS Locust, a river-gunboat which contained the Commando HQ, 'A' Company, and a demolition team, had arrived off the harbour entrance at 05.20, H-Hour. There she was promptly hit twice by the big gun on the mole, losing two men killed and six wounded. Getting inside the harbour was clearly impossible, although some 'A' Commando craft pressed on past the mole, so after being ordered to withdraw, she joined the destroyers in bombarding the shore batteries, where she was eventually joined by French chasseurs bringing the rest of the Commando. The 'A' Commando joined the Fusiliers Mont-Royal to await further orders.

Knocker White takes the story forward: 'At dawn we still hadn't gone ashore, although lots of aircraft, theirs and ours, were screaming about. Palls of smoke and murderous gunfire were coming from the beach and cliffs. We tried to force our way in on *HMS Locust*, but it was hopeless. We went back out to sea, and heard that the second plan was to be put into operation to land further along the beach and get into the dock from the rear. We transferred from *Locust* into LCAs and LCMs.'

Major-General Roberts was still receiving a stream of inaccurate or conflicting reports, of which the most critical and inaccurate was that the Essex Scottish on Red Beach had actually got into the town. General Roberts therefore decided to commit the Fusiliers Mont-Royal to exploit this apparent success. The Essex Scottish were, in fact, still pinned down, and the Fusiliers Mont-Royal were simply advancing to add themselves to the holocaust.

The Fusiliers went in at around 07.00. Their craft, flailed by artillery, were widely dispersed on landing, with a large number of men – some reports say as many as 300 – actually landing on the far (western) flank of the Royal Hamilton Light Infantry. Their commanding officer, Lt-Col Ménard, was hit on landing, and within minutes this battalion too was pinned down on the beach, sheltering behind burning tanks, among wrecked landing craft, or behind the bodies of their dead.

Major-General Roberts on *HMS Calpe* was still unaware of all this at 08.00 hrs. The reports reaching him seemed to indicate that the raid had still a chance of success. He knew that the Casino had been taken, and believed that his tanks, supported by the Essex Scottish, had penetrated the town. It also appeared that the Pourville landing was proceeding according to plan. He still had the Royal Marine 'A' Commando at his disposal, and the decision was taken to use them in support of the Royal Hamilton Light Infantry on White Beach. The orders given to Picton-Phillips were '. . . to land on White Beach, skirt the town to the west and south, and attack the batteries on the east cliff'. Jacques Mordal, a French writer, later commented that this 'over-optimistic plan needed an advance of two-and-a-half miles over ground where no one had yet advanced so much as twenty yards'. Nevertheless, it had to be attempted – the hour of the Royal Marines Commandos had struck.

Within half-an-hour, the Royal Marines had transferred from their chasseurs and *HMS Locust* to assault boats. The beaches of Dieppe ahead were still hidden behind a thick smoke screen, into which the assault craft began to move, escorted by *HMS Locust*. When the craft emerged on the far side of the smoke they were met at once with a hail of artillery fire.

'I was Second-in-Command,' recalls Major-General Houghton, then a Major in the Commando. 'My LCA contained the unit's Rear HQ, and a demolition team, which meant that it also contained a horrifying quantity of explosives. The fire which met us from the shore was very heavy, and very accurate, but we just went on.'

The Marines were embarked in two LCMs, large landing craft, and five smaller assault craft, with Lt-Col Picton-Phillips leading the way in an LCM (Landing Craft Mechanised).

'With a courage terrible to see,' says the Official History, 'the Marines went in to land, determined, if fortune so willed, to repeat at Dieppe what their fathers had accomplished at Zeebrugge.'

A Naval Officer, Lt Buist, in charge of the chasseurs, puts it another way. 'It was not long before I realized that this landing was the sea version of the Charge of the Light Brigade. A barrage of fire from the cliffs showed that the beach was under heavy fire and shells soon started to fall around the small group of (Marine) landing craft, which we tried to screen with smoke. I shouted across to ask Col Phillips if he wanted to continue, but I doubt if he heard me. Anyway, he grinned and waved to show that he meant to land, at all costs.'

'Our craft got hit and stopped,' says Knocker White, 'but we boarded another one . . . someone shouted that the Colonel was waving us back, but then another shell came in and hit our engine compartment. I saw a poor stoker leap overboard with his clothes on fire, then our OC, Captain "Pops" Manners, said very calmly, "I think we had better abandon ship lads", which we promptly did, as the fuel tanks were hissing and threatening to blow up. Luckily we drifted into the smoke which saved us a little from the murderous machine gun fire – we were only 200 yards or so from the shore.'

General Peter Hellings, then a Captain in 'A' Commando

takes up the story. 'When the fire became intense, the Colonel stood up on the landing craft to direct the remainder of the party, and lead his Commando onto the beach, under the most intense mortar and machine gun fire. As the range shortened the fire increased, until there was no doubt that any attempt to reach the town over that beach would mean certain death. The Colonel refused to turn back until he had proved it was useless to continue.'

Colonel Phillips' craft ran on to the beach under heavy fire, while the rest of his Commando, still offshore, were coming in to land. 'We were in the Colonel's LCM and were hit repeatedly on the beach,' writes Marine J. Farmer,' . . . and then I saw the bravest act I have ever seen. Colonel Phillips saw that it was hopeless, and he stood up in full view of us and pulled on a pair of white gloves and semaphored to the other assault boats to turn back. He was shot and killed in a matter of seconds.'

Sgt J. F. Knuthoffer was another Marine in Colonel Picton-Phillips' boat. 'For 10 Platoon and their companions the moment of truth followed when the LCM surged in all on its own towards touch-down – to a fireswept beach occupied by prostrate bodies and a few desperate groups clinging to cover. A look in any direction showed only too clearly that along the whole stretch of beach the landing of tanks and infantry had been smashed to a standstill. For those of us who could see over the side, the feeling at that moment was not of panic or unreasonable fear – but sheer amazement and disbelief. Not a logical reaction, but a short space of a few seconds when the brain tries to reject what has been fed in. "Get out fast – spread out – and run like hell for cover." This was someone's last gesture of optimism, as the LCM ground to a stop some way off the beach, an isolated target for everything in range. Within seconds it was down by the stern, broached-to, and the front ramp jammed shut. Even if the mind had fully registered and retained the detail, it would still be impossible to present a realistic impression of events from then on. A scene which had changed from drill book order and discipline to utter chaos in just a few minutes.

'It can be attempted only by listing some parts of the jigsaw clearly remembered. A group at the front trying to kick the ramp down. The CO, the crewman and others hit and falling about; a scrum at the back end, trying to dodge small arms fire coming down amongst them. Those looking over the shore side or trying to climb out, getting it in the head or chest and crashing back on to those behind them. Some Bren-gunners at work – one immortal bawling for full magazines – another enthusiast firing from a sitting position, threatening to shoot the head off anyone moving sideways. One survivor commented that fire from the shore in front, and a wavering stream of 1-in-3 tracer bullets past your ear from behind had a tranquillizing effect. The theory was that at this point you passed through the fear barrier; it was just a matter of curiosity to see who got you first.

'Steady mortar fire added to the pandemonium but the MLC was spared the additional agony of having bombs land on board. As the stern settled down even more, the deck was half awash, and it was not realized that this water included either petrol or diesel. Whatever it was, it ignited promptly when a burning smoke canister was dropped. The bright one who dropped the cannister probably saved several lives by forcing everyone to bale out – and it at least shifted the menace of the sitting Bren-gunner who, with his legs afire, was over the side like a flash of light – taking his weapon with him.

'Being unable to disembark either through the front ramp or over the shore side, the start of a raging fire became a deciding factor even for those who had been slow in realizing that their number was coming up. An effective smoke screen and very rapid movement meant that evacuation was carried out without many extra casualties. A quick check that those lying in the fire were dead – and then with anti-tank bombs and 36 grenades cooking and going off – instinct took over and saved the problem of planning the next move. Nobody made it ashore, except as POW's later, and the half-platoon which came back were those who were able to get out in one piece, and had the confidence to swim out towards home in the hope of being picked up.' Sgt Knuthoffer swam two and a half miles out to sea before he got onto a ship.

Richard McConkey was in one of the assault boats coming in behind. 'I was in a landing craft a few yards offshore, directly behind Colonel Phillips' boat, and we saw him stand up in murderous fire and wave us to retreat, but then we also got hit. I swam away, but I saw someone still hanging on, so a Marine called Jock Cowan and I swam back and hauled him off. He said, "I canna swim Mac", and I said, "You canna sink either, you've got a Mae West lifejacket on." That was Willy McKnight. Then a scaling ladder floated past so we put him in that and towed him out to sea, heading for home. We were picked up by *HMS Brocklesby*, and they gave us dry gear and put us below, but then their skipper came down and said, "Can any of you Marines use an Oerlikon?" So my mate, Knocker White, went up and had it blazing away. We got hit six times on the *Brocklesby* and went aground once, but they stayed to pick up survivors – what guts that skipper had. We came back to Pompey doing four knots under air attack most of the way!'

Knocker White had helped tow Willy McKnight out to sea. 'Our QMS, Wiggy Bennet, was in the water shouting, "Save your weapons, boys" – when we cleared the smoke I noticed the sea was full of jellyfish – then the ship came up, manoeuvred between us and the shore and picked us up. When the officer asked if anyone could handle the Oerlikon 20 mm, as the crew had been killed or wounded, I went up. I had done a course at Scapa Flow, and couldn't say no, mostly firing at Stuka dive-bombers – they gave us plenty of stick, and sank another ship, a direct hit amidships. The withdrawal had been fixed for 14.00 hrs, and our brave skipper made for the shore, turned stern on, to pick up any survivors. The scenes on that beach at Dieppe I shall never forget. There seemed to be hundreds of wrecked landing craft of all descriptions, tanks hardly a few yards up the beach and dead bodies, mostly Canadians, all over the shingle. Every gun was going on the ship, as gunners were letting fly with everything we had at the Spandaus in caves on the cliffs, when the skipper finally decided to shove off I thought we had had it. We were well aground, masses of shingle were thrown into the air by the ship's screws, but we eventually made it and steamed for Blighty, as fast as we could. Their bombers continued to bomb us until dark. We made it to Portsmouth, about midnight, I guess.'

In spite of Lt-Col Phillips' efforts to warn them off, the Commando continued to land. Sgt Jim Hefferson, who got ashore in an assault craft, takes up the story. 'We knew we were going in to reinforce the Canadians, and even after the Colonel was killed, we still went on. His craft was on fire and unbeknown to us at the time, we were supposed to return, but no one saw any signal. We got out over the side onto the beach, but as we lowered the ramp, our right and part of the centre sections were wiped out. The rest got away, though some got clipped on the way up the beach. There were bodies everywhere, with a yard-wide river of blood on the edge of the sea. Craft and tanks were burning, planes diving over and the mortar fire was throwing large stones everywhere off the shingle.

'After what seemed a long time, we got up behind a Churchill tank which was bogged down, and I got a bullet along my ribs, and after that a bloody grenade went off. I saw it rolling and the lever came off. Then it stopped and I got a lot of shrapnel, and worst of all, after being blind for a year in the POW camp, they took out my right eye. I have regained some sight in my left eye, but I have just lately been accepted in St Dunstans – and that is my excuse for this rotten writing. I was Corporal, acting Platoon Sergeant at Dieppe, but I never did get it confirmed. My platoon commander was Lt Smale.'

Lt Ken Smale of No 8 Platoon also got onto the beach. 'A scene of horror and carnage, where people had, quite literally, been blown to pieces. We charged up the beach and took shelter behind a Churchill tank, and I never realized I would be so keen to press my nose against a lump of steel.'

Lt Smale got back off the beach and swam out to sea, only to be picked up some miles offshore by a German E-Boat. Sergeant Hefferson was collected off the beach by the Germans some time around noon, and sent to the hospital at Rouen, before being imprisoned in the camp for blind British prisoners of war at Klosterheinan in Germany.

The Colonel's LCM and two assault craft actually beached, and all the Marines killed or taken prisoner came from these three craft. The unit Second-in-Command, Major 'Titch' Houghton, was in an LCA which was carried west, and went ashore first under the Casino, near the western end of the beach, getting off, and coming in again. Major Houghton and the Marines had hardly disembarked from the LCA when a mortar bomb hit their craft and blew it to pieces.

Ken Richardson's craft was hit close to the beach. 'We slithered over the side into the water and got ashore, still under concentrated fire, with more men being hit; the fire was very heavy, and with my heavy pack and Bren-gun it was difficult to get up the beach, which was very steep and shingly. It was a frightening sight; I saw the beach strewn with dead Canadians, abandoned tanks beached and burning, LCTs perched at crazy angles. I managed to get behind a tank, completely exhausted, with a fraction of the section and our troop commander. We could not see the enemy, but there was plenty of sniping and heavy mortar and machine gun fire from the cliffs . . . this was not what was intended.

'When we were told to go, I inflated my life-jacket and got into the water – it was very cold. I swam out towards the craft but I didn't think I would make it. The shellfire, hitting the water, seemed to numb me like an electric shock. I don't know how far I swam, but it was like attempting to swim the bloody Channel, and I was eventually picked up by an LCT full of wounded, lying all over the deck. When we got back, we were mustered into units and told to inform our next of kin. The Canadians lost a lot of men, mostly in the first half hour, and the Royal Marines Commando was seriously reduced.'

Reduced indeed; of the seventeen officers and 352 other ranks of the 'A' Commando who sailed to Dieppe, sixty-six were killed or captured on the beach and many others were injured or killed in the landing craft.

The Canadian losses were even more grievous. In the space of about six hours, the 2nd Canadian Division lost 56 officers and 851 men killed, and a further 1985 all ranks, many of them wounded, became prisoners of war. The Royal Hamilton Light Infantry, pinned down on White Beach, lost all their officers and all but a hundred men. The Fusiliers Mont-Royal were only in action for a short while, landing just ahead of the Royal Marines, but they lost 28 officers out of 31, and 484 men out of 552. Only two officers and 52 other ranks of this battalion were unwounded.

Later that day, craft began to slip into the South Coast ports, full of tired or wounded men. 'When we came into Pompey,' recalls Knocker White, 'we were ushered aboard Nelson's old flagship, *HMS Victory*, dished out with a couple of blankets and a large mug of rum, then we faded into a deep, welcome sleep. Next day we made our own way back to the Isle of Wight where our landladies came rushing down the street, hugging and welcoming us back, weeping for the faces that were missing.

'Next day we mustered for the count and I believe about twenty per cent of the unit had gone, including the CO and Major Houghton. Sadly for us we also lost our dear officer and Company Commander, "Pops" Manners, who left our company unit and became the CO.'

A few days later, Sgt John Knuthoffer received a letter from his company officer.

D2 Ward,
Brighton Municipal Hospital

Dear Sergeant Knuthoffer,

Thank you very much for your letter and good wishes which, apart from the sad news it contained, was very welcome.

It wasn't until Saturday that I learnt that most of you had got back, and you can imagine my feelings, as for the previous three days I had been absolutely certain that I was the only survivor from our ill-fated MLC.

I was picked up by a small flak ship manned by Royals who did some splendid shooting, 8 down and 1 probable (excluding an unfortunate Spit (Spitfire)).

I am as right as rain now except for a peeling face, a couple of outsize lips and two brick-red legs which I consider very lucky remembering the amount of refuse that was flying about. I am departing from this invalid's home today and am coming back on the 8th.

I am going to write to the missing lads' parents which will be very difficult as there is no definite news I can give them. Thurman gave me a description of how Alexander was killed which was quite wrong as I saw him alive five minutes after his supposed end and he had not been touched then. Can you give me further information on both him and Simmons who I know was wounded? I also know Rutter was wounded in the head and since he was just in front of Alexander I'm wondering if somebody mistook them. In fact the only one who I am certain about is poor Northern who, you may or may not know, was going to be married early in September.

I think I am unfortunately leaving 10 platoon to become 'X' Coy Cdr which, seeing the price that was paid, does not give me any satisfaction.

I reckon we leave swimming out of our training for some time now as it's perfectly obvious that you can all swim a couple of miles or more! However, regarding all new arrivals, they will have to swim (with Mae Wests) from Shanklin pier to Sandown; we can't afford to have non-swimmers or poor swimmers.

I will close now as I am about to clear out, please excuse the dreadful handwriting but it isn't my pen.

Give my regards and congratulations to the Platoon and the hope that they enjoy a well earned leave.

Hoping you have a good leave.

Yours sincerely,

H. O. Huntington-Whiteley.

Lt Huntington-Whiteley commanded 10 platoon, X Coy at Dieppe. He was killed serving with the Royal Marines Commandos in Normandy just after D-Day, 1944.

3

Sicily and Italy, 1943

He who lies far from this place died before daybreak:
but he was a soldier, and he died for his country.

Newbolt

After seven days leave, the much reduced ranks of the 'A'
Commando returned to Sandown on the Isle of Wight at
the end of August, and in the following month went back
to Deal, where they acquired a new name, becoming 40
(Royal Marines) Commando, and a new Commanding
Officer, Lt-Col J. C. 'Pops' Manners, who had been a
Company Commander at Dieppe.

'Training went on apace,' says Knocker White, 'and
then we transferred to the Weymouth area, where we
learned we were due to go on a raid to the Channel
Islands, but for some reason it was cancelled and we
returned to the Isle of Wight. Early in the New Year –
1943 – we entrained for Scotland and my Troop – 'Y'
Troop (we were remustered into Commando fighting
troops by now and issued with the green beret) – were in
civvie billets around Kilwinning in Ayrshire. There we
were brigaded with other Commandos under Brigadier
Robert 'Lucky' Laycock, and did a lot of landings,
practice attacks on radar stations, and much night work.
In early July we embarked with the other Commandos
on the *MV Derbyshire*, and sailed in a big convoy for the
landings on Sicily.'

Among these other Commandos was the second Royal
Marine unit, No 41. This second Marine Commando

Map 1 Sicily and Italy

formed in October 1942 by turning the 8th Royal Marine Battalion into No 41 (Royal Marine) Commando, which then went through the now familiar process of weeding out the RTUs, the sick, lame and lazy, and sending the remainder through the basic Commando course at Achnacarry, a process which reduced a thousand strong battalion to a Commando strength of about 450 men, organized into five rifle (fighting) troops, each of three officers and sixty-three men; a Heavy Weapons troop; a Commando HQ Company; and a Signals Platoon.

While 40 and 41 were training in Scotland, or sailing to fresh exploits in Sicily and Italy, the future of the Royal Marine Division was coming into question. According to one report during 1943, this Division was 'Mouldering away in Wales', but Maj-Gen John Owen, then a 2nd Lieutenant in the RM 3rd Battalion, did not remember it like that.

'We trained very hard, physically, with plenty of field exercises and long route-marches. We also practised minor tactics every morning, on the parade ground, doubling the men forward in groups. Rifle group forward ... then Bren group forward ... it seemed a strange way to learn or practise fire and movement.'

The problem with the Royal Marine Division was that it lacked a 'tail', in the shape of attached armour, artillery, engineers, and adequate logistical support.

Throughout 1942 this Division had been training for landing operations, while the Corps resisted pressure from the Chiefs of Staff for it to be handed over to Army command, as had happened with the Royal Naval Division in World War I. The Chiefs of Staff suggested this move, not least because the Army would then provide the RM Division with supporting units, transport, ordnance, engineers, and so turn it into an operational force. In April 1942 the Division was formed into two brigades, with some supporting artillery, manned by Royal Marines, and plans were laid to use the Division in Operation Torch, the American invasion of North Africa, but like various other schemes, this one came to nothing, although the Army Commandos were raiding the enemy coast of Occupied Europe throughout the year.

The Dieppe Raid and these continual 'pin-prick' raids by Commando forces infuriated Hitler, and in October 1942 he issued an instruction, the infamous 'Commando Order', to his senior field commanders.

Commando Order (18 October 1942)
From now on all men operating against German troops in so-called Commando operations are to be annihilated to the last man. This action is to be carried out whether they are soldiers in uniform, or soldiers with or without arms, whether fighting, surrendered or seeking to escape, whether they come into action by ship, aircraft, or parachute. No quarter is to be given. Should individual members of these Commandos fall into the hands of the Armed Forces through any other means – for example through the Police – they are to be turned over at once to the SD.

General Jodl, the overall commander of the Wehrmacht, circulated this order to his subordinates on the following day, but thought it advisable to add a note. 'This order is intended for senior commanders only and is *in no circumstances* to fall into the hands of the enemy.'

Even so, the existence of the Commando Order soon became known to the Allies, but made no difference to the Commandos. In a way, they revelled in its existence; however, it was savagely implemented by the Germans, who murdered many Commando soldiers taken prisoner in the course of the war, including the Marines captured on *Operation Frankton*, the 'Cockleshell Heros' canoe raid on the shipping at Bordeaux.

Various proposals for the employment of the Royal Marine Division were put up from the autumn of 1942 until the middle of 1943, including that aforementioned assault on the Channel Islands, but in June the Admiralty finally grasped the nettle and appealed to the Prime Minister for permission to break up the Division, which was then about 7000 men strong and, with Marines collected from other Corps roles, form 4000 into Commando units, and use a further 6000 to man the country's ever-expanding and ever-more necessary fleets of landing craft for the forthcoming invasion of Europe.

This proposal, that Marines should be used to handle small craft and assault boats, was yet another novel proposal, which met with a certain amount of opposition from the senior officers, as novel proposals often do, but the country's pressing need for landing craft crews eventually overcame all objections, and the Royal Marines have continued to man landing craft and assault boats from that day to this.

The second half of the proposal, that the Royal Marines should go over to Combined Operations, not in their traditional battalions, but as Commandos, brought even more opposition from senior officers of the Corps, so much indeed that serious attempts were made to scupper the whole idea. The Royal Marine Division was then part of Home Forces, and to keep it out of Mountbatten's clutches at Combined Ops, one suggestion was that they should be transferred to the command of the American General Eisenhower.

Mountbatten, who was, and remained throughout his life a stout supporter of the Corps in general and the Commandos in particular, finally suggested an acceptable compromise. If the Corps would agree to transfer the Marines to his command as Commandos, he would appoint a senior Royal Marine officer to overall command of the Commando Groups. This proposal was accepted in July 1943, and Maj-Gen Robert Sturges, of the Royal Marines, took up his appointment as GOC Special Service (Commando) Group in October 1943. Commando Group was later to include four Commando Brigades (1, 2, 3 and 4) each containing a mixture of Royal Marines and Army Commandos. The change from battalion to commando began at once, with 1st Bn becoming 42 Commando; 2nd Bn, 43 Commando; 3rd, 44 Commando; 5th as 45 Commando; 9th as 46 Commando; and 10th as 47 Commando. The 7th Bn, Royal Marines, was then in the Middle East, and did not return to the UK for remustering as a Commando unit until March 1944 when it become 48 Commando.

General Owen recalls what happened to the 3rd Bn. 'I joined the Corps in January 1942, at Lympstone, which was then known as Exton. By the time we had finished recruit training, I had become an acting lance-corporal, a position referred to as a "rear-rank instructor". I remember we even used to polish the soles of our boots – and not just the insteps. Anyway, I had very good boots and these caught the eye of the Adjutant. "Very smart boots there, Owen", he said. "Have you ever thought of becoming an officer?" So I went to OCTU and joined the 3rd Bn then in Wales as a second lieutenant in October 1942. We were lingering at Ashurst in the New Forest training for what we knew not when we suddenly heard of the plan to convert the battalions to commandos. This was greeted enthusiastically by most of us but less so by some of the more senior officers and NCOs. We had also heard fearful tales about Achnacarry. The unit was then divided into two, with about one third leaving us first to go "flax pulling", and then into landing craft crews and about 500 of us going to Achnacarry to turn ourselves into 44 (Royal Marines) Commando. It was an extremely tough course and we became very fit indeed. We came out with high morale at about 400 strong. Also on my course was Ross Hook, a naval chaplain, who became padre of 43 Commando and eventually a bishop, and our new CO, Lt-Col F. C. Horton who was later to lead us into Burma.'

This mustering of infantry units into Commandos on a non-volunteer basis, unlike the Army Commandos, which were always entirely volunteer formations, meant that the Royal Marine units never, or at least rarely, achieved the same dash and flair as the best of the Army Commando units. On the other hand, it should not be thought that the transformation of Marine battalions into commandos was achieved by simply changing their shoulder flash. Each battalion was re-assessed for the commando role and the unfit, the unwilling or the unsuitable were transferred to other duties, while rigorous training weeded out still more, who were replaced by volunteers for commando duty from within the ranks of the Corps. All Marine units went through the basic Commando course at Achnacarry, and were brigaded with Army Commando units for subsequent operations.

Brigadier Peter Young DSO, MC, who had Royal Marine units under command in Italy, France and Burma, can give a fair assessment. 'I would have to say that they were uneven. Some units were very good, some were, well – not so good. The good ones I can think of were 42 and 45, both very steady units. 45 Commando could be very enterprising on occasions. I would rate 45 the best of them. I have no doubt that 46 was good, because it had such a good CO, Campbell Hardy. The same applies in my mind to 48, because General (as he now is) Jim Moulton was such a good commander. I saw him at Langrune on the 40th anniversary of D-Day, standing there, a great tall fellow, in the midst of his men, all still clustered around him, and I thought to myself,

"This chap has really kept his Commando together over all these years – its rather wonderful, really. David Fellows was, I thought, a very good, solid CO for 42 in Burma, and a good friend. I rate him highly. Nicol Gray was very good. A good spirit existed in our First Commando Brigade in Normandy with 3, 4 and 6 Army, and 45 Marine Commando, and we all got on splendidly. We were led first by Lord Lovat and then by Derek Mills-Roberts, who was a soldier if ever there was one.'

With more Royal Marines Commando units forming in England for service on D-Day or in the Far East and North-West Europe, let us now return to 40 and 41 Commandos, on the high seas and heading for the Allied landings in Sicily.

The two Royal Marine units, Nos 40 and 41 Commandos, the latter commanded by Lt-Col B. J. D. Lumsden, sailed from the Clyde at the end of June 1943 to take part in Operation Husky, the invasion of Sicily, where they landed on 10 July, in support of the 1st Canadian Division, with the specific task of eliminating coastal batteries. They formed a small brigade with No 3 Commando (Lt-Col John Durnford-Slater) and were later joined by No 2 Commando under Lt-Col Jack Churchill.

The Marines could do no training, other than basic weapon training on the way out from Scotland, and had little chance of exercise, and embarked directly into their LCAs from the transport. A heavy swell was running, and in the run-in to the beaches, many men were seasick, and the landing craft became widely separated. Jim Lennon was there with 40 Commando.

'We had practised getting into the landing craft several times on the way out on the *MV Derbyshire*, because the LCAs were on the davits. We climbed in without difficulty, and were then lowered into the sea, but as our LCA touched the waves, we nearly capsized, tossing and rolling. It was awful. Weighed down with weapons and ammo I didn't fancy swimming for it. Anyway, after a bit we joined up with other craft in the dark, and we could see anti-aircraft fire going up and plenty of dull explosions where the RAF were bombing on shore, a comforting thought. I dozed off for a bit, and woke up when Paddy, my oppo, said that there was a fiver in his wallet and I could have it if he got bumped off . . . he was badly wounded about an hour after we landed.

'The order came "Get ready to land", and we thought, well, now all hell will break loose, but the only sound was the keel grating on the shingle. We had a special mission to destroy some big guns that might bother the Canadians, who were coming ashore later. On the way there we got shot up and had some wounded, but the guns were gone. They looked static on the photos, but they must have been mobile.

'Dawn was now breaking, and from our position we could see an amazing sight – out to sea, as far as the horizon, nothing but ships, big ships, little ships, every kind of landing craft. It was good to see our troops coming ashore, but we couldn't count the prisoners, there were too many.'

Frank Nightingale landed with 'Q' Troop of 41 Commando: 'Our first action was the landing in Sicily, which went like an exercise. The Italians didn't have the heart to fight and our casualties were light. I was a bren-gunner, and my No 2 was George Comley, who was with me throughout the war. After Sicily we went to Salerno, which was a different business.'

H-Hour for the landing was 02.30, but the swell and offshore currents delayed the landing and dispersed the craft. 41 Commando was carried to the east of their objective, and ended up by capturing many objectives allocated to 40, which were mostly, as Jim Lennon has recounted, empty artillery positions or machine gun posts. Opposition was light and so were the casualties, with nine killed and thirty-seven wounded between both units, most of the Italians surrendering as soon as the Commandos closed in on them.

By nine in the morning, the Canadians were well ashore, and the Commandos dug in about two miles inland, to await a counter attack, which failed to materialize, although they were heavily mortared during the day. Two days later they were withdrawn, and after a few days on board a landing ship in Augusta, where 40 Commando experienced a heavy bombing raid, were joined by No 2 Commando from Gibraltar, and the Brigade bivouacked ashore near Catania. Sicily fell to the Allied armies on 16 August 1943. The next stop was to get ashore on the mainland of Italy, and as Frank Nightingale has observed, this was to be a very different proposition, against much fiercer opposition.

With the fall of Sicily, the invasion of Italy could not be long delayed, but although the Italian armies collapsed and the country itself capitulated on 3 September 1943, the campaigns in Italy which were to follow the invasion were never less than arduous, took a severe toll of the Allied Armies and, in the build-up to D-Day in France and after, became a campaign fought as a second front, second for everything except hard knocks.

This was due in part to the Italian terrain, which is naturally suited to defensive fighting. Italy is a mountainous peninsula, with a high central spine reaching up to the 2000-metre mark, from which spurs and ridges snake out into the coastal plains which are well seamed with wide, fast-flowing rivers. As one report put it, 'Every five hundred yards there is a new defensive position for a company, every five miles a new line for a division.' The central mountains also dictated that the Allied effort was split, with one half handed over to the

American 5th Army, and the other to the British 8th Army. Against this divided force the Germans could muster sixteen well-equipped combat divisions, eight under Field Marshal Erwin Rommel, and south of Rome, in the invasion area, another eight under Field Marshal Kesselring. On 3 September 1943, the 8th Army crossed the three-mile wide straits of Messina to land in the toe of Italy. There was little opposition to the landing because the Germans had withdrawn to defensive positions beyond the range of Allied air cover, and the 8th Army promptly advanced two hundred miles up the toe of Italy without serious opposition.

For the 5th Army at Salerno it was different. It was inevitable and obvious that a major landing would follow up the initial assault in southern Italy, and Field Marshal Kesselring could easily calculate where this might fall, simply by looking at a map. The Bay of Salerno lies thirty miles south of Naples, the second city of Italy, and was (just) within the limits of the Allied fighter cover. The beaches there were wide enough to permit a full scale landing, and if Naples could be captured swiftly, the Allies would secure a major, and possibly functioning port. The Field Marshal was so sure that the Allies would land at Salerno that he not only fortified the position but also sent a crack Panzer Division there to carry out anti-invasion exercises. This division dug itself in on the heights above Salerno Bay, and was ready and waiting when the 5th Army assault formations came ashore on 9 September.

Salerno is a wide, sandy bay, closely guarded by a circle of hills which run east to west, dividing the bay at Salerno from the plain around Naples. The shortest road between the two towns runs through a pass called La Molina, which is flanked by several hills, which became known to the troops as Castle Hill, Hospital Hill and, most significant for 41 Commando, White Cross Hill.

The two Commando units, Nos 2 and 41 Commando, attached to 10th British Corps of 5th Army, were charged with the task of silencing coastal batteries, and seizing the narrow pass of La Molina. The two Commandos embarked in the *Prince Albert* and other landing craft early on 8 September and went ashore some time around 02.15 on the following day, No 2 landing first with 41 close on their heels and both units arrived at La Molina just as dawn was breaking, without encountering any serious opposition. Back in Salerno daylight brought a different story, and the Commandos soon began to meet heavy and increasing resistance. 41 Commando found the road blocked by pill-boxes and tanks, which were attacked by the leading troops and knocked out, and pushed on to take up positions around two viaducts near the village of Vietri.

'Our first bit of action was on the viaduct,' writes Frank Nightingale of 'Q' Troop. 'George and I were on the Bren, when a German troop carrier approached. us. We opened fire on it. I got hit by a grenade, not seriously. I just couldn't sit down for a while. Moggie Morgan, our Sergeant-Major, who later got the Military Medal, ordered the Marine with the PIAT to fire at the troop carrier. The Marine tried and cried out, "I can't get the bloody thing loaded!' After I had the bit of shrapnel taken out of my arse, I rejoined "Q" Troop, where we were to take this hill, and hold it. The action was pretty grim. Young Peter Heydon got the DSO here – he was only 19 – he got a very bad wound and refused morphine in case it would cloud his mind. We held on until we were forced to withdraw, then we went in again, under Captain Wilkinson . . . he got the MC. He said, "We are going to be attacked, and we are going to hold on, to the last man, and the last round", and we did. We stayed put and the Germans withdrew. I think it was supposed to be the other way round. I think we had the heaviest mortaring and the losses were very heavy. The officers, NCOs and men were terrific, people like Heydon, Charlie Stratford, another great officer, Bill Cunningham, Major Edwards . . . I could go on and on.'

Bill Tilney was there, a sergeant in 'P' Troop. 'We had already had losses when we were bombed in Augusta, when we were embarked on the *Emma* or the *Beatrix*, I forget which . . . we had a lot of casualties and Florrie Ford, the "A" Troop Commander was killed. Johnny Taplin of "P" Troop was wounded on Sicily, and Captain Halliday took over. At Salerno we had an easy landing but for the first two days it was lively, the hardest time 41 had had, or ever had; losses were very heavy. Over seventy-five per cent of 41 were "HO" Marines and we were up against parachute troops and Panzers, and I think we did a bloody good job. It proved that we were as good, but at a cost. Col Lumsden was wounded, Maj Edwards was killed, Sgt Bob Strandling was killed. The night we took White Cross, our casualties were terrific. I led my section, and came back with two men. "P" lost seventy-five per cent killed or wounded. It was a bloody night. We got pushed off, but it finally took a full Brigade to take it, and that was three weeks later. We were three weeks on Salerno and there was fighting all the time . . . we kept that viaduct open, the road to Naples . . . I remember our RSM Tierney, he was killed. When we pulled back for a bit of a rest, they put us near a gun line, with artillery, Priest guns they were, firing over our heads – not much of a place for a rest. In the end we went back to Sicily and camped in orange groves near Catania.'

By mid-afternoon on 9 September, heavy artillery fire was falling on the Commando positions at Salerno. The beach-head and town itself was under heavy pressure from German tanks, infantry and artillery, and 10th Corps were now in serious trouble. It became vital to hold the defence line at La Molina, to prevent more enemy reinforcements moving up from Naples. In the early afternoon, the Germans made a serious attempt to dislodge them, and Col Lumsden was wounded by a direct hit on 41 Commando HQ. Maj J. R. Edwards took command, and a heavy counter-attack by infantry was beaten off. The battle for the pass of La Molina continued for the next three days, when a counter-attack by 41 and No 2 finally drove the Germans back. 41 Commando had already lost ten per cent of their strength in the four day fight at La Molina, and had only been out of the line for one day when they were sent back in to deliver an attack up a steep hill to the east of La Molina, which had been occupied by the Germans. 41 took this position without undue difficulty, losing one man killed and two wounded, and named it 41 Commando Hill. No 2 soon came up to capture another hill feature and the village of Pigoletti, from which an attack was mounted on a third hill feature called the Pimple. An attack here by 2 Commando was beaten off with heavy losses, including the death of Captain the Duke of Wellington, and at dawn, the Germans used their observation point on Pimple to call down heavy fire from 88 mm guns on Pigoletti. After enduring this all morning, it was decided that 41 should attack the Pimple again that night. Although very tired by days of fighting, 41 formed up on the startline at 02.00 on 17 September, only to be struck by a heavy bombardment from their own supporting artillery, which killed or wounded a number of men, including the officer commanding, Maj Edwards, who was fatally injured. One fighting troop managed to capture the Pimple, but could not be reinforced in the darkness. When the troop withdrew from the summit at 10.00 next morning, only six men were still on their feet. Next day, a full infantry brigade was called up to attack the Pimple, but this too was beaten off, and the Germans finally withdrew on the 19th, leaving many of their dead behind.

The two Commandos, 41 (Royal Marines) and No 2 (Army) distinguished themselves throughout the ten days of intense fighting at Salerno, and paid a heavy price, losing over forty-eight per cent of their effective strength. Of the 738 men who went ashore at Marina, only 372 Commandos returned to Sicily.

While 41 and 2 were fighting around Salerno, their comrades in No 3 and 40 (RM) Commando, having been withdrawn after landing near Reggio, were preparing to land again in Italy with 13 Corps of the 8th Army. On the 19 September, as the Germans withdrew from Salerno, this half brigade, accompanied by the SRS (Special Raiding Squadron) commanded by a legendary SAS soldier, Maj Paddy Mayne, sailed from Sicily and reached Bari on the east coast of Italy on the 30th, and were briefed for Operation Devon, a landing on the east coast of Italy, at a point roughly level with Naples.

It was decided that the Commandos and SRS should seize the little port of Termoli on the estuary of the river Bifuno, a place where it was anticipated that German forces retreating from Salerno might make a stand. If the Germans could be outflanked at Termoli, and forced to continue their withdrawal, the Allied advance might continue.

The force delegated for the initial landing was extremely small. No 3 Commando had seen heavy fighting in Sicily and was reduced to less than 200 men, commanded by Captain A. G. Komrower. 40 Commando, under Lt-Col 'Pops' Manners, mustered around 400, while the SRS, even with the fighting talents of Paddy Mayne, added little to the total strength of this lightly equipped force. The opposing forces were known to include parachute troops and tanks but nevertheless, the first stages of the landing went well. A small bridgehead was established west of Termoli by 3 Commando, and the Marines of 40 and the SRS passed through this to capture the town and a road junction a mile outside the town, where the coast-road met the main road from Termoli to Naples.

For a while it looked as if all would be well. 'The Germans are quite remarkable soldiers,' says Peter Young, who discharged himself from hospital to fight at Termoli. 'Even when they are really up against it, they can usually find something to throw at you. I've also fought the Italians, and the Japanese, and the Jews. They all know how to soldier, but if you haven't fought the Germans, well, my boy, you don't know what fighting is.'

Peter Young's opinions on the enemy's formidable ability to react were to be reinforced at Termoli. The town and port were secured by 08.00 on 3 October, and nothing much happened throughout the day except for some shelling, but at dawn on the next day the enemy struck back hard. Enemy aircraft bombed the perimeter at first light, and a counter-attack developed, mounting in a rising crescendo of violence that almost swept the invasion force back into the sea. The Commandos and SRS had been reinforced by forward elements of the 78th Division, including two infantry battalions from the Lancashire Fusiliers, the Argylls and the Buffs, and some field artillery. It was just enough to hold the beach-head.

Termoli was the key to any defensive line on the river Bifuno, and the Germans were determined to retake it. In the middle of the morning a heavy attack came in on the perimeter from the 26th Panzer Division, supported by infantry, and by 14.00 the position was serious. Enemy tanks of the 26th Panzer Division had reached the SRS positions on the road junction, 3 Commando was under mortar and artillery fire, and 40 was under pressure from advancing infantry. Action continued all around the perimeter during the afternoon and throughout the night, and heavy fighting continued throughout the next day as the enemy flung everything they had at the British perimeter.

'Some people didn't fancy it at all,' recalls Peter Young. 'At one point, Peter Hellings, who was then Second in Command of 40, and I had to draw our pistols in order to persuade some gunners to get back and fire their weapons at the advancing enemy tanks.'

Roy Farran of the SRS, recalls sending an officer back to call up some help from the 78th Division, and meeting an infantry brigadier who had just assured him that '. . . everything is under control, old boy', when a Spandau machine gun began to fire into Brigade Headquarters at close range, sending the Brigadier diving under an armoured car. Farran 'did not feel that the situation was at all under control'.

Ken Richardson of 40 Commando, whom we last met at Dieppe, agrees with this. 'We got ashore all right, but landed on a "false beach" and we drowned our radios crossing the deep channel between that sand-bank and the shore. We caught them by surprise all right on the 3rd, but next day was different. My section joined the perimeter around Commando HQ and before long we saw dark figures advancing down the road. I remember our password was "Surrey . . . and England", but we got fired at. The enemy came in real close, and we were throwing grenades at each other, and I got hit . . . My left arm was shattered. I was hit in the femoral artery as well and lost a lot of blood, very quickly. I got dragged into the HQ, which was also a First Aid station – there were our own and German wounded all over the place. I think the battle went on for four days. They were para-troops and Panzer Grenadiers, and they blasted us with

Tiger tanks, but we held on till 8th Army came up. I was flown out to an American hospital at Bizerta in North Africa, and eventually I got home, my fighting days being over. 40 went on to the Garigliano, where I am led to believe they were once again seriously diminished. Our CO in 40 then was Lt–Col Manners, a fine officer, very daring and direct.'

Richard McConkey remembers the lull after the landing. 'After taking it we handed over to a Brigade and went drinking around the dockside, then an officer came round to tell us to report back at the double; Jerry was counter-attacking and advancing fast. We went up to meet them and our Colonel "Pops" Manners was in the lead as usual. There were British soldiers streaming back, young officers and all. "Pops" threatened to shoot them if they didn't turn back. Anyhow, we manned their guns and all. Then we fell back and finished up fighting in a cemetery; we shoved them back and more troops came up. I finished sniping from an old house. They were blasting us with Moaning Minnie mortars. Well, this Corporal wanted a message taken to HQ and said, "You'd better take it, Mac". I told him he didn't know his job, but though I grumbled, I went in the end. I didn't even know where HQ was, but an officer said, "Follow me Mac", and as we were going up a passage, a bullet killed him. We buried him there, but not deep, about a yard, as they would shift him later.'

Jim Lennon, who was in 'A' Troop of 40, wrote down his impressions of Termoli soon after the battle. 'They told us our objective was a port about fifteen miles in front of 8th Army. We had to take it and hold it until the Army could link up. We were to land at 02.00 and the Army would arrive about 09.00 (we hoped).

'Our beach was a mile or so past Termoli and the water was chest-deep and very cold. We crossed over the sand and passed through 3 Commando, then through a railway siding. The rest of the Commando made for the town. Our Troop went for the crossroads to form a road-block. It was a fast march, walk and run. It's nerve-racking to be behind enemy lines and we could hear small arms fire from the town and wondered how the rest of the lads were getting on. We hit the road and began to dig in and that warmed us up. At dawn a Jerry truck came in towards Termoli so we opened up with Bren, tommy and rifle, killed the three in the cab and put them in the ditch. Our officer drove the truck off the road. We lit fags and waited. We knocked out another truck and took the occupants prisoner: both were wounded, a Parachute officer and a trooper. We dressed their wounds, and the officer offered me one of his shirts as a souvenir.

'The next truck along was a bonus, full of chocolate and cigarettes, and the next held the garrison mail! It didn't get through, nor the man riding shotgun. It was now noon and we had shot up a lot of trucks but no 8th Army arrived. We found out later that the bridges were blown.

'At nine that night, a Recce Regiment came along and we were relieved, our job finished, or so we thought. We had gone back about a mile towards Termoli when we heard the artillery, and looking back, we saw the crossroads under fire. We heard that the Army boys had a lot of casualties. The next few days were bloody sticky! Jerry hit the whole line with everything he had, tanks, guns, mortars, planes. "Hang on", we were told by Maj Hellings, who came tearing past in a jeep, throwing out packets of fags. We were told that Monty was mounting a big attack from the west. On the fourth day we were relieved only to be sent to the right flank to cover an Army Brigade (38th Irish), who were moving in to attack. The attack was successful, and Jerry was on the run. We had our losses, but after refitting we were ready for another job.

'Knocker' White of 'Y' Troop, gives another graphic account of the landing and battle at Termoli. 'It was a filthy night and heavy seas were running. As soon as the ramps were down we were up to our necks in rough seas; however, we made it, no opposition. I don't suppose they expected any landings under those conditions. We tore up the beach and just ahead of us was a freight train chugging out of a cutting. Some of the lads jumped onto the footplate and they said the driver slit his own throat and committed suicide. Our section then advanced up the railway, towards the town and searched the houses along the streets for any Germans. Most of the fighting seemed to be around the town square and a hotel near the railway. We then got back along the rail track, where there was a brick wall between us and them. There were several Germans in the top rooms throwing grenades about, so Charlie Cooper, our Section Corporal, said "Put your grenade cup on your rifle and see if you can lob one or two into the windows"; so I did, and after a couple of tries got the range spot on. This quietened them down. Then we all leapt over the wall, rushed down towards the hotel, which had a large steel shuttered blind drawn down over the doorway, so we all got our bayonets out and prised under the bottom until we forced it up, then rushed in. No Jerries down below, so we decided that the Bren-gunners would fire upwards through tne ceilings, while the rest of us rushed upstairs bursting open the doors and throwing grenades in. This did the trick, except for one wounded Jerry who, although badly wounded, fired his Schmeisser as one of our boys entered a room; fortunately he only received a stomach wound, but needless to say, the German was finished off. Thus Termoli was taken.

'During the day more British forces landed. Six Sherman tanks got through, before a bridge was blown, and we established a bridgehead some five miles in depth. Things were quiet for a day, then they hotted up as a counter-attack began – at first, heavy mortar and

Landing craft before the assault on Dieppe.

Royal Marines of 43 Commando moving up to their next objective, Lake Comacchio, Italy, April 1945.

German gun emplacement at St Aubin-sur-Mer.

D-Day memorial at St Aubin-sur-Mer.

48 Commando's landing beach at St Aubin-sur-Mer, 6 June 1944.

Lieutenant-Colonel Jim Moulton directs tank fire on to the Langrune strong point.

Lieutenant Paddy Stevens standing before 'A' Troop, 41 Commando, on D-Day.

Royal Marines Commandos moving off the Normandy beaches during the advance,
6 June 1944.

Troops of 1 Commando Brigade moving inland from the beaches to their first objective
after landing in Normandy on 6 June 1944.

Amphibious vehicles on the beach during the assault on Walcheren, November 1944, showing some of the defensive obstacles in the background.

Marines of 'A' Troop, 41 Commando, advancing through Westkapelle to their objective – the lighthouse visible in the background (Walcheren, November 1944).

Royal Marines Commandos land in the Arakan, Burma.

Terry Brown about to go on patrol with 42 Commando in Malaya, 1950.

Marines of 41 (Independent) Commando inspect damage to an important enemy supply line in North Korea, after demolition with explosive charges, 10 April 1951.

41 (Independent) Commando Royal Marines on the march from Chosin; Lieutenant-Colonel Drysdale is in the centre of the picture.

Machine gunners of 'S' Troop, 45 Commando, in the Libyan desert, 1954

Air Troop, 41 Commando, in Cyprus, 1969.

The first wave of Royal Marines Commandos embark in helicopters on the flight deck of HMS *Theseus* for the airlift to Port Said (Suez, November 1956).

artillery barrages, then the tanks and infantry, but the boys held out, until on the fifth day the main force broke through.

'After it was all over, General Montgomery came over and congratulated us, and said the Germans had done exactly what he wanted them to do, move a complete armoured division from the Naples area to our bridgehead and try and drive us into the sea.'

40 Commando's battle report on Termoli shows that the Commando were in action within a few hours of landing, and after that brief lull on 3 October, stayed in action for four days, with much of the fighting at very close quarters. Consider these extracts from the Unit diary: '"A" Troop advanced to the bridge, and attacked an enemy HQ with very close fighting; the enemy were cleared with grenades . . . Lt Hill badly wounded in the legs.

. . . 20 Germans killed and 30 captured, including a paratroop colonel. Captain Marshall took two sections and assaulted the German position on the ridge, held by approx. 40, with 2 MG and other automatic weapons. Enemy fell back leaving 10 dead, 20 prisoners taken.'

The Germans put in one final attack against 40 early on the morning of 6 October, but once again they were beaten off. By mid-day they were in full retreat, and the battle of Termoli was over. The Commandos and SRS had prevented the Germans making a stand on the Bifuno, and General Sir Bernard Montgomery, the 8th Army Commander, was duly grateful.

'Take your boys back to Bari,' he told Brigadier Durnford-Slater, 'where there are plenty of girls and plenty to drink.' The Commandos withdrew to rest at Barletta near Bari, and took the General's advice seriously to heart. Out of the line, or when no action was pending, life in 40 was like that in any other unit, a round of training, inspections, sport and, if possible, a spot of local leave. 'Q' Troop of 40 also produced a magazine, *Victory*, and the issue dated 22 December 1943 makes interesting reading. In *Unit News* it records the departure of 'our late 2 I/C Major Peter Hellings DSC, MC, and wishes him God-speed', and comments on the prevalence of strikes in the factories and mines in England. The column 'For Jazz Lovers' comments, 'Most of you will have heard the buzz that a guy named F. Sinatra is stealing Bing Crosby's thunder in America. Don't let it bother you. It is this correspondent's firm conviction that Sinatra is a nine days wonder.' A fashion note concludes that 'zip fasteners will be a big thing in men's clothing after the war'. This rest period, like so many others, did not last long.

40 Commando's next two 'jobs' in Italy were in the heavy infantry role, which was not one for which a World War II Commando unit was well equipped. All Commandos in Italy, both Army and Marine, suffered continually from the inability of certain senior Army officers to appreciate that a Commando unit is trained and equipped for a specific role, and lacked both the logistic element, and indeed the manpower, to maintain itself in the line for any length of time, like a full-strength Army battalion. It was also necessary for the Brigade to rest, re-equip, and recruit more men. The Army Commandos raised theirs by calling for 8th Army volunteers, while the Marines recruited from the landing craft crews, and detachments of the Fleet.

'Prior to joining the Commandos, I served for two and a half years with the East Med Fleet and saw far more action there, serving on the aircraft carrier *Formidable* and then the *Coventry*, where we got sunk in a raid at Tobruck. In fact, I would say I was bomb-happy by the time I joined 40 . . .' writes Marine B. J. Smith of Lancaster.

While all this was going on, changes were taking place at a higher level. Brigadier Bob Laycock was promoted to the command of Combined Operations after Lord Mountbatten went to take over South-East Asia Command, at the end of 1943, and Brigadier Tom Churchill arrived to take over the newly formed 2nd Commando Brigade which, with 3 and 41 returning to England for D-Day, would consist of 2, commanded by his brother Jack Churchill, 9 commanded by Lt-Col R. J. F. Tod, 40 (Royal Marines) under the redoubtable 'Pops' Manners, and the newly arrived 43 (Royal Marines) Commando raised from the 2nd Battalion Royal Marines, under Lt-Col R. W. B. Simmonds RM. This force was completed by the Belgian and Polish Troops of No 10 (Inter-Allied) Commando.

The Brigade's first operation after Termoli was in the infantry (as opposed to the Commando) role, in support of the operations then developing around the town and monastery at Cassino. In late November 1943, Tom Churchill joined his Brigade at Molfetta, and to give them battle experience, sent the Belgian and Polish Troops of No 10 (Inter-Allied) Commando into the line, which then lay along the river Sangro, where they did very well. Then early in December, Churchill received the order to send one Commando to assist 10th British Corps across the Garigliano river, on the left flank of the American 5th Army in the opening phase of the Battle of Cassino. This task was delegated to No 9 Commando, which had seen no action, and they landed on the beaches north of the river on 29 December 1943; 9 Commando created a considerable diversion, and drew down a lot of enemy fire, forcing the enemy to divert forces from the Cassino front, and as a result of this the 2nd Commando Brigade (still called a Special Service Brigade at this time), was switched from the eastern (8th

Army) coast to the western (5th Army) coast, and concentrated near Naples.

Twelve days after No 9 returned from the Garigliano it was the turn of 40 Commando, who were sent to assist the 56th (London) Division in a main crossing of the river.

'We formed up a couple of miles from the river,' writes James Lennon, 'and the assault was to go in at 22.00 hrs. 40 Commando was to be the first over, and alongside us was a Battalion of Ox and Bucks Light Infantry, a good bunch of lads. We moved off at 21.00 hrs going at a steady pace towards the river. After about ten minutes the earth seemed to split and everyone dived for cover. There was a tremendous cacophony of noise. We awaited the crump of shell and mortar – nothing. Then we heard our own shells screaming towards the enemy. We breathed again, our own barrage going in to soften up the enemy. Soon we were at the river, and no fire from Spandau or mortar met us. "Maybe he's gone," some optimist shouted, but our "Intelligence" knew exactly where he was. As we slid down the river bank to man the assault boats, Jerry let us have it, red tracer lines patterned the night around us. We were lucky the tracers were passing well above us and soon we were across the river; we climbed up the opposite bank, the REs accompanying us with their mine detectors and white tape, and soon had a safe path for us to advance on. By this time Jerry was mortaring the river banks. We advanced about a hundred yards, then were ordered to wait for the rest of the assault to come up and then to advance on our objectives. Ours were the heights directly to our front. The noise from the British and American barrage was deafening, but we were being hit by mortar and shell fire from the Germans. At the briefing we had been ordered to by-pass the Spandau nests, leaving them for the following troops to mop up. "Keep going, get on those heights." We were moving pretty fast now; we were almost amongst our own barrage. After a pause we were ordered to move on again. A Spandau gunner had us in his sights and began that familiar stacatto barking . . . someone close by got one. We took cover behind a small house, but before we had time to catch our breath we were ordered to cross the orchard. Several of our section had been hit now, and one or two were missing. There was nothing we could do, we had to keep going. We crossed the orchard and learned later that it had been mined and booby trapped, yet not one of our men had hit one.

'Several Spandaus were now firing, one of them directly to our front, about a hundred yards along a track. Several of our troop crawled as near as they could and then rushed it, killing the crew and took two or three prisoners who had taken all they could – they came willingly.

'Dawn was breaking and our barrage wasn't as intense. We rested a while, and then began our climb to our objective, the heights, maybe two thousand feet. We found some abandoned machine guns unattended in their "nests", the crews had scarpered, wise men; we were in no mood for taking prisoners. We were hampered by snipers, and the mortars and "Eighty-eights" had got our range. We were ordered to dig in – some hope, in that rock-hard terrain! We did the next best thing, built "sangars", rocks built up around our bodies – they afforded some protection against flying shrapnel – and we lay there waiting for the one with our number on it, mouths and tongues dry. Then the shelling stopped. Later, looking back over the few miles we had covered, the whole scene was littered with countless shell holes: it didn't seem possible that any German, or for that matter any living thing, could have survived that terrible barrage of ours.

'We made a welcome and well-earned "Brew" and wondered about our casualties and what the immediate few hours had in store for us; a few enemy planes buzzed us and dropped several bombs, while our planes machine gunned and bombed enemy positions. We rested in a shallow ditch running along a narrow lane. We slept fitfully under straw we had gathered. It was cold with only a leather jerkin on top of our uniform.

'(Fifth Day). Some Army boys to our right and front had taken a real hammering from the German shelling. We were ordered up to reinforce them on Monte Domiano, a hard slog which took us two or three hours. We were under fire all the way up, and by the time we reached our new positions our section was sadly depleted. I could count about nine or ten; Jerry was about eighty yards in front of us behind a stone wall. We were now on the crest of Domiano and built our sangars and waited for the next order. As the order came in, a frontal attack on three Spandau nests some distance behind the wall, I looked at three dead "Tommies" lying out there. Our Troop was ordered to storm that wall and silence the Spandau. Before we went over the wall we threw smoke grenades and took what cover we could. We could hear the bullets whining past us through the smoke, while our tommy guns and rifles were blazing in the opposite direction, aiming through the drifting smoke to where we thought the Spandaus were. Through a break in the smoke I caught a glimpse of a mountain range, and in that same split second I saw the blurred outline of two of the enemy both in the act of throwing stick grenades. I fired at the shadowy figures and fell flat. The grenades exploded on either side of me . . . I raised my head to see if any of my pals had been hit. The smoke was still drifting around me . . . there was a hell of a racket coming from further to my right. I put my hand to my head and felt the blood coming from a wound. I decided to get back over the wall before I passed out, if I could make it. I made a dash for the wall and expected a burst in my back, but I made it. I was told that at about the same time that we attacked the wall, Jerry had counter-attacked on our right, the troops who should have followed us had their hands full with that lot. My best pal Tommy Grey was one who didn't come back over the wall. He was killed as he went over, firing a Tommy gun.

'I went back to get my wound patched up at a first-aid post, then I was sent back for further treatment down the mountain, making my way down with a fellow with a leg wound. We walked with army stretcher bearers carrying badly wounded men. They did a marvellous job, leaving the stretcher cases at the bottom of the mountain, then going back for more. There were plenty of snipers about, but they didn't fire on stretcher bearers or walking wounded, but at reinforcements going up the mountain.'

To see the purpose of the landings at Anzio it is necessary to recollect the previous comments on the defensive nature of the Italian terrain. Fighting up the 'leg' of Italy was exactly like hitting one's head against a brick wall, and when the Germans made a determined stand at Cassino, the Allied advance, which had never been rapid, came to a complete halt.

Cassino was a terrible battle. It lasted for over six months, and the defences mangled some fine Allied divisions and Corps. The 36th (Texas) Division of the 5th Army were badly cut up early in the first battle, the 2nd Indian Division and the New Zealanders came up and pounded away fruitlessly in their turn, taking heavy losses. To break this stalemate it was decided to try another landing, and put a strong force, the US 6th Corp, which consisted of the US 3rd Division and the British 1st Division, under the American General Lucas, on the beaches near Anzio. Even if these landings did not succeed, it was calculated that they would draw off enemy forces from Cassino, and that might, just, tip the scales there in the Allies' favour.

The details of the Battle of Cassino, and the long-term effects of Anzio fall outside the scope of this book. Let it suffice to say that although the initial landings at Anzio took the Germans by surprise, they reacted with their usual promptness and ferocity, and proved themselves quite capable of containing both the Anzio beach-head and the Allied line at Cassino. The fighting at Anzio was particularly bitter and fought at very close range, often in deep gulleys which soon came to resemble the Western Front trenches of World War I.

The forces which landed at Anzio on 22 January 1944, included three battalions of the American Rangers, the US equivalent of the British Commandos. They advanced rapidly and seized the initial perimeter. No 9 Army and 43 (Royal Marines) Commando, who landed from *HMT Derbyshire*, crossed the beach unopposed at 05.30, well before dawn. They crossed a flat coastal plain, seamed by deep gulleys, killing a number of despatch riders but meeting little opposition, and were on the lower slopes of the Alban Hills, which were supposed to mark out the beach-head. That night they handed over to the US 3rd Ranger Battalion, and were withdrawn to Naples.

This was only a short respite for after a few days 43 and 9 were sent to the Garigliano front to help the 46th Division develop their bridgehead across the river. The Division held two six hundred metre peaks, Mount Turlio and Mount Tuga, but these two were dominated by three taller mountains, to the north and west, Mount Ornito and a nameless mountain known as Point 711, while beyond these two lay Monte Fiato, the tallest of the three at over 1000 metres. The capture of these three peaks was allotted to 9 and 43; but to even get to the lower slopes they had to cross a valley 300 metres wide. The task was formidable.

Brigadier Churchill made two recces of the battlefield, and decided to attack from the flank, with 43 taking Ornito and Point 711, and 9 coming through to assault Monte Fiato. The attack went in at 18.30 on the evening of 2 February 1944. Before they could move, 43 were shelled by an 88 mm and advanced in bright moonlight; they soon met heavy mortar and machine gun fire. The CO leading from the front, took 'A', 'B' and 'D' Troops into the attack, leaving 'C' to mop up the opposition on the lower slopes. Among the ranks of 'C' Troop was a young Scots Lance-Corporal, Tom Hunter, who was to win the VC a year later at Lake Comacchio.

The assault was uphill and over very broken ground but Ornito and 711 were eventually secured, and over thirty prisoners were taken. Meanwhile, 9 Commando were coming through, under 'hellish fire, which killed their Second-in-Command, and wounded the CO, Colonel Tod'. The Germans were by now 'thoroughly roused' and 9 were forced to withdraw from Fiato and take up a defensive position with 43's HQ on the lower slopes of Mount Ornito. During the day, both Commandos endured heavy shelling and mortar fire.

The Germans counter-attacked on the 3rd, sending in a company of Panzer Grenadiers, but 43 counter-attacked at once, and threw them back. At 21.00 the Commando was relieved by a battalion of the Hampshire Regiment, and withdrew across the Garigliano, having lost seven killed and twenty-six wounded in twenty-four hours of fighting.

There was no rest in Italy for the Commandos – or at least, not for long. Nos 9 and 43 began training again, and at the end of February were sent to join the Yugoslav partisans on Vis, but 40 Commando were sent back to Anzio where every rifle and the guns of the Fleet were needed to hold off the relentless German attacks on the now beleaguered beach-head.

'Knocker' White gives a graphic account of life in the line at Anzio. 'After Termoli we pulled back to Molfetta for a spell over Xmas '43, then shortly into the New Year we trans-shipped round to the west coast of Italy, near the Naples area. Prior to this period the Commando had been involved in the crossings of the Sangro and Garigliano rivers, but "Y" Troop was not involved, being held in reserve.

'Some time towards the end of February, 40 Commando were called to Anzio; we were held in reserve on the initial landings, which we had learned were going well and with a bit more enterprise Rome may well have been taken. But gradually the Germans regained the initiative and with reinforcements being rushed in, pushed our forces back into a tight perimeter, within which, not a square yard was out of range of mortar and artillery fire.

'This was the scene that greeted 40 when we landed on 2 March 1944. The weather was filthy, wet and cold and everywhere a quagmire. First night there, somewhere up at the front, I don't know where as we hadn't seen any maps, or the territory in daylight, we ("Y" troop) were called up to do a fighting patrol. I remember we waded up a river, water knee-deep, for some two hours until we came to an army post on top of the river bank. It was very dark by now; and after Captain Laidlow, our OC, had been briefed by the Army's OC, he came back and told us "Well lads, somewhere out there in No Man's Land, are a group of farm buildings which a strong German patrol occupies at night, playing hell with the troops here, so we've got to go out there and eliminate them."

'After a brief rest, we were all set to go, and just as we went over the top a thunderstorm broke. It thundered and lightninged and rained, but I didn't mind because I'd often found that the filthier the weather, the more likely you were to get away with it, and so it was. The going was hard, as every yard was pitted with mortar and shell craters, and then suddenly there were the buildings, and we were in among them before they knew what had hit them. They were all killed, except one whom we took back as a prisoner. We had to make a long circular detour to get back to our lines, mostly by compass, and every now and again having to halt and investigate silhouettes of knocked-out vehicles and tanks before carrying on. We eventually found our lines, a British mortar team, ensconced in a hut, and after the challenge and correct password, they made us a very welcome brew of tea. We then got further back and while having a meal and awaiting further orders, a single mortar bomb fell among us, killing one of my pals, "Yorky" Towers, and wounding several more, a sad episode after the night's work. Next move, we boarded some trucks and churned our way along white taped lanes and directed by Red Caps to I don't know where. I heard someone mention "Pontine Marshes" and that's all we knew. After unloading, Captain Laidlow came to me and said, "I want you to take an advance party, Knocker, with this guide, to some gulleys, to relieve the army." So away we went into the gulley, were shown the dugouts, the manned slit-trenches, the direction of the enemy, and that was that; as the guide went off he said, "Best of luck, mate. Am I glad to be getting out of here!"

'By the end of the night, the rest of the Troop had arrived, and I showed Lt Beadle our section officer, our dugouts and manning points. Most of the slit-trenches had dead bodies buried in them and were sited nearly at the top of both sides of the gulleys. The dug-outs where you rested off watch were just dug into the sides of the gulley with a sandbagged surround at the entrance. As the weather was so wet, the gulleys were rushing with water, so your feet were always wet and grit got between your toes and skinned them. At the bottom of our gulley was a T-junction, which we were told meant certain death to venture into, while up from there the ground rose and circled around us like a horseshoe, behind which was the enemy; and they let us know it, mortaring was constant (the Moaning Minnie type) to keep your nerves on edge. At night, armoured track vehicles kept clanging about, making you think an armoured division was coming at you, and every so often a barrage of smoke shells came at you, making you think an attack was coming.

'We were getting quite a few casualties, mostly when in the open, changing watches. So I suggested we changed the watch at the odd hours, as evidently Jerry knew our tradition of changing watch at the even hours. Getting the wounded back to casualty clearing was a business too. After getting them on to a stretcher, you had to get to your end of the gulley, wave a big white sheet on the end of a pole, then emerge into the open, hoping they had seen you. This was the practice before we took over, so we continued it. You had to carry no weapons, dump your wounded at casualty clearing (about 1 mile to the rear), all in flat, open country, then return with the same numbers that were carrying. As soon as you reached the gulley, you all had to run like mad to your nearest dugout, as they rained mortars at you. After about ten days things were getting grim ration-wise, as the mud was so bad – even a Jeep only got through to us now and again. Water was a problem too, you couldn't use the gulley water as along its edges were buried American soldiers, the whole length. It looked as if they had been ambushed and taken a real battering at some time. At the entrance end of the gulley, several sapling trees were growing, so we dug underneath their roots, clearing them, until we got a good trickle of water to hang a tin under. We used to get enough to make a brew-up. Eventually we augmented our rations by finding some in the dead Yanks' haversacks. We found their tins of self-heating stews particularly handy and packs of glucose tablets.

'As the days went by, the inactivity of the war of attrition began to tell on all of us. Our 25-pounders used to put down a barrage now and again to quieten them down, and we did a bit of patrol work – as did they. One night after there had been an exchange of fire during the night, a German Red Cross party waved from the ridge, as it was our practice to let them come and get any dead or wounded. On this occasion, our TSM "Bangalore" Hawkins, went out with his runner, and parleyed with them; his runner then came back with his T. Gun and said he was going back with the party, helping them with the stretchers. Time rolled on, but no "Bangalore" returned (we called him Bangalore because he was tall and streaky). Then during the late afternoon a loud-hailer from the ridge shouted, "Englander, Englander, we have letter for you", which was on the end of a pole coming over the ridge. Lt Beadle's runner went and retrieved it and brought it back to him. The contents were to the effect that after they had reached their lines that morning, they had searched "Bangalore" and found a Beretta pistol concealed on him. This had contravened some section of the Geneva Convention and so they had detained him.

'I met "Bangalore" Hawkins in POW Camp in Germany later on in the war and could tell you another tale about him, but that's another story . . . another day. Well, the weeks dragged on, the weather didn't improve and casualties mounted. "Pops" Manners came up some evenings to have a chat to keep our morale up etc., but couldn't relieve us yet. However, after 26 days we did get relieved, by one of our Troops, and like the army chappie, I was glad to be out of there.'

4

The War for the Islands, 1943–44

There is full many a man that crieth
War! War! that knows full little to what
war amounteth. War hath its beginning . . . but
what befalls thereafter it is not light to know.

The Melibee

While the Eighth and Fifth Armies were battling their
way up the Italian peninsula, a curious little war was
developing further to the East, in the scattered islands of
the Adriatic and along the coast of Yugoslavia. The
politics of Yugoslavia in the years before and during the
early part of the war were of Byzantine complexity, but
by 1944 the situation was at least definable. The Germans
had occupied the country in April 1941, and behaved
thereafter with considerable ruthlessness, so that the entire population, not noted for passivity at the best of
times, was soon roused against them. The Yugoslav resistance came from two main parties, the pro-monarchy,
right-wing Cetniks, under Draja Mihailovich, and the
Communist Partisans under a dedicated Communist,
Josip Broz, better known to history as Marshal Tito. In
the early days of the occupation these two groups worked
together, but their mutual antipathy soon grew to the
point where their followers were fighting each other. At
first, Britain supported the Cetniks, but when Tito's
Partisans were seen to be the more effective and active
force, British aid was transferred to the Communists
who, after defeating the Germans, intended to establish a

Communist state in Yugoslavia after the war, and were eagerly awaiting the arrival of the Red Army, then fighting its way into the Balkans. The Germans had quickly conquered the mainland, although they were never able to subdue the Partisans high in the mountains or on the islands. By early 1944, Tito's main force was deployed in a string of islands off the Dalmatian coast, where various British units, among them Nos 2 and 43 (Royal Marines) Commandos, were sent to their assistance.

In December 1943, Brigadier Fitzroy Maclean, who headed the Allied Military Mission to the Partisans, had arrived in Italy, and went to see the GOC, General Alexander. He told the General that help was needed if the Partisans were to keep the Germans out of the Dalmatian Islands, and that while some might fall anyway, one of them, Vis, could be held if the Partisans were immediately reinforced. This seemed to be an ideal role for a commando unit, and the first troops of 2 Commando landed on Vis on 6 January, followed a month later by 43.

43 Commando had been raised from the 2nd Battalion Royal Marines in August 1943, and was the first Commando to go through the training centre at Achnacarry as a complete unit. The unit, commanded by Lt-Col R. W. B. Simmonds, sailed from the Clyde on the *Monarch of Bermuda* on 13 November 1943, for 'destination unknown', which turned out to be the Bir Hakiem transit camp outside Algiers. 43 joined Brigadier Churchill's 2nd Special Service Brigade just after Christmas 1943, and saw action at Anzio and on the Garigliano, before being sent to the island of Vis, in the Dalmatian group, where they arrived on the night of 28/29 February, 1944.

'When daylight broke on the 29th,' says the 43 Commando history, 'the sight that met our eyes was incredible. There, spread out on the sea to the north, south and east of us, were many islands, all occupied by thousands of enemy troops, who far outnumbered us, here in our last fortress. A grim thought was that we were almost out of range of our own aircraft, while the enemy had many aircraft close to Vis. However, we had a small but intrepid Royal Navy, in MLs, MGBs and MTBs, with whom we were to fight many battles against the enemy.'

Vis is a rugged, mountainous island, rising steeply out of the blue Adriatic. It has two ports, the only towns of any size on the island, Vis, to the east, and Komiza to the west. The small central plain, covered thickly by vines and surrounded by mountains, eventually became an airstrip, and the hills around the airstrip became the Commando's home. Here they dug in and pitched their bivouacs. The weather was cold, wet and windy, as their shelters flapped under the relentless tugging of the *boras*, the Adriatic wind. By the end of March it was very hot, the nights were shorter, food supplies were uncertain, but the Commando was active. During the first month on Vis, 43 carried out eight raids on neighbouring enemy-occupied islands, some at troop strength, and reconnoitred many more with a view to future raids, while supplying boarding parties for the patrol craft which went out each night to harass enemy shipping. All this was a prelude to major raids and operations.

'The Navy were there, and a section or two of us would go out with them. The MGBs would lie up quietly off the Yugoslav coast and wait for Jerry convoys creeping down. Then they would dash out and attack the escorts with guns and torpedoes, and come alongside the convoy, so we could leap aboard and secure crew and cargo . . . many a prize was taken like this, including a cargo of butter one night,' writes Knocker White of 'Y' Troop, 40 Commando, which had arrived on Vis in April.

Lt-Col Simmonds then became Head of Planning for

the Commando Brigade, and 43 was commanded by Major N. G. M. Munro. On 21 March the entire Commando, accompanied by a 3000-strong Yugoslav Brigade, embarked for Hvar to attack the 250-strong enemy garrison at the port of Jelsa, the Commando's first major operation with a Yugoslav unit, the whole force being commanded by Lt-Col Simmonds.

The enemy were already withdrawing when 43 attacked, and the two forces exchanged a huge volume of fire before the Germans retreated to the east coast, to collide there with the newly-landed 1st Dalmatian Partisan Brigade, where the fighting became hand to hand. The Commando mortar platoon put in a good shoot in support of the Partisans, while 'A' Troop and Commando HQ beat off a heavy counter-attack, dispersing the enemy and inflicting many casualties. The Commando withdrew that night to Vis, having killed 50 and captured 80 of the 200-strong Hvar garrison. They had also had their first experience of working with the Partisans, an experience all the Commandos were to remember.

Tito's Partisan army was a wild, fiercely disciplined force, drawn from the many nationalities of that Balkan State – Slovenes, Croats, Serbs, Montenegrins – and containing many women and children, who also played a full part in army life, including the fighting.

'Death meant very little to them,' writes Ross Hook, then the padre of 43 Commando. 'The small German *schu* mine was deadly, and widely employed before their defences, so Partisan units would go into the assault preceded by waves of children, some no more than twelve years old. I remember the shock I had when I saw small boys being brought into the temporary hospital in Brac. I told the interpreter it was barbarous to send small children into battle but he replied, "But it saves the lives of the soldiers . . . we don't have many men, but we have plenty more boys."

'Trifling with Partisan women could prove dangerous, even fatal. Three men of 2 Commando had to watch while the Partisans shot three women for the crime of pregnancy, and the normal way of warfare was equally unsparing, with few prisoners being taken on either side.'

'We took prisoners, of course,' said Norris Peak of 43, 'but getting them back wasn't easy. We might put twelve on a Jug boat for Vis and only six would arrive. 43 smuggled back to Italy a naked German who came crawling into their lines one night, the sole survivor of a group of German prisoners. They had been forced to strip before execution, and the task of shooting them had been given to a girl Partisan and a boy of thirteen, "as a privilege to shoot Fascist dogs".'

The British troops found the Partisans hardy if unreliable fighters, as indifferent to wounds as to death. Ross Hook again: 'When I was at the hospital at Gruz, the doctors told me of Jugs arriving on foot with two-week-old gangrenous wounds. For all their unreliability (and their maddening conviction that only the Russians were really fighting the war – their high opinion of the Russians went through a rude shock when the Red Army entered Belgrade with rape and pillage), the Jugs were honest. I lost my wallet the first day on Vis, and a Jug who found it gave it back to me the next day, intact. They gave us a very good white wine, which was potent stuff, as those Marines who downed it like beer discovered to their cost, although it never gave anyone a hangover – which might strike some as a kind of paradise – and a special drink called *racchia*, which was about 95 per cent proof and was used by the MO to sterilize his instruments.

'They enjoyed a game of "futbol" too, but they could be temperamental. When our referee, the OC of "B" Troop, gave a penalty against the Jugs, their team walked off, and their supporters swarmed onto the pitch, all armed to the teeth . . . there were no more penalties after that!

'The Partisan women, the *drugovistas* . . . I recall one, squat, square, solid as a Gurkha, wearing a khaki side cap, a red star in the middle, square on her close-cropped head. She wore an Italian field tunic, German breeches, and British army boots. From a leather belt hung four Italian "red devil" grenades, her legs were wrapped in puttees, and over her shoulder was slung a Sten gun, complete with silencer.'

Charles McNeill of 40 Commando, recalls similar sights. 'The Partisans were a hard lot, wearing any uniforms they could lay their hands on – Italian, German, British. They were armed with all sorts of weapons, mostly German, grenades, knives . . . especially the women, youngsters, 12 to 14 . . . all were the same. The head man in the group I was with had only one arm; the story went that the Germans cut it off for no reason. When the Germans took Yugoslavia they did terrible things, so the Partisans did not take prisoners, and the Germans would not surrender to them. When we attacked on Brac we shouted we were British, with the idea that the Germans would surrender to us, (no chance).'

Raiding and reconnaissance patrols continued throughout April, but the next major operation began on 22 May when 43 and 2 Commando embarked on a 24-hour operation against the island of Mijet. This operation was not a success, partly because the plan underestimated the time necessary to cross the difficult terrain, partly because the enemy were reinforced by SS troops from the Yugoslav mainland. The Commando re-embarked on the second night, their clothes and boots shredded by the undergrowth and razor sharp rocks. The 43 Commando history records that, 'Mijet was the most exhausting operation the Commando ever undertook, and achieved little conclusively.' May ended on a sombre note, but one bright spot was the arrival on Vis of 40 Commando.

On 30 May word was received that the Germans were mounting an all-out operation against Marshal Tito's HQ in Bosnia, and an order arrived, directing the troops on Vis to mount some major attack in order to draw off forces from the mainland. It was therefore decided that a Commando plus two Partisan brigades would mount an assault on the strongly-held island of Brac, which the Germans had re-occupied and reinforced. This task was first allotted to 2 Commando but switched to 43 a few hours before the force sailed. 43 were accompanied by a troop of 40 Commando, and 1300 Partisans.

43 got off to a good start with a difficult but un-opposed landing, and made a swift nine-mile march to their start line in the mountains, a considerable feat since the troops were carrying full scales of kit and ammunition, plus 3-inch mortar bombs, and Bangalore wire-cutting torpedoes, while the Heavy Weapons troop was man-packing their mortar and Vickers machine-guns. The objectives were two strong German positions on 1800-foot mountain tops, both well defended by well-trained troops. Artillery support came from 'a very fine battery of the III Field Regiment', and their FCO (Fire Control Officer); Major Turner MC, RA, who marched with the Commando and had fought at El Alamein, took one look at the German defences and remarked that eight regiments of field artillery would be needed to reduce them. Lacking this kind of firepower, the Commando attacked with what it had in the early afternoon, after being accidentally strafed by a flight of British Spitfires from Vis.

Their attack was supposed to be made in conjunction with that of the Partisans, but the Commando were soon mystified to realize that all the enemy fire was concentrated on them. Just as their forward troops crossed the enemy's outer defences, a Yugoslav woman interpreter arrived at Commando HQ bearing the message that the Partisans had decided not to attack. The Commando hurriedly withdrew as the enemy counter-attacked, and were mistakenly strafed yet again on the way out. Having taken up defensive positions facing the enemy they spent a fairly quiet night.

On the next day, Lt-Col Manners arrived with three more troops of 40 Commando, but their time was spent bickering with the enemy and fruitlessly attempting to co-ordinate attacks with the various Partisan brigades, which culminated in a night attack against three hill positions, codenamed Pts 542, 557 and 622, the latter being the task of 43 and 40 Commando. B, C and D Troops of 43 attacked 622 first with great elan, and had blown gaps in the wire and minefields before it was again obvious that the Partisans had not moved. All the officers of C and D Troops were killed or injured on this assault, which was finally driven home by the C and D Troop Sergeants, Gallon and Pickering, although both were wounded. 43 lost six officers and sixty other ranks killed, wounded or missing during this action, and most of 43 then withdrew. The B Troop commander, Captain Schooley, had also been hit, but continued to command his Troop, which was joined during their advance by two fighting troops of 40 Commando, led by Col 'Pops' Manners, and accompanied by the Colonel of 2 Commando, Lt-Col Jack Churchill, who was the British force commander for the Brac operation.

Exactly what happened after that is still not clear. Apparently there had been some failure in wireless communication, which was very common in that mountainous terrain, and 43 were unaware that their attack should have been supported by 40 Commando as well as by the Partisans. Whatever the details, and however the situation occurred, the result was that the two units, 43 and 40, attacked 622 in succession rather than simultaneously, and the enemy were able to deal with them in detail.

The second attack was led by Colonel Jack Churchill, playing his bagpipes, who ordered B Troop of 43 to attack 622 from the right flank, while he led Y Troop of 40 directly to the assault, sending word for 43 to follow in support of 40. These arrangements made, the attack went in. 'Y Troop of 40 were magnificent,' Churchill wrote later, '. . . all in line, shouting, firing, just like on the assault course at Achnacarry.'

Knocker White was in that Y Troop charge. 'We had laid up all day, hoping to keep in touch with other units, but communication was very bad, and we didn't have much success. We tried to raise 43 who were to attack another part, with no success, so Col Churchill decided to push on. Someone who had been probing for mines called out "Mines sir!" but Col Jack Churchill said, "To hell with the mines. When I open up on the pipes, in you go", and he did and we did. Y Troop made a charge, all strung out and every weapon firing, grenading any foxholes. We killed all opposition on the hill and put up a green Vereys. I was in one of their slits with the Bren group, Jack Hopley and his No 2, Marine Holloway. Everything went deathly quiet and then there was a mighty cry, like "Ra-Ra-Ra", and a line of Germans rose up and put in a counter-attack. They pounded right past us, everything going.'

B Troop of 43, with the two troops of 40 Commando, had overrun the German positions on 622, and put up the success signal when 'all hell was let loose onto the objective, with (German) mortars, shells and rifle grenades'. It became obvious that in the continued absence of Partisan support, two strong German companies were counter-attacking from the flanks, and casualties began to mount. Lt-Col Manners was severely injured. Col Jack Churchill was captured, and Captain Schooley was last seen charging into the enemy. 40 Commando was driven off the hill, but eventually got back to the start line, having lost seventy men in this brief action alone, including the much-loved CO 'Pops' Manners. 43 Commando and the rest of the landing force, now under Lt-Col Simmonds, withdrew to the beach, accompanied by dispirited Partisans, carrying their wounded, as the few mules they had had collapsed with the heat. The withdrawal from Brac was completed on the 4 June.

Brac succeeded in diverting German forces and attention from the mainland, and Marshal Tito made good his escape, but the battle inflicted grievous losses on the British units involved, notably on 40 Commando.

Knocker White takes up the story of the hilltop of Brac. 'When the Germans had swept past, we got out of the slit, to see if we could join up with the rest of the troop, but something, a bullet or a piece of mortar bomb hit me in the neck. I heard one of my mates say, "He's had it", and when I came round, two Germans were prodding me with bayonets. When they saw I was alive, they put a field dressing on my neck and took me off the hill to their HQ. It had a big radio in there called Telefunken . . . I can see it now. Then their doc looked in my mouth and said, "Ah, you are lucky, it has missed the carotid artery". There were about ten or twelve of us in there. I asked for water but their doc didn't have enough. On the next afternoon they took the lads out, gave Colonel Churchill his bagpipes (he had been caught too) and they had to dig a mass grave for our dead, and Col Jack played the lament, the *Flowers of the Forest*. When they came back I learned that poor old "Pops" Manners was dead . . . and so we started our journey to the POW camps.'

Richard McConkey picks up Knocker White's tale.

'When Knocker got shot in the neck, his mate thought he was dead, and had died in his arms . . . anyway, he got back to 40 and wrote to Knocker's wife and said, "Knocker died in my arms" . . . Knocker's wife was on widow's pension for six months before word came through that Knocker was a POW in Germany. The government then tried to get her widow's pension back, not successfully, I can assure you.'

'Our fine Colonel, "Pops" Manners was killed on Brac,' writes Jim Farmer. 'Actually he was so severely wounded, he died under treatment from the Germans. They sent us word that they had done everything they could for him, but to no avail.'

Another Y Troop Marine, Charles McNeill, rounds off the story of Brac from 40's point of view. 'We held the hill for a few hours, but for some reason, the Partisans called off their attack, and we were counter-attacked from the flanks and had to get out quick. We carried our wounded back to the beach and got away to Vis. There we went back to our holes in the ground around the airstrip, two bods to a bivvy, covered with a groundsheet . . . I thought I would throw that in.'

43 Commando, unsupported by the Partisans, and unaware that 40 Commando were in support, reached their objectives on Brac at considerable cost, including the loss of seven officers and seventy men, but owing to the difficulties of the terrain, received no supplies or ammunition during the second day of the battle. They were the last Commando to withdraw, and covered the beach until the rest of the force had re-embarked.

The rest of the month of June 1944 was spent training and improving the defences of Vis against the possibility of an enemy attack, activities briefly interrupted by the arrival of Marshal Tito, who had escaped from Bosnia. Other visitors included the GOC Commando Group, Major-General R. G. Sturges, who inspected the

Brigade, and brought them news of the exploits of their colleagues on D-Day, news which left some of the Commandos somewhat depressed.

'We felt rather sad afterwards, that all our efforts, against climate, terrain and the enemy, sometimes with little support or planning, would be for ever dwarfed by the glamour of the other Commandos, and would go unrecognized by posterity.'

Meanwhile, with Vis secure, the raiding went on. The Commandos went back to Hvar, overran a German camp and returned to Vis with eighteen prisoners. A party from 'A' Troop 40 went out with the Navy, boarded four lighters in succession under heavy fire, returning to Vis with 'great booty in stores and Danish butter'. Jim Farmer remembers this: 'We went on MTB patrols from Vis, cruising up and down the coast. There was a crazy Lt Commander who, when he could get no response from the shore-batteries, would sound his klaxon to wake them up . . . we often wished him great ill health.' In July, Major Munro took a party to Korcula, where they stayed for two weeks, 'skipping about to avoid capture', and the same pattern of activity continued throughout August and September, with raids on a long list of enemy-held islands.

On the night of 16 September, 'D' Troop 43, landed on Solta, led by Captain B. I. S. Gourlay MC. They were engaged by heavy machine-gun and mortar fire, but were joined on the following night by the rest of 43 Commando and next day the unit attacked the main enemy position. 'C' Troop of 43 was led by Captain R. B. Loudoun, who later became a Major General. Captain Gourlay, who eventually became Commandant General of the Corps, was wounded during this attack, but led his Troop onto the objective and won the MC as did the OC of 'E' Troop, Captain Parkinson-Cumine. Many men were injured here by the little *Schu* mines, which had been scattered about by the enemy, and the Commando also suffered from heavy artillery fire from coastal defence guns on the nearby mainland. Five days later the enemy abandoned their positions on Solta and withdrew to the mainland, although only about one third actually got away, the rest falling prisoner to 43 and the Partisans.

In mid-October, 43 Commando, again briefly commanded by Major Munro, was withdrawn to Italy, and ordered to prepare itself for further operations on the mainland of Yugoslavia and Albania. They landed at Dubrovnik on 28 October, and from then on assisted the Partisans in harrying the retreating Germans out of Yugoslavia. Commanded now by Lt-Col Ian Riches, they took on a wide variety of tasks, repairing roads to get the artillery forward, and even acquiring a troop of 75 mm guns, with which they proceeded to harass the enemy still further.

During this period, relations between the British troops and their Partisan allies began to deteriorate, for the Germans were clearly on the way to defeat and with the Red Army entering the Balkans, the Communists felt able to dispense with their British allies.

'The Partisan attitude became increasingly intolerant as our stay lengthened . . . early curfews, barring us from Dubrovnik, refusing us admittance to bars, forbidding civilians to talk to us, all made our position invidious, and arrests were made on the slightest excuse.' On January 20 1945, 43 Commando were withdrawn from Yugoslavia, and arrived in Italy, for a short spell of leave and a month's field training, before being committed to 8th Army, which they joined near Ravenna, at the end of February 1945, meeting up with their old friends in other units of the now veteran 2nd Commando Brigade.

The years have mellowed 40 and 43's memories of their campaigns in Yugoslavia, while in no way diminishing their admiration and affection for the local people, who also remember the men in green berets and welcome them back year after year to visit the old battlefields.

Knocker White recalls a recent visit. 'Well, the Partisans gave us a great welcome. Four little girls met us at the airport with flowers, and we spent the first week on Hvar, with coach tours, the hills all covered with lavender and sage. On the Thursday we went to Vis for the VE celebrations. The village band and councillors came to meet us, and the children sang their hearts out with the old Partisan songs . . . then to Komitya, where Major MacCallum unveiled a plaque; then a great luncheon with all the wine you wanted. On Trogier we saw the stables where the Germans held us prisoner . . . that brought back memories.'

Other men of the 2nd Commando Brigade have similar stories, and whenever 43 have their reunion dinners, the guest of honour is a representative from the Yugoslav Embassy. 'You always remember the good times, and the lads . . . we'll never forget the lads – you know – the ones who didn't make it.'

While 43 were fighting their brisk little wars on the islands or mainland of Yugoslavia and Albania, the other Royal Marines Commando, the veteran 40, had not been idle. As already related, 40 arrived on Vis to join the rest of 2 SS Brigade in May 1944, and were summoned from there to assist 43 Commando and the Partisans on Brac, where Lt-Col Manners was severely injured and later died of his wounds. After Brac, 40 Commando withdrew to Vis and there took on the task of harassing the enemy on the island of Mijet, under a new commanding officer, Lt-Col R. W. Sankey RM, who took the unit back to Italy to rest and retrain, before they joined No 2 Commando for operations on Corfu and the nearby coast of Albania, where they arrived on 24 September, to be greeted by the most atrocious weather.

'Although I had served in Burma during the monsoon, I have never seen anything like it,' writes Brigadier Tom Churchill. 'Torrential rain fell day and night, for ten days and nights, while the lightly equipped troops lay out on the mountains, clothes soaked, boots cut by the rocks. Twenty-five per cent of the brigade fell victim to exposure or trench-foot, and when the rain finally ceased on 3 October, the force's effectiveness was much reduced.'

Commandos are a resilient breed, and by 6 October 1944, after two days of sunshine and the chance to dry their clothes and weapons, the small Brigade were ready to move against the port of Sarande, on the mainland opposite Corfu, with 2 Commando attacking artillery positions and 40 moving directly against the port. The attack began at 04.00 on 9 October with an artillery and Naval bombardment.

By dawn 40 had got through the enemy wire and outposts, and were fighting their way house to house through Sarande, finally locating the core of the enemy resistance in a large building which fell after the Commando had assaulted it 'with the utmost determination.'

'We endured continuous rain for days before Sarande,' says Jim Farmer, 'and there was still heavy rain when we roped up, climbed the cliffs overlooking Sarande and hauled up the 3-inch mortars and baseplates. The SRS took up small howitzers the same way. Needless to say, the Germans were taken by surprise and surrendered within the day. Then we took Corfu without a fight . . . nice change.'

Once Sarande had fallen, 2 and 40 embarked at once in their assault craft and set out across the straits for Corfu, arriving there just as dawn broke, to find that the Germans had already surrendered. After a tumultuous welcome from the joyous Greeks – and Corfu is arguably the most pro-British of all the Greek Islands – 40 Commando were left there for a while to garrison the island and enjoy a well-earned rest. Here, as elsewhere in the Eastern Mediterranean, political factions were emerging as the battlefield fighting moved further away, and the Marines had to maintain the peace between the rival Royalist and Left-Wing Greek factions, before they returned to Italy at the end of February 1945 to join the other units of 2 Commando Brigade for their last great fight, at Lake Comacchio.

The 2nd Commando Brigade, now commanded by Brigadier R. J. F. Tod, late of 9 Commando, consisted of four units, Nos 2 and 9 (Army) Commandos, and Nos 40 and 43 (Royal Marines) Commandos. For the operations at Lake Comacchio, this force was joined by various support units from Eighth Army, including elements of the SBS under the fighting Dane, Anders Lassen. 2 Commando Brigade spent a few weeks in the line and moved up to Lake Comacchio on 2 April 1945.

Lake Comacchio is a vast, flooded area, a swamp rather than a proper lake. It is fairly shallow, so that children could paddle out for miles were it not for the thick, sucking mud. With an average depth of two feet, Comacchio was too shallow for large assault craft, and too deep and wide to wade, apart from being dissected in parts by deep channels. As a military obstacle it was formidable, but it barred the way for an advance north into the valley of the Po, and had to be taken.

The plan, Operation Roast, called for 40 Commando to hold the line on the river Reno, which flows out of Comacchio, while 2 and 9 crossed the lake in shallow storm-boats, and took the north bank of the Reno, and 43 first took the long tongue of land between lake and sea, then crossed the channel onto the west bank of Comacchio, to join with 2 Commando and advance north.

The attack went in on 1 April, and soon became confused. The water level in the lake had fallen, so that the

Commandos of 2 and 40 had to manhandle their craft through knee-deep mud. 40 Commando began their attack at 04.45 and, under cover of their activity, elements of 2 and 9 got across the lake.

Jim Farmer remembers it: 'Lake Comacchio was our last operation, and I would say the worst and fiercest since Dieppe. The support we expected did not materialize and our casualties were heavy. The reinforcements to my troop were killed to a man . . . I never even knew their names.'

43 swept up the tongue of land and crossed the Reno by the evening of the first day, joining up with 2 Commando, and taking over 400 prisoners. On the second day the advance north did not start until after mid-day and was made against increasing opposition, during which Corporal Tom Hunter of 'C' Troop, 43 Commando, attacked the enemy positions with the Bren, clearing one after another until he was killed. For his actions at Lake Comacchio Corporal Hunter was awarded the Victoria Cross, the only Royal Marine VC of the war.

Tom Hunter is remembered by his Troop Commander, Captain Loudoun: 'Hunter was a Scotsman, and joined the Corps in 1942, after a spell in the Home Guard. He was a forthright, outspoken man, a likeable fellow, and a useful member of 'C' Troop. The Troop had been in action since the early hours, and casualties had been moderately heavy, from the shelling . . . the death of about half-a-dozen men had given the Troop a fervour amounting almost to fanaticism.'

According to the Commando history, 'C' Troop came under murderous fire from at least eight Spandau machine guns, and Hunter engaged them with his Bren, calling for more magazines as he went on, the rest of 'C' Troop charging up behind him.

The 2nd Commando Brigade were relieved on 3 April, but brought back into the line on 10 April, when 40 Commando were sent across the lake to attack an enemy strongpoint and bridge at Marete. 'Y' Troop led the attack, losing two officers before the bridge could be taken; the Troop finally crossing on a bridge formed from toggle ropes, to assault the strongpoint and kill the garrison.

Six weeks after Comacchio, the war in Europe ended, and in the months that followed, Nos 40 and 43 Commandos were, for a while, disbanded, although 44 Commando was later renumbered as 40, and 43 Commando was reformed in the 1960s. These two wartime Commandos were great units, with 40 fighting from Dieppe to the final weeks of the war, and 43 soldiering on solidly, taking every task that came its way, and gaining for the Corps Britain's highest military decoration. They still are great units, holding themselves together even now, forty years or more after the peace, and the reasons for that are best expressed by the '43' padre, Ross Hook, who won the Military Cross while serving with 43, and eventually became a bishop.

'What do I remember? I remember we were fit, very fit, all of us . . . we were Commandos, and felt proud of it, but there are other memories stored up in my mind, of the cheerfulness, the courage, the many simple kindnesses, all the things that made up the community of 43 Commando. I remember one Marine, a Bren gunner, who used more swear words than anyone else I know . . . he went to hospital and when he came back he handed me a parcel, saying, "Take this, your other one is bloody awful . . ." Inside was a beautifully-made altar cross that just fitted into a haversack. I still have it.

'As time goes by, I forget the bad times, but I remember all the gallant lads, from Corporal Hunter downwards, who gave their lives . . . many of them I buried. After the war I was talking to an ex-43 at a wedding, and I asked him about his life and work, and he said, "Well, you know, padre, Civvy Street is all right, but I still miss the lads". I, too, still miss the lads, and will always remember what a grand bunch of lads they were.'

5

D-Day, 6 June 1944

Cheerily to sea; the signs of war
advance . . .
No King of England if
not King of France!

Shakespeare: Henry V

D-Day, 6 June 1944, is arguably the most significant date
in the history of Combined Operations. This is the day
that Combined Operations was born for, during the dark
months of 1940, this was the day for which all previous
raids and training had been but a preparation. The day
when the Allied armies stepped again onto the shores of
France was the final justification of the concept of Combined Operations, without which the great mass of the
Allied armies would not have gone ashore.

The Allied armies, under the overall command of the
American General Dwight Eisenhower, were commanded on that day by Britain's leading field-commander,
Field Marshal Bernard Law Montgomery. Montgomery
commanded a landing force drawn from three armies,
one American, one British, one Canadian. The ranks of
this multi-national force included three Army Commando Units, Nos 3, 4 and 6, and five Royal Marines
Commandos, Nos 41, 45, 46, 47 and 48, in 2 Brigades
(Nos 1 and 4). With the exception of 41 Commando,
which had seen action in Italy, these were newly-raised
Marines Commando Units, although the men in them
had seen service either with the RM Division, the

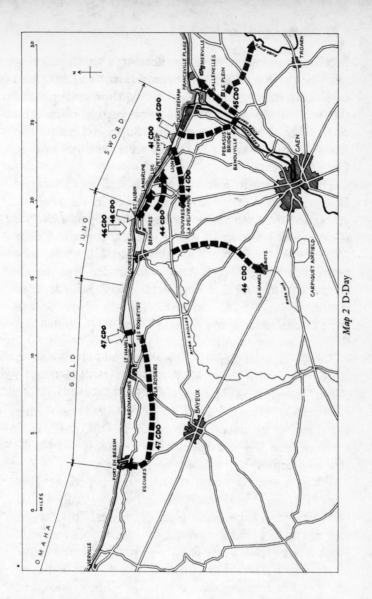

Map 2 D-Day

MNBDO or with units of the fleet. It is worth pointing out that the Royal Marines deployed some 17,000 men on D-Day, many in landing craft, or manning the guns of the fleet, or serving in beach control parties, or in tanks of the Royal Marines Armoured Support Group. The Royal Marines were at D-Day in force, and not only in Commandos.

The Commando forces at the disposal of Combined Operations had expanded considerably in the last two years, and they were now formed into a Special Service (Commando) Group of four Brigades, commanded by Maj-Gen R. G. Sturges CB, DSO. No 2 Brigade, consisting of Nos 1, 9, 40 and 43 Commandos, had already been active in Italy and Yugoslavia. No 3 Brigade, consisting of Nos 1, 5, 42 and 44 Commandos, were sent to the Far East. Nos 1 and 4 Special Service (Commando) Brigades were committed to the D-Day operations.

No 4 (Special Service) Brigade, commanded by a Royal Marine Brigadier, B. W. 'Jumbo' Leicester, was a Royal Marine Brigade consisting of 41, 46, 47 and 48 Commando. No 1 (Special Service) Brigade under the command of Brigadier the Lord Lovat DSO, MC, consisted of Nos 3, 4 and 6 Army Commandos, and No 45 (Royal Marines) Commando.

'When I started to go through the papers I have,' writes Lt J. E. Day, 'I was reminded of how badly 45 has been treated in subsequent Corps histories. This may be due to the fact that we served in an Army Commando Brigade, or because very few ex-45 officers stayed in the Corps after the war. I do not claim that 45 was better, or saw tougher fighting than other RM Commandos, but we had a rough time in Normandy; 1st SS Brigade had an important task, and we took our fair share.'

No 1 (Special Service) Brigade were charged with landing on Sword Beach beside the river Orne, on the left flank of the Allied Armies, and seizing the port of

Ouistreham, before pushing inland to join with the 6th Airborne Division which had been dropped in to secure the flank of the invasion force on the left bank of the Orne, and seizing and holding the crucial bridge, across the Caen canal – Pegasus Bridge.

No 4 (Special Service) Brigade was deployed to the west of No 1, and directed to seize a number of coastal resorts, St Aubin, Lion-sur-Mer, Luc-sur-Mer and Langrune-sur-Mer, deploying laterally to link up the various divisions of the British and Canadian invasion force; No 47 Commando had the special task of operating on the extreme right of the British army, and seizing the fishing port of Port-en-Bessin, while No 46 was to be kept offshore as a floating reserve, and came ashore on D + 1 (7th June).

On this occasion the Commando forces were not the first to land. To penetrate the German Atlantic Wall, the first ashore was a mixed force of tanks, line infantry and special armoured units, who had the task of seizing beach-heads and penetrating the coastal defences. The Commando units came ashore up to an hour and a half later, supposedly onto secured beach-heads, and with the tasks of overwhelming strongpoints and extending the beach-heads laterally, to either flank.

'This concept was correct, but based on a false premise,' says Maj-Gen Moulton, who commanded 48 Commando on D-Day. 'The Atlantic Wall was not a continuous line of fortifications, but a series of strongpoints – the villages – surrounded by minefields, overlooked by artillery, and defended in depth. Think of a strongpoint as a medieval castle, and then think of lightly equipped units trying to scale the walls . . . that will give you some idea of our problem. We would have done better to land out in the flanks, not head-on into the defences, as the Canadians and 48 did at St Aubin.' Jim Moulton's comments are borne out by the views of other Marine officers who went ashore on D-Day.

The plan for the Allied invasion of Europe, Operation Overlord, had been worked up steadily since 1942. After various alternatives had been considered, the planners finally elected to go ashore in the Bay of the Seine, on a fifty-mile front between the Cherbourg peninsula and the river Seine itself.

The overall plan was as follows: American airborne divisions would land at the foot of the Cherbourg peninsula (the Cotentin) on the night of 5/6 June, followed at dawn by the 4th (US) Infantry Division, who would land on Utah beach, east of Ste-Mère-Eglise. This force would secure the right flank of the invasion, and pinch off the port of Cherbourg. (The invasion was actually postponed by 24 hours.)

On the left flank, the British 6th Airborne Division would land on the left bank of the Orne, to secure the other flank, with a glider unit, capturing Pegasus Bridge by *coup-de-main*, as a first strike shortly after midnight on 5/6 June. With these flanks secure, the main invasion forces would come ashore, strongly supported by air and naval units.

The plan called for the troops to land at half-tide, on a flood (rising) tide, and since the tidal set in the Bay of the Seine is from the western, or Atlantic, side the American forces landed first. The beaches of the Calvados coast are wide and sandy, gently shelving, with a line of cliffs to the west, broken by gaps at the little town of Port-en-Bessin, and four miles of beach north of Vierville. This beach, 'Omaha', saw much of the most bloody fighting on D-Day, when the US 1st Infantry Division were badly mauled during the initial landings.

East of Omaha came the Gold beaches, where the British 50th Division would come ashore, accompanied by 47 (Royal Marine) Commando, which was charged with the capture of Port-en-Bessin, the link-port between the British-Canadian and American forces. East again lay

Juno beach, the landing area for the 3rd Canadian Division and, at St Aubin, Lt-Col Moulton's 48 Commando. Finally, in the area between St Aubin and Ouistreham came Sword beach, where 41 and 45 Commando would land with the 3rd British Division. The final unit with which this book is directly concerned, 46 Commando, sailed from Cowes on D-Day, and came ashore at Bernières in the Canadian Juno area on 7 June.

The German forces and defences which were to resist this assault were formidable, not least in their commander, Field Marshal Erwin Rommel, sometime commander of the doughty Afrika Korp. Rommel was appointed to command the defences of the Atlantic Wall in the spring of 1944, and soon began to strengthen them considerably. Rommel intended to defeat the Allies on the beach, and began his work by increasing the offshore obstacles and laying overlapping minefields. In three months his troops laid four million mines along the invasion coast and had time permitted, he intended to lay fifty million. He increased the artillery on the beach-head areas, concentrating especially on the formidable 88 mm anti-tank guns, and ordered his troops to entrench themselves well forward and, wherever possible, enfilade the beaches to turn each one into a killing ground. Finally, as Jim Moulton has pointed out, he turned the coastal resorts into fortresses, evicting the inhabitants, reinforcing the houses and cellars, blocking the streets with wire, mines and concrete walls, moving in anti-tank guns. Finally, he insisted on securing an adequate number of well-trained troops to man these defences, including a number of Panzer Divisions equipped with the latest tanks. On D-Day the German forces on the Calvados coast of Normandy mustered six infantry divisions, two Panzer divisions, an airborne regiment and some Russian units. These were dug in actually on the beach and landing areas. In reserve were three further infantry divisions, a parachute division and two more Panzer units – 12 (SS) Panzer, and an exceptionally fine unit, Panzer Lehr. These troops belonged to the German 7th Army. Just to the north, across the Seine, lay the 15th Army, consisting of two further Panzer Divisions, and mustering a total of 250,000 men. During the spring of 1944, these forces trained hard, dug deeper, and worked continually to improve and thicken their defences. To overcome them would be a formidable task indeed, but the work began on the 5/6 June 1944, when the landing units of the Allied Armies sailed from their ports along the south coast of England.

'Anyone talking about his memories of D-Day will start with rude words about the crossing,' writes Maj Dan Flunder MC, then the adjutant of 48 Commando. 'In our case it was indeed abominable. We were in LCI(S) – Landing Craft Infantry (Small) – these were wooden craft which gave the impression of bouncing on the water, rather than floating on it, like a proper boat. In the rough conditions of the Channel that night, they rolled and swooped and swung in a most exhausting way.'

Col Paddy Stevens, then a lieutenant in 41 Commando, remembers sailing from the solent with 'A' Troop of 41 Commando. 'We sailed out from Spithead in LSIs, past the place where my father used to watch the shipping . . . it was pretty rough, but the sight of all that shipping, cruisers, destroyers, all kinds of landing craft, all moving out, forming into line, was quite unforgettable . . . the troops seemed happy enough, they were a tough, resolute crowd.'

C. S. M. Tilney, then in 'P' Troop, 41 Commando, also remembers the weather. 'It was rough – *very* rough – lots of people were seasick, but we sat up most of the night, playing cards, trying not to think about it. As it got light, the sights, the crowd of shipping was tremendous; you couldn't describe the amount of shipping. I remember also, how young we all were. I was only 23, and a Troop Sergeant-Major – being a Commando soldier was a great game, if you were fit.'

So they set out, through the darkness; over the stormy seas, sailing in their darkened ships, looking up, straining to glimpse the hundreds of aircraft pouring overhead to bomb the beaches, or drop the parachute divisions. Presently, it began to get light.

41 (Royal Marines) Commando had been raised from the 8th Royal Marine Battalion in October 1942, the second of the Royal Marine Commando units, and had seen service in Sicily and Italy before returning to UK for the Normandy landings.

'Our CO was Tim Gray, a first-class professional soldier and the youngest of the Marine Commando COs,' recalls Paddy Stevens. 'He had seen to it that we had a lot of training, and been thoroughly briefed with lots of lateral air photographs, but although the shore looked familiar, it was somehow still unexpected.'

41 Commando's task was to assault Lion-sur-Mer on Sword beach, the most easterly of the three British and Canadian beaches, but they actually came ashore, under heavy fire, some two hundred yards west of their chosen area, and landed over a beach swept by shell and mortar fire, and littered with burning tanks.

'I remember a line of detached houses, seen through smoke, two or three tanks burning, troops on the beach, and some bodies in the water. There was a lot of shelling and machine-gun fire, not aimed specifically against our craft, but a nasty pause before we got off the ship, and I had to wade a bit. I have vivid memories of the burning tanks, and many of the assault battalions were still on the beach. We lost quite a few men on the beach. I remember standing up because I thought I was just as good a target lying down ... anyway, it was expected.'

The task of 41, once ashore, was to split into two parts, designated as Force 1 and Force 2. Force 1 was to eliminate the German strong point near Lion, which was found to be deserted. Meanwhile Force 2 attacked a château, set among houses, inland to the west of the town, which was strongly defended. Three officers were killed in the assault and the château did not fall for another twenty-four hours, when it was captured by the 5th Battalion, the Lancashire Regiment. Meanwhile, the combined forces of 41 had moved on to their final D-Day objective, to link up with 48 Commando further west, and attack the radar station at Douvres. This was said to be the strongest position on the coast, with defences that had taken three years to construct, and 41 were not able to take it until 17 June when they required the support of flail tanks to clear mines, and a naval bombardment.

Many Marines of 41 never got that far. Marine Frank Nightingale was on the beach with his Bren: 'I got hit a couple of times, once in the water and then on the beach, so apart from seeing dead bodies all over the beach, I can't tell you much about the landing. I rejoined the unit much later, and Peter Heydon got me into "Y" Troop.'

T. S. M. Tilney remembers some casualties. 'We lost David Barclay and the RSM, Horace Belcher, one of the real characters of 41, on D-Day or D + 1. Horace was a sea-marine, well liked, well respected. We got bogged down near Luc-sur-Mer, and Lt-Col Tim Gray was wounded and the Second-in-Command killed. Eric Palmer took over as CO and Burnett became the RSM. The radar station we had to take was wired in and heavily defended ... we needed tanks and 25-pounders to get in, but we took it and 200 prisoners.'

Denis Fawcett also went ashore with 41. 'At the time I

was Troop Sergeant-Major of "Y" Troop, 41 Commando, commanded by an extremely able and enthusiastic Captain, Peter Howes-Dufton. Our landing at Lion-sur-Mer was wet, but relatively trouble-free, considering the very unfriendly reception given to our arrival. The LSI beached some distance from the water's edge and the Troop made a hurried departure down the port and starboard ramps. Nobody was keen to linger, and several fell off the ramps half-way down to almost disappear into what seemed to be, when we touched bottom, about three feet of water. We made our way across a fairly short stretch of beach and gathered ourselves together into some semblance of order beneath a not very high sea wall. As far as I can recall, up to that point, our Troop had suffered no serious casualties, although there was plenty of evidence that others, in the shape of both men and machines had not been so fortunate. Some of the bodies bore resemblance to comrades from another Troop, which had preceded us, and this aroused a momentary pang of grief. After making a quick exit over the sea wall and off the beach, we moved inland along a road with houses on either side, and it was here that our progress was interrupted by a shower of mortar bombs, some of which landed in the road and caused our first casualties. The Bren gunners of the sub-section, advancing on the left of the road, were killed instantly, and several others badly wounded, including one from my little lot in Troop HQ, which was ahead of, and on the right of the stricken section. Meanwhile Capt Howes-Dufton at the head of the leading section had pushed on undaunted, but regrettably was killed by machine-gun fire during the attack on an enemy strongpoint. I have a press-cutting which reports comments made by our CO, Lt-Col Tim Gray (himself wounded on D-Day) in a letter to Peter Howes-Dufton's parents, which pays tribute to this very gallant officer.'

Paddy Stevens, who won the Military Cross on D-Day, describes what happened to him. 'You have to realise that battle is very confusing. One minute everyone is there, the next minute they have disappeared. There's a lot of noise and confusion. Some people seem to have total recall, and can still remember where every Bren gun was sited . . . I can't do that. I remember the din on the beach, but once we got off onto the road behind, it was a different world, total silence. We went west, two troops along the coast, one troop inland, about a mile behind the beach, into houses by the radar station, looking straight down the main street. We ran into a lot of Germans, with an armoured half-track, and took cover in the houses. I remember Peter Powell walking across the road, very calm, bullets flying everywhere, already wounded.

'In street fighting it is extremely difficult to see what is going on. I got separated from the rest of the Troop, with about seven others. The Germans tried a rush, with one running down the centre of the road firing a Schmeisser. I shot at him and so did the rest . . . he fell in the road outside and died. We withdrew for a while then came back, getting close to the half-track which was still firing. I threw a grenade into it, then beat it back into cover as fast as I could.

'What else? We saw a massive glider drop across the Orne, bringing reinforcements for Sixth Airborne. When we withdrew that evening, still trying to find the rest of the unit, we passed a churchyard full of dead British and German soldiers. I found the German we had shot in the road and took his Schmeisser; I kept it for some time. Finally, we met two tanks and I asked them, "Where are the Commandos?" They directed us towards a hedgerow a couple of hundred yards away, but when we got there we saw a lot of Germans in the field beyond. We fired into them and they beat it. We rejoined the unit just before dark and found heavy casualties. "A" Troop was down to 30 men from over sixty, and with the other officers wounded, I became Troop commander. The Colonel, Tim Gray, brother of Nicol Gray, had been wounded – but 41 did well on D-Day . . . we pulled ourselves together and got on with the job.'

Bill Sloley went ashore at Luc-sur-Mer at the head of 'P' Troop: '41 was a good unit . . . Tim Gray, Nicol's brother was the CO, and John Taplin was the Adjutant, with David Barclay a 2 I/C. People in "P" Troop you will have heard of were W. E. Tilney, George Elsom, our TSM, who was killed at Walcheren, and "Sticks" Dodds, who was a Sergeant then.

'As you know, the landing was put back a day, and the sea was very rough. One "P" Troop officer was so ill with seasickness, he couldn't go ashore – we bundled him up and left him on the LCI. As OC I had to be the first down the ramp, up to my neck in water, so it was hard to keep the weapons and radios dry. We were certainly fired on, but we got off the beach, courtesy of the AVRE tanks . . . people were being shot or killed all about us. I remember one chap from "A" Troop wandering about with a stomach wound, looking for the RAP – he died later – there was a lot of fire, smoke, noise, gun flashes. The houses had been converted into strongpoints with concrete and wire.

'The Commando was split into two groups, one under Tim Gray, one under the Second-in-Command, David Barclay. We got through Luc all right. "Sticks" Dodds' section was leading "P" with myself right behind when we got held up. I then tried one of those classic left-flanking attacks, among the houses, but the flanking section ran into more trouble. I got a message back to David Barclay but he had already been killed, so the half-Commando came to a halt. I went back for an "O" (Orders) Group, to find that my friend, Peter Howes-

Dufton, had been killed. A bomb fell on the CO's "O" Group, wounding Tim Gray and the Adjutant . . . Eric Palmer took over as CO, and we stayed where we were for the night.

'Later on, the entire unit went inland to Douvres, to surround an occupied German radar station. Attempts were made to make them surrender, but they refused until we were putting in a full-scale assault with a troop of tanks – they were an arrogant bunch. I lost Sergeant Rush h:re – he was hit in the arm on a patrol and died of gang.ene. Once we got to Sallenelles, across the Orne, we got down to patrolling. "Sticks" Dodds was very good at that, and I remember the heavy bombers going over to flatten Caen. Then we took part in the break-out to the Seine, the whole Commando marching by night, in single file. At Troarn our sniper's favourite trick was to shoot at the Germans when they came out for a pee. Later on, we were withdrawn from Normandy and sent to De Haan, near Bruges, to prepare for Walcheren.'

Out on the eastern flank of the invasion, 45 Commando had landed on Sword beach with the 1st SS Brigade, which was specifically charged with advancing inland to link with airborne forces astride the Orne, crossing the Caen canal by rubber boats if necessary. Fortunately, the airborne forces had taken the bridges and still held them, so the link-up was speedily achieved, although the CO of 45, Lt-Col N. C. Ries, was picked off by a sniper, and his 2 I/C Major Nicol Gray, took over the Commando.

Once across the Caen Canal and the Orne, 45 were sent north along the coast to Franceville Plage, near Merville, and dug in near the famous battery which had been taken at dawn by the 9th Bn, the Parachute Regt, but later re-occupied by the Germans. This put 45 out on a limb, beyond the main perimeter of the Allied armies.

Captain Day served with 45 until he was wounded on

D + 6. 'In April 1944, our Brigade Commander, Lord Lovat, decided that every Commando unit should have one troop trained as parachutists. In 45, this was "E" Troop, and the parachute training gave us the cohesion we had lacked previously. The other Fighting Troops were formed from the equivalent companies of 5 Bn RM, but E Troop was formed from miscellaneous elements of that battalion. All ranks in the Troops volunteered for parachuting, except Private Dunlop, RAMC, our medical orderly. He was soon persuaded that his friends didn't want to lose him, and in volunteering against his wishes, he displayed the spirit he showed on 6 and 7 June, tending our wounded, and staying with them when we withdrew from Franceville.

'45 went to Normandy in 4 LCI(S). "E" Troop shared their craft with the machine-gun platoon of "F" Troop, under Lt Colin Fletcher. We went onto the beach at La Breche. It was not easy to see what was happening, but shell splashes appeared around us. None came near us, but two other 45 craft were hit. I left my group in the stern and went to watch the Troop go ashore, with Ian Beadle, out Troop Commander, ready to lead his men ashore . . . then we scraped the beach and the ramps went into about three feet of water. It was nearly two hours after the initial assault before we got ashore, but the beach was still not a good place to linger.

As the tide had come in quickly, it took little time to crunch over the sand and follow the green berets heading for the checkpoint 1000 yards inland. We came under fire from "Moaning Minnie" mortars, which landed astride the Column, but caused no casualties. I met the CO Col Ries, who had clearly had a wet landing. We reached Benouville, dumped the dinghies we had been carrying, and crossed the (Pegasus) Bridge, which was under fire from

the south. My Sergeant was wounded. I met Captain
Beadle who told me "E" Troop had already lost one man
killed and three NCO's wounded. I think Marine Speight
of "E" Troop was the luckiest – or unluckiest – marine.
He was wounded on 7 June as we moved through
Sallenelles to attack Franceville Plage. He returned to the
unit in August, in time for the breakout from the
beach-head and was wounded on the first day, at
Criqueville. He came back *again*, when we were at
Bexhill and was wounded on 23 January 1945 at
Montfortbeek. Speight's time under fire could be
measured in minutes, but he got hit three times!'

45 Commando were sent out from the 1st Brigade
area towards the coast at Franceville Plage, and were
then pulled back to Merville, digging in near the
Merville battery. One of the little-known incidents of
the Normandy landings is that two Marines, Lt Peter
Winston and his MOA (batman) Marine Donald,
parachuted into Normandy with the 9th Battalion,
the parachute Regiment, with which 45 expected to
make contact on D-Day. On 8 June, 45 withdrew from
Merville back to the Brigade perimeter at Le Plein
where Capt Day arrived after accidentally walking,
quite unharmed, across a minefield.

'Maybe it was a false minefield, but the presence of
mines in our area was brought home to me after the war, at
the Commando Reunion in 1983. I was sitting at the 45
table, when a man in a wheelchair came across from the 6
Commando table and offered us all a drink. He told us that
during the move inland he had walked into a minefield,
and lost his legs. His own troop had moved on to the
attack, but two men eventually saw him and came into the
minefield to rescue him. He had no idea who they were,
but remembered they wore 45 Commando flashes. He
never saw them again, but would always buy a drink for
anyone from 45 (Royal Marines) Commando.'

45 beat off a heavy German attack around Franceville, and lost a steady stream of men while holding its share of the perimeter, patrolling out by day and night to probe the enemy defences. From the landing on D-Day until 8 June, 45 had 32 killed, 62 missing, and 90 wounded, about fifty per cent of their strength. In Day's 'E' Troop, the losses by the time Day himself was wounded, a week after the landings, were 11 killed, 23 wounded and 5 missing. A fighting troop consisted of 65 All Ranks, so Ian Beadle had 24 remaining out of the 64 who left Warsash with him. Among the missing, was that gallant RAMC orderly, Pte Dunlop, the reluctant parachutist, who stayed with the Commando wounded in Franceville Plage.

Fred Harris was a Marine in 'A' Troop 45 Commando. 'I joined the Royal Marines in 1942, and was demobbed on 22 May 1946. Our Colonel was Lt-Col Ries, my Troop Commander was Capt Grewcock, with Lt Armstrong and a South African, Lt Thomas, as the Section Commanders. Our TSM was QMS Falconer. I was support group bren, with my "oppo" Don Winter. Brian White, the Adjutant, took over after Captain Grecock was killed - and was killed himself in the advance beyond the Dives. Capt Day was a subaltern in E Troop and wounded at Le Plein. On 5 June 1944, work came to move out, and we were transported to Hampshire, where we were given tea and entertained by the Brigadier's Piper, prior to going aboard the LCIs. We were soon all aboard and making for the open sea. This was *IT* then, no turning back. Shortly after sailing we got news of the actual landing areas; our unit was at Queen Red Beach, right of Ouistreham, and our objective was to knock out the Merville Battery if it hadn't been done by the Paras, and take the coastal town of Franceville Plage.

'The crossing was rough, if spectacular, with craft of every description. On the run-in I had my own thoughts as, I am sure, did everybody else. There was no chatter now, mostly silence, and certainly nervous tension. The landing wasn't bad but there was a heavy surf which twisted the ramps, and we landed in waist-high water. With my load I stumbled on the ramp and in I went, completely submerged. Sgt Gray, however, saved the day and yanked me to my feet, dumping me on the beach. After a few press-ups I managed to get to my feet and struggled up the beach. Small cross-fire and shelling was fairly heavy. There were dead bodies being washed up and wounded being attended to and my first sight of Germans were some badly frightened prisoners. We passed through the infantry that had landed earlier and reached the RV, and I felt a sense of relief and welcomed the rest it afforded – my ducking had almost doubled my weight.

'So far, so good, although it all seems so confused, not a bit like the briefing at Southampton but somebody obviously knew what was happening as we were once more on the move. Passing through a small village, a few Frenchmen appeared, shouting "Vive La France!" and waving the odd rifle in the air, also scrounging a cigarette. They called themselves Free French, and were identified by armbands.

'We were now on our way towards the Orne bridges, and Paras were in evidence along the way; they looked weary and had obviously had a hard time; they were pleased to see us, that's for sure. The Paras had captured the bridges which were still being sniped at, and getting the occasional mortaring. On crossing the Canal bridge I recall seeing some the dead crew of an anti-tank gun position and the gliders which had landed smack on target. Col Ries, we heard, had been wounded, and Maj Gray had taken command, as we pushed on towards Merville, the rest of the Brigade then went off in their particular directions.

'The Battery, having once been captured, had been retaken by the enemy, and so we stayed put for the night around the village of Merville, having passed through Sallenelles, where there was further shelling. Dawn came and we had orders to withdraw, back through Sallenelles, which seemingly changed hands several times. We met up with the Army Commandos and dug in. However, this didn't last long as we were soon on the move. I recall not being sorry, as we were continually being mortared during our short stay. We were now on our way to Franceville-Plage, and once again went through Sallenelles. On the way back to Merville we were heavily shelled.

'Our rucksacks were now discarded, ready for us to go in action (hopefully we would see them again), and we made off by-passing Merville and on the road to Franceville-Plage, a coastal town with a main road code-named "Piccadilly". The objective was to go through the town to the beach and take up positions to the east and west. Several of the other Troops had already made their way up "Piccadilly" and had fanned out. "A" Troop started to make its way and we now saw some of our own casualties. RSM Grimsey and Cpl "Spot" Watson had been killed by shellfire and several other wounded were lying around being treated.

'Small arms fire was intense now, and the troops spread out to the right along the houses and chalets, pushing out, garden by garden, towards the beach. One minute there was a crowd of us, next it seemed each man was on his own. I could hear names being called, and the occasional sighting of "one of ours". Finally, I reached a garden with concrete tank traps at the rear end, whereby I set up position and was joined by Derek Cakebread, our troop sniper; Jimmy Lovatt and "Nipper" Lea appeared at the rear of the house where they stayed put. Again, there was this air of confusion, things obviously weren't as they should be, information was scarce, but we did hear that our German-speaking Commando from 101A Cdo had called on the Germans to surrender. They obviously didn't want to know, as soon after they counter-attacked to our right, and suddenly a German jumped out from a hedgerow, shouting and shooting – at the same time he threw a stick grenade, which Derek and I shared; rolling over, I managed to drop him with a long burst of fire. We both suffered slight wounds, although my arm felt as if it had been torn off. I made my way up the garden to where Jimmy and "Nipper" Lea were. Derek had gone off elsewhere, probably to do a bit of sniping. It seems very chaotic; the enemy were obviously in great strength and out among us; small-arms fire was coming from all directions, and a Spandau was constantly raking the road in front of us.

'Word was passed on that the Troop was to pull back down "Piccadilly", and we decided to cross the road under cover of smoke. Jimmy had a smoke bomb, which he threw up the road. Unfortunately the smoke was ineffective; nevertheless, we made a dash for it. I gathered up my Bren, doing a hop, skip and jump. I was confronted by a fence, which I cleared like a gazelle. My arm had stiffened up by now and I could do little more than carry my Bren, so I made for some First Aid. Jimmy and "Nipper" joined some other stragglers and we heard later that "Nipper" was killed by a mine.

'The First Aid Post was pretty busy with some badly wounded, but I was fixed up with a dressing for a shrapnel wound under the armpit. I remained there, helping out generally, but mainly filling magazines for the light machine-guns. It appeared we had been hit very hard by a considerable force, and there were attacks and counter-attacks well into the evening, until instructions were received that we were to make our way back to Merville. Search patrols went out to locate stragglers, unfortunately there were quite a number missing, — my pal Jimmy Lovatt included. We learned later from the local people that a number of Marines had been killed, having fallen asleep, among these were Jimmy and Derek's pal, L-Corp Freddie Stallwood.

'Around midnight we left Franceville-Plage and reached Merville, where we spent the rest of the night. Dawn, however, started with shelling from what we learned were 88 mm SP guns, and we learned to fear these in the months ahead. I went out with a patrol to try to recover ammunition, and whatever else from the spot where we had offloaded our rucksacks, only to find the Jerries had looted them, and in fact some had been carried off; we saw several prisoners much later, carrying our rucksacks, minus the frame.

'Meanwhile, we heard that two German ambulances drove in to HQ area, the drivers apparently unaware we were in charge. Some of our badly wounded were loaded onto them and they were forced to drive in the direction of Le Plein. Unfortunately, they were intercepted by the Germans and the wounded men were taken prisoner.

'Later we moved out again and headed towards Le Plein, and in spite of a few skirmishes and sniping, we reached our goal, where we were billeted in a church and received our first meal since landing, three days ago. Sleep was all most of us wanted, and we bedded down. So much for our first spell of action. We now knew what it was all about.'

48 Commando, the last Marine Commando to be formed and the first to land on D-Day, had an unlucky beginning, but one which illustrates what a difference leadership can make to a military unit. The Commando was formed in the spring of 1944 from the 7th Battalion, Royal Marines, a unit which had, to say the least, been mucked about a bit. Raised early in 1941, it joined the

Royal Marine Division in 1942, and was then sent to perform guard duties in Southern Africa, where a South African General refused it permission to deploy. It was later discovered idle in Durban, and sent on to Egypt, as part of a logistical unit with the unglamorous name of No 31 Beach Brick. In 1943 the 7th Bn sailed with this unit for the invasion of Sicily.

On 19 July 1943, the 7th Battalion were detached from their duties with the Beach Brick, ordered to reform as an infantry battalion, hurried to support the 51st Division, and committed to battle, supposedly against weak Italian forces. These turned out to be most aggressive elements of the elite German Hermann Goering Division. The battalion were given no opportunity to get organized and had a very bad time. Later evidence reveals that the 7th Bn did as well as anyone could have done, and better than most, but even so, rumours circulated in 8th Army. The battalion was shunted about Italy for some months and then, much to their surprise, ordered home to England to reform as a Commando, where their fortunes took a turn for the better, not least in the appointment as their commanding officer of Lt-Col J. L. Moulton, who set out to make 48 Commando into an outstanding infantry unit.

Lt-Col Moulton met his Commando for the first time on 3 March 1944, barely twelve weeks before the invasion. The men, he records, were wary and suspicious, and he told them bluntly that there was a lot to do, and a lot of training to fit into the available time, but they would get their long-promised and long-overdue spot of leave, and if he, Col Moulton, decided that they were not adequately prepared when battle came around this time, he would say so, in no uncertain terms. This established, re-equipping and training began at once, with a number of officers and men returning early from leave, eager to make a fresh start. 48 Commando went through

Achnacarry and received a good report after what Col Moulton describes as 'the usual torments'. The unit then went into civilian billets at Gravesend for more training and then on 25 May into the Commando marshalling camp, where they were briefed for the landings. Their objective was to land at Nan Red on Juno beach, before the resort of St Aubin-sur-Mer, behind the North Shore Regiment, a Canadian infantry unit, which would be supported by tanks of the Fort Garry Horse. 48 were to pass through the beach-head of the Canadian units, and turn east (left) towards Langrune, and tackle the coastal defences from the rear, before linking up with 41 Commando which had landed on the right flank of Sword beach and turned west (right) towards Langrune. The unit embarked at Warsash, Hampshire, on 5 June and sailed that evening for France.

What went wrong? Looking back, Col Moulton can think of two basic errors in the plan. 'First of all, we were in the wrong landing craft. LCI(S)s were designed for back-up infantry, not as assault craft . . . you landed by gang-planks over the bow, quite useless for heavily equipped men in rough water, while going into the assault. Secondly, the intelligence was poor. We were told of a continuous line of fortifications along the shore, but it wasn't like that. The Germans built concrete strong-points in the villages, and we landed right in front of one. We should have landed either side and not directly under their guns . . . it was a fairly murderous affair. Then the naval and air support was inadequate . . . look at that coast, even today, and it is still lined with pre-war houses, virtually untouched in 1944. You also have to realize that if a shambles develops in the assault, there is no way of stopping it . . . craft keep pouring in, men keep coming ashore. You just have to sort yourself out and get on with the job. That's what 48 did . . . we pulled ourselves together and marched on Langrune with what we had.'

Dan Flunder was the unit Adjutant. 'As Adjutant, I was

OC troops and spent the night with them in a cramped little mess-deck; almost everyone was sick. I had the men up on the superstructure early, because I thought the fresh air would restore them and because men are always happier when they can see what is going on. Soon we were running into the beach, and I walked up and down the bows keeping an eye on the Navy people responsible for lowering the ramps. The sea was covered with craft as far as the eye could see. The shore was under bombardment, craft were sinking, and from where I stood, it certainly didn't look as if the Canadians had secured the beach – things didn't look good at all.

'I didn't realize we were under fire until I saw two men collapse and fall over the starboard side. By then it was too late to beat a retreat, and I later found three bullet holes in my map case . . . they must have passed between my arm and body during that period. The tide was high and we had craft hitting the beach obstacles . . . the CO had our 2-inch mortars firing smoke from the bows, so at least we were not getting aimed fire. When we grounded, we got the starboard ramp down, which wasn't easy with the waves thrashing the stern about. I was half-way down when a big wave lifted the bow and somersaulted the ramp and myself into the sea. I saw the great bows coming over me, and the next thing I remember is walking up the beach, soaking wet, with some of my equipment torn off, including my pistol . . . I still clutched my stout ash walking stick. When I got to the top of the beach, I was violently sick.

'The beach was covered with casualties, some Canadian, some ours. The surf was incredible, with beached and half-sunken craft wallowing about in it. Offshore, other craft came steadily on. Some tanks struggled ashore and some bogged in the shingle. Those that were advancing had their turret lids shut and were heading for a large group of wounded. I was sickened to see one run over two of our wounded and it was heading for our good padre, John Armstrong, who had been badly wounded in the thigh. I had spoken to him on the way up the beach; typically, he had been vehement that I should not stop by him, exposed to enemy fire. I ran back down the beach and hammered on the turret, to get someone to put his head out. When this failed I stuck a Hawkins anti-tank grenade in the sprocket and blew the track off – that stopped it.'

Marine C. L. Pitt remembers the incident. 'Nobby Hall and I went down the gangway . . . one of the sailors was hit . . . then up the beach like the wind, until we reached the sea-wall, and Nobby was right with me. We were pinned there by machine-gun fire from pill-boxes at each end of the beach and their 88s had the range and had put some tanks out of action. A few yards back, a couple of Canadian tanks were at a standstill and two of our wounded lads were lying in front of them. We already had more than enough casualties to deal with. Without a word or waving on the front tank moved forward, right over one lad, and taking the arm off the other as he rolled clear – it was a flash of split second time that stays in my mind. We were just a few feet away when it happened, but Nobby and I couldn't do anything about it.'

The history of the North Shore Regiment records another view of the scene. 'I noticed the LCIs loaded with Royal Marines Commandos approach our beach; they put the ramps down, but from somewhere a German machine-gun opened up and cut them down all along the port side. They fell overboard as though they were a row of wheat sheaves tumbling into the water. Those men who had not been hit, jumped into the water to swim ashore.

'Subsequently, the Commando passed my HQ in the coast road, and I spoke to the CO and asked how he had got along. He said he had lost 50 per cent of his strength in the landing. I was able to report that St Aubin was in our hands and his start line was secure. He thanked me and went on with his job.

'About the time I decided to move off the beach, a Fort Garry tank moved off the beach to go inshore. It had only gone a few yards, when it ran over a mine and its track was blown off.'

Col Moulton realized that '. . . the Commando was meeting something like disaster' even before coming ashore. He thanked the officer commanding the landing craft before descending the ramp, dragged a wounded man out of the surf, and then walked up the beach to the sea wall, waving his men on. Readers should know that Col Moulton is six feet two inches tall. Once by the sea wall, he began to assess the situation, when a mortar bomb landed close by and splinters struck him in the leg, hand and arm. Deciding that the splinters had done him "no serious harm", he set about sorting out his men.

Hardly any of 'Y' Troop had got ashore. 'Z' Troop was there, and so were elements of 'B' and 'A', both much reduced. Of the heavy weapons, 'S' Troop had no machine-guns and only one 3-inch mortar, but the sole survivor of its crew, Marine Thornton, brought this into action, planting the baseplate then going back down the beach to retrieve barrel and bipod, before mounting the weapon, laying out what ammunition he could find and reporting, 'No 1 mortar, ready to fire, sir.' Col Moulton gave his men twenty minutes to sort themselves out and find what weapons they could, then he led them off the beach.

'The beach was an amalgamation of death, with mangled trucks, burning tanks, wrecked craft and dead Canadians and Royal Marines,' writes C. L. Pitt. 'Then our CO appeared before us, revolver in hand, an example of cool, calm competence under fire, rallying his troops.

"Come on, lads, we have to get off the beach", and he led the way to the exit on the right of the sea wall – we got off just in time before an ammo truck blew up not far from us. At the assembly area we sorted ourselves out and went through the streets of St Aubin towards Langrune, dealing with snipers on the way. A French lady came out of a house along the road with a tray of glasses of wine, and bread and jam.'

At the assembly area, Col Moulton discovered that his unit had lost forty per cent of its men, including one complete rifle troop, 'Y', which had been rescued from their sinking craft by an LST and taken back to England. Some men of that troop jumped overboard and attempted to swim ashore to join their unit on shore, but all drowned in the surf. One must conclude that there was not very much wrong with the fighting spirit of 48 (Royal Marines) Commando.

'Think of the Langrune strongpoint as a medieval castle,' says Col Moulton, 'a block of old houses, streets full of wire, mines, plenty of troops with mortars and machine-guns, a castle virtually impossible to breach without artillery, but we had a go. The Commander of "B" Troop, Jim Perry, was killed by a sniper. We used our only mortar – then a supporting tank shed a track and blocked the road. Men kept coming in, including RSM Travers, who had swum ashore but been swept east by the tide and had actually landed under the guns of the Langrune strongpoint.'

Dan Flunder remembers the advance to Langrune. 'Leaving the beach on D-Day, "A" Troop was led by their Troop Commander, Mike Reynolds, a remarkable sight. Both his arms were strapped across his chest and his battledress was soaked with blood. He had been quite badly wounded in the arm and one shoulder, but insisted he was mobile and quite able to cope. And cope he did, until a direct order from the CO sent him back for proper treatment. Some days later, after the Troop had already had two other Commanders, the CO sent for me and said, "Dan, I'd like you to take over 'A' Troop and I suspect you'd like it too, wouldn't you?" Indeed I would, and with a light heart I picked up my rucksack and set off for the troop position. That was the beginning of my time with my beloved "A" Troop, which lasted happily through many actions until VE Day.'

48 hammered away at the Langrune starting point for the rest of the day, losing more men, until the Brigade Commander, 'Jumbo' Leicester, came up and ordered them to stop and take up defensive positions in anticipation of an armoured counter-attack. As the day ended there was much to do, not least in collecting the wounded.

'Our MO David Winser from the RAMC did wonderful work,' writes Dan Flunder. 'He was the quintessential Wykhamist, with lots of that quiet lazy charm. I saw him collecting the wounded from before the strongpoint – the road was under rifle fire but David just carried on working, all over the place, even in the minefields.' David Winser won the Military Cross on D-Day, but was killed at Walcheren five months later.

Col Moulton sent a patrol to the east, searching for 41 Commando, which returned without making contact, but the expected German counter-attack did not materialize either. The next day, Col Moulton took what was left of his Commando back into Langrune and captured the strongpoint.

46 Commando, commanded by another outstanding officer, Lt-Col Campbell Hardy, spent the night of D-Day still at sea. 46 had been trained and equipped for a special task, to climb the cliffs east of the Orne, and assault the heavy German batteries there, then fight their way through to the perimeter of 6th Airborne. However,

this task was cancelled because the enemy batteries were not firing with any effect into the invasion fleet. 46 Commando eventually came ashore on Juno, the Canadian beach, on the morning of D + 1, and were used to assault strongpoints east of Langrune, and successfully reduced a major obstacle near Petit Enfer, taking sixty-five prisoners.

The Commando were then placed under the command of the 3rd Canadian Division and given the task of clearing the enemy from the valley of the little river Mue, a tidal stream which flows into the Bay of the Seine at Courseulles. The valley is a heavily cultivated area, with thick hedgerows and orchards, perfect for defence, and their task which they shared with the French-Canadian Regiment de la Chaudière, was to sweep through it and evict the enemy from the villages of Le Hamel and Rots. Since their troops were mostly Panzer grenadiers from the 12th SS (Hitler Youth) Division, the opposition was both fierce and professional.

'The battle for Rots and Le Hamel will be forever in our minds,' writes Reg Bettis of 46. 'We were certainly up against a different kind of enemy from on the coast – the Waffen SS of 12 Panzer, who were well trained. 46 showed that Royal Marines Commandos were better, but the fighting was very bitter. Marine Tom Vardy was awarded the MM for that action; he was killed the next year, just before VE Day. After we took Rots, we were there during the night, awaiting a counter-attack which never came, much to our relief, and I can remember the eeriness of the night, with a burning tank by the church in the village square.'

The attack, which called for close co-operation between tanks, infantry and artillery, wore the enemy down, and after two hours, Le Hamel fell to 'Y' and 'S' Troops, after which 'A' and 'B' Troops, with artillery support, moved on against Rots, where the leading sub-section of 'A' Troop were mown down by machine-gun fire from a Panzer tank. 'A' and 'B' Troops worked their way round the village, while the tanks fought it out in the north, and after 'X' and 'Z' Troops arrived in support, the Germans withdrew. 46 lost twenty killed, nine wounded and thirty-one missing in this final one-day battle, but they gave a good account of themselves as the following letter from the Canadian Division to Brig 'Jumbo' Leicester clearly shows.

HEADQUARTERS 3RD CANADIAN INFANTRY
DIVISION

15 June 1944

To
Comdr
4th SS Bde.

Dear Brigadier Leicester,

Just a note to thank you, your staff, and your Commandos for the excellent work you carried out for us and also for your loyal and enthusiastic co-operation during the successful assault.

During these last few days I must ask you to congratulate for me Lt-Col Hardy and his 46 Commandos, for their thorough dealing with the enemy in and along the river line (Rots and Rosel): my R. de Chauds buried 122 Boche done in by your chaps.

Be assured we appreciate all this and will always deem it an honour to be fighting alongside and preferably with, the Royal Marines Commandos.

Signed: R. F. L. Keller
         Maj-Gen, GOC
         3 Cdn. Inf. Div.

The last Marine Commando to go ashore on D-Day had perhaps the most difficult task of all. 47 Commando had to capture the vital little harbour of Port-en-Bessin, which lay tucked into the chalk cliffs, half way between the American landing beach on Omaha, and the most westerly British beach, Gold. Port-en-Bessin was important for two reasons. Firstly, it marked the junction point for the American and Anglo-Canadian forces. Secondly, and more importantly, it was to be the French end for an underwater petrol pipeline that was to carry vital fuel to the ever-thirsty tanks and trucks of the Allied armies. This pipeline, codenamed 'Pluto' (Pipe Line Under The Ocean), was to be unrolled across the Channel as soon as Port-en-Bessin was secured and since a direct assault from the sea, *pace* Dieppe, was deemed impossible, 47 were to land near Arromanches and make a ten-mile march inland through the enemy-held countryside and assault Port-en-Bessin from the rear.

47 Commando, commanded by Lt-Col C. F. Phillips, embarked for D-Day at Southampton, on 2 June and their leading ships, the HMLSI's *Princess Josephine Charlotte* and the *SS Victoria*, were off Arromanches about 05.00 on 6 June. The unit embarked in LCAs and set off for the run in to Jig Green beach at Arromanches. A mile offshore it became apparent that the beach was still under fire, and deserted except for four support tanks. At this moment the assault craft came under fire from a heavy battery by Le Hamel, and the LCA containing men from 'Y' Troop, was hit and sunk. The rest of 47's craft were ordered to turn east, and land wherever they could and, as 47's history relates, 'It soon became a case of every craft for itself. The beaches were crowded with every type of craft, all types of vehicles and equipment, mostly wrecked or drowned.'

'The CO told us the party was on the day before,'

writes Bill Andrews. 'We go ashore at seven a.m. and home for Christmas! We started the run-in, but it was clear they didn't want us to land, shells started to come down with accuracy and exploding on the water. Capt O'Hare was by the ramp and kept saying, "Piece of cake, piece of cake", then the ramp went down. We saw a bulldozer get a shell in the side. We were making our way to a gap, passing a body or two. One had been hit by a shell in the chest; I did not even feel sorry then, but I do since. There was a German officer in an MG bunker dead as a doornail and two Ox and Bucks sergeants in a slit, who landed before us. I asked our Sergeant where the rest of the unit was and he said, "All around somewhere".'

Offshore, obstacles were very thick and several craft were holed, others were hit and one ran onto a mine and had its bows blown off. Of the 14 LCAs of 47 Commando that set out, only two returned to the parent ships. In the onshore shambles it took 47 half an hour to get ashore, with the LCAs scattered down a mile of beach, and it was not until 11.00 that the majority of the Commandos were assembled, and set off for their march on Port-en-Bessin, arriving at their start line at La Rosiere at 17.30. When heads were counted it appeared that 47 had lost five officers and seventy-three other ranks. 'X' and 'Y' Troops were reasonably dry and equipped, although 'Y' had only one officer, 'A' Troop was present but without weapons, 'Q' was at half strength but 'B' was almost intact. The Commando had also lost all their Bangalore torpedoes and most of their 3-inch mortar ammunition, and had only one mortar, which had lost its dial sight. In addition, most of the wireless sets had been drowned by immersion in the sea. The Commando dug in near Port-en-Bessin and spent a quiet night, although 'A' Troop captured and cheerfully disarmed two Germans who walked into their lines.

By mid-morning on 7 June, communications were re-established and the assault on Port-en-Bessin went ahead at 16.00 with many of the 47 Marines, especially those in 'A' Troop, equipped with German weapons.

Fred Wildman tells what happened to him with 47 Commando: 'On 5 June 1944 the Commando found itself aboard two ships, HMLSI, *Josephine Charlotte* and the *SS Victoria*. The *Josephine Charlotte* had been a Belgian cross-Channel ferry before the war and the *Victoria* had been on the Irish Channel run. They had been adapted to Assault Landing Ships and were carrying 14 LCAs between them. My own troop, Heavy Weapons, was on *Victoria*.

'Most of the day had been taken up with intensive briefing on our task. We had been issued with maps in the holding camp just outside Southampton, but all the place-names had been in English. Once we had boarded the ships at Southampton Docks the maps were replaced with the genuine article. These were amazingly detailed indicating ditches, barbed wire, LMG positions etc. It became apparent that 47 was not going in with the rest of the Brigade which was to attack the area to the east of the British landing sector. 47's target on the other hand was to the extreme right of the British sector with a 10-mile gap between us and the nearest American troops. Our target was Port-en-Bessin, a small port well defended from a seaborne landing by a high feature each side of the town. Both east and west features had gun emplacements sited out to sea and it was decided to attack these from the rear after landing at a little place called Le Hamel, some way to the east of the port.

'Sitting at the briefings it didn't look as though it was going to be too much of a task, especially in view of the massive fire power that was to be hurled at the enemy. As details began to emerge of naval and air support, we began to feel almost sorry for the Germans who were to be subjected to an enormous barrage of fire power from the greatest invasion force in history.

'As the ship began to move on the evening of 5 June, we looked a rather unusual sight for His Majesty's Royal Marines. On orders from the CO no one had shaved for at least 3 days, and when we put our camouflage paint on, we looked the sort of thugs no one would like to meet on a dark night. The hope was that this would be true of the Germans.

'We anchored about seven and a half miles from the beaches at about 05.00. They began to lower the LCAs and we prepared our equipment for the climb down the scramble nets into the boats. The weather was still very rough but we got into our craft without too much trouble. By this time the bombardment had started and the whole of the coast seemed to be erupting with a noise that really was indescribable. The sea was a mass of all shapes and sizes of craft and the sky seemed hardly less crowded with bombers, fighters, and gliders being towed towards the bridgehead. The nearer we got to the beach the less inviting it looked. It seemed to be a mass of crippled, burning, and sunken craft, and clear landing areas seemed to be at a premium. We began to wonder if our sympathy for Jerry hadn't been a trifle misplaced.

'As we moved closer to the beach, we came under fire and the boat next to us blew up and disappeared. It became obvious our original landing target was not on, and the boats were ordered to turn east and look for a better area. It soon became a case of each craft for itself and we started a run into a likely spot. As we closed on the beach there was a helluva bang, and the front of the boat disappeared; as it started to settle, most of us decided it was possible to wade ashore and went over the side with full equipment plus, in my case, a mortar sight. Unfortunately, appearances were deceptive and I found myself struggling in eight feet of water. I managed to rid myself of the mortar sight but couldn't get the buckles undone on my equipment. I began to think my own personal invasion was ending there and then, but after a lot of struggling and gasping, my feet touched the sand and I made it to the beach. Looking back to the sea, we discovered our boat was still above water at the rear, being kept afloat by the watertight engine compartment.

'Perched on top of this was one of our lads, a non-swimmer who had decided to take a chance on the boat. He wasn't a bad judge, being the only one to get a dry landing. Someone found a rope and swam out to the boat and we soon had it hauled up to the beach. The mortars were recovered but all the sights were lost, a devastating blow to our ability to support the attack later on.

'By now, all the Commandos had landed, but were spread over about 1500 yards of beach. We heard later that only two of the 14 LCAs returned to the parent ships. Soon we left the shambles on the beach and moved up to the small road running parallel to the dunes. As pre-arranged, we started to move west in small boat-load parties to the RV at Le Hamel. After a while, the Commando assembled at a road that led inland from the beach to Les Rocquettes. The enemy were still occupying Le Hamel and were defying the efforts of 231 Brigade to shift them, so it was decided to change our route and travel via Les Rocquettes. It was on this road that Marine Lamsden was killed by a sniper. Most of the Commando were by now carrying German weapons and ammunition picked up from casualties and the prisoners we were collecting as we slogged towards our destination. Our own casualties were mounting steadily as we came under mortar and MG fire from isolated spots along the way. We reached La Rosière about five miles east of Port-en-Bessin about 17.00, resting up and taking stock.

'At 19.45 the Commando set off across the country

over the Masse de Cradelle, and as darkness set in we reached Point 72, a hill a mile and a half from the port and overlooking the approach road. We started digging in for the night on and around the hill. Midnight arrived and the end of D-Day saw HW Troop in defensive positions in a small wood overlooking the road to the port.

'Etched on the memory? Our first sight of bodies *en masse* in the water and on the beach. A flail-tank beating up a minefield just off the beach. Amidst all the bombardment, a farmer with two horses calmly ploughing a field. A group of veteran Desert Rats nonchalantly under fire, knowing exactly where the shells were going to land. An expertise we soon acquired in the bridgehead. A small car that had been driven over by a tank and the driver's remains still in it. A badly wounded German asking, "Ich Kaput?" and men grinning reassuringly, nodding their heads and saying, "Yes mate, you'll be all right". Luckily I knew enough to say "Nicht kaput," and shake my head.'

Next day, Fred Wildman helped to take Port-en-Bessin, using the 3-inch mortar without a sight. 'During the night the Commando was spread along a ridge that encompassed Point 72. There were dugouts on the feature that had obviously been German aid posts, and these were quickly converted to our own RAP and HQ billets. There were various alerts during the night as the enemy began probing our positions with small patrols and reacting to our own patrols. Most of us managed to squeeze in a couple of hours sleep, but could have done with a great deal more. Daylight arrived and preparations began for the move to the Port. The Forward Observations Officer arrived in a Bren-gun carrier to co-ordinate support fire from a 25-pounder battery, and some destroyers deployed off the coast towards Arromanches. Arrangements were also to be made for some dive-bomber attacks on the feature each side of the port. After a number of conferences attended by Bill Titmuss, the mortar Sergeant and Taffy Williams for the machine-guns, a clear idea of the battle plan began to emerge of the attack as a whole, and our own role in particular.

'"A", "B" and "Y" Troops were to be in the initial attack on weapon pits and the eastern and western features. "Q" Troop to be in reserve and "Y" Troop holding Point 72. The axis of advance was down the road from Escures to Port-en-Bessin, the start line being Escures. The MMGs were to give covering fire from Point 72 and we with our 3-inch Mortar with no sight, hopefully to give support with smoke and HE from Escures.

'The attack was due to go in at 16.00. At 14.00, the Navy started bombarding the port and the features each side of it, and at about 15.50 a squadron of Typhoons gave the feature defences a pasting. The Field Battery started firing on the eastern feature and soon grass fires added greatly to the smoke cover. As the leading Troops left the cover of Escures, they came under increasingly heavy sniper fire from the château at Fosse-Soucy. Prelanding briefings had indicated there were some HQ Troops in this château, hardly likely to give much trouble. In the event, it turned out to be a Sniper's School, and they gave us more than enough trouble. "X", "A", and "B" Troops advanced down the road in quite deep ditches and managed to reach the town in reasonably good order. "X" Troop were immediately successful in their attack on some weapon slits and took about twenty prisoners. "A" Troop passed through the town and turned left along a track onto the western feature. Directly they reached open ground they came under heavy fire from two flak ships in the harbour.

'This, combined with MG fire and grenades from the top of the hill, made their position untenable and they retired to the cover of some houses with some casualties. A small party was detached to deal with the Flak ships and this operation, coupled with attacks by two boats from the destroyer *Ursula*, was successful. After an initial foray up the Eastern feature by Capt Cousins and ten men, he reported to the CO that he was confident of getting to the top, given another twenty-five men or so. The CO allocated "Q" Troop, who had been badly depleted by the landings, only about half getting ashore. After some covering fire from the MMG and not very successful smoke cover from us with our 3-inch mortar, which we were trying to operate without a sight, "A" and "Q" went into the attack. They got to the top of the ridge and "A" turned left towards the sea. After dealing with a number of pill-boxes they came under heavy fire. Capt Cousins took four men to deal with this. He was killed by a grenade and one of the men wounded. By this time the Germans had had enough and started to surrender. "Q" Troop had wheeled to the right on reaching the ridge top and charged along the top firing from the hip, and very soon began taking prisoners. It was by now about 23.00, and the eastern feature was effectively ours. In the morning "X" Troop were ordered to clear the western feature but found it largely deserted and after some initial firing from a pocket of the enemy, the Germans were persuaded to surrender. This is a very general picture of the attack gathered from documents and other people afterwards.

'The Heavy Weapons task started in the woods of the hill topped by Point 72. The MMG had been set up to give covering fire for the attack on the eastern feature and our mortar was on the slope facing the port. During the day the enemy had started probing the positions on and around the top of the hill and as the day progressed, mounted a determined attack supported by mortars and machine-guns. Bill Titmuss ordered us to take up firing positions on the slope of the hill but our position soon became untenable and we retired to the other side of the hedge into a quite deep ditch on the road bordering Escures.

'The Germans must have had a view of us because the mortar bombs began exploding almost on top of the ditch and we decided to get cover in the village. It became obvious the positions on and around Point 72 were on the receiving end of a determined German counter-attack, and we decided to join up with the main body at Port-en-Bessin. As we went down the road we passed Lt John Bennet and three Carriers, making their way towards Point 72 RAP on the CO's orders. We told him the situation looked a bit dicey with the Germans attacking the area with mortars and MMGS. We heard after that he managed to get to the RAP and off-load supplies and eventually arrived back at the port to help in the attack. We met with the CO on the outskirts of Port-en-Bessin and he ordered us to set up the mortar and range on the Eastern feature to cover the attack. Without a sight we needed rather more time and ammunition than the CO could give us, and he soon ordered us to stop firing. Back on Point 72 the enemy mounted a sustained attack and managed to overrun the position causing casualties and taking a few prisoners. When a patrol was sent in on the following morning, the enemy had withdrawn, having looted everything in sight and leaving some of our dead to be recovered and buried. This was effectively the end of the Port-en-Bessin battle. After the war, General Sir Brian Horrocks, in one of his television talks, said that if he were asked to pick a battle that typified World War II, he would pick the assault on Port-en-Bessin by 47 RM Commando.'

Supported by the guns of *HMS Emerald*, 47 Commando had soon captured two of the three strongpoints which defended the port though the fog of war that had surrounded 47 since it arrived off the landing beach, hardly abated. About 16.20, just after the attack had started, the CO received a report:

'(a) that "A" Troop had got up on the Western feature.

(b) that "B" Troop were stuck in the town.

(c) that "X" Troop had not crossed their start line . . .'

This part of the unit history concludes tersely: 'The CO decided to go forward himself and find out the true position.'

'A' Troop's task was to pass through the town and attack the enemy on the western feature. The RSM was wounded during the advance, and once in the town they came under heavy fire, first from the eastern feature and then under more fire from German flak ships in the harbour as they advanced to the cliff edge.

'B' Troop had a fierce fight in the town, especially near the harbour basin, and had to subdue flak ships in the harbour, while 'X' Troop made its way through the western outskirts of the town and attacked weapon pits below the western feature. The Germans then counter-attacked and recaptured some ground, before Capt Cousins took 'Q' Troop and assaulted the eastern feature, which fell at around 22.00, though Capt Cousins was killed in the assault.

'Our troop was fired on from the road as we went into Port-en-Bessin,' writes Bill Andrews, 'and I saw Sgt Farr of the 10 I-A Commando talking to some twenty prisoners. He said they expected us well before this time and they did not know what was going on . . . it's a bit of a blur from then on. I heard Capt Cousins was killed, and met a Yank artillery officer who came to tell us his "stuff" was not ashore, so he couldn't support us. There were droves of German prisoners coming in, and they were told to empty their pockets into a farm barrow, which was full of binoculars, watches, rings . . . the boys soon made that lot vanish. That night we took turns guarding the area, and then we went off to La Deliverande, and then to Sallenelles.'

The Battle of D-Day cost the Allied armies some ten thousand men, killed, wounded and missing. By the evening of 6 June, the Allies were ashore on a fifty-mile front and established in parts to a depth of seven miles. The Commando units suffered heavily in the landings and in spite of hopes that they would be swiftly withdrawn and sent back to England, this never happened. 47 Commando, who expected to be 'home for Christmas', stayed in the line and did not actually return to England until November 1945.

41 Commando captured the radar station near Douvres on 17 June with the support of artillery and tanks. The 4th SS Brigade crossed the Orne and took up defensive positions near Sallenelles, where they recall being greatly plagued by mosquitoes. When the breakout began in August 1944, the 4th Brigade advanced towards Dozule by night, and then made a memorable night march, in single file, to St Maclou on the Seine. Paddy Stevens (then of 41) remembered this march twenty years later when he was commanding 45 Commando in the Radfan, but on 31 August, the Brigade crossed the river Seine and advanced up the French coast, a cheerful advance after the bitter fighting on D-Day and the steady attrition among the woods and orchards of the Normandy countryside. The 1st Special Service Brigade went back to England in early September, taking with it 45 Commando. The much reduced 46 Commando, which had suffered so severely at Rots, took part in operations round Dunkirk, returning to England in October, changing with 4 Commando which joined 4th SS Brigade for the next major Commando operation of the war, the assault on the island of Walcheren.

6

Walcheren and the Rhine, 1944–45

A city consists of its men, and not its walls.
Nicias: Speech to the Athenians

On 4 September 1944, the 11th Armoured Division entered the port of Antwerp, and the finest harbour in Western Europe was at last in Allied hands. Antwerp was the second largest port in Europe, the third largest in the world, and the only one capable of adequately supplying the Allied armies, which already numbered over two million men, during their advance into Germany. The capture of Antwerp was therefore good news but there was, as ever, a snag.

Antwerp lies on the river Scheldt, some forty miles from the sea. The river pours out into a vast estuary which is divided into two parts, the East and West Scheldt by a long peninsula, South Beveland, and two islands, North Beveland and Walcheren. All three were held in strength by the German Army. Until the banks of the river and these islands could be cleared of the enemy, the great port of Antwerp was useless. The task of clearing them was entrusted to the 2nd Canadian Infantry Division, the 52nd British Division, and the 4th (Special Service) Brigade, which now consisted of Nos 4, 41, 47, and 48 Commandos, plus two troops of No 10 (1-A) Commando. 4 (Special Service) Brigade were charged with the capture of Walcheren.

Walcheren has the shape of a battered triangle. The

interior of the island lies below sea level, behind an encircling rampart of high sand-dunes and dykes. There are two main towns, Flushing on the south coast, and Middelburg, which lies in the centre of the island. Both had been fortified. The natural defences were strong and as usual, the Germans had added to them with concrete blockhouses, pill-boxes, minefields, wire, machine-gun posts and heavy artillery, so that the island had been turned into a formidable fortress.

The force sent against Walcheren consisted of 4 (Special Service) Brigade, commanded by Brigadier 'Jumbo' Leicester RM, aided by tanks, engineers, and ancillary units, a total force of something over 8000 men, who were carried to the assault by a strong naval force, Force T, which included the battleship *HMS Warspite*, and two monitors, *HMS Erebus* and *Roberts*, which carried 15-inch guns, plus a host of support craft. The landing force would be put ashore in tracked amphibious vehicles, known as Weasels and Buffaloes, and the assault would be preceded by air attacks which had the aim of breaching the island's dykes and flooding the low-lying centre. The attack itself was scheduled to go in on 1 November 1944, by which time the port of Antwerp had been free of the enemy but quite inoperative for nearly two months.

The plan called for No 4 Commando to land on *Uncle* beach, at the south of the island and take the town of Flushing, while 41, 47 and 48 landed at the western end of the island and attacked Westkapelle. The great dyke at Westkapelle was well supplied with defences, including artillery, and these had survived a heavy attack by the RAF on 3 October, though the dyke itself was breached and the island flooded. 41 Commando intended to land three troops on the north side of this breach, and then advance along towards Westkapelle. The rest of 41, plus two troops of No 10 (1-A) Commando, would then clear

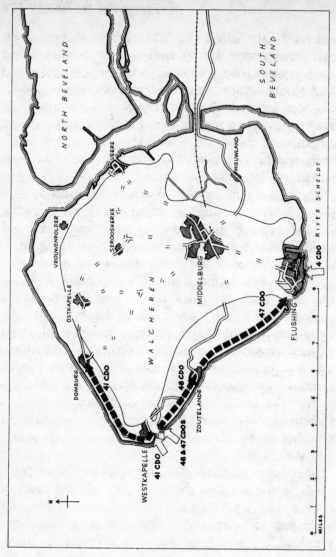

Map 3 Walcheren

the port itself. Meanwhile, 48 would land south of the gap, move south to Zoutelande and 47, landing in the same place, would pass through 48 to push south and join hands with No 4 at Flushing. Artillery support would be supplied by Force T and by Allied batteries and field artillery from the southern shore of the Scheldt. All in all, it was a good plan.

Force T sailed from Ostend at 03.15 on 1 November, and four hours later were hove-to off Westkapelle while *HMS Warspite* and the monitors pounded the dyke with their heavy guns, and rocket-firing assault craft moved in to provide close support. These were immediately engaged by enemy guns on the dyke. LCF 37 soon exploded and the crews of the other craft took heavy casualties while finding that their guns and rockets were largely ineffective against the reinforced concrete of the German strongpoints, even when the support craft went so close inshore they sustained hits from rifle fire. This battle to silence the batteries by rocket and naval gunfire went on until the afternoon, by which time the inshore support craft had taken heavy punishment. Only seven out of twenty-seven support craft were still in action, and casualties among the crews amounted to nearly three hundred killed and wounded. As they withdrew, the attack was taken up by rocket-firing RAF Typhoons.

Frank Nightingale won the DCM on Walcheren. 'As I told you, I got hit on D-Day, but I returned to 41 in France and met up with Peter Heydon, who got me into his Troop, 'Y' Troop, as a corporal, with my old mate George Comley, as my Bren-gunner. We then went on to do the worst landing 41 took part in, at Walcheren. We landed at Westkapelle – I have never seen so many craft get hit, ships, landing craft . . . anyway, we finished it with an attack on a battery at Domburg, where my troop commander, Peter Heydon, who got the DSO at Salerno when only 19, was killed . . . my troop seemed to be going down like ninepins. My section officer, Lt Holmes, got badly wounded in front of the battery, so I went out to fetch him in and I had to crawl with him (I couldn't tell you the distance). I don't think it was far but it seemed like bloody miles. After fetching him in, I had to borrow a German Schmeisser because my Bren was full of sand. I thought I got the DCM for fetching the officer in, but you can read the citation and decide from all the bullshit, which part is true . . . I went on and got hit again . . . that was the fourth time.'

Unit . . . 41 (RM) Commando
No. and Rank . . . Ch/x 101330 Mne (A/Ty/Cpl)
Name . . . Frank Lewis NIGHTINGALE

At 1545 hours on 5 Nov 44, Y Troop 41 (RM) Commando as part of a Commando attack, assaulted Battery W.18 at DOMBURG on WALCHEREN which contained some 200 Germans. During the fighting in the battery, Cpl Nightingale was forward with his section officer and one other marine. They were heavily engaged by enemy MG and rifle fire from the surrounding woods, and the marine was killed and the officer seriously wounded. Cpl Nightingale attempted to carry on the fire-fight with his bren gun but this fired only a few rounds and stopped. Cpl Nightingale seized a captured German MB 34 and continued to fire this until the enemy was forced to withdraw. After a while the enemy counter-attacked in a determined manner but Cpl Nightingale once again drove them to ground and alone held on to this flank until the remnants of his section were able to advance and join him. Through this NCO's personal disregard for safety, and his determination to kill the enemy, the troop was able to hold on to the position.

Paddy Stevens, who had won an MC on D-Day, commanded 'A' Troop at Walcheren. 'We were based with the Brigade at De Haan, and did plenty of training for Walcheren, and were anyway a much more useful, battle-hardened unit. Westkapelle was overlooked by a great lighthouse for the Scheldt, and that was "A" Troop's objective. On the way in, in an LST, there was a lot of firing from the Navy, and I remember the flickering of gunfire from the shore batteries. As we went into the breach in our Buffaloes, the support ships were really close in, engaging the batteries at point-blank range. Two hundred yards in front of our craft, a rocket ship blew up, the sea was boiling with explosions. Well, we got ashore, first in the Buffaloes – they are tracked amphibious vehicles – then when we came under shellfire, I got the men out. Although a Marine unit, we had several army Commando officers and some South Africans. The village was half under water, and the lighthouse was at the end of the street. The enemy were firing from the top, dropping grenades, and our Vickers fired back. Eventually, CSM Stokell blasted the door in with a PIAT, and they came out. We took about eight or ten prisoners. Peter Heydon was killed at Domburg taking a battery. I remember seeing part of 47 Commando picking their way round to join the rest of their unit after they were split up on landing. Domburg was a set-piece attack, but we ran into a minefield. I saw a shell burst ahead and I saw, I actually saw, a piece of shrapnel flying towards me. It hit a phosphorous grenade on my chest, ignited it . . . I snatched it off and threw it away. We had a ripple of casualties from D-Day on. I was a subaltern on D-Day, a Captain on D + 1, a Major after Walcheren, that's all in five months. There was always a heavy toll among the officers. They were expected to lead from the front and they did.'

Bill Sloley was still commanding 'P' Troop of 41 Commando. '41 was then about four hundred strong, because we had received reinforcements all the time in Normandy to make up our losses. Some of these were sea service officers, like Paddy Brind Sheridan – we also had a lot of excellent South Africans, like Denys Ranger, Jock Mackenzie, Sam Burder, Fouché; Jock Mackenzie was killed going ashore at Walcheren.

'We embarked at Ostend and landed at Westkapelle in broad daylight, without much air support as I recall, but the monitors and *Warspite* were hammering away, and the small gun and rocket ships were firing at the shore batteries – every enemy gun was in action and they took heavy losses supporting us.

'Those German strongposts were like forts, or castles, several storeys high, linked by tunnels – anyway, in we went – I remember Ranger waving to his pal MacKenzie in the next craft, which then received a direct hit. We got ashore and clambered up over the dyke. I carried a German Schmeisser, which was faster than a Thompson and not so ready to jam with sand. "P" Troop had to go left flanking up the dunes, which we did. The nearest gun emplacement had received hits and the Germans were withdrawing towards Domburg, and we followed. Brind Sheridan was killed attacking one strongpost, and Peter Heydon was killed attacking another – he was miles out in front of his troop, bringing them on, and a sniper got him; Marine Moses went out to help him and got killed as well – our casualties were heavy. Then a lot of 48 Commando were killed when one of their Buffaloes went over a mine.

'When the battle was over, my troop went to Veere, and from there we mounted raids across the water against Schowen – TSM Elsom was killed on one of these and Denys Ranger was wounded. I was only hit twice, but nothing serious.'

Dennis Fawcett was with 41 Commando at Westkapelle: 'Perhaps my most vivid recollections of this action were, firstly, the run-in to the gap in the dunes at Westkapelle. From my position in the amphibious landing craft, a Buffalo, I believe, I could see as we approached a semi-circle of fire from coastal defences landing on the seaward side of the gap, and recall thinking something like, "Bloody hell – we have to go through all that lot!" Luck was with us, and we eventually trundled up the dyke on the northern side of the gap, scrambled quickly from the craft and made off towards the inland lighthouse. Later, in attacks on concrete emplacements on the approach to Domburg, we were given terrific support by RAF rocket-firing Typhoons. We wore yellow squares of cloth on our backs to indicate how far the leading troops had progressed, and the Typhoons screamed in and fired almost over our shoulders, marvellous for morale, and made things somewhat easier.'

41 Commando, landing north of the gap, under intense fire, had landed half an hour late, and lost two craft to artillery fire during the run in. 'B' and 'S' Troops got ashore about 09.00 and outflanked one of the more aggressive batteries, and by 11.15 the rest of the Commando, with tank support, had taken Westkapelle, where they at once came under artillery fire from a large German battery, 'W17' at Domburg, which shelled them remorselessly for two hours until the Typhoons silenced it with rockets. The Commando then advanced on Domburg and took it by 19.00 that evening, although 'X' Troop lost their Troop Commander when the Germans counter-attacked.

48 Commando, under Lt-Col Jim Moulton, landing south of the gap, had also taken its first objectives. Captain Dan Flunder of 'A' Troop, explains what

happened. 'Right from the start it was obvious that Walcheren was going to be a difficult operation. The great importance to the whole campaign of opening Antwerp was quite clear – to the Germans as well as us. We would be fighting round the rim of a saucer with a flooded centre, and would be outnumbered four to one during that process. Not that extra troops would help – there wouldn't be room to deploy them.

'Incidentally, it isn't easy to believe in premonition, but Derek de Stacpoole hated the idea of Walcheren from the start and often said so when we were out together. He and I had a quiet dinner in Bruges just before we embarked, and he said he'd never felt like it at the prospect of action before. I put it down at the time to the effect of the rotten wounds he got on D-Day following even worse ones when he was sunk on the Med . . . When we were training at De Haan for this action, "A" Troop fired over 55,000 rounds of .303 – and I think other troops did the same. We used everything for targets – steel helmets, bottles in the sea . . .

'It was with rather special attention we listened to our first briefings, although, as always, confidence increased as we listened to the plans in detail. It was very much the sort of amphibious assault we existed for, but of high technical difficulty, and in every way a bit special. We were still ourselves well under strength in spite of some welcome reinforcements during our pre-operation training period at De Haan. "A" Troop embarked just fifty-five strong.

'The CO had managed to avoid the hated LCI(S)s we had had on D-Day, and the plan was for us to land in amphibious vehicles called Buffaloes from tank landing craft. We were to land on one side of the gap at Westkapelle made by RAF bombs through which the sea had flooded the island.

"A" and "Z" Troops were to land as a second wave,

the first assault being made by "B", "X" and "Y". "A" Troop was used to leading, or being in the van, and I felt the second wave was a great indignity. I found Tom Nuttall of "Z" Troop was also a bit upset, so we went together to complain to the CO. Wise as always, Jim Moulton wasted no time talking about "mutiny" or questioning of his orders, but blandly asked us which of our troops we preferred to keep ready under our own hands in a difficult operation – the best or the worst? I left feeling outsmarted, but nevertheless a bit mollified!

'As we ran in on a cold, grey, breezy morning, there was a lot of evidence of hard times ahead. The usual smoke and shellbursts looked pretty thick, and there were a number of sinking landing craft. Our supporting LCGs (essentially tank landing craft, but mounting a 3.7 gun for the close support role) had heroically (not too strong a word) taken the inshore passage right under the German heavy batteries to try to keep the heat off us and paid the price. Although the debris looked bad from where we were we soon heard that our leading Troops were ashore and had taken the immediate beach defences. 41 Commando, just to our left were also ashore and fighting in Westkapelle.

'We soon came under fire ourselves. Several craft in our wave were hit, including my own, and as we limped in at reduced speed there was a Buffalo on fire behind me. "A" Troop had ten casualties before getting ashore, and shells were beginning to fall pretty thickly in the gap as we landed. But we got ashore and started up the dunes. As I looked back, I saw our Buffaloes burning fiercely, so that was the end of our packs. Of all things, when you lose your few personal belongings, like that, the razor is probably the most important to morale, so captured German razors became a matter of some priority. We managed very well.

'As we moved along the dunes towards the sounds of

battle ahead I became conscious of the film of fine blown sand which was covering our weapons, and which was a nuisance throughout the battle. I had thought it might be a problem, and before we embarked I had got from the armourers a supply of graphite. We had tried to clean the oil from our weapons and replace it with the graphite. Judging from my own rifle it didn't seem to have made a fat lot of difference, so we stopped in a hollow behind the forward troops and cleaned weapons. I remember saying something swingeing to the effect that a jammed weapon would constitute a disciplinary offence. While we were doing this I was summoned by the CO – the first attack on the big Battery W11 by "Y" Troop had failed, and the Troop Commander, my great friend Derek de Stacpoole, had been killed right up against the heavy concrete emplacements. I passed the rest of the operation in a bitter vengeful mood and, as always, the Troop caught it from me. Because of our friendship the two Troops "A" and "Y", had looked upon themselves as "chummy Troops", so they took it hard as well.

'The dunes widened a little at this point, and the CO told me to work as far round to the left as I could to give covering fire to the next attack. One of my subalterns, Wally England, got one Bren gun right out into a rather exposed position on a spit of sand almost in the flood, and they had a great early success in nailing the whole crew of the German 81 mm mortar which had caused so many casualties among our leading troops – at this time, for example, "Z" Troop's senior surviving rank was a Corporal.

'While preparing for the next assault, by "B" troop, we had some supporting back-up from the Navy, and finally fighter-bombers put in a classic dive-bombing attack. By this time we had worked a good bit further round the flank and were well within any normal safety limits. The nearest bombs were certainly less than fifty yards away. I was lying flat as they came in, and I remember the extraordinary feeling of the ground coming up and thumping me as it shuddered with the exploding bombs. But "B" troop were on their feet and on their way in and we were firing everything we had – there was no time to ruminate over safety limits. They did very well and were quickly successful, as "X" Troop followed them up and cleared the rest of the position.

'In helping to search the position and marshal the seventy-odd prisoners, I remember being struck by the difference between the strapping, big, well turned out, coastal gunners, and their somewhat dishevelled infantry defenders. They stayed separate in their groups, too.

'Early in the bitter cold night which followed, I went to look for Derek's body. As I looked down at it, I felt none of the pangs I had expected, and realized I should have known better by then – a body from which life has departed never has any meaning. The person has gone. But my anger remained.

'The next morning "A" Troop was sent forward to clear a defended Oerlikon position and then make what progress it could. The next major position was the village of Zoutelande, just over a mile ahead. Mike Aldworth came with me with a detachment of 3-inch mortars. We took twenty prisoners from the Oerlikon position after a rather half-hearted defence by them, which caused us no casualties. There was some other small-arms fire coming from positions between us and Zoutelande, but this didn't amount to much until we got closer to the village. A persistent single bullet kept cracking round me at fairly regular intervals, and I thought I had been singled out by a good shot for special attention. Once I thought I saw a head move just after a shot, about five hundred yards away on the summit of a high dune, so I prepared myself and waited. I had always scored well with a rifle, and was big-headed enough to carry a sniper's rifle as my personal weapon. When I saw a movement again I squeezed off a shot but had no idea whether or not I had hit. As we moved on there were no more of those distracting cracks round me, so I forgot about it.

'We were making steady progress using fire and movement (and Mike's mortars) until about three hundred yards from what was increasingly obviously a well-manned strong point; I thought the landward side of the dunes was becoming untenable and we crossed over to what seemed better shelter on the seaward side. I speeded up the advance then to get as far as we could before we ran into heavy close range fire and realized we were running out of shelter as the dunes curved in. So in to the minefield we went, gambling on them being anti-tank mines deeply covered by the drifting sand. About fifty yards from the strong-point, running as best we could in the soft sand, we came upon two single strands of wire, presumably marking a path through the minefield. I gestured to those behind me and we ran up the path in single file. I passed over a little crest and jumped down into what was obviously the command post of the whole fortification. There was no further resistance and we rounded up over 200 prisoners. At my feet as I jumped down had been the body of a Feldwebel, still holding his rifle, with a neat hole through his steel helmet in the centre of his forehead. I felt rather like the winner of an old fashioned duel.

'Mike's mortar covering fire had been a big help in keeping heads down, and the occasional arrival in the village of a 15-inch shell from *HMS Erebus* could have done nothing for the defenders' morale. I sent a patrol further on up the dunes to try to find the next defended position, and spoke to a much relieved CO on the radio. I was told to stay where I was and let 47 Commando pass through. While searching the concrete fortifications we found the civilian population huddled in a big bunker which had been a store. I found an interpreter, and announced that I was a British Captain. There was a surprised murmur accompanying broad grins – I was after all in a parachute smock, with camouflage paint on my face, a cap-comforter on my head, and a rifle in my hand, with no badges of rank visible to them. Perhaps nettled by the murmur, I said pompously, "Would you please tell the Burgemeister you are now safe from the guns of the British Navy?" The pleased acknowledge-ment of this romantic statement was interrupted by a noise like a train, while everything shook and filled with dust as another salvo from *Erebus* arrived. I was told later that the CO's language as he watched this happen from back up the dunes had to be heard to be believed, but it did succeed in convincing the Navy that they really shouldn't do it again.

'I returned to the Command Post in time to greet the CO of 47 Commando as he came through, and to tell him where my forward patrol was. He was in a foul mood and was extremely rude – presumably cross at having his first objective taken by a single Troop of another Commando. I got a chilly reception too, the next day when I was sent up to reinforce them after their first attack on the next big coastal battery (W11) had failed.

'I was none too pleased, therefore, to be given what I thought was the dirty job of getting round to the flank in the dunes, overlooked by the whole position, to give covering fire to the next assault when it went in. Starting to move in the dusk before dawn I nearly fired at a dim figure ahead of us – only a wish not to betray our movement restrained me. It was a good thing, too, be-cause the figure was the Brigadier, quite alone, and looking piratical with a blood-stained bandage round his head. He was full of good cheer, if, I thought, a bit startled at our task, and his congratulation on our exploits the day before mollified me no end. It was not easy getting round to the position I had picked out – as soon as it was light we were under fire all the way, there was not much cover and I had to resort to "pepper-potting" – which means small groups making random dashes and diving into cover. Almost incredibly we got there without casualties, although I was out of touch with 47 Commando because my signallers were pinned down by a light machine gun, and when they did make a desperate dash got a bullet through the radio!

'It was a great relief to find that the small group of buildings I was making for were unoccupied. I had expected I would have to attack them, and didn't like the thought of the wrath of the CO of 47 if I held him up while I did so. I quickly disposed the Troop and then we unleashed such a blast of fire as to relieve our frustrations, and to inform 47 Commando we had arrived. They put in a fast, hard attack, and we loosed off everything we had just ahead of them. It was all too much for the enemy, who quickly gave up. Just before the attack started there had been a very accurate artillery shoot from the other side of the Scheldt – we were now just about far enough along the coast to be in range.

'Prisoners told us the Dutch would hate us for flooding their island. It simply wasn't true, then or now. They regarded it as the price of freedom and told us we had to do it, or the battle would have been much worse both for them and us. One incident illustrates their feelings. During the night after our attachment to 47 Commando we stopped for the night at a farmhouse under the dyke which had been pretty well demolished by a shell from the old Monitor – *Erebus*. The farmer and his wife were dead in the ruins. We disposed them decently and covered them, and made ourselves as comfortable as we could in the farm buildings. During the night I was awakened to be told there was a light approaching through the flood, and soon the sentries brought in two young Dutchmen, who had waded through the mostly chest high flood from Middleburg – some five miles. They were the sons of the house, and I had to show them their parents and express sympathy. They were pathetically grateful for the little we had done to extricate the bodies and cover them up, and prepared to return through the flood. Before they left, I apologized for the troops eating the apples we had found in the barn, and explained that because of the bad weather we had had few supplies landed and were getting very hungry. They begged us to take anything we could find and left for their cold and wet five mile wade. Just before first light I was awakened again, and it was our same two young friends, who had returned with a sack of bread they had collected from friends and neighbours in Middleburg . . .

'There is only one more story to relate of "A" Troop's Walcheren, and it is a very sad one. We crossed the Westkapelle gap and waited in Domburg in case 4 or 41 Commando needed help in the assault on Veere. I was ordered to take the Troop through the flood in Buffaloes to try and make contact with 52 Div, who should by then be making headway towards Veere on the other side of the island. We had a terrific welcome in the little village of Serooskerke, but at the last crossroad as we left the village, my Buffalo, which was leading, had to swerve to avoid two men in a punt. The second Buffalo, fifty yards behind, came straight across and blew up on a booby-trapped 11-inch shell the Germans had put in the flood. The tragedy was that, thinking of mines, I had taken only my Sergeant-Major and a Bren group in the leading vehicle, and loaded heavy fire support into the second vehicle in case we bumped into the infantry somewhere. Eighteen men were killed, and nine wounded. As I waited on the radio to report before resuming the patrol, Commando HQ were telling all Troops that the formal surrender of all enemy forces in the island had now been received.

'There is a postscript. Forty-one years later, now aged 63, I stood one golden evening in the military cemetery at Bergen-op-Zoom, looking at a small grey stone. On it was carved simply:

Major D. R. W. de Stacpoole
Royal Marines
Aged 26 years
1st November 1944

My admired senior and very good friend – just twenty six years old. It was a poignant moment, and after all those years it still hurt.'

The first wave of 48, 'X' and 'Y' Troops landed south of the gap at 10.05, and were led ashore by Lt-Col Moulton. The offshore shelling had so far caused only slight casualties and they found their first two objectives, a group of concrete blockhouses and a radar station, empty and undefended.

As Dan Flunder has said, the second wave, consisting of 'A' and 'X' Troops, with the Machine-Gun platoon, were not so lucky. One Buffalo received a direct hit on the way in which destroyed all their Vickers MMGs. The shelling and mortaring continued as the Commando re-grouped and 'Y' Troop was virtually wiped out by machine-gun fire when assaulting an enemy battery, W13, which was still firing at the landing craft offshore. The Commando needed more support to reduce this strongpoint, but their radios were not working, their tank support bogged down on the dunes, and of their two fire-control officers who were to control supporting gunfire from the ships, one had already been killed and the other had lost his radio. Casualties included Captain Mackenzie of 'X' Troop and the unit doctor, David Winser.

With 'Y' Troop decimated, 'Z' Troop went into the attack, and lost half their men to mortar fire. At 15.45, 'B' Troop had a go, their assault supported by the main artillery of the 2nd Canadian Division from across the Scheldt, who had been contacted by Lt-Col Moulton. 'B' Troop advanced in the gathering darkness, took the position, captured thirty prisoners and went on to overrun the German battery HQ, capturing the commander, his second in command, and seventy gunners. The Commando consolidated their position around the battery, and stayed there throughout the night.

Colonel Moulton had been quite determined that 48 Commando should not come ashore in the LSIs which had proved so disastrous on D-Day. 'We put the unit in Buffaloes, tracked amphibious craft, a great improvement, although they were petrol driven, burnt well if hit, and their tracks dug deep and dug up mines. 48 had hardly any casualties on the way in, three troops in the first wave with "Y" Troop in reserve, under de Stacpoole . . . but we were shelled heavily after we got ashore, and the radios were unreliable. Stacpoole was killed attacking the battery. Finally, we contacted the Canadian artillery across the Scheldt, and worked out a fire plan. Then "Z" Troop, under Tom Nuttall, an Army officer from the Devons, got mortared and Tom was wounded, so "B" Troop went in. We smoked out the target and "B" went across the minefield and into the battery. There was a lot of loose sand, jamming the weapons, lots of mines. One officer tried to shoot a German with his tommy-gun, found it wouldn't fire and hurled it at him instead. We took a lot of prisoners there, gunners mostly – they didn't have many infantry. Dan Flunder – a man who knew how to handle infantry – took his "A" Troop on to Zouteland next day.'

The last Marine Commando to enter the gap was 47 under Lt-Col C. F. Phillips, who swept into the assault at about 11.00. In the general confusion, three landing craft put their marines ashore on the north side of the gap, separated by hundreds of yards of turbulent water from their comrades on the south side and also from the direct route 47 were to take to Flushing.

'B' Troop, on the south side, lost four Buffaloes to shell fire on landing, and it was 18.30 that evening before 47 were finally assembled, south of the empty radar station overrun that morning by 48. They had suffered very few casualties, but lost all their radios. There they waited, while 48 Commando hammered away at the W13 battery, awaiting the capture of Zouteland.

Fred Wildman gives an account of 47's action at Walcheren; '47's task was to land on the south side of the gap and with 48 clear the dykes towards Flushing, where No 4 Commando had landed. Covering fire was to be given on the run-in by the battleship *Warspite* and the Monitors *Erebus* and *Roberts* along with a variety of rocket and gun ships. Air cover was promised, but in the event, the clouds were so low it didn't materialize.

'We boarded our LCT soon after midnight on 1 November at Ostend and after some initial rounding up by our escort force outside the harbour, set sail for Westkapelle in the early hours. Soon after dawn our escort destroyer gave us the go ahead for the landing. The scene at this stage was impressive, to say the least. The shells from *Warspite* and the monitors were whizzing overhead and the rocket ships were tucked right up to the dunes and were firing directly up to the huge gun batteries at the top of the dunes. The Germans were replying and replying accurately it seemed to us, as boat after boat went up in flames. We heard afterwards that the Navy had lost four out of every five of these craft.

'As we approached the beaches we came under fire and suddenly the whole front of the LCT appeared to go up in flames. What in fact had happened was that one of the Buffaloes carrying spare fuel had been hit. Mindful of my enforced swim on D-Day, I was soon up on the bridge with my bootlaces and equipment undone ready to go overboard. To my amazement, I saw the Buffalo I should have been on, sailing round the side of the boat with Captain O'Connel mouthing epithets in my direction. Somehow or other he'd managed to get it past the flames and over the ramp. He brought it alongside and after chucking my rifle down, I leapt after it. Lucky for me there were plenty of bodies to cushion my fall, but it seemed the bodies in question had a different view of what was lucky. We headed for the gap and trundled up the beach, fortunately on the right side. Two of the LCTs had discharged their cargo of Buffaloes and Weasels to the north side of the gap. By the time everything was re-organized on the right side, it was approaching evening and we had only three left out of our twenty Weasels and had suffered some thirty casualties. One very grievous loss to the HW Troop was Jimmy Day, a cheerful, out-going, seemingly indestructible character, whom every-body liked and respected. He'd been killed outright by an 88 mm shell.

'Bearing in mind the whole centre of the island was flooded, leaving the perimeter of dunes and one small coastal road to advance along, it was obvious we were in for a tough time, and so it proved. On the second day, 47 advanced through 48, towards the huge W11 battery. After covering fire from HW mortars firing smoke and HE and support from the machine gun section, an attack was mounted at 17.00 which was repulsed with casualties which included all five Troop Commanders of the fighting troops. After some re-organization, the Commando settled down for the night. It was while recce-ing for a good mortar position, that our Mortar Section came under fire and Corporal (Lofty) Rippener was killed. The enemy counter-attacked our forward sections during the night but were repulsed. The battery was attacked again on the morning of 3 November, this time successfully and many prisoners taken. The interior of the battery looked a gruesome sight having had what looked to be a direct hit from one of the support battleships. This proved to be our final major battle on the island and we moved forward to join up with 4 Commando at the Flushing Gap. On 11 November, 47 returned to the old billets at Wenduine to refit. From there, on 25 November, we moved to an ex-German Barracks at Bergen-Op-Zoom, which proved to be very comfortable after our recent exertions.'

Allied losses in men, tanks and landing craft were very heavy, not least because the heavy bombing, while failing to reduce the German resistance, had pitted the ground with deep, water-filled craters in which several tanks drowned, and could not be recovered. The Lothian Horse, which landed ten flail tanks and nine bridging tanks to help the Commando's advance, lost seven flails and eight bridging tanks by the end of the day. During the night more tanks were landed, though more were lost, so that there were only four tanks left to support 47 and 48 during their advance south towards Flushing, which began the following day.

At dawn on 2 November *HMS Erebus* pounded Zouteland with her 15-inch guns, and 48 moved in to the attack. At 11.00 the garrison surrendered, and 47 promptly passed through 48, which was consolidating on the objective, and were soon fighting their way into the outskirts of Flushing. Here their advance was held up, as low cloud and poor visibility prevented the use of air support, and 'Q' and 'Y' Troops of 47 lost a dozen men in the street fighting, though 'A' and 'Y' Troop, advancing along the dunes made good progress until held up by mortar at the battery. Dan Flunder took 'A' Troop of 48 up in support, and infiltrated forward into a good firing position, overlooking the battery and with their support, 47 took it by assault. That night, as Fred Wildman relates, 47 beat off a heavy counter-attack and on the following day, the outer defences of Flushing fell; and that evening 47 joined up with No 4 Commando which had captured the rest of the town. On 4 November the heavy fighting finished and minesweepers began clearing the channel up the Scheldt to Antwerp. No 4 spent the next few days mopping pockets of resistance in Flushing, while the three Marine Commandos advanced to the north coast of Walcheren, winkling out enemy positions on the way. The fighting finally ended on 8 November, when the last stronghold, battery W19, fell to the Brigade. Casualties among the Brigade had been very heavy, especially in 41 Commando.

After Walcheren, the 4th (Special Service) Brigade returned to Ostend to rest and re-equip, and on 6 December this Brigade, like the others in Commando Group, dropped the much disliked 'Special Service' description and adopted the word 'Commando' as the Brigade title.

A month later the German Army counter-attacked in the Ardennes, in the so-called Battle of the Bulge, and 47 Commando were sent to reinforce 1st Corps along the river Maas, where they were soon joined by three troops of 48 Commando. In mid-January, 47 raided the island of Kapelsche Veer in the middle of the Maas, which was held by a spirited battalion of German paratroops. The battle lasted all night, with the Commando withdrawing just before dawn, in good order, but with its ammunition exhausted. The Kapelsche Veer position fell two weeks later and it took two Canadian infantry battalions to overcome the defences. The Canadians found the graves of 150 Germans killed in the 47 Commando raid.

Fred Wildman again: 'Towards the end of December, the Commando moved up to the Maas and began a period of patrolling and defence activity, heightened by news coming through of a German breakthrough at Ardennes. Although there was no major battle at this time, the constant patrolling produced a steady stream of casualties. On 30 December Maj Donnell was promoted to Lieutenant-Colonel and took over Command from Lt-Col Phillips.

'Our period of relative inactivity came to an abrupt end in the middle of January 1945, in one of the most vicious and harrowing battles of 47's history. Kapelsche Veer was a small island formed by the Maas on one side and Oudermaas on the other. The Germans had crossed the Maas on Christmas Eve and dug in on a 25-foot high dyke which broadened out to quite a wide plateau where they were dug in. We found afterwards the troops consisted of Paras and Waffen SS, which explained quite a lot. A Company of the 1st Polish Armoured Division had tried to shift them and been severely repulsed. The Poles were to give covering fire for our attack and to build a bridge over the Oudemaas which was almost frozen over. There was no role for HW Troop in this operation and we were deputed to be stretcher bearers. Quite a large section of the Troop were on leave at this time, but not being one of these fortunates, I found myself allocated to 'X' Troop along with Tommy Wallace and a stretcher. It seemed to take the Poles ages to construct the bridge and they didn't seem to make much effort to keep the noise down. The Germans must have been well aware of what was coming. As we sat in a barn waiting for the bridge, it seemed to me virtually everybody around were young replacements, and I found it difficult to pick out any of the original 47.

'Eventually the bridge was completed just before midnight and we moved over with some difficulty and began the move to the attack position. "A" Troop soon bumped a small enemy outpost and wiped them out with some speed and a great deal of noise. Eventually everybody was lined up at the base of the dyke near the defended area and the barrage from the mainland opened up at 00.55. It ceased at 01.00 and the rush up the dyke began. Some of the lads mistook the attack signal at one point, and Tommy and I found ourselves at the top of the dyke with nothing but a stretcher for company. We proved it possible to jump down a 25-foot dyke in two jumps. The enemy fire was vicious, sustained and accurate, and only "Q" Troop managed to get on to the plateau for a while. Captain Stickings was killed, and it became obvious the task wasn't possible in the time available which was by daylight. By this time there were many casualties lying around and in serious trouble, because of the freezing conditions.

'Tommy and I picked up one casualty who had a bullet through his jaw, and it turned out to be a fellow stretcher bearer from HW troop – Ken Kitson. We began the long haul back to the first-aid post at the river. It became obvious it wasn't physically possible for two men and we quickly picked up a couple of volunteers to help. Even so, carrying a casualty along the narrow top of a frozen dyke under fire proved immensely difficult and I am afraid the poor chap was dropped a few times. Speaking to Ken after the war he assured me he didn't remember any of that journey at all. I shall remember it as long as I live.

'The Commando retired hurt from this battle with 49 casualties. We learned that the position was eventually taken by 10th Canadian Infantry Brigade, supported by tanks, and at a cost of 350 casualties. This proved to be the last major battle for 47, and the rest of the year consisted of rest periods and leaves, interspersed with patrol activity which contributed its share to the casualty list. On being disbanded in 1946, the names of the dead on the 47 Commando Roll of Honour numbered 115, and of the original 450-odd men who set off for D-Day, there were only 88 of us left in the unit when the war finished.'

Throughout the early winter of 1945, 4 Commando Brigade continued to harry the Germans. In February, 4 Commando attacked the island of Schouwen, and 48 Commando alone carried out no less than five separate raids in the first two weeks of March. Apart from keeping the enemy on his toes, these raids provided useful experience to the new Commando recruits now arriving fresh from Achnacarry and the 4 Commando Brigade continued to harass the enemy for the next two months, until the War in Europe ended on 8 May 1945.

After over two months in Normandy, and eighty-three days of action, 1 Commando Brigade had returned to England with the intention of refitting for the war in the Far East. The Brigade was now commanded by Brigadier Derek Mills-Roberts DSO, MC, a veteran of Dieppe, 'a fighting soldier if ever there was one', says Brigadier Peter Young, and he soon brought his Brigade, which now contained 3, 6, 45 and 46 (Royal Marine) Commandos, to the peak of efficiency. 'If a morning exercise went well,' recalls one of his officers, 'the afternoon was free. If it went badly, we repeated it until we got it right – however long it took.'

The Brigade returned to Western Europe and took up positions along the river Maas, and fought its next serious action on 23 January, when No 6 Commando crossed the Juliana Canal on the ice, and occupied Maasbracht, and No 45 occupied the village of St Joosurg, near a small stream, the Montforter- beek.

45 came under heavy fire and were soon pinned down

here with the most forward troop, 'A' Troop, engaging the enemy with rifles and Brens, losing two killed and thirteen wounded. The wounded were aided by L-Corp Harden of the RAMC, who went forward three times to dress wounds or rescue wounded men. Wounded on his second sortie, he went out again, across the fire-swept snow and was shot in the head and killed. For his actions here with 45, L-Corp Harden was later awarded the Victoria Cross.

45 and 6 Commando beat off a counter-attack that night, and drove the enemy back next day to the banks of the Montfortbeek stream, and No 3 Commando came up to enter the town of Linne, which fell on the following day. The fighting in and around the Montforter beek is well described by Captain Day of 'B' Troop, 45 Commando.

'As this is now one of 45's "Memorable Days", this story needs to be told accurately. It is only worthy of being a "Memorable Day" because of Eric Harden's VC; apart from this it was a straightforward "Advance to contact" engagement with fewer casualties than we had, for example, on the three Troop raid on Belle Isle a few days later. I saw nothing of the "A" Troop action and Harden's great gallantry and, unfortunately, Wiggy Bennett MM, the "A" Troop TSM, who was a key witness, died last December.

'When we left Echt, on a cold, clear morning, the order of march was "A" Troop, commanded by Captain E. W. D. Coventry of the East Lancashire Regt, "E", "B", "C" and "D" Troops. 6 Commando led the Brigade (46 Commando was not with us as they had been detached to Antwerp) and entered Maasbracht without opposition. We passed through them and moved on to Brachterbeek without incident. At this point our column came to a halt and while in that village we were subjected to some mild shelling. Nicol Gray was forward with "A" Troop, so our orders came over the radio. We assumed from the sounds of small arms fire that "A" Troop had run into trouble; "E" and "B" Troops were told to follow the line of an embankment running east from Brachterbeek and gain a foothold on the Montfortbeek feature. We set off in single file with "E" Troop in the lead, moving on the north side of the embankment which gave us cover from the Montfortbeek.

'About 600 yards from Brachterbeek I heard heavy bursts of small arms fire ahead of me and saw that "E" Troop had come to a halt. I moved forward to find Ian Beadle and discover what had happened. Ian was standing in a small indentation in the embankment which gave a modicum of cover from the front. As I reached him I saw a small group of men returning towards us round a slight bend in the embankment. The "E" Troop leading sub-section had been badly hit. Three men had been killed and three wounded. One of the wounded was being carried by Captain M. C. Brockbank. Chester Brockbank had only recently joined the Commando and at this time was a supernumary attached to "E" Troop. Later this day he took over "C" Troop when Captain P. D. Barnard of the Gordon Highlanders was wounded. Brockbank was killed during the battle on the river Aller, in April.

'The wounded were placed on the snow in the small indentation where Ian and I were discussing our next move and other casualties later that day were also initially put down here. It was only some weeks later, when the thaw came, that we discovered this small area was littered with *Schu* mines which, presumably because the ground was frozen, had failed to detonate when we were walking all over them.

'While I was with Ian, my TSM, B. M. Aylett MM, came up to us and said four tanks had arrived with "B" Troop. I told Ian that I would probe forward on the left, over a frozen marsh, and he said he would come back and talk to the tank Commander when he had sorted things out in his Troop. I returned to "B" Troop and told my two subalterns, Peter Riley MC, and E. Y. McDonald as much as I knew of the situation. I told Riley to take his section and probe forward over the marsh towards the Montfortbeek, taking care not to get involved at this stage. Until I was sure that the marsh was a possible line of approach, I did not want to commit the whole Troop to it.

'Almost as soon as Peter had set off, Ian Beadle appeared and we both went over to talk to the Tank Troop Commander. Almost as soon as we made contact with the tank man there were bursts of small arms fire in the direction of Peter Riley's advance. I asked Ian to get the tanks to fire at the positions that had held him up, shouted to "B" Troop to follow me and dashed off after Peter, mentally cursing him for falling into the same sort of trap that had caught "A" and "E" Troops.

'There was no problem in crossing the marsh, which was well frozen, and I soon found myself jumping the small stream that was the Montfortbeek. A few yards from the stream I saw Peter Riley and some of his men searching a group of Germans. A quick word with Peter confirmed that he had the situation under control and I left him to it, concentrating on getting "B" Troop into a defensive position before the expected counter-attack. We were in possession of a wooded triangular gully, with the apex, some 100 yards from the stream, pointing towards Linne, which I knew was one of the Brigade's objectives. The base of the gully was as one with the wooded Montfortbeek and thus provided an easy, covered approach to our position; this weakness was my chief worry throughout our stay in the position. Having sited the Troop on the north and south sides of the gully, where they began digging in on the rim with good fields of fire, I returned to Peter Riley. As he advanced towards

Montfortbeek he had seen some dozen Germans retiring from the direction of "E" Troop's position and had immediately attacked them, killing three and capturing five. Incidentally, contrary to other reports which have been published, the tanks played no part in our battle. Although I had asked for them to fire on the known enemy positions, they had not been able to do this and as far as I am aware they did not open fire all day except to knock the top off the windmill which overlooked "B" and "E" Troops' positions.

'Before dark, the Colonel, Nicol Gray, had come forward to me and told me to hold the position, sending "D" Troop (Maj R. H. W. Kirby RM) to reinforce me. "D" Troop took over the northern rim of the gully and "B" thickened up the southern side, the apex and a position to our rear, on the other side of the stream. This rear position gave us some depth but could do little to cover the approaches along the Montfortbeek itself.

'A hot meal had been sent up to us and with two Troops well dug in we seemed fairly secure, though the wooded approaches to our rear still worried me. At about 21.30 we were subjected to a short but intensive bombardment which showed that the enemy knew where we were. "B" Troop had no casualties but "D" had one man killed and the TSM, R. Hanes, was seriously wounded. A little after this, 3 Commando patrolled north of us, towards De Villa, and met some opposition, incurring casualties. It was very cold, some degrees below freezing and we had no greatcoats. However, I found that the anti-gas cape we all still carried provided good insulation and, snuggling down in my slit trench some ten yards from the rim of the gully, I fell asleep.

'I was woken up by someone whispering that Marine W. K. Laidler, a Bren gunner on the southern rim of the gully, thought he could hear movement in the field in front of him. I scrambled up and moved across to

Laidler, about ten yards away. The night was overcast and I could see nothing significant in the snow-covered field but I could hear an occasional metallic clink. I decided to put up a Vereys flare, sent a message to Bunny Kirby and quietly warned those on the southern flank to be ready to open fire, including the Troop PIAT. Apart from the PIAT there were three Bren groups and some twenty riflemen awaiting my signal. When the flare burst it illuminated a closely-bunched group of men in snow suits, about 50 yards in front of us; my impression was that there were about 20 or so of them. In case anyone in "B" Troop had any doubt about the action to be taken, I yelled "Fire!" at the top of my voice and for a brief spell everyone seemed to be joining in. I put up a couple more flares and the scene was further illuminated by the PIAT whose bombs provided a brilliant and lethal pyrotechnic display against the dark background. Enough was enough I decided, and checked the fire.

'While B Troop had been enjoying itself, my thoughts had switched to the approach from the Montforter beek; I loathed the thought of the uncontrolled mêlée which would result if the Germans burst upon us from that direction. Artillery fire seemed the only answer and so leaving Peter Riley to watch the open field, I went back to the Signallers' trench and spoke on the radio to Commando HQ, asking for a Troop shoot on the Montfortbeek. The co-ordinates I gave put the aiming point just 50 yards south of us. I knew this was tantamount to bringing fire down on our own position, but reckoned it was justified as we would have the shelter of our slit trenches. I yelled a warning to everyone to take cover and squeezed in myself with the uncomplaining two signallers in case I had to use the radio again urgently. The RHA's response was speedy and re-markably accurate, though a few shells landed around us. My heart sank when I heard calls for Gethin, the Troop

Medical Orderly who, although a Marine, was trained to RAMC standards. Throughout our campaigns, I would hear his name called and this quiet, self-effacing but courageous man would unfailingly answer the call, dashing into the smoke, debris or whatever else remained of the catastrophe which required his presence. On this occasion two men had been wounded by our own shells, both from the sub-section on the other side of the stream, and I suspected my warning shout was not heard there. One of the wounded was Sgt Jimmy Baines, who became RSM of 45 some ten years later. ("Sticks" Baines was a drill instructor on the parade at Eastney when 45 spent a month there in October 1944. He was so mad keen to join the Commando that Nicol Gray arranged for him to come straight to us without doing the usual Commando training.) I walked a short way along the Montfortbeek before we were relieved the following morning and found three dead Germans there. There may have been more further on, so I felt my action in calling for artillery fire so close to us had been justified. There were also twelve dead Germans, including one officer, in the field in front of our position.

'Early on 27 January we received orders for the raid which was to take place that night. In brief the intention was that "E" Troop less one section would form a firm base on our side of the Maas, a section from "E" Troop would take up a bridgehead position on Belle Isle and "D" Troop would assault the enemy position which was thought to be in the area of the lock. Once this part of the operation was successful, "B" Troop would cross to Belle Isle, carry assault boats on sledges over the snow and cross the Maas again on the far side of Belle Isle. "B"'s objective was to land in the area of Drift and seize a prisoner in the Merum area. We had no intelligence on what we were to expect in this area but after the war I was in correspondence with a Dutchman who was writing an account of the liberation of Limburg Province. He was living at Merum at the time of our proposed raid and said it was the HQ of the Hubner Parachutist Group, the men we had been fighting at Montfortbeek, so we would probably have had a warm reception.

'"D" Troop had a very bad time, clearly in serious trouble, although the CO had no reports from them. The "B" Troop raid was cancelled and I was told to reinforce the small bridgehead section and fix a line across the river so that a ferry service could be started. Despite three attempts, with a mixed crew from "B" Troop and the RM Engineer Troop, I was unable to get a line across, but Bob Aylett took one boatload over to reinforce the bridgehead, which was under attack while I was still struggling in the river. The CO ordered the evacuation of Belle Isle and I returned to my Troop which was sheltering behind the river embankment. I was wet, cold and dejected at my failure.

'All became quiet after a while and we lay in the snow for what seemed like hours, thinking that we had been forgotten, when I heard someone calling for me to report to the CO; Nicol Gray told me that Ian Beadle had taken a patrol across to Belle Isle and returned with a prisoner and without encountering any live enemy. Now Sgt Fenwick of "D" Troop had been heard shouting from the area of the now deserted bridgehead saying he had a badly wounded Marine with him; I was to go across quickly and rescue them. I dashed back to "B" Troop, called for volunteers and grabbed the first five men who moved towards me in the darkness. I found these to be Bob Aylett, Sgts Johnny Bastable and Jack Sinclair, and Marines Ogle and Denny. I had to dissuade Ogle from bringing his beloved PIAT with him and then set off to find a boat.

'We had no difficulty getting across the Maas. After

my earlier efforts with the line the assault boat now seemed to move like a skiff. Fenwick met us as we landed and said Marine Hannah was about a hundred yards away but could not move. I sent Bob Aylett with the two sergeants to fetch Hannah, told Ogle to look after the boat and took Denny with me to the top of the nearby embankment so that we could provide some cover if we were attacked. There was no sign of the enemy and it was not long before I saw the group carrying Hannah coming towards the boat. As they drew near Denny and I returned and he embarked. I stood with Ogle, holding the boat steady as the others approached to put Hannah on board. Suddenly a machine-gun opened up and bullets struck the twelve inches of water between me and the boat. There was a marked scurry as the unfortunate Hannah was hurried aboard and Ogle loosened his hold but then seemed to grab the boat again. The machine-gun was firing again but his aim seemed higher now. I told Ogle to push the boat off and he scrambled aboard rather clumsily. I shoved him further in the boat and squeezed in myself. Aylett had distributed the paddles and I had the steering oar. As the machine-gun continued to fire in our direction we struggled to turn the boat against the current and head for home. All were paddling furiously except for Ogle who was sitting motionless in front of me. I commented harshly on this lack of activity to be met with the rather aggrieved response, "I can't sir, I've been hit in both arms." By now the "B" Troop Brens had opened up to give us some covering fire and we reached our own side of the Maas safely, though swept some way downstream. We found a gate to use as a stretcher for Hannah and made our way back to the firm base, accompanied by long range enemy machine-gun fire whistling harmlessly over our heads from the direction of Merum.

'Unknown to me at the time, R. W. Thompson, a war

correspondent for *The Sunday Times*, crossed the Rhine in a Buffalo with "B" Troop. He produced a graphic account of the crossing in his book *Men Under Fire*, which includes the following:

> "We are Butcher Troop, 45 Royal Marine Commando", yelled a broad Commando by my side. But he had to cup his hands and yell it into my ear. All around me, crouched in the assault craft, the faces were eager and there was not even a sign of tension. These men are terrific."

'At Wesel 45's position was based on a factory on the north-eastern outskirts of the town. "B" Troop's location was in and around one of the factory buildings. Those of us inside the building could not dig in because the factory floor was of concrete but there were a number of steel sheets lying around which we used to make rough and ready shelters. In the afternoon of 24 March we were subjected to a short but intensive bombardment, a high velocity gun joining in with more conventional artillery. It was much more frightening being shelled in a building than in a slit trench. There was much steel work in the building and shell fragments, hitting the steel girders, whanged around with an alarming noise, adding to the sounds of crashing shells and falling masonry. Three men were wounded and evacuated, one of whom later died of his wounds; others had minor injuries but stayed with us. One shell hit the front wall of the building, making a hole about four feet in diameter. This was immediately above one of our Bren positions which was a key position as it was the only one with a view directly to our front. As soon as I saw what had happened I went forward to assess the damage. Gethin was ahead of me tending two of the Bren group who had been wounded. Corporal J. Sykes MM, the NCO in charge of the Bren group, covered in brick dust, was clearly shaken by the near miss.

The position had to be manned again and I was preparing words of comfort like lightning never striking in the same place twice. However, Sykes was already calling for another man to join him, checking the Bren and getting his position back in working order.

'Early on 1 April, 45 arrived at the village of Greven, about ten miles north of Munster. Alf Blake, now commanding the unit, sent for me and said that the BBC had announced that Munster had been captured. This conflicted with the information available to Brigade HQ and I was to proceed to Munster and clarify the situation. I took two jeeps and a dozen men from "B" Troop, all of us very pleased at the opportunity to swan around the countryside for a change. I chose a route approaching Munster from the west and passing through a small village, some five miles from Munster, I noticed a concentration of US Airborne Troops and tanks from the Guards Armoured Division in the village. About half a mile beyond the village, I passed some Americans resting by the roadside. After another couple of hundred yards I stopped the jeep; I had realized that the Americans were not resting but looked singularly alert and rather surprised as we swept past them. I turned back to the American parachutists and in answer to my questions they said they were awaiting orders to advance on Munster. With a muttered curse on the integrity of the BBC and someone in the jeep making a rude comment about April Fools Day, I drove back to the village, reported to the Brigadier commanding the Armoured Brigade and returned to the Commando with my news.

'During 45's withdrawal to the small bridgehead held by a company of the 1st Bn The Rifle Brigade, at about midnight, "B" Troop had acted as rear-guard. Having reached the bridgehead, "B" was in position on the right flank, my right hand group on the river embankment. The platoon we were relieving had an outpost position

200 yards ahead of the main position and I sent Eric McDonald and his section to take this over. The rest of the Troop began digging in new positions, the previous ones not being very suitable. It was the third time we had dug in since mid-day and we were thankful the soil was light and sandy. About thirty minutes after Eric had taken his men off to the outpost, and while the rest of us were still digging in, a small arms battle broke out in the direction of the outpost and some fire was directed at us from upstream. It was a tense situation. My right flank was protected by the river and the Rifle Brigade officer I had relieved had told me that the outpost covered my left flank. I had not, however, visited the outpost and did not know the precise location of the Troop on my left. The Troop position was just in front of the supporting pillars of the road bridge which had been destroyed and I knew that if we did not break up the attack the enemy would be right amongst the sappers who were working on the Bailey bridge. I could not call for close artillery support as we were not dug in and I did not know the situation at the outpost where firing continued. I yelled some exhortation at the Troop and then the Germans were upon us, rushing at the forward line of "B" Troop.

'There were rapid bursts of fire, much shouting, and the firing ceased. We had been shooting at the Rifle Brigade men returning from the outpost after being relieved by Eric McDonald. Three men had been hit but I never discovered how seriously they had been hurt as they were carried away immediately by their comrades. It was a tragic mistake, for which no one could be blamed. A contributary cause of their failure to identify our own troops was the fact that, unlike us, the Rifle Brigade men wore greatcoats, as did many of the Germans we fought against. Shortly after this, Eric McDonald reported on the radio that the attack on the outpost had been beaten off. On the following day we found seven dead Germans around that position.

'On 7 April it was fairly quiet, except for periodical

shelling, which caused some casualties among 45 and also the Royal Engineers, who had already suffered badly. During the day someone discovered, in one of the buildings in the bridgehead, a lavatory that still flushed. This unexpected luxury proved very popular despite the fact that the lavatory door was missing and anyone making use of the usual facilities was completely open to enemy view.

'45 crossed the Elbe in the early hours of 29 April, after 6 Commando and 46, and passed through 46 on the outskirts of Lauenberg. "B" Troop was in the lead and our objective was a battery of Light AA guns situated on the Furstengarten, a high cliff overlooking the proposed bridging site. It was still dark when we turned south in the centre of the town and I was moving cautiously, anxious to maintain surprise, too cautiously for Nicol Gray, who came forward to me, urging me on and reminding me that it would soon be daybreak. For the last stretch of some 400 yards our route was down a very narrow street. Not wishing to have the whole Troop caught in this defile, I told Graham Partington, a 19-year-old subaltern who replaced Peter Riley when the latter went off to command the re-constituted "D" Troop after Belle Isle, to take his section down the backs of the houses, parallel to the main Troop route. I took Graham up an alleyway, pointed out the direction to him, and to emphasize the need for speed, I gave him a gentle push to send him on his way. Graham took about three paces and disappeared into a pit containing an evil-smelling liquid. Leaving him to deal with this unexpected problem, I went back to the Troop and we set off quickly towards the Furstengarten. Without any response from the enemy we swept into the courtyard of the AA battery HQ building. Bob Aylett and the Support section went for the building and Eric McDonald and Graham Partington, the latter stinking but only slightly delayed, went past me with their sections, heading for the gun sites. Surprise was complete and the resistance negligible. Our first prisoner, taken by Aylett, was a dishevelled unarmed German soldier who, so I was told later, was on his way to wake the unit's cook. A few scattered shots were fired at us but in minutes it was all over. We had no casualties but there were 10 dead Germans around the guns and we took some 50 prisoners. "B" Troop remained on the high ground of the Furstengarten while the rest of 45 cleared the town. By mid-day the unit had collected some 300 prisoners and the only resistance came from the Luftwaffe which bombed the bridging operations. The FOO attached to us from the 1st Mountain Regiment RA got the captured guns into action and claimed a hit on a Focke-Wolf 190.

'Graham Partington bore me no grudge for his unfortunate mishap during the advance but turned respectfully resentful, a difficult attitude, but Graham managed it nicely, when I told him to retrieve his Tommy gun which he had dropped while taking his unexpected bath. Having done this successfully, he remained naked for the rest of our short stay, except for a borrowed German blanket, while his loyal MOA did his best to clean his clothing and equipment. Even so, over the next week or so we always knew when Graham was approaching!'

'In a broadcast on 4 May 1945 the BBC referred to the Brigade as follows:

They are led by a dynamic officer, Brigadier D. Mills-Roberts. No comfortable HQ for this commander. He has his own slit-trench beside his men up in the front line. British Generals have showered their praises on the Commandos. The summing up is "their timing is perfect; their nerve unlimited; and they always achieve surprise". Many a captured German Garrison Commander has put it this way: "I never dreamt that you would come in that way".

'Personally, I have no doubt whatsoever that the Brigade's achievements and their relatively light casualties during the four months of the 1945 campaign were due to the high standard of leadership, tactical skill and determination of Derek Mills-Roberts, coupled with the courage, resourcefulness and high morale of all those in 1 Commando Brigade.'

The German defences lay on a line of fortifications north of Linne, which formed part of the last German redoubt, the Siegfried Line. To obtain information about these defences before ordering a general assault, the Brigade were directed to raid the enemy positions on Belle Isle on the Maas, and this task was entrusted to 45 and a detachment of No 10 (Inter Allied) Commando.

Since the country was in the depths of winter, the Marines were provided with white snow suits, and sledges were constructed to haul the assault boat for the crossing. In spite of this, the assault party were spotted by the defenders, and a fierce fire-fight broke out on Belle Isle, which forced the main force to withdraw.

In February, the snow and ice melted, plunging the armies into a sea of mud, but in mid-March the brigade assembled at Venray, on the east bank of the Maas, and began to train for the Rhine crossing. The Brigade's objective was the city of Wesel which lay on the east bank of the Rhine at a point where the river was fast-flowing and about three hundred yards wide.

Mills-Roberts decided that the assault should be led by 46 Commando with Brigade Headquarters, in Buffaloes; 46 would secure a beach-head on Grav Isel, a common about two miles west of Wesel, followed by 6 and 45 Commandos in 'storm boats', (small assault craft) with 3 Commando bringing up the rear in Buffalo amphibious vehicles. The assault would be covered by an air and artillery bombardment, after which 45 and 6 were to assault the town. If the Brigade could seize and hold a bridgehead, Buffaloes would ferry the 1st Cheshires over at dawn, and finally the 17th US Airborne Division would drop north of Wesel at 10.00 and link up with the Commandos on the next day. H-Hour for the Commando assault was 21.30 on 23 March 1945.

The RAF Lancasters dropped their bombs about 18.00 and the artillery bombardments commenced, until the clear evening sky over Wesel was draped with a great cloud of dust and smoke. Promptly at 21.00, 46's Buffaloes dropped down the banks into the water and began to thrash across the river towards the German shore. The barrage and bombing had dazed the defenders and 46 got across with few casualties, and they had seized their bridgehead at Grav Isel within half an hour; 6 Commando, coming behind, had a more difficult task as the enemy revived and met a hail of fire which sank several boats, including the three into which their RSM had jumped in turn as his previous boat sank. Nevertheless, 6 and 45 Commandos were soon ashore and formed up for the attack as the second Bomber Command attack rained bombs on the city. When this stopped, the Brigade advanced into the town.

By midnight 1st Commando Brigade were established in Wesel, and entrenched in the north and north-western suburbs. On the following morning they were reinforced by the 1st Cheshires, and elements of 17th US Airborne. Sniping and street fighting continued for two days but by the evening of 25 March, Wesel had fallen. The Brigade had killed several hundred Germans, and taken eight hundred prisoners, at a cost of eleven dead, sixty-eight wounded and seventeen missing, and that night the GOC Commando Group, General Sturges, arrived in the Brigade lines to bring his congratulations and help consume part of a large barrel of hock which someone had unearthed from the ruins.

After the Rhine crossing at Wesel the war in Europe had now only six weeks to run, but 1 Commando Brigade were in action right to the end, taking part in one final action against the 12th SS on the Weser, and 46 Commando capturing the town of Hademstorf, against fierce resistance.

Fred Harris was still soldiering on with 45 Commando and also recalls the final confrontations in Europe. 'The New Year 1945, changed our destiny, as in January we went back to Europe via Ostend and after a very cold train journey and a road journey, we were soon in Holland. It was very cold now and our front was close to the river Maas; at night, unless you paid attention to the action of your weapons, they quickly froze. Shortly after arrival we were on the move to Maastracht and Brachterbeck with No 6 Commando. These were cleared quite easily, the latter by "A" Troop 45 Commando, who then made off towards the railway station with Lt. Thomas in the lead. Some 100 yards or so before reaching the station, the troop came under heavy small arms fire and mortaring. We dived for cover at the sides of the road where the banks fell away, affording some cover, but not before Sgt Thomas had dropped a German in his tracks. It was a sticky position, and although a Spandau was raking the roadway, Don and myself decided to break for some cottages across and up the road, about 30 yards away.

'The leading section was now bringing some fire down on to the Germans in the area of the station, and we took advantage of this. Jumping to our feet, we made off. My intention was to smash my fist at the door; unfortunately it didn't turn out like that, I bounced off a very stout door and my Bren clattered to the ground. Don had dived through one of the front windows and was inside. The German machine gunner, having spotted us, sent several bursts down the road. A small recess in the doorway afforded some cover, but the machine-gun was raking the building and one burst of fire took away the corners of the recess and parts of my leather jerkin and parachute jacket went with it, as did two "mills" grenades which dropped out of the ripped pocket. It was definitely hairy, and I made a break for the window next door, after which I recovered my Bren with the aid of a "twig" broom. The leading section had also managed to get some cover. Neil Patrick, a Scot, had kept the Germans occupied by charging them, firing his Bren from the hip. He was later awarded the MM.

'Some of the chaps with Lt Cory had been caught out in the open and were badly wounded and still under heavy fire. A jeep came charging down towards us, and as it reached the cottages, it was shot up and the driver wounded; the jeep was also carrying the Medical Officer, who immediately dragged the wounded man into the cottages, and having seen to him, made off at high speed towards (as we learned later) "A" Troop HQ where L-Corp (Doc) Harden had gallantly gone out into the open to recover the wounded, Lt Cory and his men, ably assisted later by Marines Dickie Mason and Jimmy Haville. Unfortunately, on one of the return trips, Doc was shot in the head by a marksman and killed. He was later awarded a posthumous VC. Jimmy Haville was mentioned in despatches. "A" Troop, it would seem, was completely pinned down, and any movement brought further small arms fire and mortaring. Don and I exchanged fire from a windmill at the rear of the cottages, which eventually fell quiet.

'Some news eventually got through to us, and it appeared that the other Troops were engaging the enemy from other directions, one of these being known later as "Riley's" gully, after an attack by "B" Troop's Lt Riley. "A" troop were instructed to stay put and pull back after dark. This was done with the aid of some white bed sheets to give cover against the white snowy background, and a couple of civilians for guidance. It had been a fierce battle, with considerable casualties and much courage on the part of many members of the unit, whose gallantry was suitably rewarded. Heavy casualties were inflicted on the enemy; this was seen at daylight, when the unit was relieved by 6 Commando.

'Several other moves took us to Linne, Belle Isle being the next action. Belle Isle was so named as a result of the Maas forming a horseshoe shape with an island in the centre. The attack unfortunately resulted in casualties, both to the enemy and ourselves. I was never sure what else was achieved. A stark memory of this was seeing our dead brought back (the Jerries allowed us to go over and collect them), in grotesque shapes, having frozen in the position they fell and died. We remained in this area for a short while, watching the Maas from a place called the "Ice Box". It was extremely cold and duty here meant a pretty lonely night. We were spread thinly on the ground. I seem to recall we "lost" the odd man or two picked up by German patrols and there were a few clashes when the Germans came over the Maas on the ice, often caught out by our trip flares. It was a particularly nerve-racking time. The only contact sometimes, was hearing the constant cocking of automatic weapons, not to do so meant they might be frozen solid when you needed them. Eventually, we were relieved by Americans. An entire Division, no less!

'A few more moves, then leave started; forty-eight hours in Brussels. The 21 Club and the Montgomery Club brought some light relief, then it was off again, and we were getting towards Germany. Boat training had taken place and seemingly this was for the Rhine Crossing, which we soon learned was to be at Wesel. The big day came and we moved off to our positions. Shortly, a huge bombing raid commenced on the town of Wesel, followed by an artillery barrage which virtually shook the very ground under us. It was very difficult not to be anything other than nervous and almost shell-shocked as we were virtually sitting under the bombardment. I remember of all things, mail coming up, which for me was in the shape of a food parcel, a homemade cake . . . This was duly cut into umpteen pieces and passed round.

'Our turn came; we clambered into the Buffaloes (a swimming tracked vehicle), and we were on our way down the bank and into the river. Since nothing could be seen from these vehicles, only the night sky and tracers overhead, there was little to do except try not to think about being sunk.

'Eventually we landed and set off for Wesel (out came the white tape) as in night infiltrations. There seemed little opposition, the occasional short fire fight, then on again by daylight. "A" Troop had got a position in what appeared to be a railway siding, where we stayed for a while, getting harassed by an 88 mm SP gun, which drew in, fired a few salvos and was gone. On one occasion I fired a few bursts at the gun, unfortunately attracting some return machine-gun fire which killed Marine 'Scouse' Ord, who was positioned inside a railway truck.

'Moving on from here, we attacked and took up a position in and around a place known as the Factory. A few recce patrols revealed the extent of the bombing damage; it was one mass of craters and bombed buildings. God knows how anybody survived it, and how many troops and civilians were killed. American para-glider troops were also wandering around, no doubt dropped outside their zones. It was not unusual to hear "Hey Mac, have you seen our outfit?"

'We were into Germany proper now, prisoners were more frequent and in fairly large numbers. It was noticeable how very young or very old the majority of them were; the old looked very frightened and the young (many of them only boys) had a rather arrogant look about them. We ourselves were sensing victory, and the tempo was speeding up, journeys were made by TCVs (Troop Conveying Vehicles) more frequently, hence our arrival just outside Osnabrück where a night march took us into the town. Snipers had been left behind – the Germans were said to have pulled out – and unfortunately, they took their toll; several casualties fell. Lt Wright was killed. Don and I, having set up a position, were quickly joined by three nervous-looking Germans, creeping along the road with a little white flag. They were reluctant to leave us, having been captured, but having made them understand we didn't intend shooting them, they went off to the "cage". The Germans were now retreating quite rapidly, making a stand here and there at such places as Leese near the river Weser, where a particularly heavy battle took place for its capture. There were many young fanatical Germans who didn't want to give up and unfortunately, they were still causing us problems. Not too many of the original Troop that landed in Normandy now remained, many of the casualties of the last weeks were young, and we hardly knew their names, like the Corporal who poked his head over the river bank on the Aller.

'The end was in sight now. We moved to Lauenburg and had a short rest, then off towards the Elbe, which we crossed by Buffaloes; the many gun positions on the opposite bank were deserted, weapons and stick grenades being left intact. However, it seemed necessary to keep going and several other places were overrun, hundreds of prisoners were now on the march. We met some British POWs, and released European prisoners were causing trouble. Finally it was over, and we moved to our final destination in Germany, a town called Eutin, where we were charged with keeping the peace, rounding up troublesome displaced persons and interrogating and questioning Germans about the concentration camp at Neustad.

'To go home meant probably going out East, so we made the best of things, and hoped eventually to get in on the Berlin Parade. This wasn't to be, however, and soon we were on the road again to Ostend and England.'

On 19 April, 1 Commando Brigade reached the town of Lauenburg, and began to prepare for their last attack, a night crossing of the river Elbe. This took place on 29 April, with No 6 leading the way, followed by 46, 3 and 45. The crossing was made under fire, with enemy infantry gathered on the bluff above, hurling grenades down onto the narrow landing beach. 46 cleared the Germans from the cliff, and the Brigade began to clear Lauenburg of snipers and machine-gun posts as soon as it got light. Resistance finally ceased on 30 April, and 1 Commando Brigade finally stopped advancing in the early days of May, when they stood, triumphant, on the shores of the Baltic.

7

Burma: The Arakan and Kangaw, 1944–45

The greatest difficulty of a Commander, at any level,
in this type of country, is to know what is
happening. The fog of war is nowhere more dense
than in the jungle.

Report: 7th Australian Div 1945

No 3 Special Service Brigade, which became 3 Commando Brigade in December 1944, is the only one of the great fighting brigades of World War II which still survives. As 3 Commando Brigade, Royal Marines, it lives on as the cutting edge of the Corps of Royal Marines.

The Brigade was raised on 6 November 1943, and was composed of two veteran Army Commando units, Nos 1 and 5, which had seen action in North Africa and Madagascar, and two newly-formed Royal Marines Commandos, Nos 42 and 44, formed from the 1st and 3rd RM Battalions. The Brigade sailed for India a week later on 13 December, bound for the war in South East Asia. Half the Brigade, the HQ, Nos 5 and 44 (Royal Marines) Commandos, reached Bombay without incident on 22 January, but the ship carrying 42 and No 1 (Army) Commando was bombed in the Mediterranean, and had to put into Alexandria for repairs. It was not until September that they were re-united with the other units of the Brigade.

The Brigade Commander, Brigadier W. I. Nonweiler, fell ill in the autumn of 1944, and was eventually invalided home, but Colonel Peter Young arrived from Normandy as Deputy Brigade Commander in October, and commanded the Brigade until Brigadier Campbell Hardy arrived in mid-December.

'Campbell Hardy was already celebrated throughout the Commando Group for his exploits in Normandy,' writes Peter Young, 'where he twice won the DSO in three months. He was a formidable looking character, with iron-grey, close-cropped hair, and an aquiline nose which gave him a Prussian air, but since people seldom crossed him, he was usually pleasant and lighthearted. The greatest gift a commander can have is the gift of making his men feel that if *he* takes them into battle, they can't possibly be beaten. Campbell Hardy soon had 3 Commando Brigade thinking that way.'

When Peter Young, fresh from commanding No 3 Commando in Normandy, arrived in the Far East, he found the Brigade in half, but Nos 44 and 5 had already seen action.

The war in Burma is still a half-forgotten war. Not for nothing did the men of 14th Army refer to their force as 'The Forgotten Army'. Their war was fought in the jungle, a very long way from home, and against the savage, often fanatical Japanese, who gave little quarter and asked for none at all, a formidable adversary to meet in such a demanding and unfamiliar terrain. While waiting for the rest of the Brigade, Nos 5 and 44 were soon in action in the Arakan, which lies on the western coast of Burma, south of what is now Bangladesh.

On 11 March 1944, 44 Commando landed in the Arakan to attack Japanese positions south of the main Maungdaw-Buthidaung road, an important supply route. The 14th Army stood at the end of the line for equipment, and even the landing craft which took the Commando ashore were creaking and leaking, but by dawn, in spite of harassment from snipers, the Marines had taken their objective, the village of Alethangyaw. Probing forward, a Marine patrol lost one wounded man, whom the Japanese dragged out into an open paddyfield, where he lay all day as bait for other men of his unit. Local villagers finally brought him in after dark. On the following day, 44 Commando sent patrols into the surrounding jungle, finding the easiest access along the bed of a *chaung* (river) which ran across their front, and withdrew as the Japanese counter-attacked their abandoned positions just as the Commando re-embarked.

Maj-Gen John Owen, then a Lieutenant in 'C' Troop 44 Commando, remembers the early days of 3 Commando Brigade. '5 Commando were then a much more professional bunch than we were in 44 Commando, having had previous operational experience. We were fit enough, but our military skills at troop and unit level were still weak and, initially, they didn't care for Marines very much either; perhaps because unlike us, Army commandos were all volunteers and some had to drop a rank or two just to get in. But soon it was mostly just a friendly rivalry. We did a few operations together, *Screwdriver 1* and *Screwdriver 2*. Later we were at Silchar in Assam during the time of the Kohima battle. 'A' Troop were kept on a tea estate where the manager, K. O. Smith, just couldn't do enough for us – officer or marine. We patrolled from there – we even had elephants on the unit strength at one time, but the weather was foul. In the monsoon, we once had 17 inches of rain in 24 hours!

'From Silchar, we went through India by train via Calcutta to Bangalore. It took six days and, although the officers were pretty comfortable, the men were overcrowded; it was extremely hot. After about two days we were running some twelve hours late, so Dickie Acton, the MMG officer, and I got into the engine cab and drove the train all day until we made up the time.

'After several small-scale actions in the Arakan, before

Kangaw, 44 and 5 withdrew to Ceylon, where they were joined by 1 and 42 Commandos. The Brigade then began to plan a series of raids along the west coast of Burma, which began with a raid by a troop of 42 on Elizabeth Island in November 1944, where they killed ten Japanese for the loss of one Marine captured. Peter Young commanded this operation.

'We prevailed upon General Christison, Commander of XV Indian Corps, to lend us a Eureka, the type of craft used at Dieppe. I decided to accompany this expedition myself, and Douglas Drysdale, the Brigade Major, insisted on coming as well. What casualties were inflicted, I can't say, but the Marines returned without a prisoner, and the withdrawal was complicated by the Eureka breaking down. Douglas Drysdale and I stood on the beach and watched it drift away. A gallant Indian seaman cleared weed from the propeller and the craft came to life again. Even so, we had to swim for it and it says much for the discipline of those Marines that not one of them lost his weapon.'

During the remainder of that month, 1 and 42 carried out several more small patrols and raids along the coastal plain, while the 14th Army gradually jostled the Japanese south until, by mid-December 1944, the Japanese were in full retreat, but still capable of turning ferociously on their pursuers.

In December 1944, the command of what was now 3 Commando Brigade, passed to Brigadier Campbell Hardy DSO, who retained Colonel Peter Young as his Deputy Commander. The Brigade were first ordered to seize the island of Akyab, but fortunately the Japanese had fled before the Brigade arrived offshore and they therefore landed unopposed, although 5 Commando found and wiped out a strong enemy patrol. With Akyab secured, the Brigade were next sent to the Myebon peninsula. The Brigade began to land on the morning of

12 January 1945, and though the Japanese opposition was slight, they soon ran into an unexpected obstacle – mud. 42 and 5 Commando landed when the tide was high and got ashore without undue difficulty, losing only a few men to mines, but their supporting tanks soon stuck in the mud, and had to be left in the landing craft. 5 Commando came ashore half an hour after 42 and passed through 42's beach-head, to a hill in the jungle, where they were held up by Japanese machine-gun positions. Meanwhile, back on the beach, the tide was going out, and when 1 and 44 came in to land, they aimed by mistake for the beach used by 5 and 42, and their craft ran aground four hundred yards from the beach. Wading that short distance took these fit, tough men no less than *three hours*.

Gen Owen was one of those who landed: 'After some hard training and a move to the Teknaf Peninsular, we set off again. Akyab? The Japs had fled. Myebon? It seemed to be all mangrove swamp and we had to wade in for four or five hundred yards which took over three hours. The mud sucked our boots off and we were exhausted and covered from head to foot in mud. I remember the CO of 42 being wounded and carried off swearing that he would return. "Fight on lads. I'll be back." Campbell Hardy was the brigadier and I saw him there leading from the front as usual. I was in one of the assault Troops when 44 was about to attack a small hill feature, and he appeared, standing along side us, and said: "Stand by 44 – let's go!" and he led us into the attack – quite a man! Peter Young was there, too. Another remarkable man; he would go off with his orderly stalking Japs. Just the two of them, armed with rifles. Crazy really!'

Fortunately, there was little opposition because the landing area was in a mangrove swamp, which was turning into an ever-wider sea of mud as the tide went out. The Commando lost a few men from mines and shell fire, but by the time 44 landed, the mud was anything from knee to waist deep, and they toiled through nearly 400 yards of this before staggering ashore. Henry Brown landed there with No 1 Commando. 'Under fire it would have been murder. We clambered into the water and sank up to our waists in three feet of slimey mud, covered by a foot of water. It was almost impossible to move. There was the sound of fire from the beach, but luckily none of it came in our direction. If it had, there is nothing we could have done about it.'

44 followed 1 into the mud, and landed even later when the tide was at its lowest. When they finally reached the beach, the men were completely exhausted, their clothes and weapons coated with a thick layer of drying mud. Their tanks could not get ashore at all, and were eventually landed at dusk on the far side of the peninsula, while Gurkha Engineers slaved all night to hack out a road through the jungle. 5 Commando attacked the hill feature at first light and took it with tank support, killing many Japanese.

42 Commando, commanded by Lt-Col David Fellows RM, now took over the advance and entered the village of Myebon, which was unoccupied, but the enemy were located dug in on three nearby hills to the north. The Commando attacked these with tank support and drove the Japanese off, though Lt-Col David Fellows was wounded in the assault. 1 Commando occupied another hill, Point 200, and 44 moved up into front line reserve.

3 Commando Brigade now spent three days resting and consolidating around Myebon. The Brigade's next task was to advance on Kangaw, which lay across a series of *chaungs* and swamps overlooked by a commanding feature, Hill 170, where they received a number of reinforcements which included Lt George Knowland, late of No 3, who went to 4 Troop of No 1 Commando.

The object of the battle of Kangaw was to cut the Japanese lines of communication for their 54th Division, which was falling back along the road from Myohaung to Dalet, and kill as many Japs as possible. The Brigade landing craft took them up the Daingbong Chaung, landing in front of a long ridge, Hill 170, two miles from Kangaw. No 1 were able to reach the lower slopes before they were halted by enemy fire. 42 then took the neck of land between the chaung and Hill 170, and 44 advanced to pass Hill 170 on exposed position on a far hill, code-named Pinner, where some failed to dig in adequately and were heavily shelled all night and attacked by infantry, losing about 60 men. Pinner was held during a grim night and 44 were relieved by an Indian battalion and withdrawn to behind Hill 170 which had been previously secured by 1 Commando.

John Owen again: 'From Kangaw we went up the Daingbong Chaung in LCAs. 1 Commando took Hill 170 which had no height – only 170 feet – but it was a long jungle-covered feature. I felt then that something was building up as we moved on to a feature code-named *Pinner*. We were hot and tired and regrettably many of us did not dig in as well as we should have. We sat resting and brewing up in and around our trenches until stand-to, and then, at about 20.30, suddenly all hell was let loose. Shells were bursting in the trees around us and I remember seeing a Marine hit in the pouch where he had a phosphorous grenade. Terrible. The next day, just to add to our problems, while we were burying our dead, the hill was hit by shells, this time from an Indian sloop. Someone sighed and said, "Sailors never could shoot straight". The battle for Kangaw went on, reaching a climax after ten days and, when it was over, one or two others and I were called back to Brigade HQ to be sent back to England on leave. This was in the middle of a campaign – and the only time I have ever won a raffle. Amazing!

With 42 and 5 Commando coming up to join No 1, Hill 170 was consolidated by the evening of 18 November, although the Japanese kept the hill and the Chaung to the rear under heavy shellfire for the next ten days. Many of these shells were duds, and the Japanese made no major effort to dislodge the Commandos, until at 06.00 on 31 January they attacked No 1 Commando in earnest with a relentless succession of artillery bombardments and infantry assaults, which mounted in ferocity by the hour. No 1 Commando, the most experienced unit in the Brigade, fought back tenaciously.

'With more intuition we should have realized that the Japs would try to blast us off the hill (Pinner), and slaughter our remnants in the valley below. We stood-to till dusk and settled into our trenches for what we hoped would be a quiet night.

'At 20.00 a mortar opened up on our north flank, then a red Vereys went up and the attack started. First an MMG swept our forward trenches, then artillery blasted us point-blank and then the Japs swarmed in . . . their own shellfire must have killed a lot of them, but they came on. Their shells were hitting the trees, spraying fragments into our forward trenches. Every time a gun flashed from the paddy, a shell exploded on us, close, frontal fire, while the Japs crept in on us. After ten minutes or so, it seemed like an age, the artillery stopped and the Japs came in with grenades and machine-gun fire. The men were magnificent and held their fire wonderfully until the Japs were within a few yards of our trenches, then let them have it . . . the Japs were shouting "Come into the open, Commandos." A porcupine, shaken by the shelling, fell into the RSM's trench, and left quills in that regimental hide – we had 26 killed and 44 wounded before we beat them off.'

The Japanese left 20 killed before or among 44 Commando's position, but no wounded or prisoners. Only one Japanese soldier was captured during the ten days' fight at Kangaw, and he had already lost a foot.

F. W. Homan served in the Arakan in 'X' Troop of 42 Commando. 'Speaking for myself and perhaps many others, I think Col Fellows, who was a Maj-Gen when he died in 1984, was the finest CO I ever served under. I remember Peter Young in Burma, and Hiram Potts . . . a great character, and Bert Welsh who was a good boxer, and a tower of strength, getting wounded at Kangaw. He got the DSM for his actions there and no man was entitled to it more.

'As to Myebon and Kangaw . . . it was one of the Jap supply bases . . . I remember a long hill with a pagoda-like temple perched on top. We got our baptism of fire at Myebon. No 5 and 42 Commando were luckier than 1 and 44 – those poor devils got bogged in the mud. A machine-gun raked us but it was captured by a couple of troops; I'm not sure from which Commando. When we got up the hill, the view was magnificent. If *we* had the hills and they had attacked them, we would never have let them land at all – that was Myebon.

'After being on this Pagoda hill a couple of days, we – "X" Troop – went out on patrol but found no enemy, and went to Hill 170. "X" Troop formed a perimeter around some artillery on the edge of the *chaung*, with the enemy in close proximity. The tide came in as the machine-gun and artillery fire got worse, so we had a choice of shellfire or drowning in a trench full of water . . . the trench won. We got on well with the Army Commandos, and I sincerely hope they got on well with us.'

Marine J. Waldheim served in HQ Troop of 44 during the Arakan campaign. 'The Japs were up to all sorts of tricks, driving cattle into our lines or calling out "Johnny, come down and fight." I was in "C" Troop of 44 when we changed from the 3rd Bn then I went to HQ Troop

and became the Colonel's runner. He was in charge of
the Brigade landing and led the advance to *Pinner* at
Kangaw. I remember Willie Gallacher from Glasgow . . .
he bumped into four Japs and gave them a burst, killing
all four of them. Lt-Col Stockley wrote to me after the
war, and I read some time ago that he died of lung
cancer. We were always very friendly. I enclose also a
letter I wrote to my wife a day or so after Kangaw.'

> Dearest Doris,
>   I see that you have read or heard on the radio
> that our unit was at Kangaw. Well, dearest, I will
> not dwell too much on that episode but God was
> watching over me. During that night I never
> thought I would see the light of day again, for the
> Japs surrounded the hill feature we were on and
> attacked us with everything at their command.
> Their guns were firing at point-blank range. . . . I
> never thought anything so horrible could happen. I
> write to tell you that I am alive but many I knew,
> friends, have laid down their lives . . .'

Peter Young, who fought throughout the War to gain
the DSO and three MCs, recalls the Battle of Kangaw as
the fiercest of his experience. 'I was deeply impressed
with the murderous onslaught of the Japanese, and the
staunchness of the men (of 4 Troop, No 1) who held the
key to the position.'

After a heavy opening bombardment, the Japanese
sent in strong infantry attacks, which fell directly on 4
Troop of 1 Commando, and eventually overran them.
Counter-attacks by 42 and 1 Commando failed to retake
this troop position at first, but two troops of 5 Commando finally retook 4 Troop's position in the late afternoon.

A Troop of 1 Commando, which took the brunt of the
first Japanese assault, contained Lt George Knowland of

The Royal Norfolks. With less than 40 men he beat off attacks by three hundred Japanese infantry, supported by machine-guns and artillery, and continued to fight on, encouraging his ever depleting force, until he was shot down. For his gallantry on Hill 170, Lt Knowland was awarded a posthumous Victoria Cross.

A Troop's stout defence prevented the Japanese from penetrating the Brigade line, but they remained on the hill and repeated counter-attacks by 1 and 42 could not dislodge them. In one attack, 6 Troop of 1 Commando alone lost half its men. So it went on, with attack following counter-attack, as each side strove to drive the other off the hill. The Brens were vital to the defence, and were manned continually, one man replacing another as the gunner was killed or injured; at one Bren, twelve men were shot down in rapid succession. 'It got so that a man who came scrambling up the hill with ammo one minute was being carried back down on a stretcher the next minute.'

The Japanese put in assault after assault against the Brigade throughout 1 February, but by now the Commandos were well dug-in, and could not be dislodged, though the fighting was hand to hand, with great slaughter among the Japanese, with the British 3-inch mortar crews dropping bombs on them at minimum range and their 25-pounder field guns firing into the Japanese infantry over open sights. In spite of their losses, the Japanese continued to swarm up the hill, digging in frantically behind any spot of cover, then sweeping forward again, inching their way up the hill. This pattern of attack continued all day.

The fight for Hill 170 raged all day, and when dark fell both sides were still clinging to their own blood-soaked patch of hill. That night the Japanese withdrew, and when 5 Commando advanced to take over the ground next morning from the gallant, much-reduced No 1

Commando, they found the bodies of over four hundred Japanese lying in an area less than a hundred yards square. The Commando units lost forty-five dead and ninety wounded in the ten-day fight for Kangaw, and when the battle was over, the GOC XVth Indian Corps, General Sir Philip Christison, of which 3 Commando Brigade formed a part, issued a Special Order of the Day:

> The battle of Kangaw has been the decisive battle of the Arakan campaign. It was won due very largely to the magnificent courage of 3 Commando Brigade on Hill 170.

3 Commando Brigade withdrew from the Arakan and were preparing for Operation Zipper, the invasion of Malaya, when the War ended in August 1945.

Commando units did not exist when the Second World War began, but from the date of their formation until the day that War ended, they were never out of the fight. Now this history takes leave of the Army units but it should be remembered that, in the beginning, in 1940, the Commando spirit and tradition was the creation of the Army volunteers, joined later, in 1942, by the Commandos of the Royal Marines. In 1946, the Army Commandos were disbanded and the task of maintaining the now proud tradition they had done so much to create passed to the Royal Marines, who have maintained it from that day to this.

The Army Commandos have passed into history, and the men who served in their ranks are growing old now. The Royal Marines who saw them in action during the war have never forgotten them, but if those who came after want to know what they were like, they need look no further than the Commando Memorial in the cloisters of Westminster Abbey. It is a small monument, the simple statue of a Commando soldier, but the quotation upon it, from the Second Book of Samuel, speaks for all the wartime Commandos, Army or Royal Marine.

They performed whatsoever the King commanded.

8

Palestine and Malaya, 1948–52

I have true-hearted friends, not mutinous in peace,
yet bold in war: these will I muster up.

Shakespeare – Henry VI

One of the apocryphal stories told in Service circles is of
the senior officer who emerged from his dugout on
Armistice Day and, having surveyed the battlefield, turns
to his subordinates and remarks, 'Now that's over,
gentlemen, perhaps we can get back to some real
soldiering.' That attitude reappeared as soon as hostilities
ended in 1945.

Demobilization commenced almost at once, and the
Royal Marines, which had reached a wartime strength of
over 70,000, shrank rapidly to a post-war total of around
13,000, which was soon whittled down even more. The
Army Commandos were swiftly disbanded, and the
Royal Marines Commando units reduced from eight to
three. After some uncertainties and delays, 3 Commando
Brigade became 3 Commando Brigade, Royal Marines, a
formation which by 1947 was made up of 45 Commando
from the old 1st Special Service Brigade, 42 from the
wartime 3 Commando Brigade, while 44 was
re-numbered 40 Commando to keep alive the memories
and traditions of the original Royal Marines Commando.
Meanwhile, the Corps and the Royal Navy were
shrinking to a size suitable for a post-war role and in
danger of reverting to a pre-war mentality, which included the proposal that the Corps should be disbanded.

The war had expanded the functions of the Royal Marines, keeping them in capital ships but putting them also into landing craft and Commandos, but the old Sea Service spirit resurfaced strongly after the war when, as the authorized history delicately puts it, '. . . there was some animosity between the wearers of the "green" and "blue" berets.'

'When I joined, and for a long while afterwards,' says Fred Heyhurst, 'there were plenty of people in the Corps who thought that the proper place for a Royal Marine was manning a 6-inch gun on a battleship or standing about in best blues and white gear, guarding the keyboard on a cruiser. Luckily, I had a Heavy Weapons rate, so I was able to keep off Big Ships entirely.'

All the 'Hostilities Only' ranks who had served in the Corps throughout the war had been demobilized by the end of 1946, but they were replaced by National Servicemen, who began to appear by early 1947, and served in the Corps until National Service ended in 1960, by which time some three hundred officers and 9,000 NS Marines had served in the Corps, the majority in 3 Commando Brigade.

By the end of 1947, the Corps had settled down into three broad functions: Commandos, who rotated between the Commando School, which was first at Towyn in Wales and later at Bickleigh near Plymouth, and 3 Commando Brigade, wherever it may be; Amphibious, the landing-craft Marines, who were based first at Eastney and later on at Poole, and manned various types of landing craft, organized into Raiding Squadrons; finally, though they were declining in numbers as the capital ships were phased out, came the Sea Service Marines. All regular Marine recruits were trained initially at the Royal Marines Depot, Deal, and the Infantry Training Centre at Lympstone, until detailed for further training in one of these three roles, while all retained, as they still retain, a strong link with the Royal Navy, of which the Royal Marines form an intrinsic part. This is the broad picture, but there was plenty of movement, and it was by no means unknown for a Marine to serve one commission of two and a half years at sea, and follow it with a similar term in the Commando Brigade.

By 1948, the total strength of the Corps stood at 13,000 men, of which only 2000 were at sea in cruisers or aircraft carriers. In that year the Corps formed a Reserve, the Royal Marine Forces Volunteer Reserve, which later became the Royal Marines Reserve. This held its first muster Parade on the Artillery Grounds in the City of London, where the Admiral's Regiment had been formed almost three hundred years before. The Reserve soon established centres in various provincial cities, which were organized unitially into Wings, duplicating the activities of the Corps; Initial Training, Amphibious, Sea-Service and Commando, with the Commando Wing designated for a while as 48 Commando under the inspiration of Major Dan Flunder MC, who served at the City of London RMFVR Centre where he was soon in the company of such stalwarts as Frank Nightingale DCM, Bob Richmond, Harry Barlett, 'Daisy' Adams and plenty of ex-wartime Army Commandos. By joining regular Commando units on attachment, RMR ranks have since served in Aden, Borneo and many other operational theatres.

Meanwhile, 3 Commando Brigade had moved from Hong Kong and returned to the Mediterranean, where it was assigned to cover the withdrawal of British forces from Palestine at the ending of the British Mandate. 40 Commando were the first to arrive, and took up peace-keeping duties in the port of Haifa.

This was no easy task for, apart from the daily task of keeping the Jews and Arabs from each other's throats, the Brigade was subjected to a steady diet of sniping, ambushes, riots and ground attacks, which caused some casualties, while giving the Corps useful experience of similar situations, which would arise during the 'Withdrawal from Empire' actions over the next twenty years. Life in Palestine, if difficult, was never dull, as Robin McGarel Groves, then in 42 Commando, recalls.

'42 had only just returned from three most enjoyable months of desert training in Tripolitania and had barely got rid of the sand which seemed to have got into everything. The only literally sour memory was our scheme to bring back a quantity of the local Tarhouna red wine in one of the unit's small water trailers. The Officer's Mess had financed the project but sadly this 'red infuriator' did not improve with travel, having turned to vinegar and becoming quite undrinkable on arrival at St Andrews Barracks, Malta. To add insult to injury, this led to a very unsatisfactory correspondence with the local Ordnance Depot concerning the after effects of wine on the water trailer, which was only brought to an end by our departure from the island.

'40 had left for Palestine before we got back to Malta and accounts trickling back of the goings on in Haifa caused some of us to try and transfer to 40, but Lt-Col Ian Riches, our CO, who probably knew more than we did, would have none of it, so we concentrated on enjoying the fleshpots of Malta and picking up our local sporting fixtures.

'Our fun did not last long, for only a few days later we received orders to embark as soon as possible for Palestine in the *LST Messina*. There is a well-known Commando catch-phrase which says, 'The impossible we do immediately, miracles take a little longer.' The packing of Troop stores proceeded apace to a pre-arranged plan, as did the packing of our own personal kit and possessions that we were to take with us. It was in the packing of what was left behind that things were difficult. Having only recently arrived in the unit I managed to get the things that I was leaving behind into the trunks and suitcases I had. What I was taking with me just about fitted into my Bergen rucksack and a large suitcase. I remember that we were told to take 'blues' and I am so glad that I did not take my best suit, as that, amongst most of the rest of the contents of my suitcase, disappeared at Port Said, when unwisely, I became separated from my baggage some two months later.

'About four hours after the order to move was given, the whole unit, less a small rear party and, of course, the long suffering married families, were sailing out of Grand Harbour bound for Palestine. We were all very excited by the prospect and thanks to good administrative planning, had with us more or less all the things that we were likely to need. Our wretched Rear Party were not so lucky as they were exposed to all the pent up complaints of the married families left behind. They also had to try and cope with the depredations of the Officer-in-Charge of Barracks, who descended on St Andrews Barracks, noting every blemish that could possibly have been caused by our occupation and sudden departure. The ensuing correspondence was still going on when I left the unit some 30 months later.

'Time passed quickly and by the time we arrived in Haifa some six days later we were ready for anything, or almost anything. In response to a signal, the CO went ashore to report to HQ 1st Guards Brigade, under whom we were to serve during the first part of our time in Palestine. The Second-in-Command, Maj Dickie Birch, a former Fleet Air Arm pilot of distinction, was left to give the orders for our move by road to Jerusalem.

'The orders took quite a long time to deliver as it involved listing every vehicle in our convoy of which there must have been about 80, stating who was to travel in each, and listing the stores that they were to carry. I think that we started just after 18.00, which coincided with the opening of the bar for the first time since we left Malta. Unwisely perhaps, the 'O' Group, which had been expanded to include all officers, were permitted to use the bar during the proceedings. By the time we had reached vehicle number 60, attention was definitely wandering, and it was nearly 22.00 when the 'O' Group was over and we all disappeared to brief our troops and get them ready for an early start the next morning. My Troop Commander in 'X' Troop was Maj Willy Aston, another former Fleet Air Arm Pilot, who had had the traumatic experience of seeing his wife and child killed in front of his eyes, when their plane crashed at Gibraltar. Despite this, he had a wicked sense of humour with little respect for authority. He used to tease the CO and Second-in-Command unmercifully. The other subaltern in 'X' Troop was Tony Stoddart, who had a similar disregard for authority and they understood each other very well. Both were very popular with the men, who respected their leadership qualities and highly individualistic styles. It was a good set-up. The Troop Sergeant-Major was TSM Abrams, who had seen wartime Commando service. He was the sort of chap with whom one would like to find oneself in a tight spot. He was a first-class leader and a member of the unit football team, and very fit. He also provided that vital link between the officers and the men of the troop. When he became my acting RSM in 45 Commando in somewhat unusual circumstances some 15 years later, I tried to get him rated up permanently, but unfortunately I was unsuccessful. 'X' Troop also provided another member of the Commando football team in the person of the goalkeeper, Cpl Sandy Powell. He was a large, red-headed man as his nickname suggests. He was the terror of opposing centre-forwards, for when charged, he lowered his shoulder and raised it smartly under their rib cage, usually effectively reducing their capabilities for the rest of the game. Maybe he was one of the causes of the rule changes about charging goalkeepers.

'The convoy was already lined up in its order of march, with vehicles marked with chalk showing their number in the convoy. In addition the convoy was divided into groups by troops. As I remember it, 'X' Troop Group consisted of the Troop Commander's jeep, towing a trailer, a Dodge Weapon Carrier and water trailer with the TSM and ammunition, a Chevrolet 3-tonner with the TQMS and Troop Stores, towing a trailer, and five Troop-carrying vehicles (TCVs) with Tony Stoddart and myself in the front of two of them. I suppose that we might have been a little suspicious of the wisps of steam from the bonnets of these well-worn TCVs driven by RASC drivers. They had obviously seen the best of their lives in the Western Desert before being nearly driven into the ground in Palestine. Our own vehicles were probably still suffering from three months desert training and were a very mixed bag with examples of most US and British makes still in service in the British Army. The last vehicles of the convoy did not arrive until well after midnight. The Palestine Police looked after us very well. They assisted our cooks to get us a meal and allocated us areas where we could doss down for the night.

'Next morning, after a skimpy wash and a shave and a mug of tea, in which a spoon would stand up, we moved off to take up a position on Mount Scopus. We debussed near the skeleton of an unfinished building, believed to be the start of a new hotel, which was immediately christened 'Herod's Palace'. My half-troop was deployed to 'Tony's House', a most attractive villa with a lovely garden, belonging to an Armenian lady called Madame Antonius. Opposite was the house of the Grand Mufti of Jerusalem, who someone remembered had spent some of the last war in Berlin. Both houses were unoccupied. All

Madame Antonius' furniture was stacked in a locked room. Our orders were to establish a road block in our vicinity on the road leading to the Hadassar Hospital, which towered above us on a nearby hill. I remembered that the School of Infantry, Warminster had recommended the use of 40-gallon oil drums filled with stones. As there were plenty of these at Herod's Palace and loose rocks lay everywhere the job was soon done, a row of barrels half way across the road on the near side, another a little further on, half way across the road on the off-side and two more similar rows, taking care that it was not possible to avoid the road block by detouring on either side, and that large vehicles just had room to get through. Each end, where vehicles should stop, was covered by a PIAT in a makeshift stone pill-box. Only two Marines were normally in the open to frisk vehicles in either direction, with a further five in reserve. Arms and ammunition were what we were looking for. The following extract from the road block log for 10 May 1948 gives an idea of the sort of things that went on:

0700 Road block opened

0730 Jewish lorry No. M129K from Hospital with 6 men, 2 women and furniture

0745 Armoured ambulance to hospital with 1 corpse, 2 wounded men

0810 Mufti's brother and 5 Arabs arrived to continue repairs to house

0900 Blue Kaiser car for hospital with 3 men

0927 2 British 3-tonners for hospital

0940 2 British 3-tonners from hospital, turned back by Jewish road block

1000 Heavy explosion in area MR904557

1005 Armoured ambulance from hospital driver and one man

1600 Second and third Arab defensive position observed in same area

1700 3 Jewish lorries to hospital with bedding, food, firewood and 10 men
1715 1 Jewish lorry No M129K with 3 bodies 8 wounded men, 6 nurses
1730 Explosions and machine gun fire from direction Old City
1745 Mufti's brother and 5 Arabs left

'One of these vehicles was a massive armoured ambulance, painted black with a Star of David on either side. This had an iron girder instead of a bumper and caused us to reinforce the two outward rows of our road block. There was a curfew at night, but nights were quite exciting. It seemed to be British policy to site our positions between those of the Arabs and Jews. This had one obvious disadvantage, as when they fired at each other, some of it came our way and with tracer this risk becomes more visible. I have been told that you cannot see tracer if this is being fired directly at you . . . I remain unconvinced. The telltale noise of a German Schmeisser or a British Bren gun, together with scattered rifle shots through the night, produced no shortage of volunteers to fill sandbags the following morning. Fortunately, we received no casualties, apart from the odd chip of stone, but the stucco on Tony's House was going to need some repair. If the shooting became too close, one solution was to shoot back at where the worst seemed to be coming from, and then for good measure, have a go at the other. I managed to take a small number of 'X' Troop to have a quick look at the Old City of Jerusalem, which was an unforgettable experience. As time went on and the end of the Mandate approached, this nightly firework display increased in intensity. While we were in Jerusalem, the unit came under the command of 1st Guards Para, commanded by Col John Nelson, a most dashing and impressive soldier. He took a particularly dim view of all this shooting and decided that one way of stopping it would be to eliminate the Jewish forces in the Hadassar with an attack by 1 Guards Para and 42. The hill on which it stood was steep and there was little cover. At the top of the hill was the surrounding wall of the hospital. Apart from both units' 3-inch mortars and Vickers machine-guns, there did not seem to be that massive fire support that the School of Infantry included in every exercise. As for a night attack, the Israelis seemed to be able to turn night into day with an almost un-limited supply of Verey lights and flares. It was a great relief when the whole thing was called off because we were pulling out. The rest of the British Forces in Jerusalem were ordered to withdraw south to Egypt. 42, however, were told to withdraw north to Haifa to rejoin the rest of 1 Guards Brigade in Haifa, to cover the final evacuation.'

The last unit to leave Palestine was 40 Commando, commanded by Lt-Col R. D. (Titch) Houghton, who had returned to active duty after his capture on the beach at Dieppe in 1942. The British Mandate, which had been granted by the League of nations after the 1914–18 War, finally ended on 24 May 1948. 45 Commando withdrew on 12 May, and 42 withdrew into the Haifa perimeter on 15 May. The last units, covered by the Support Troop of 40 Commando, were evacuated on 27 June. 40 Com-mando gradually drew in their perimeter around the dockyard at Haifa, with the 'S' Troop mortar platoon setting up their last base position on a sand-backed platform set in the bows of the *LST Striker*, which, with its sister ship, the *Reggio*, was to carry the Brigade around the Mediterranean, on and off, for the next fifteen years. Lt-Col Houghton received the OBE and Capt Dennis Aldridge, later of 41, the MBE for their work in covering the withdrawal from Palestine. Within days of the British departure the Arab-Israeli War broke out, and has gone on intermittently ever since.

Robin McGarel Groves continues: 'The journey back to Haifa was much less exhausting and also much quicker this time as we had reliable vehicles. We were, however, withdrawing for the last time, leaving the land to be fought over by Jews and Arabs; thus, any vehicle that broke down and could not be recovered, had to be abandoned and destroyed. One such casualty was Willy Aston's trailer, which burst a tyre. This, together with his jeep, was the pride and joy of his driver, who kept both in immaculate condition. In those days, trailers had no spare wheels and no other wheels were interchangeable. The trailer was quickly unloaded and the load piled into the back of the jeep, and it was was then pushed over a cliff to the dismay of Willy's driver.

'Back once more in Haifa, we found ourselves scattered around the city. Commando Headquarters and the Headquarter Mess was in the Wade and Nusnas area, with a magnificent view of town and harbour and within easy walking distance from the main shopping area. 'A' Troop was split between the area to the west and the main coastal road below Mount Carmel. 'B' Troop was spread around Northern Carmel. 'X' Troop was in the Old Town and near the docks in Barclays Bank and the Sailors' Home. 'Y' Troop was more or less in reserve near Commando Headquarters. 1 Coldstream Guards had been withdrawn into Peninsula Barracks in the Bat Galim area, prior to withdrawal. Milpal, as the Headquarters of Gen Macmillan GOC Palestine was known, was in the Carmelite Monastery. When visiting there, I met one of the monks who was still living in the building and who knew my father when he had been stationed in Haifa for a short time during the war. On the strength of this, I had a fascinating conducted tour of this very ancient building. Nearby in the Palazzo was the Headquarters of COMPAL (Commodore, Palestine): Commodore ATGC Peachey (he had been my Captain in the cruiser

Enterprise) who was responsible for intercepting illegal immigrants and co-ordinating the loading and sailing of ships carrying military stores and troops.

'Our task in Haifa was to man various roadblocks as well as carrying out patrols both in vehicles and on foot. When we finally withdrew we left these road blocks *in situ*. Their strength was tested and found to be effective the night after we left, as we heard that no less than three white United Nations jeeps had been written off through collision with them in the dark.

'As by now the Israelis had eliminated all serious Arab opposition, life became rather less exciting and we reverted more to a peacetime existence. We managed to organize quite a lot of football and hockey. We also ran bathing parties out to Athlit, where the Irish Guards had a camp. I found myself the member of a Court Martial trying a Mauritian Pioneer Corps soldier for a very gory crime with a knife. Among the Mauritians this did not seem all that out of the ordinary. The evidence was given in English, French, a sort of Mauritian patois, Arabic and Hebrew. Fortunately, the President of the Court Martial had sufficient mastery of all these languages to persuade the various interpreters to say what the witness actually said rather than what they thought he ought to have said, which those who know the Middle East accept as one of the local hazards.

'Prossi's restaurant on Mount Carmel Avenue was a popular spot for Sunday lunch. The cooking was superb and their Brandy Sours made an excellent aperitif. There was also an attractive night club on Mount Carmel called the Piccadilly, which was popular with the younger officers of 42. One night we were enjoying a quiet beer, as was our wont, when a large number of Irgun Zui Leumi came in, wearing denison smocks, carrying sten-guns and dripping with grenades. They had just returned from capturing Acre and had come to celebrate. Very soon they started being rude, so as we were heavily out-numbered we decided that discretion was the better part of valour and left very swiftly via the open window. After this the Piccadilly became off limits.

'Our main problem, and one which affected all British forces left in the Haifa enclave, was the security of our own weapons and equipment. There was a semi-official black market price, varying from £20 for a pistol to about £20,000 for a Comet tank. This last prize is what two mistaken tank crews were believed to have been offered when they drove their tanks through the wire at Ramat David by the Airport and defected to the Israelis. They had also been promised that they would be made Captains, but ended up as batman before (it is believed) coming to a sticky end. The two tanks were reported in various battles with the Arab Legion, eventually being blown up by an ex-British 17-pounder, which the Arabs had acquired by equally dubious means.

'All this time the vast stockpile of military stores was being withdrawn and as the perimeter decreased, so further units left Palestine. Having a farewell drink with someone from 6th Airborne Division, I was offered a couple of Deerhound armoured cars and two ex-Palestine Police armoured cars. As these were in excess of their G1098 scale they could not take them with them. A bottle of whisky clinched the deal and I felt very proud of my new possessions when I drove them up to Commando Headquarters. Ian Riches however, took a rather different view; in fact, I think he was rather horrified. However, after explaining what super mobile pill-boxes they would be and how useful in supporting our vehicle patrols they would prove, we were allowed to keep our armour. Sadly before we left, together with others, we had to set fire to them in a disused quarry and complete their destruction with explosives. Much later, I saw one of these Deerhounds abandoned on an airfield in Malta –

possibly 40 Commando may know something about this?

'One of the more interesting duties was manning the big road block just below Mount Carmel, where a vast number of vehicles were searched each day. Mr Kaiser's cars seemed to be one of the most popular makes and we used to run a small sweep each day on the car with the most passengers. I think the most we ever found was 27, including those on the roof, bonnet, and in the open boot. One night five British 3-tonners disappeared, which I am glad to say were not ours. The GOC was furious and ordered us to detain the first 10 ten-tonners that passed through our road block and to hold these until the British vehicles were returned. Needless to say, our 3-tonners were never seen again so the confiscated 10 ten-tonners were eventually burned. The main Israeli Army, Haganah, were really in charge outside the Haifa enclave, and we got to know some of them quite well, particularly those who had served with the British Army during the war. In fact, we established quite a good working arrangement with them, but obviously it had its limitations. Recovery of missing vehicles, arms and equipment was beyond its scope, but it proved to be most helpful when 42 found itself the last unit in Palestine and were able to embark in good order with all our arms and equipment, though it was strained when we were seen helping to push the fleet of black Palestine Police Humbers into the harbour.

'Although all three commandos of 3 Commando Brigade were sent to Palestine, the Brigade Headquarters remained in Malta. The only representative of Brigade Headquarters who spent much time in Palestine was the Brigade Major, Bill Heald, a Major in the Dorset Regiment, who was a most agreeable and lively companion. It was through him mainly that we maintained our links with Haganah via an ex-British Army Officer known as

Henry. Bill Heald had some interesting tales to tell of his visits into Jewish-held territory.

'There is a song we used to sing in the Mess that goes to the tune of 'My Darling Clementine' which gives the flavour of our life at the time. It was written by Tony Stoddart and as far as I can remember, went like this:

> Fifty pounds just for a Sten gun
> It's the same old ruddy line
> He's a hooked-nosed robbing bastard
> And he comes from Palestine.

> Half a million for a Churchill
> Bring along the crew as well
> Haganah will make you Captains
> Better pay than IZL.

> Piccadilly on Mount Carmel
> All the girls are Haganah
> Where the BM did do business
> Propping up the (two syllables) bar.

'The vessel chosen to take us to Port Said was the *Empire Vigour*, a ship that had been in the news earlier for transporting illegal immigrants back to Germany. The accommodation was basic to say the least. The holds had been fitted with staging for the immigrants to sleep on. There was a trough on the deck, presumably for washing, only in our case there was hardly any water. Sanitary arrangements were minimal and most used the leeward side. We fed from our field cookers, which roared away on deck. The unit dossed down where they could, avoiding the lower reaches of the hold. When all should have been on board, I noticed that one officer was missing. I knew he had discovered a very hospitable Armenian lady, and feared that he might have overslept, but I was wrong, for he appeared, looking terrible, and found the first place he could to go to sleep. Here he remained for the whole of the voyage, making up for the sleep he had missed over the last night – and several nights previous.

'At last Port Said hove in sight. Our journey only took twenty-four hours, but it seemed much longer, and we were a pretty grimy and itchy bunch by the time we took the special train from Port Said to Shandur on the Little Bitter Lake, where we were to be based for the next year.' Marine R. S. Dobbs also joined the Brigade in Palestine: 'My first introduction to Cdo life was at Gibraltar Camp, Llanegryn, Wales, where at the age of 30, I went through the Cdo Course with a squad of tradesmen, mostly aged around 20. I completed the course and returned to Chatham to await further drafting. In December 1947 I was drafted to Cdo School at Bickleigh, where I completed another Cdo course.

'I was eventually drafted to 3 Cdo Brigade on 25 February, 1948. I was to be the SA Armourer in 40 Cdo who were stationed in Haifa, Palestine. My first stop was St Andrews Barracks, Malta, for final briefing before joining the main body in Haifa.

'At first, we had a camp alongside the law courts on the main Jerusalem Road. The camp appeared to be between the Jewish Quarter one side and the Arabs on the other. Very often we heard gunfire pass over our camp as someone from either group poked a weapon out of a window and fired at the opposite side. The weapons used were of a great variety. We knew this because while the courts were in session, we used to comb through the long grass and confiscate those we found hidden by the people brought before the courts on various charges. Some of these weapons appeared to be home-made and I would imagine would be more dangerous to the firer than anyone else.

'We later moved our camp into Haifa dockyard itself, and took over control of traffic in and out of the docks.

We also mounted night patrols to combat pilfering from the various sheds and stores. Another job was carried out by our PTI Sgt 'Sticks' Dodds, who was a great swimmer and carried out many underwater searches on ships for mines. Our CO, Col 'Titch' Houghton, had many meetings with the headmen of both the Arabs and the Jews trying to keep peace with both sides.

'When it was decided to withdraw all British Troops from Palestine, it was agreed they should pass through Haifa and 40 Commando would be the last to leave. This took place and Col Houghton performed the last act by toppling the large crane on the dockside. The Palestine Police had been one of the first units to be disbanded and leave.

'We then moved to Dekelia Camp, Cyprus, and looked after illegal immigrants to Palestine who were being kept in compounds until they were returned to the places they had come from. Most of our runs ashore were spent in Larnaca, where brandy was very cheap, around two shillings a bottle. I met one character who owned a bar in the market place. His name was Steve and he was very friendly and spoke good English. As soon as you went into his bar he would bring food and a bottle of brandy and would sit and talk with you. It appeared to me that people just came and helped themselves to food and drink but never seemed to pay anything and when I asked him about this he said that when the people harvested whatever crop they produced and sold it then they would come and pay him. This was the way of the Greek Cypriots. I never saw him or they mark it down on a slate or book, so I cannot say whether he went broke or not. He told me never to mix brandy and ouzo, as this was fatal. I never did, as I had seen the effect of ouzo drinking on Greeks.

'We did not stay on duty in Cyprus very long, but returned to Malta for another short period of rest and re-organization.'

Malta was the 3 Commando Brigade base for much of the 1950s, and Robin McGarel Groves describes his first introduction to the post-war Commandos: 'My posting to 42 Commando came through on the day we completed our Commando Course at Bickleigh. January and February on Dartmoor had been wet and cold, but there had really been little time to think about personal discomforts. We were young and by the end of the course we were very fit. Sandy Macpherson, Eric Scott, Johnny Bishop and Arthur Meny-Gibbert were also destined for 42, but being the only bachelor among them, it was obviously thought that I needed less pre-embarkation leave. Thus, two weeks later and considerably less fit, I found myself embarking in the troopship *Otranto* at Southampton.

'Relying on past experience I quickly settled myself in, relieved that I appeared to have no responsibilities for drafts. My fellow passengers seemed to be a cheerful lot, mainly destined for Egypt and the British Mission in Greece. As the ship's entertainment officer was returning to Greece, the ship's loudspeakers played incessant Greek music, which I for one found most agreeable. There were one or two nurses and members of the women's services as well as daughters of senior officers, so the time passed all too quickly, and seven days later we found ourselves entering Grand Harbour. There were still many wartime wrecks visible including the tanker *Ohio* anchored in Bighi Bay. There were also further signs of the heavy aerial bombardment ashore, where many buildings were still in ruins.

'I took my time over disembarkation to ensure that I had all my baggage with me. Also, I got the ship to signal the unit to send transport to pick me up, as unless one stood over one's baggage once it was ashore, there was always the risk of things disappearing. I arrived at St Andrew's Barracks and reported to the officer commanding the Rear Party, for the unit was still in Tripolitania doing training. They seemed quite surprised to see me, as apparently I was not expected for two weeks; however, a quick exchange of signals resulted in me being booked on a boat to Tripoli in a week's time.

'This gave me a wonderful opportunity to look up old friends and also to look up addresses given to me by my father, who had been in Malta for most of the siege. One of these was the Archbishop of Malta, Monsignor Gonzi, who was most charming. Another was the Baroness Inguanez, who lived at Casa Inguanez at Medina, in the centre of the island. She had been a great beauty in her time and on her piano were photographs of most of the crowned heads of Europe just before the Great War. There was even a photograph of our King Edward VII. The house was filled with many precious things and seemed almost a time capsule. Just listening to her reminiscing was quite fascinating. She, of course, pressed more addresses on me of people nearer my own age. The week passed very quickly and then it was time to leave for Tripoli.

'I found that I had to take a draft with me for 42 and we duly embarked in the *Empire Peacemaker*. She was a converted frigate that had been uses as a convoy rescue ship. Because of her antics in any kind of a sea, she was inevitably known as the *Empire Sickmaker*; however, we were fortunate. It was only a short overnight trip and the sea was like glass. The accommodation was a bit of a contrast to the *Otranto* as we slept in racks or hammocks, but on a lovely sunny morning we arrived at Tripoli. This time we were expected and my draft and I got aboard the two unit 3-tonners for the 60-mile drive to Tarhouna, where 42 Commando was based. There seemed to be no speed limits so we belted along, the Austin 3-tonner emitting that high pitched gear noise for which they were notorious. The only time we slowed down was to negotiate where a bridge had been demolished, and again where sand had blown over the road.

'When we arrived at Tarhouna, we found that the unit had just returned from an exercise, the last part of which was called "Busy Bees". This seemed mainly concerned with the tactical siting of the Officers' Mess Tent and involved the officers dining in full white mess kit. As the CO put it, it was to exercise the Officers' Mess staff and to keep up standards. As I was not "tactically loaded" it took a little time to disinter my rather crumpled mess kit.

'I had not met Lt-Col Ian Riches before. He had been Adjutant at Plymouth Division early in the war and had won a DSO commanding 43 Commando in Italy. He sent for me the next morning and gave me a long and serious talk about my duties, which were, among other things, to include carrying out the duties of Senior Subaltern. Having spent most of the war at sea, the greater part as an Acting Captain, this was outside my experience. I listened carefully to all he had to say, but from what I had seen of the other subalterns the previous night, I doubted whether a heavy-handed senior subaltern on the pre-war pattern envisaged by my CO would cut much ice. I decided to move slowly.

Tarhouna was an old Italian barracks. After the Italians left and before the British arrived, someone had removed all doors and windows and, of course, every plug from every basin. It is interesting that even today, every sensible traveller in the Middle East carries an assortment of plugs. Tarhouna was a delightful spot situated in an oasis. There was even a waterfall and for part of the time there the Unit had bivouacked near by. The surrounding village also boasted an *albergo* or inn which sold a very drinkable local vino, which was a little stronger than expected with a nasty form of accompanying headache.

'I had only been there a day or so, when I was sent off on a vehicle patrol to Garian, Yefren and Giado up on the escarpment above the coastal plain. The patrol consisted of three 15-cwt Chevrolet trucks of that flat-fronted variety shown in so many pictures of the 8th Army. These could well have been driven from El Alamein to Tunis and back. They were certainly not in the first flush of their life. With me were 12 men from "X" troop. We took all our own petrol, food and water, so as to be quite self-sufficient. We also had a selection of vehicle spares and tow ropes.

'The ascent of the escarpment to Garian was very spectacular and a living tribute to the Italian engineers who had built it. The road consisted of a series of hairpin bends, which carried the track up some 4000 feet. Garian was quite a small town with a few trees and houses built in the style one sees in the south of Italy. On arrival we made our number with the District Officer, who allowed us to bivouac in his compound. At Garian we met the members of the Quadripartite Commission, French, British, American and Russian representatives who were visiting all the ex-Italian colonies in North Africa to make recommendations on their future. In Libya, British influence was strong in Tripolitania and Cyrenaica; French influence was strong in the Fezzan, in the south. I have no doubt that the Commission worked very hard during the day. They certainly played hard at night. I found myself caught up in a party which started at 6 pm and was still going strong at 1 am, when I baled out.

'The senior British Representative was called "Puff Puff" by everybody. I never did discover his proper name. He was a most amusing and cheerful character with a good grasp of French and Arabic. The Commission seemed to split two ways. The British and the Americans hung together, while the French seemed to chum up with the Russians. While the Commission had been in Italian Somaliland they had been the centre of quite a serious riot. As a result they had now been given an escort. I met the escort commander, who seemed to be showing signs of wear and tear. He complained bitterly that these parties were a nightly occurrence. They were however where many of the difficulties identified during the day were resolved.

'We left Garian at an early hour. The track was dusty but hard and corrugated. At about 35 mph you ride over the top of the corrugations and it is not so bumpy. The desert was relatively featureless with a brown gravelly surface, yet there were variations in colour and here and there undulations, so that all the time the terrain had variety. As the day grew hotter, a heat haze appeared, making any other vehicle coming towards us appear a wobbly vertical apparition, lacking any constant width. Before long, we came to Yefren, another small village at the top of the escarpment, with a "Beau Geste" style fort overlooking the coastal plain. The fort had been an Italian Police Post and we halted near by to top up with petrol and water and to check tyre pressure, which in the desert can get dangerously high. There was also a shop selling Coco-Cola, where we refuelled the inner man. Proceeding onwards we came to a troglodyte village, where we again stopped. Here we were offered coffee, served in very small cups and with a very black, bitter taste. Care had to be exercised not to find yourself chewing your way through the grounds, which nearly half filled the cup. Here we did our first "hearts and minds" work, as our sick berth attendant treated a number of people with sores. The whole population lived underground in caves and it was eerie to see the white eyes peering at us out of the dark holes in the ground. The people of the village were Berbers, fine upstanding men and women with good features, survivors of the ancient race which was once dominant in this area. After a second cup of coffee, we moved on to get clear of the village before stopping for the night.

'The desert can get very cold at night and it really paid to dig a scrape to get below the cold surface desert wind. Apart from the noise of the wind, it was wonderfully quiet and far more stars seemed to be visible than in more civilized surroundings. Even our compo rations tasted better under such conditions. After a quick wash and shave and a further compo meal, we set off again, this time to Giado, another small ex-Italian police outpost with a white crenellated fort, surrounded by a pleasant village. The map showed "eau potable" and there were several wells supporting quite a large area of cultivation. Little square whitewashed houses were dotted around, presumably built by Italian colonists, but now occupied by Arabs. This was our furthest point and we started back on a track further inland, stopping the night at Gasrel Hag, an insignificant point on the map where two tracks met.

'The next day, nearing Garian, an Arab girl chasing a camel ran in front of one of our trucks and got knocked down. Fortunately she did not appear to be badly hurt, but nevertheless we put her in the back with her father and took her to the small hospital in Garian. I then made my way with the father to the District Officer's house to report what had happened. The District Officer was obviously an old hand, for listening to both of us he berated the father for allowing his camel to stray out of control on to the track and get in the way of vehicles. The more he went on the worse I felt, though we were not really in any way to blame. Fortunately the girl was released from the hospital, with only sticking plaster to cover the graze. I longed to offer some sort of compensation, but knew that this would be misinterpreted as acceptance of blame. When I got back to Tarhouna I reported this accident and got ribbed unmercifully by Willy Aston for "bashing a bint" so soon after joining the unit.

'Life at Tarhouna was not all work, for in the afternoon we ran sightseeing parties to places like Leptis Magna, Tripoli and Sabratha to see the Roman ruins. The road to Leptis was a tarmac one and regularly marked with white kilometre stones, and there were more of those square white houses amongst the cultivation. It was really quite impressive how much the Italians had done to improve the country in the way of roads, public buildings and agriculture. Having been engulfed by sand and only recently excavated, Leptis Magna was very well preserved and gave a good impression of what a Roman City must have looked like. The silted-up harbour was an attractive picnic site and somewhere to study the guide book I had acquired on a "run ashore" in Tripoli. The name Tripoli came into being when the inhabitants of Leptis and Sabratha, driven out by a combination of encroaching sand and Berber attacks, moved to Oein, which was re-christened Tripolis or the three cities. We also got invited to a "cous cous" held in an orchard with all the blossom out. Coloured rugs were spread out for us to sit or lie on and others were hung to provide shade. Our "cous cous" was mutton and chicken served in a 3-foot dish of fine safron rice. Only the guests fed initially, the hosts picking out special morsels with their fingers and handing them to each of us. Having been trained in these niceties we carefully only ate with our right hands as the left hand was considered unclean, being used for other more basic purposes. My fear that I should find myself presented with the sheeps' eye was fortunately not realized, but it did happen to one of the others, Major Bill Teak. He, being the man he was, swallowed it down whole without a murmer, to the admiration of all of us and probably our hosts. While our hosts had their meal, we lay on our backs belching contentedly, in the approved style. The orchard was quite near what had been a famous international motor racing circuit in the days of Mussolini but now it was occupied by the Americans Airforce and was known as Wheelus Field. Fortunately today there was no air activity to disturb the peaceful atmosphere.

'The final exercise before 42 Commando returned to Malta was to be the capture of Castel Benito Airport in a dawn attack. Castel Benito, renamed soon after this Castel Idris, after the King of Libya (and renamed again after the revolution deposed him), is now known as Tripoli International Airport. The plan involved being transported by truck to within 10 miles of Castel Benito, making an advance in Commando snake formation (one behind the other in single file), forming up within sight of the objective and putting in our attack as it got light. All leaders had a white patch sewn to the back of the collar of their denison smock to assist those behind. I think that Ian Riches must have chosen this formation out of nostalgia for the action at Lake Commacchio in Italy, where he won his DSO, but it did have some snags. Those at the tail of the column frequently found themselves almost doubling to keep up, then there were unexplained halts. It was a little discouraging to see the head of the column passing us heading in the opposite direction with the unfortunate Intelligence Officer who was doing the navigation leading, presumably having taken a wrong turn through the maze of orange trees. What with all the stop-starts and the loads we were carrying, we were quite tired when we reached our start line and far from a dawn attack, it was now broad daylight. Despite it all we put in a spirited attack across some 400 yards of open ground. "X" Troop captured their objective, which was the Control Tower. The troop wag, Sgt "Snaky" Boyne, hoisted a Union Jack and the exercise was considered ended, which brought to an end that inevitable exercise situation of "Bang you are dead! — No I am not, I shot you first". Nevertheless, one could not help feeling that one good man with a machine-gun could have eliminated the whole commando as they charged in line abreast across the airfield.

'We then proceeded to a bivouac area on the outskirts of the airfield, where the Commando cooks had prepared a most welcome breakfast. We then settled into our troop bivouac areas, where we were to remain until we embarked for Malta. As Tripoli was quite close, leave was given for a final shopping spree and general look around. There was quite an amusing Officers Club, called the Wadaan, which served quite good food and had a well-stocked bar. Near by there was also the Del Mahari Hotel, which was very popular with the officers. As Mahari is Arabic for racing camel, it was always known as "The Sign of the Racing Camel". My fellow subaltern in "X" Troop, discovered the Public Baths, where he was offered a "Bagno Vegetale", which he accepted, not quite knowing what to expect. He was somewhat surprised when a young Arab girl entered his bathroom and tried to wash his back. Anyway, that is what he said. As no one had had anything except a shower since leaving Malta, the Public Baths did a roaring trade. Laden with Libyan carpets and sheepskin rugs, the unit embarked in the Landing Ship Tank, I think the *Salerno*, for our return to Malta, and St Andrews Barracks.'

The early summer of 1949 saw the Brigade back in Hong-Kong, patrolling the border with China, and carrying out the usual round of guards and parades that make up peacetime life for garrison troops, but this idyll lasted only six months, until May 1950, when the Brigade was sent to fight against the growing Communist insurrection in the jungle of Malaya.

The 'Emergency' in Malaya had its origins in the Independence struggle of the pre-war years. At that time, the Malayan Communist Party had been banned, but after the Japanese invaded the Malayan peninsula, and the British garrison of Singapore surrendered in 1942, the Communists took to the jungle and began the fight against the Japanese, an effort the British were obliged and willing to recognize and support. The Malayan Peoples Anti-Japanese Army (MPAJA), was, in fact, a largely Chinese force, with minimal participation from the native Malays or the immigrant Indian population. British officers from Force 136 were parachuted in with arms and supplies, and they armed and trained the bands of MPAJA, which fought against the Japanese until the end of the war.

When the war ended and the British Army landed once again in Malaya, discreet steps were taken to disband and disarm the MPAJA but, as in Yugoslavia and Greece, the open aim of the Communists, after defeating the Germans or the Japanese, was to seize the country for themselves, expel the Imperial power, and impose a Communist dictatorship. The MPAJA faded back into the jungle, re-named itself the Malayan Races Liberation Army (MRLA) and took up the fight again, this time against the British. This jungle war lasted for ten years, until Malaya became independent, and still sputters on along the northern frontier with Thailand.

The Communists organized for the struggle by splitting their forces into three interdependent sections. First, in the jungle were the MRLA units proper. Although theoretically organized into brigades, they operated in groups of between three and fifty strong. The Marines usually referred to these as 'bandits' or 'CTs' (Communist Terrorists). Then came the 'Min Yuen', undercover Communist supporters who lived and worked in the villages, and helped to supply food to the CTs. Finally, came the 'Lie Ton Ten', the killer squads, who executed traitors or informers, kept waverers in line with torture and beatings, and in their spare time carried our minor acts of sabotage by cutting telephone wires, slashing rubber trees, or organizing riots.

According to Chairmen Mao, the guerrilla swims among a friendly population like the fish in the sea. The Communists certainly drew support and supplies from the native population, but very little of this was due to political persuasion of the merits of their case. Terrorism and extortion were the twin pillars of their policy, and to remove the native population from the threat of coercion, and to cut off the CTs from their supplies, the villagers were eventually moved out of the jungle edge into protected villages, where they could be both policed and protected. With this done, the infantry units of the British Army and the Commando troops of the Royal Marines carried the war into the jungle.

3 Commando Brigade Royal Marines, commanded yet again by Brigadier Campbell Hardy DSO, who had led the old 3 Commando Brigade at Kangaw, arrived in Malaya in May 1950, and was at once deployed in the northern part of the country, in the State of Perak.

Perak is roughly the size of Wales, a state with mixed terrain where flat plains, rivers and high jungle-cloaked mountains mingle with rubber estates and tin mines, a microcosm of Malaya, but with two particular military disadvantages. Firstly, the population contained a high percentage of Chinese who, willingly or unwillingly, supported the CTs, and secondly, the nearby frontier of Thailand offered the CTs a refuge in times of stress, as well as a source of supply. Bandit acitivity was therefore rife in the State of Perak, and the bandits proved difficult to subdue.

Each Commando was given an area to patrol and control, with 40 Commando based in the north around Kuala Kangsar, 42 in the centre of Perak near Ipoh, the State capital, and 45 at Tapah in the south, each Commando deploying its Troops around the area, often in bases or 'locations' up to 50 miles from Commando HQ. From these locations the Marines went out to patrol and ambush, operating usually at half-section strength of about ten men. Patrolling in Malaya was hard work. The climate is enervating, humid and hot, with regular drenching thunderstorms. In primary jungle, under the tall trees, the vegetation is difficult enough to penetrate, but where the top cover has been cleared away, the secondary jungle flourishes, and can only be crossed by following animal tracks or hacking a path with a machete. Throw in high, steep mountains, swamps, mosquitos, leeches, rushing torrents and shattering heat, and campaigning in Malaya was difficult enough even without the constant possibility of ambush and enemy fire.

'X' Troop of 40 Commando spent three weeks of April 1951 patrolling in this sort of country, hunting for a CT group which had attacked a Malay *kampong* or village at Temengor, thirty miles east of their base at Grik, and killed three villagers. One day, the Marines, with their Iban trackers, covered twenty-four miles through the jungle, following elephant tracks while carrying full packs with two days rations and full ammunition scale, and on another a Marine was swept to his death in a river. The bandits fled, but the patrolling went on.

Jeremy Moore remembers this patrol very well. 'We stopped very late, after crossing the Perak river which was very fast-flowing. We kept going until people started falling over, and then we sat beside the track for most of the night. When I took my jungle boots off later I counted 50 leeches on my right foot alone.'

Apart from patrolling, ambushes were a favourite way of interrupting CT movement and increasing the unit body-count, and the story of this one, by a sub-section from 'Y' Troop, 42 Commando, is typical in style, but untypical in its success.

The 'A' Troop Commander, Major Anthony Crockett, had decided to put an ambush on a track beside a pipeline, largely because a small trickle of intelligence reports seemed to indicate that bandits, or at least supplies for bandits, were moved along it from time to time. The ambush task was delegated to a corporal, and it took his sub-section a full day to hack their way through the jungle and infiltrate up to an ambush position which overlooked track and pipeline.

Since the fumes and smell of their Hexamine tommy-cookers would carry for hundreds of yards, cooking was forbidden, and since the position was waterless, each man carried two water-bottles which had to last for at least forty-eight hours. They lay on the jungle edge overlooking the track for twenty-four hours before their chance finally came.

Two men, talking loudly, came walking down the track, each carrying a large knapsack and both armed, one with a carbine, the other with a rifle. The Marines waited until they were in the centre of the ambush, and opened fire, the Bren gunner firing a burst full into the leading man's chest. As he fell, his companion flung off his knapsack and dived for the cover of the pipeline to fall in a hail of fire from the rifles and Bren of the Marines fire. . . . 'Jets of water from bullet holes drilled in the pipe sprayed high into the air and over the blood-stained bodies lying in the sunlight'. Communist guerrillas were hard to kill. One Marine put a full 28-round magazine into a bandit who still managed to run over a hundred yards before he dropped. Up at the sharp end, it was a rough little war.

Marine Sherratt was a driver in HQ Troop of 45 Commando: 'I joined the Corps in 1947, aged seventeen and three months. I had two brothers in the Royal Marines, and I used to play at Commandos when I was a kid in the woods. I went to Bickleigh and joined 45 at

Suez, and went to Malaya in 1950, to Tapah. I don't recall any jungle training to speak of. I hear the Welsh Guards had Marine instructors in jungle warfare, but we didn't. Maybe some of the other troops or units did, but we certainly didn't.'

Terry Brown, then a signaller in 42, tells the same story. 'When we arrived, our training consisted of a lecture from an officer in the dining room. "It's simple," he said, "when we get fired at, we go straight at 'em!" I remember thinking, bloody hell, what manner of men are these?'

Marine Sherratt drove a 'Dingo' scout car. 'They were heavy, and we would wear out a set of tyres in a month or so. I was armed with a pistol, and our job was dropping off patrols and picking them up again.'

Occasionally, Marine Sherratt had to pick up other things. 'For identification purposes, the patrols had to bring back the bodies of any CTs they killed, so, since that was hard work, lugging a body through the jungle, the Ibans – or Dyaks – the trackers from Sarawak, used to slice off their heads and hands with a parang . . . all went well until some Marine had his picture taken holding a head in each hand by the hair . . . the Press got hold of it and all hell broke loose.

'We had one bad ambush, I remember, when we had two Marines killed, just after Christmas 1950. One was a mate of mine, Topsy Turner, from Birmingham. He was near Tapah, travelling towards Ipoh, when their vehicle was overtaken by a police vehicle full of CTs disguised as police. They flagged our truck down, then opened up on it as it stopped. SBA Sprules, the sick bay tiffy, ran for it and was wounded, but Topsy and another Marine were killed. Jock Henry was killed a bit later, in the Cameron Highlands, during an ambush, and the section was pinned down . . . Jock went to get more ammo and someone shouted, "Go left, Jock", but he went the wrong way and was killed. We caught the decoys that led us into the ambush and the Marines wanted to kill them . . . they didn't . . . I remember Alan Hardman of 'A' Troop, 42, who took Arthur Helliwell, the Fleet Street reporter out on patrol once. It was a good unit, 45, but I reckon 42 was the Brigadier's favourite.'

More and more National Servicemen were entering the Corps and finding their way to the Brigade, and Terry Brown was one who found his way to 42 Commando. 'When I joined the Royal Marines, I was interviewed by an officer who asked questions about one's background. . . . What were my hobbies before I joined up, he asked. When I told him that I did a bit of ballet dancing, he gave me some good advice. "I wouldn't mention that to the chaps if I were you," he said. How true!

'Commando training involved a lot of climbing. Our instructor was the formidable Capt Joe Barry, who used to make us skip among the boulders, strewing wild flowers about like a lot of fairies in order to improve our balance, much to the delight of the onlookers. I had done quite a bit of climbing before I joined, but I was unprepared for the Commando method of roping down a cliff, namely to run the rope between one's legs and over the crook of the arm, turn round and face down the cliff and run as fast as you could. We used dories, raiding craft, LCPLs and LCAs in our training, a lot of which was in bad weather off Plymouth.

'Our journey to the Far East was in *HMT Empire Pride* and, as usual, the troops, forming the bulk of the passengers, were squeezed into the quarter of the ship forward of the bridge. The remainder was occupied by married families and officers. The weather was foul. I spent four days in the hammock locker going through the Bay of Biscay and if I could have thrown myself over the side, I would have cheerfully done so. We lived on mess decks of twelve men, all of whom had a full complement of eating irons to start with. When we arrived in Singapore three weeks later, we were down to one set between the twelve of us. In those days most of the ports of call were coloured pink on the map, Port Said, Aden etc.

'We went up-country on a train resembling those that you see in wild-west films. Standing guard at night on the open platform at the end of the carriage as we crossed into Malaya from the causeway, with the smell of rotting vegetation and hearing the noises of the jungle for the first time, was like something out of *Wide World* magazine. The carriages all had notices in English, Malay, Chinese and Tamil, to the effort that one should lay on the floor if coming under fire from the track-side. This, I might add, was a pretty frequent occurrence.

'After a lot of hanging around, we finally caught up with 42 Commando in Perak. I was sent to "A" Troop, a spectacular setting surrounded by huge limestone crags. We were kitted out with our G1098 gear, consisting of jungle green shirts, shorts and long trousers, jungle boots, jungle hat, set of 1944 equipment, one blanket, machete with sharpening stone, toggle rope, face and wrist veils, white 42 Commando lanyard and garter tabs. Sitting on top of this lot was a small square of the Naval General Service Medal ribbon, the old "four by two".

'My jungle training consisted of the Section Sergeant telling me that if I got lost, the first thing to do was to brew up. He also said that we could forget all that right-flanking section attack business. Our tactics on coming under fire were to go straight for the enemy and get stuck in!

'After a spell in Perak the unit was relieved by the Worcester Regiment and moved to Kajang in Selangor. I was sent to "S" Troop and took up my duties as the signaller to the Assault Engineer Section. I carried a "68" set which weighed about 20 pounds. This, together with weapon, ammunition and rations proved to be a hell of a weight to lug around the jungle. Communications were always very difficult as the sets were pretty useless and the mountainous jungle in which we operated was not conducive to good radio reception. We used our own makeshift aerials consisting of a piece of D8 telephone cable with a stone or piece of wood on the end, slung up in a tree, of which there were no shortage. I was amused when, on returning to the signal store at Eastney, I found that this aerial was being produced in an authorized version. I worried about what I would do on coming under fire, carrying this huge load. I need not have worried – at the first shot the set was ditched and I was taking cover.

'Our weapons were No 5 jungle rifles, Bren guns, American M2 carbines, Australian Owen guns, silenced Lanchester carbines, shot-guns, 9 mm Browning pistols and 36 grenades. The Sten was universally disliked and we had a pretty free hand in the choice of weapon. This proved a bit embarrassing, because on one occasion, when ordered to fix bayonets to attack a jungle camp, only one man was discovered to have a rifle. Each troop had a Dingo scout car equipped with twin Vickers K-guns.

'I palled up with our troop Iban, Tan Yan. These trackers from Borneo were a fearsome sight, short brown bodies, heavily tattooed, long black hair reaching down to below the waist, which was tucked into their jungle hats when on patrols. Each carried a parang with which he would willingly lop off enemy heads. Around their waists they carried a weird assortment of knick-knacks, a test-tube with a bit of twig in it, and scalps. They were excellent trackers but had pretty short fuses when in action. "Hello, you old rubber tapper", I would greet Tan Yan. "Me no pucking rubber tapper, You pucking rubber tapper", he would riposte. I took him ashore on one of our rare visits to Kuala Lumpur. He was dressed in jungle green shirt and shorts, black and green football socks, plimsoles and green beret. As we proceeded down the street, the pavements cleared magically.

'While I did see one tiger, one crocodile, one monitor lizard, one python, which we found stretched out across the track, having just eaten a wild pig, the main menace were mosquitoes in every shape and size and red ants with a bite like an electric shock, and of course leeches. I counted 56 of these on my legs one day. We frequently saw whole families of wild pigs, and monkeys would accompany us high in the trees.

'Films never seem able to convey the absolutely knackering effects of heat. Any prolonged movement was exhausting and we sweated constantly. The only time when the temperature was bearable was when operating high in the mountains. If you were lucky, the going was through rubber plantations or *lalang*, but usually progress had to be made by the exhausting business of taking turns to hack your way through what we called thickets with a parang or machete. Some of the plants had little hooks growing along the under side of their fronds, which dug into the skin and clothing. It rained nearly every day in head-aching deluges. I remember standing in one of these downpours trying to get through on the radio after a contact, sending my call sign 9F, "dah dah dah dah dit di di dot dit", over and over and getting electric shocks all the while. All this for twenty-eight shillings a week!

'Getting wounded was not a pleasant prospect. It took four men to carry a litter, and we were mostly operating at section strength, about eight to ten men. At night the racket was appalling, an incessant hum of mosquitoes and all the other insects, the larger mammals crying, yelling and crashing about. Every so often of tree would fall over somewhere with a crash. Bits of decaying wood glowed eerily on the jungle floor, rather like the fluorescence one sees at sea sometimes.

'One particular night was memorable. We were trying to ambush a gang as they came down from the hills to get food. After a fruitless vigil for several hours, getting eaten alive by mosquitoes and seeing no-one, the patrol commander crept around the section and told them to stand by to move. The last man in the ambush turned his rather surprised face to our Corporal, yelled, and took off down the track at a high rate of knots. The patrol commander yelled and ran off down the track in the opposite direction. I'm afraid the rest of us just lay on the ground and laughed until the tears came. How that bandit got where he was, will always be a mystery.

'After a long and exhausting spell of patrolling and ambushes, I decided not to go on the ambush one night, but to spend the night with the driver, guarding the truck which we parked at what was euphemistically called a planter's bungalow. This huge, two-storeyed, neo-Tudor pile, stood in a rubber plantation miles from anywhere. The driver and I spent a happy couple of hours, drinking the planter's beer on the verandah. The planter then asked us if we would join them for dinner. While the opportunity to get some good grub was not to be missed, I was a bit worried about my dress. The planter got changed into a white tuxedo and his memsahib appeared in a fetching *décolletée* gown. I was wearing a faded and dirty pair of jungle green trousers, held together at the crutch with a safety pin, jungle boots and a grubby green vest, over which I wore a battered denison smock, heavily impregnated with mosquito repellent. I was in a dilemma, to take off the smock, or not. It was like a scene from a Somerset Maugham story which had gone terribly wrong somewhere.

'The time came to leave Malaya. The rest of the Brigade had depated for Malta long ago. Although many of my troop had served in 41 Commando in Korea, most of the men had been stuck in troop locations for two years and the reunion of the unit was a memorable event. We held a Memorial Service to honour the men who wouldn't be coming home, and the next day was given over to celebrating our departure. The festivities lasted all day, and when we reached the ornate oriental railway station at Kuala Lumpur, we were all totally and gloriously pissed. We finally embarked after the whole unit had danced a conga, led by the Colonel all round the station, in and out of the "White Other Ranks" toilets, the "Asian Other Ranks" toilet, onto several locomotive footplates and up and down the railway tracks. The band of the Royal West Kents was persuaded to play the unit song, "We're a Shower of Bastards", and the whole event became a rollicking sods opera. When we finally steamed out of the station to the strains of "Auld Lang Syne" we left platforms of planters and other well-wishers all sobbing their hearts out – and I think somewhere at the back of the crowd our old enemy, Lew Kom Kim, the "Bearded Terror of Kajang," was shedding a quiet tear too.

'We spent a fortnight in Singapore recovering, pale, thin creatures compared with the tanned garrison troops. The campaign had taken its toll and a lot of men were in poor shape. However, a fortnight of swimming and Tiger beer did wonders for us and we sailed on *HMT Dilwara* for Malta looking somewhat less emaciated.'

Colour Sgt R. S. Dobbs recalls some events in Malaya: 'Various Naval ships transported us to Malaya to try to combat the bandits infiltrating down through Thailand. We landed at Penang and moved into barracks which also housed the KOYLI and a battalion of Scots Guards. That, if I remember, was where the Commandos were given a two-week course in jungle fighting. I was not required to do this, as my job was to make sure that the weapons used were in first class order. Our first tented camp on the mainland was at a place called Grik, which was adjacent to the Thai border. Conditions were pretty primitive at first, having to keep ourselves clean by jumping in the river for a wash and bath. Fortunately, our Assault Engineers were very good and rigged up showers. The piped water on the surface soon heated up in the sun and became quite hot. We just seemed to have made the place into a reasonable camp when we moved to Kuala Kangsar.

'I had one interesting incident during this spell of duty. While spending a rest weekend period in Penang, I was touched on the shoulder by Paddy Hornibrook, who was one of the rookies like myself at Deal in 1935. While we had a drink in the hotel garden, he told me he had been in the dockyard police at Singapore but had transferred to the prison service and was stationed at Ipoh. It was his day off with 100 dollars to spend because of the duty he had done on the previous day. It transpired he was the hangman for North Malaya and had just removed a bandit from existence.'

Eric Blyth served in 42 Commando in Malaya, first with 'S' Troop and then for a while with 'B' Troop. 'I always wanted to serve in the Commandos. My father did thirty years in the Queen's Bays and one of my grandfathers was in the Guards. I joined the Corps in 1947, went to Palestine with 42, when 40 were there under "Titch" Houghton. In Malaya we were at Tapah and then with "B" at Ipoh. On Christmas Eve 1950 we got ambushed and Brian Eathough, another Marine, got shot . . . the Chinese were good at it, make no mistake, and the Western Ridges, jungle covered up to 2-3000 feet, were their base – notorious for Commies. If you sat on your arse and waited you got hit all the time, so we went out patrolling and went in after them.

'About the heads . . . when we started, we carried

cameras to take photos of the dead . . . taking heads wasn't done, and then at a place called Malim Nawar, after three months with no contacts, but finding plenty of trails and food dumps, we got lucky. One morning – I was Acting Sergeant then – we saw the trails through the dew on the *lalang*. I got the lads and the Iban tracker, and we followed, ten of us, up the track and into them, about thirty . . . I got the first one . . . then three rounds hit my M1 carbine and broke it, so I smacked the next Commie over the head, and my carbine started to work and went off, hitting the Marine behind me in the hand. He shouldn't have been there anyway. So afterwards, the Iban sliced the heads off and I took them down to the market in Malim and showed them to the crowd and said, "This is what will happen if you don't stop helping the CTs".'

From Ipoh, 42 went to Kajang, an area terrorized by a Chinese bandit rejoicing in the title of 'The Bearded Terror of Kajang'. The story went, says Eric Blyth, '. . . that he was a schoolmaster, educated at Oxford, and with a red beard, very unusual in a Chink. His atrocities were quite unique, burnings, the lot . . . still we went after him into the "gunong", big mountains full of caves. One time up there I trod on the body of a bloke I'd shot three weeks before. You could carry any weapon you fancied, so I carried a Bren with seven magazines; heavy, but lots of fire-power.'

Marine Harwood, a regular Marine, went to 45 Commando, and records an unusual method of selecting volunteers. 'I started with 504 squad and broke my foot badly and ended up in 507, but this turned out to be a lucky break, as in those days the even numbered squads went to sea and the odd numbered squads went to the Brigade. We moved from Hong Kong to Malaya just before the Korean War started, and I volunteered for 41 but we had to go to Malaya. We were stationed at first on the Malaya-Siam border. It was fairly quiet there, then we moved down to Perak, one of the hot areas. 45 Commando HQ was at Tapah. "Z" Troop, of which I was a member, were based at Kampar in a derelict rubber plantation-manager's bungalow. We were so under-strength, space was no worry.

'We started the squatters' resettlement programme off; one idea to cut the supply of food to the bandits. The squatters lived miles from roads, way out in the jungle. Small patrols went out to ferry them and what they could carry back to enclosed villages that were built for them. They were given housing, schooling, medical care, plots of land, with the government buying the surplus produce.

'I became a leading scout in charge of our Dyak or Iban trackers. We had one or the other, but never together, as they were enemies. They are the real headhunters. At one camp we caught a young wild boar, so we started to fatten it up for Christmas. When the time came to kill it, Saleh, the head Iban, tried to grab it, but it bit his hand, so he lost his temper, his parang flew out of its scabbard, his wrist did not move more than six inches, then he was doing his victory dance with the boar's head in his hand.

'Our main job was to hunt the Communist terrorists that were trying to take over the country. In this we had great success. The terrain was very varied, from huge swampland, virgin jungle and small mountains, rubber estates, etc. The roads were known by colour, according to the chance of ambushes. We had a curfew going and at dusk six of us with Brens, Stens, Carbines and Owen guns in a 15-cwt used to race round the high risk roads, blazing away at each bend to deter any ambushes. I lost some good friends through ambushes. We lost two of our mates when they were ambushed in the main road of a small town.

'On one patrol (which normally was made up of two trackers, a scout, one Bren gunman, NCO or officer, and about three others) one of my Ibans came face to face with a bandit. The bandit let go with his Sten, which luckily jammed after a few rounds. Entap (the Iban) was trying to fire his rifle, but could not push his safety catch forward (he was pushing the back of his bolt). So down went the rifle, out came his knife. He threw it like a javelin, hitting the bandit's webbing. The bandit dropped his Sten and ran; as it was very thick scrub rubber he was lost in a couple of strides. We had to hold Entap back at gun point, as he wanted his knife back, which was a family heirloom, over 100 years old, but the risk of ambush was too great. He went missing that night when we got back to camp, and turned up two days later with his knife but would not tell us what happened.

'When we shot any bandits we had to take the bodies back for identification. If that was not possible, the Ibans took the heads off. Once, when we had shot two, the Ibans wanted the scalps. They had to be kept back at gun point, but when we stepped out onto the road to identify ourselves to the arriving transport, they were quick as a flash and had the scalps in their hands in less than a minute.

'The other natives we employed were the local Sakai, the aborigines of Malaya. Again, they are very small in stature, but very, very strong. Their weapons are blowpipes with poisoned darts. The men are about five feet tall, their blowpipes twelve feet. They can hit a small, flying bird at fifty yards with no effort. Shortly before we arrived in the area, the bandits had raided a Sakai village, when the men were hunting; they raped and killed the women and ransacked the village. When the men came back, all the Chinese villages in the area were put to the torch. (Most of the bandits were Chinese.)

'One of our patrols was in the area a few weeks after

this happened, and before they could identify themselves, two of the lads had darts in them. Luckily it was just a mild poison which they used for birds and animals. They make very good trackers.

'The area we did not like was the swamps, with the leeches etc. The leeches used to suck your blood without you knowing. I used to carry a tube of Iodine to dab them off me, as you could not pull them off without leaving the head in, which would fester. We were charged by a water buffalo once, when we were on squatter resettlement, it made a right mess of our three-ton truck. But the worst of the lot were the mosquitoes – our fingers used to swell with their bites.

'We had plenty of close shaves. Once, after a skirmish, shooting two, we found a food dump, but being cautious as always, we noticed wires leading from the pile. They were connected to jars of old nails, glass and bits of steel, packed tight with Amatol X all around the area. (Amatol X was a fairly new explosive then.) A nasty booby trap.

'Two days before I left the unit (end of commision and medical report came within two days of each other), three of us were out on patrol, when I saw a bandit running towards a swamp. I shouted "Stop!" but he still ran, so I fired one shot over his head. He still ran, so I fired once more, saw him jerk, by this time the other two had come up to me, firing as we ran up to him by a fallen tree. He was trying to pull the pin out of a grenade. His intestines were hanging out – he got the pin out but on examining the grenade later, we found it to be cracked and wet. Another lucky escape.'

Malaya did have its lighter moments, and Christmas, as always in the Services, was a chance for the Brigade to let its hair down a little, while officers, NCOs and Marines all together settled down for a party. Anthony Crockett gives a vivid description of a Christmas Eve spent with 'S' Troop of 42 Commando.

'Christmas Eve 1951 – the canteen was bulging. Men were bursting out of the doors and crammed along the window ledges. A figure stood on the table in the middle of the room wearing boots, a sarong, a pale pink brassiere and a jungle hat, singing a most indelicate song and beating time with a large, slightly sodden cigar. He threw a wink in our direction, waved us to the front of the throng and continued with his song. Bottles of beer appeared from nowhere, and were thrust into our hands. We all joined in the chorus. Then, of course, we all had to do our own party piece, and were hoisted, one by one and none to gently, onto the table, while half the room shouted for order and the other half just shouted . . . the rest of the evening is a bit of a blur.

'At one time I remember several of us sitting on the bed of a Marine who lived in a small room at the back of the canteen, drinking foul Chinese brandy out of a cigarette tin and helping him eat the contents of a large tin of shortbread his mother had sent him from Edinburgh. We had an extraordinarily heated discussion on the subject of Scottish nationalism.'

Jeremy Moore, who later commanded the British land forces which retook the Falklands, was then a lieutenant in 40 Commando. 'I joined the Corps in 1947, mainly because I wanted to fly, and this was a way into the Fleet Air Arm, which Marine Officers could join in those days. Later on this policy was dropped, but by then I had found out what super blokes Marines were, so I went to the Commandos. The great pleasure of my service was serving with Marines – men rather than machines.

'I had a tremendous time in Malaya, absolutely smashing. I managed to extend my tour and serve three years with the Brigade. I arrived on the trooper *Empire Halladale* in November 1950 and joined "X" Troop of 40 Commando. Frank Bristow was the Troop Commander, and Lt Elvie was the other subaltern. We shared a mess with "C" squadron of the 4th Hussars.

'As reinforcements we had no jungle training, but back in England, John Owen, who was then an instuctor at the Commando School, took us on a JEWT (Jungle Exercise Without Trees), on Exmoor, but that was it. I went out with the Troop to patrol with Lt Bill Mansell, to pick up a few tips, but my MOA was so unfit he simply couldn't keep up and in the end I had to bring him out. The next time I took a patrol out, I was in charge.

'I'd have to say that we were bloody inefficient. We didn't understand the jungle, but, Thank God, the blokes were jolly good, a lot of them National Servicemen, willing to have a go, often very imaginative . . . but we hadn't tackled the training in the painstaking way we do now – as for, say, Northern Ireland, where the units have six weeks training before they go there *every time*.

'Nevertheless, we did achieve successes, but there was more courage than skill in many of the things that went on. We lost a number of people who, in later years, we wouldn't have lost.

'Now, to go back a little, when 40 arrived in Malaya, the CO was Bertie Lumsden, a flamboyant character, who got some good initial successes against the bandits. Then. as things progressed, 45 started to get more kills. People were very kill-conscious, so to keep morale up, while the bandit score flagged, 40 set out to win every sporting contest in the Far East, which we did. Then Lumsden was relieved by Lt-Col Martin Price, a very upright officer – he used phrases like 'An order is an order, and must be obeyed'.

'By then, I'd had a long time in the jungle, and would take new arrivals, like Pat Wilsey and Peter Whiteley for a look at it. I found this a marvellous opportunity, because they were much more experienced officers than myself, and I learnt a lot about soldiering from them. All the time we were thinking of ways to get back in the game, by setting ambushes that would succeed by staying out longer.

'One day we received a surrendered terrorist, who told us of a bandit camp that was probably occupied, so I took a small patrol out to ambush one of the tracks leading to it, at a place where the CT had a "post box" – a place where they collected rations, messages and so on. We took the surrendered terrorist with us, but it soon became obvious that we were on the wrong track. When this became clear, we were on the edge of the jungle, near some rubber, and I felt exceedingly exposed, so I led the patrol up to a bank which overlooked the track, and we were just getting into position – I was actually briefing the Bren group Corporal, when somebody signalled and "lo and behold", there they were, coming down the track out of the jungle, three scouts in front, a bigger group still in the trees behind. This leading guy came on down the track which was about twenty yards in front of our position. We just froze . . . and they were opposite us when one of them suddenly saw the Bren gunner. He was there, squatting over his gun. He realized he'd been seen, flung himself behind the gun, cocked it and shot the CT in the groin. We killed two of them, and tackled the rest of the party, but they got away. Martin Price was over the moon that his Commando had got a kill – well, two kills, and after that I could do no wrong.'

For this patrol action, Lt Jeremy Moore received the Military Cross. 'How much that had to do with my MC I couldn't say, but jungle soldiering is hard work and it could be dangerous. Another "A" Troop subaltern, David Langley, was in hot pursuit of a gang, when they turned on him. He lost a Corporal and two Marines and got four bullets in his body. I particularly remember my MOA, Marine Derbyshire, one of nature's gentlemen, a boxer and a good shot – you can't do better than have a man at your side who can carry your pack if need be, knock down anyone who gets in your way, shoot the enemy, and is a good companion as well!'

During their two-year stint in Malaya, 3 Commando Brigade killed or captured 221 terrorists at a cost of thiry Commandos killed. They received, in return, over thirty awards for gallantry and over sixty Mentions-in-Despatches. 'A record of hard work, devotion to duty and comradeship of which the Corps has every reason to be proud,' as Sir John Harding, the Chief of the Imperial General Staff, wrote later.

The Royal Marines Commandos were to return to the jungle again, during the confrontation with Indonesia in the 1960s. Even today, they regualarly send companies to train in the jungle, and keep that hard-won expertise alive.

9

Korea, 1950–52

Chosin was a battle unparalleled in US military
history – an epic of great suffering and great
valour.

Time Magazine

At dawn on 25 June 1950, the North Korean Army
crossed the 38th Parallel and advanced into South Korea to
begin a bitter three-year conflict, the first, and so far the
only, all-out clash between the democratic nations of the
world and forces from the Communist block.

Like so many conflicts since 1945, the war in Korea
arose out of World War II itself. When the Japanese
surrendered in August 1945, the Russians advanced rapidly
into Korea from the north, and had occupied all of that
country as far as the 38th Parallel before the Americans
could enter the country from the south. As was their
practice, the Russians then established a firm frontier along
the 38th Parallel, and made it clear that they intended to
use this line to divide the country permanently into two
seperate zones. For the next two years the United Nations
strove to make the Russians leave and so unify the entire
country, but the Soviets flatly refused, even stating that
their occupation of northern Korea was no business of the
United Nations. Meanwhile, they set about imposing
Communist rule, installing a puppet regime, and equipping
and training a vast North Korean Army with the obvious
intention of invading the south when the American forces
left and occupying the entire country.

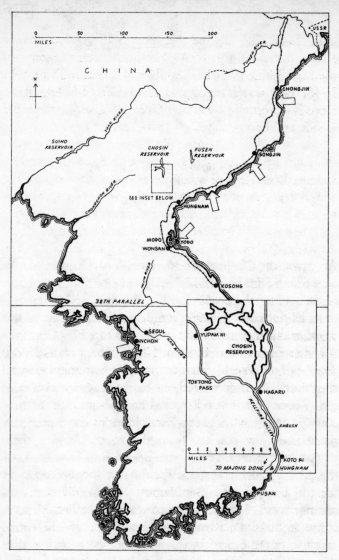

Map 4 Korea

In 1948, the United Nations ordered elections in Korea, but these only took place in the south, leading to the establishment of the Republic of Korea in December 1948. This government was accepted as the legitimate Korean goverment by all the United Nations, except the USSR and her satellite and vassal states.

During 1949, following the election of the new government in South Korea, the US Army withdrew, leaving behind only a small force of advisers and training teams who, at the request of the South Korean government, were to train the Army of the new Republic. This embryo South Korean Army took over the task of guarding the frontier along the 38th Parallel and, given the growing animosity between the two sides, border incidents began and multiplied during 1949 and the early months of 1950.

At the end of May 1950, the United Nations made yet another effort to unify the country, and a UN Commision met representatives from North Korea on the 38th Parallel, and were pleased to obtain a statement that all the North Koreans wanted was a peaceful unification of the country. Three weeks later, and without a declaration of war, the North Korean Army rolled south across the frontier.

Korea is a long, curving peninsula, just over 600 miles in length, and varying in width from 120 to 200 miles. To the north lies Manchuria and Soviet Russia; to the south, a hundred miles across the sea, lies Japan, while the east coast faces the Sea of Japan, and the west looks towards China. The northern boundary of the peninsula lies along the Yalu River, which separates Korea from Manchuria and fronts onto a short, ten-mile gap which leads directly into Russia.

The terrain of Korea is mountainous, with a large range in the north and north-east, where the peaks run up to 8,000 feet, and a continuous range of hills down the east coast from north to south from which spurs jut out west across the country. The climate offers four distinct seasons, which occur at the same time as they do in Europe, but as Korea lies to the east of the Asian land mass, the weather tends to be extreme. Spring and autumn are pleasant but short, summers are hot, and the rains, which come in July and August, tend to be torrential, with up to twelve inches of rain falling in two weeks, often accompanied by typhoons when the winds get up to 120 miles an hour. In winter, the temperatures are well below zero, and there are frequent heavy snowfalls.

When the war broke out in 1950, the total population of Korea was around thirty million, of which about two-thirds lived south of the 38th Parallel. The capital of the South was and is Seoul, which lies forty miles south of the Parallel and had a population of something over one million. In the southern part of the peninsula lies the port of Pusan, which was the second city of Korea and had the only proper harbour. Finally, on the east coast, and in Communist hands, were two other towns of some importance, Hungnam, an industrial centre, and Wonsan, a road and rail terminal. Wonsan stands within an excellent natural harbour, and contained oil refineries and other industrial installations.

The Koreans are of Mongol descent, a short, tough, industrious people, and good soldiers. When the war broke out in June 1950, the South Korean Army consisted of just eight divisions, all of them positioned along the 38th Parallel. Some of these existed in name only, or at little more than battalion strength, while some could muster a brigade; none had any armour or adequate artillery. Against this force the North Koreans hurled seven full-strength divisions and four brigades, all well trained and equipped with Russian T34 tanks, artillery and air support.

This is the story of the Royal Marines Commandos in Korea, but a broad picture of the war, from its outbreak to the arrival of the Royal Marines must be sketched in quickly.

Seoul fell to the North on 30 June, after four days of fighting. Meanwhile, the UN Security Council had ordered all hostilities to cease, and commanded the North to withdraw. The North igonored these appeals, and continued their advance.

The Security Council – in a decisive act which will surprise, if not amaze, those who have heard its pronouncements in the years since – thereupon called on all member states of the United Nations to render every assistance possible, military, political, economic, to the Republic of South Korea.

This UN call was promptly taken up by President Truman of the United States on 27 June, when he 'ordered the United States Air and Sea Forces to give the Korean Government cover and support'.

On the same day, the British Prime Minister, Clement Attlee, expressing similar sentiments, placed all British naval forces in the Far East under US command. It is interesting to note that by the time the Korean War ended, no less than twenty-two nations had committed troops, ships or aircraft to the struggle on the side of South Korea: the USA, Great Britain, Australia, Canada, New Zealand, South Africa, India, Norway, Denmark, Colombia, Bolivia, Puerto Rico, the Phillipines, Thailand, Ethiopia, France, Turkey, Greece, Holland, Belgium, Luxembourg and Sweden – a United Nations indeed. It will probably never happen again, but it ought to be remembered.

In the first phase of war, from June to September, the United Nations forces were in full retreat. The vast bulk of the Allied forces were always to be American, and the first to arrive in Korea was the US 24th Infantry Division, which arrived from Japan on 30 June, five days after the invasion. This Division went into action at once, but was steadily driven back, and although reinforcements continued to arrive, they could not stem the Communist advance. The 25th Infantry, and the 1st US cavalry, an armoured unit, arrived at the end of July, and the British 27th Infantry Brigade arrived in Pusan at the end of August, as did the US 2nd Infantry Division and, of particular significance to the Royal Marines, the leading elements of a very special unit, the 1st Marine Division of the United States Marine Corps (USMC).

The major task for these units was to hold the port of Pusan. If Pusan could be held, then reinforcements could come in through the harbour there in ever-increasing numbers, and a counter-attack against the Communists would soon be possible.

It was a near-run thing, but they did it. On 1 September the Communists launched one last, all-out effort to break through the Pusan perimeter, and managed to advance five miles before they were held, but held they were. With their strength growing daily, the UN forces then prepared to strike back. Two weeks later the United States Marines swept in from the sea and landed on the West coast, at Inchon; among them were a number of Commando troops from the Royal Marines.

In early August the British Admiralty had called for volunteers for raiding duties, intending to draw men from the Far East Fleet, and sent Lt E. G. D.Pounds RM out to take command. His unit, which became known as *Poundforce*, consisted of just ten marines from the Far Eastern Fleet. They spent three weeks at Camp McGill, a USMC base fifty miles south of Tokyo, learning to handle American weapons, and were then attached to a Raider company of the US Army, and embarked with them on the *HMS Whitesands Bay*. Their task was to survey the Inchon landing beaches for the 1st Marine Division; they carried out this task successfully, although their boat was holed on a reef and they came under machine-gun fire as they withdrew from the beaches where, two days later, the United States Marines came ashore.

The call to raise a larger force for raiding duties in Korea came from the First Lord of the Admiralty to the office of the Commandant General, Royal Marines, in early August 1950, when Col J. L. Moulton picked up the phone. The order concluded with the remark, 'Now let's see what the Royal Marines can do.'

At this time, 3 Commando Brigade were heavily committed in Malaya, but since the Admiralty wished to raise a Commando for raiding duties in Korea, something had to be done. Lt-Col D. B. Drysdale was ordered to raise a special unit, designated 41 (Independent) Commando, Royal Marines, at the Commando School, Bickleigh, and at Stonehouse Barracks in Plymouth.

Douglas Drysdale had joined the Royal Marines in 1935, after spending some years working on his uncle's estates in Argentina. 'My father's side of the family were Anglo-Argentine and the idea was that I would learn the business and then take over running an *estancia* . . . I loved the life, but not the people, so I came back to England, did a final year at Stowe, and then joined the Corps.'

By 1944 Drysdale was Brigade Major of 3 Commando Brigade, and served with it in Burma, under Brig Campbell Hardy, before taking over command of 44 Commando in 1945, when the Brigade was preparing for Operation Zipper, the invasion of Malaya.

'44 were not then a happy or efficient unit. I had to sack a lot of people, but we were ready for "Zipper" when the Americans dropped the Bomb. An indifferent CO can get by if he has good company commanders, but really the character of the CO is crucial to the character of the unit – fundamental, really. The whole tone of the unit is set by the CO as in civilian life – a bad managing director can't run a successful company. How do you do it? Well, by being absolutely honest. If those you command know you are straight, you are half-way there – it's slow, but it works; it also helps to have a sense of humour.'

In 1950, when the orders came for Drysdale to report to London, he was Chief Instructor of the Officers' School at Stonehouse Barracks, Plymouth, with the rank of Major. He hurried to London for an interview with Lt-Gen Joe Hollis, the Commandant General Royal Marines. Hollis told him to raise a Commando from overseas drafts and Corps establishments in the UK, for service in Korea. 41 was not to be a full Commando, but a small unit of 200 men at first, later 300, and Drysdale was given just two weeks to put it together.

'Now it's up to you,' said General Hollis. 'Interview whom you like. You will need signallers, heavy weapons, cooks . . . but get volunteers.'

Drysdale's first three recruits were Captain Dennis Aldridge, then Adjutant at Plymouth, Lt Gerald Roberts, then the Adjutant of the Commando School, Bickleigh, and Capt Ralph Parkinson-Cumine. A request for volunteers was posted on unit orders at Royal Marine establishments throughout the UK and the response was instantaneous. Capt Dennis Aldridge said: 'I wanted to join the Royal Marines to have the best of both worlds – by sea and land – and possibly to fly. In 1950, I was the adjutant of the Royal Marine Barracks at Stonehouse, when the offer of 41 Commando came along. I volunteered because, quite frankly, I was a bit bored with the job I was doing and I thought Commandos were the best thing since sliced bread. Most of my time up to then had been with Combined Ops or at sea, and I first went to the Commandos after the War, joining 44 Commando in Hong Kong.'

Among the first to apply was Colour Sgt James 'Sticks' Baines, who became the unit RSM, and the unit held its first parade at Bickleigh on 16 August, and flew out to Japan on the 1 September, in BOAC civilian aircraft. As these were flying through the air space of neutral nations it was decreed that 41 Commando should travel in civilian clothes.

'This was a small problem, and a bit of a farce,' says Col Drysdale. 'In those days, quite a lot of Marines didn't even have civilian clothes, so the Admiralty had to stump up and buy them. Then, when we got ready to fly out, half the Marines were either wearing boots or carrying kit-bags with *1234 Marine Boots* or whatever, clearly stencilled on the bottom.'

Thus, thinly disguised, the major element of 41 (Independent) Commando flew out to Japan, and made its way to Camp McGill. When 41 was finally concentrated it contained three main components: firstly, the handful of men in Poundforce, known as the Fleet volunteers; the UK contingent, and finally a contingent of specialists, taken from a draft already en-route for 3 Commando Brigade. Among these was Marine Fred Heyhurst.

'I joined the Corps in 1949 at Deal, signing on for seven years with the Colours and five on the Reverse . . . did the usual training with a six-weeks Commando course, and a Heavy Weapons Course, and was sent with a big draft to Malaya . . . you remember how it was done? We marched out of Stonehouse Barracks and down Union Street, six hundred of us behind the Plymouth Group Band. I remember it played *Colonel Bogey*. We sailed on the *Devonshire*, a troopship, from Liverpool. We had lectures on board, and learned to use and strip the jungle carbine. I'd heard a bit about Korea at Stonehouse, but I didn't even know where it was when, on leaving Colombo they cleared lower decks (i.e., ordered a general assembly) and read out a list of sixty or seventy names, mine included, for a "unit", now being formed "somewhere". That's all the volunteering I did for 41.

'For the next few days we lived on "buzzes", but all the people needed had specialist rates; Sigs, Assualt Engineers, Heavy Weapons. There was one officer, Lt Bill Pearce, and several NCOs. We left the ship at Singapore, and went directly to RAF Changhi. It took three flights over four days to get to Japan, but this included two nights at Clark Air Base in the Philippines, our first introduction to the Yanks – marvellous!

'Food in the Corps then was atrocious, but at Clark AFB it was fantastic. I remember thinking that the steak they put on my plate was for four of us – when we found out there was one each . . .! Anyway, then to Okinawa, and so to Tokyo. There was no one to meet us there, but Bill Pearce got us to Camp McGill, and then we ran into someone I recognized; he'd been a Colour Sergeant at Bickleigh when I did my training, and was to be our RSM, Jimmy Baines – he finally put us in the picture.'

As 41 was to serve with the USMC, it was to be equipped with American arms, and the men would wear American uniforms, except for badges of rank and green berets. 41 assembled at Camp McGill on 15 September, and began a frantic programme of training on their new weapons, training that frequently went on round the clock.

'I suppose there were then about 200 of us,' says Fred Heyhurst, 'organized into four fighting troops, and a Headquarters Troop, which contained Commando HQ, Heavy Weapons, Signallers, Medics, and the Assault Engineers. We had to learn American weapons, from the

M1 carbine to the 81 mm mortar and the Browning .5 machine-gun. We were training maybe eighteen hours a day, but there was a will to learn I never came across again. We were there for a purpose and if it was necessary, we'd start the drills on a new weapon at midnight, all of us, officers and the men, the Colonel, Dennis Aldridge, who was an Acting Major, and my officer, Peter Thomas, a Heavy Weapons man, the lot.

'They were a magnificent bunch,' recalls Colonel Drysdale. 'I never had any trouble with them, and they pulled together very quickly. RSM Baines was the lynch pin of the unit, then and later . . . a marvellous man. I'd met the USMC during the war and when we arrived they were all keyed up for Inchon. They asked me how long I needed to convert and train and I asked for a month.'

On 2 October, 41 embarked on two destroyers, the *USS Wantuck* and *USS Bass*, and a submarine, the *USS Perch*, for raids against the North Korean railway which, since Korea is such a mountainous country, runs close along the eastern shore. Lt-Col Drysdale took 'B' Troop ashore from the *USS Perch* and laid charges under the railway lines which were heard to detonate as the Troop withdrew, for the loss of one man. Three nights later, on 5/6 October, 41 struck again. The targets were two tunnels, both well north of the 40th parallel, well behind the enemy lines. The destroyers stayed over the horizon until dusk, before closing the coast and sending off the raiding parties in landing craft.

The Commando force, 125 Marines, led by Lt Pounds and Lt Peter Thomas, under the command of Dennis Aldridge, and accompanied by American naval officers from an Underwater Demolition Team (UDT), went ashore in ten-man inflatable dinghies, nine or ten in a line, towed by a Landing Craft Personnel. Lt Thomas left the dinghies offshore and swam in through the surf to check the beach, and as it was clear, signalled the Marines to land. 'C' and 'D' Troops of 41 came ashore a few minutes later.

Two tons of explosive were manhandled out of the boats, through the surf, up the beach and into the tunnel, and by 01.00 the Commando re-embarked. Lt Pounds was burned when cutting through some electric cables, but thirty minutes after the fuses were pulled on the charges, ' . . . a vast orange red burst of flame and a banging roar' indicated that the East Coast railroad was definitely out of action, for a time at least.

Fred Heyhurst was on this raid. 'We'd been well briefed with air photos. It was a pebble beach, hard to hump all the explosives up. We were ashore about eight hours. When we got back on board a US sailor said, "Thank God you're back, the waiting has been hell", and he gave us each a small bottle of medicinal brandy – US ships are usually dry. Next day, Corporal Hall and I were transferred to the *USS Bass*, and told to start learning how to handle a 3.5 rocket launcher; we hadn't seen one before. We took that on the second raid, stayed ashore about four hours, then we went back to Japan.'

'C' and 'D' Troops landed again the next night to blow up another section of the line, but although this time they were detected and fired upon, they withdrew into the dark without loss. Other Marines landed from the submarine *Perch*, and blew up the railway on another part of the coast, but by now, early November 1950, the UN advance had succeeded in securing the coasts and had advanced well into the North, with 10 (US) Corps, which included the 1st Marine Division now based at Hungnam.

The raiding season was temporarily over, so 41 were then sent to join the US 1st Marine Division, where they were supposed to serve as a reconnaissance unit.

The 1st Marine Division was well forward from the 10

Corps base at Hungnam on the east coast and established around a reservoir sixty miles inland from the coast at a place called Chosin. Two weeks earlier, China had entered the war in force on the side of North Korea, and in many parts of the front, the UN forces were yet again in full retreat. Although the 1st Marine Division was a strong, well-trained and well-equipped formation, their position was precarious in the event of attack, because the troops were not concentrated but strung out along the narrow road, often little more than a track, which ran from Hungnam, all the way to Chosin and beyond. The 10 Corps command did not believe that significant Chinese units had as yet penetrated this far; however, as 41 arrived to join them, the men of the 1st Marine Division were in fact about to enter the fight of their lives. The 1st Marine Division asked for 41 as a reconnaissance unit, and so 41 was shipped first to the 10 Corps' base at Hungnam, arriving there in the third week of November. The US Marines were now established with the HQ at Hagaru-ri, well to the north-west, near the Chosin Reservoir, with two regiments fifteen miles further north-west at Yudam-ni. Between Chosin and the sea were several more marine battalions at Koto-ri, while another battalion lay a little to the south of Divisional HQ guarding the road. Early on the morning of 10 November, at least two divisions of the Chinese Army struck at these scattered units of the 1st Marine Division, and blocked the road which linked them to each other, and with 10 Corps.

On that very day, 41 were due to leave Hungnam and drive north in trucks to join the Division, but when they attempted to move they found that the Chinese had already cut the road beyond Koto-ri, effectively cutting off the 7th Marines from Divisional HQ, and Divisional HQ from all contact with the rearguard at Koti-ri, and were obviously preparing to chop up the 1st Marine

Division into its component parts and destroy it piecemeal. That night, as the Chinese continued to advance and infiltrate forward to the road, 41 took up positions around Koto-ri. It was bitterly cold, and snowing.

Colonel Drysdale takes up the tale: 'The UN forces had driven the NKA over the 38th Parallel, and so, as there was no need for raiding, we were sent to Hungnam, enroute for the 1st Marine Division. We were about 300 strong by now, in three fighting troops, a heavy weapons troop and HQ. The Marine Division were all strung out on a long line of communications up to the Parallel, and had started to take Chinese prisoners, which showed that Chinese units were on our front, but no one at 10 Corps would believe us. We got up to Koto-ri where the 9th Marines were based under "Chesty" Puller (Lt-Col Lewis Burwell Puller USMC) – a great character, he became a General – and his 1st Regimental Combat Team. I liked him a lot. Chesty was as tough as old boots, and drank a lot of whisky. Anyway, Chesty sent for me and passed on the orders from General Smith, commanding the 1st Marine Division. I was to take 41, a company of US Marines and a US Army Company, plus some Marine Corps tanks, and hack through from Koto-ri to the main base at Hagaru-ri.'

When formed, Task Force Drysdale consisted of 900 men mounted in trucks with 17 tanks. Their task was to drive ten miles up the narrow road to Hagaru-ri, through the mountains and across country which was crawling with infantry of the Chinese Peoples Army, in ever-increasing numbers. Before marching out, Colonel Drysdale amazed the Americans by parading his Commando for inspection and insisting on the daily shave. 'I always insisted that my men shaved at least once a day, not in the mornings maybe, too bloody cold, but at least every day. That staggered the Americans at first, but before long they started doing it themselves – it freshens you up, that's why I did it.'

The operation closely resembled an advance up the Khyber Pass against the wily Pathans during the good old days of Empire. The Chinese, occupying the heights, were able to fire down directly into the cabs of the trucks, so Drysdale first dismounted his men and sent them leap-frogging forward, clearing the hills on either side as the column advanced; starting with 41 clearing one hill, then moving the US Marines through on to the next, then putting in the US infantry, then bringing 41 forward once again. It was sure, but it was slow and by early afternoon they had advanced only two miles. Then a message was recieved from 1st Marine Division HQ that a breakthrough that day was imperative, so the men were recalled to the road, and the entire force, mounted in the trucks, struck out towards Hagaru-ri, in the face of ever-increasing resistance, the tanks leading, with 41 Commando directly behind, and the others in the rear, all under heavy fire from machine guns and rifles in the hills on either side.

Colonel Drysdale: 'It was very cold indeed, bloody cold . . . 30 degrees below or worse, so cold you had to keep engines running all night or the oil would freeze, and water bottles had to be kept inside our Parkas. I set out to clear the heights, but it took too long, so we got back into the trucks and set out to barge our way through. The Chinese were coming closer. I saw one jump out of the ditch and chuck a grenade . . . I caught some splinters and a US Marine in my jeep (I was just behind the tanks) said, "O.K. Colonel, I'll sit here by you. Maybe God likes me better than he does you." We were ambushed several times and the Chinese finally manage to cut off Pat Oven's troop and the Army company. Pat got most of his troop back to Koto-ri after a pretty average massacre. The Chinese closed in on the road. The doctor and Ralph Parkinson-Cumine were killed there. The Chinese had two divisions up there on the heights, and once it got dark we had no air cover. We went on, forever stopping and starting.'

Dennis Aldridge: 'on the way up we were under constant attack by hundreds of Chinese, swarming down the hillside in the moolight. They were there for the shooting, but there were so many . . . I remember "B" Troop had a battle later at Chosin and they found five-hundred-plus Chinese bodies in the valley before their position, some of the Chinese wearing equipment they had taken from our dead. The USMC were absolutely splendid, but we served our purpose by showing that they were not alone – we were only 230 among what . . .? . . . twenty-plus thousand – but the effect on their morale, of having British Marines along, in our green berets, was out of all proportion to our numbers.

'I have one rather sad recollection: It was so cold, and when we arrived at Hagaru-ri I remember taking one young, wounded Marine out of a truck and dropping him into the American RAP. He seemed quite chirpy then but later on, when I asked after him, I found out that he had died. This poor kid had had the most awful wounds, but . . . well, under those thick winter clothes, no one had noticed . . .'

Fred Heyhurst was one of the wounded. 'We had our Thanksgiving Dinner, an American festival, with the USMC before we went up. It's very barren up there, mountains, the road just tracks and bloody cold. I'll tell you what I wore, right? One set Naval underwear, issue; long johns; an angora shirt, string vest, UK battle-dress; US combat-suit, a fur-lined Parka . . . eight layers of clothing, and I was *still* frozen. Their boots, Shoepacs, were useless – your feet would sweat inside and the sweat froze. You had to wash your socks out and dry them somehow – and Mum seemed very far away. My shoulders ached with the weight of my clothing and we had to keep easing the working parts of our weapons or the oil froze.'

'We had four 3-inch mortars and could see the Chinese, but the ground was too frozen to take the baseplates . . . we couldn't bed-in. I was given an LMG and went with Colonel Drysdale, though we used the mortars later to disperse the Chinese on the hills. Anyway, off we went, nose to tail in transport, under fire from the hillsides. In the late afternoon the tanks ahead shot off, and then all hell was let loose. I got into the ditch, then we went up, on in a hail of fire. I was in a 30-cwt when it happened. It was too cold to feel much, but I turned to Buck Taylor and said, "I think I've been hit." A truck ahead blew up, an ammo truck. Buck gave me morphine . . . I'd been hit in the leg. It was like the Wild West; we were the waggon train, they were the Indians . . . and no cavalry to come to the rescue. I fell out and did a forward roll into the ditch and came down right beside our SBA, Bill Stanley from Barrow-in-Furness. I was pleased to see him. "Bill," I said, "I've been hit." "No favouritism," said Bill. "See me at sick parade, eight a.m. tomorrow."

'What else . . . I remember seeing Dick Twigg, a Heavy Weapons rating, firing from the bonnet of the 30-cwt. He got the MM . . . the airstrip at Hagaru-ri all lit up like Blackpool . . . ours was the last vehicle to get in, but others came through the lines on foot later . . . we lost a lot of men though.'

Fighting every inch of the way, Force Drysdale had still only made another three miles when dusk fell, early in the winter afternoon. By now the Chinese were putting in mass infantry attacks against the column, pouring down the hillsides in their hundreds. These attacks were only driven off with the help of strafing USMC fighter aircraft, and the attackers were sometimes shot down right onto the road. The Marines still kept going, against all odds, and at 01.30 that night, the survivors entered the Marine Corps perimeter at Hagaru-ri, still full of fight.

Force Drysdale had lost 321 men and 75 vehicles, but as the USMC account records, 'To the slender garrison of Hagaru was added a tank company and 300 seasoned infantry.'

'The British Marines were the only ones to make it and still join us in condition, and willing to fight,' wrote a USMC sergeant later. 41 had, however, suffered heavy losses; 61 men, killed, wounded or missing out of the two hundred who had left Koto-ri that morning. The Chinese had also succeeded in cutting the road and splitting Force Drysdale in two. Those cut off were wounded or killed, with only a few survivors (including Captain Oven's troop), after leaving a group of soldiers who were preparing to surrender, making it back to Koto-ri. This incident provoked an interesting exchange between Corporal Dave Brady of the Assault Engineer platoon and Captain Ovens. 'Look here, Brady,' said Ovens, 'never mind what they do . . . We're British, and we're not going to surrender.' 'Well, actually sir, I'm half-Irish,' said Brady. They both got back to Koto-ri.

While the USMC evacuated the wounded from Hagaru-ri, and held the base perimeter against strong Chinese attacks, their advance regiments fought their way back down from Yudam-ni, while the remnants of 41 joined in the perimeter defence and on the day after their arrival, staged a counter-attack back down the road to drive off a Chinese attack.

The position of the 1st Marine Division was still precarious, and their main tasks were first to hold the Hagaru perimeter until the Regimental Combat teams of the 5th and 7th Marines could fight their way back from Yudam-ni, where they had been under heavy attack for several days. 41 Commando went out to meet the Marines coming from Yudam-ni, and as their unit history recalls, 'those who were privileged to meet them will have an abiding memory of the splendid USMC infantry marching into Hagaru alongside their wounded, after fighting for a week in sub-zero weather, driven by a screaming north wind.'

With the bulk of the Division back within the Hagaru perimeter, the next task was to break out to the sea.

Col Drysdale: 'Hagaru was a very big perimeter, and we held our share of it, did fighting patrols and so on. It was still terribly cold and so we had warming tents, where you could, in small numbers pull back and get warm for a while. They were still working on the airstrip, and we got the wounded out by air.'

Fred Heyhurst: 'It's a bit of a blur after that, but Bill McKay, one of our sergeants, got me off the 30-cwt and into a hut. Then, the next thing I remember, I was in the morgue. I came round in a hut, or tent, surrounded by corpses. I got out of there quick. We were carried down to the airstrip that night, British and US wounded, and counted off into loads, the count for the first flight stopping just short of me. That aircraft took off and flew straight into the hillside. I flew back to Japan and into hospital, hobbling by then. The bullet fell out of my clothing a week later, having gone right through my leg and stopped in my thick clothing. I gave it to my nephew when I came home.'

'X' Corps authorized the USMC Division to abandon its equipment and return with all speed to the coast, but Gen Smith decided against this suggestion. At dawn on 6 December, after a week at Hagaru-ri, 41 had shrunk to about 100 men, and on that day the 1st Marine Division, now amounting to about 10,000 men and 1,000 assorted vehicles, set out for the sea, bringing with them their weapons, their wounded, even their dead. Since the word 'retreat' does not figure in the USMC lexicon, this move was referred to in General Smith's orders as 'an advance to the sea' or 'an attack in a different direction'. The advance would be led by the 7th Marines, while 41 Commando formed up with the 5th Marines as part of the rearguard, and so the 'advance' began. It was a great feat of arms. The temperature was well below zero, the enemy active, the odds considerable. 41 and the 5th Marines held the Hagaru-ri perimeter while the Divisional column got under way, beating off attacks until dawn on 7 December. When the Chinese finally drew back, 600 dead lay in the snow before the Marines' position. Two hours later 41 and the Marine rearguard began their withdrawal, but they were now cut off from the rest of the Division, and had to fight their way through a roadblock, which was only cleared after another two-hour battle. In the early dusk, 'C' Troop of 41 left the road to attack Chinese machine-gun posts, and fought its way back to the rearguard perimeter well after dark, arriving at Koto-ri where they were met by Captain P. J. Ovens and twenty-five Royal Marines, who had fought their way back there after being cut off in the convoy battle of the previous week. When 'Chesty' Puller at Koto-ri reported the strength of his command to General Smith, he found it worthwhile to mention that his garrison of 4200 men included 100 Royal Marines.

This long fighting 'advance' down 'Hellfire Valley' has become a classic in the annals of the USMC, which records that even as the Chinese scattered the column here and there, so the Marines would form fresh defence perimeters, beat off the attack and then 'withdraw' over the hills, in the dark or hidden by blizzards, and made their separate ways down to Koto-ri. Here there was still no rest for 41 Commando, which was sent to hold the high ground above the road, and stayed up there all night in two feet of snow, as the temperature plunged to minus 20 degrees Celcius.

Next morning, stiff with cold and gaunt from lack of

sleep, the 5th Marines and 41 left Koto-ri at 09.00, and after one brief fire fight at the head of the pass, the 1st Marine Division reached the 10th Corps perimeter at Majong-Dong.

Dennis Aldridge: 'The march out – we were getting the usual sniping as we left, and Colonel Drysdale sent out a party to chase them away, a group of about 30 men with no support, just sorting out the enemy and coming back, doing it all the hard way, on foot. I hate napalm, but My God, it saved my life up there. When we got back to the coast, I slept for twelve solid hours.'

41 and the 1st Marine Division had been marching and fighting for three days and covered some sixty miles. Apart from the wounded, many men were now suffering from frostbite or exposure, but like the 1st Marine Division itself, 41 still remained intact as a fighting unit. For their part in this epic struggle, 41 (Independent) Commando were later awarded a US Presidential Unit Citation, and a host of other awards, British and American, for the officers and men.

Much reduced, 41 was withdrawn to Japan to rest, re-equip and receive more men, among them Eric Blyth, a volunteer from 42 Commando, who arrived from Malaya to serve in the Heavy Weapons Troop of 41. 'I volunteered while I was with 42 in the jungle, when I heard they needed Heavy Weapons rates, and found them at Wonsan, after Chosin was over. Lt-Col Drysdale was a gentleman and a fine officer; he made us shave and keep ourselves smart, which made the Yanks look up anyway. I arrived in a New Zealand frigate with the beer, very popular. 'Sticks' Baines was the RSM and Peter Thomas the HW Officer. We had 81mm mortars and two .50-calibre machine-guns, lots of firepower to strafe targets on the mainland. 41 Commando were an excellent unit, good in its role, but I'd rather have the jungle, when you're on your own more, in little units and patrols. I'll tell you something else . . . I did thirty-eight years in the Royal Marine Commandos, and you want to know if it was worth it? Yes, every second.'

Colonel Drysdale remembers one incident in Japan. 'I have to say how well we were looked after by the USMC, and by our own Ambassador to Japan, Sir Julian Gascoigne. Shortly after we returned from Chosin, we received an invitation to a cocktail party at the Embassy, requesting the presence of "Colonel D.B. Drysdale RM and 41 (Independent) Commando, Royal Marines". I looked at this for a while and then I rang Mary Follett at the Embassy and said, "This is a bit ambiguous. Does he mean the whole unit?" She said, "His Excellency means the whole lot." So we put the 300 of us into trucks and off we all went to the Ambassador's cocktail party, hurling down his Dry Martinis impeccably.'

By April 1951 the unit strength was up to 300, and 41 were ready to go out again. Since the Chinese had now pushed the UN forces south of the Parallel again and re-occupied much of the coastline, 41 had trained yet again for coastal raids.

Early that month 41 landed on the east coast of Korea near Hungnam, drove off an enemy patrol that came to investigate, and blew several gaps in the coastal railway line. Then, after returning to Japan, the Commando began to prepare for a more ambitious undertaking. In July, 'C' Troop landed on Yodo Island, in the area of Wonsan harbour, eighty miles behind the enemy lines, and set up a base. In the next few weeks other Troops of 41 occupied other islands near Yodo, with 'E' Troop getting established on Modo, although they were shelled from the mainland, and from other islands in Wonsan Harbour occupied by the enemy. 41 were joined in these operations by South Korean Marines, who added their .5 machine-guns to the armament of 41's Heavy Weapons

Troop. The Mortar platoon were particularly active at Wonsan, setting up night fire bases on islands close to the mainland, and subjecting the enemy batteries to a thorough bombardment, before slipping away at first light. This activity and probing raids along the coast soon obliged the North Koreans to reinforce their positions, and by September there were heavy troop concentrations on the mainland. Ships supporting and supplying 41, which included the cruiser *HMS Belfast*, were subjected to shellfire from coastal batteries, but 41 continued to go ashore on the islands or on the mainland, often by canoe, losing two men killed and twenty wounded during their time in Wonsan.

Dennis Aldridge again: 'We spent Christmas with the USMC and the British Embassy in Tokyo were marvellous to us. In the New Year we went back to Japan, into a tented camp, and when we left, we left it spotless – another thing the USMC thought was marvellous. Their General, O. P. Smith, said to us, "Anyone can live in a shithouse, but you guys really keep things neat and really comfortable." Then we were in a Commonwealth Division camp for a while, and did another raid, nothing overwhelming, and then to Wonsan. One of the islands in Wonsan Bay was a leper colony. We raided the coast in craft of all sizes, from canoes to LCAs, and generally made a bloody nuisance of ourselves to the Chinese.'

In December 1951, 41 Commando, now commanded by Lt-Col F. N. Grant, handed over their base at Wonsan to South Korean Marines and withdrew to Sasebo before returning to England where it was formally disbanded at Plymouth, on 22 February 1952.

41 Commando had been first raised during World War II and was to re-appear again in the 1960s, but few periods in the ever-eventful life of this particular Commando can

match that of Korea. As always, there is a price to be paid: 31 men were killed in Korea, or died in captivity, while 17 more spent harsh years in Korean prison camps before returning to Britain, and many of the unit were wounded. In return, 41 Commando gained a Presidential Unit Citation, and among other awards, a DSC and two Silver Stars for Col Drysdale, and MC and a Silver Star for Dennis Aldridge and Gerald Roberts, MCs for Captains Marsh and Owens, and Military Medals and Bronze Stars for many NCOs and Marines, including RSM Baines, and the DSM for QMS R. R. Dodds – a total of 30 assorted decorations in all.

However, perhaps the best appraisal of this remarkable unit can be given by the men who served in it, or saw it in action. Col Drysdale: '41 was undoubtably the best unit anyone could hope to command . . . they did everything I ever asked of them.'

Dennis Aldridge: 'What do I think of 41 Commando as a unit? In all my years of service, it was probably the best unit I ever served in – it had many great people in it – we produced at least seven RSM's for the Corps, and as you know, the Warrant Officer is the backbone of any organization and the RSM is the supreme example of this. The other day, I got a note from Fred Heyhurst, telling me what had happened at the last 41 Reunion when the pennant from the *USS Perch* was presented to the Royal Marines, and Fred said, ". . . even if only two of us were left alive, we'd still get together", and that's my feeling too.'

Fred Heyhurst: 'With twenty-three years' service in the Royal Marines, I know that 41 was a unit second to none.'

General O. P. Smith of the 1st Marine Division USMC: 'I am familiar with the long and glorious history of the Royal Marines. The performance of 41 (Independent) Commando will take equal rank with the past exploits of the Corps.'

Finally, a member of the USMC who saw the 'Chosin

Few' in action: 'May a poor, slogging American Marine say a word of thanks for a job well done? I walked into Hagaru from Yudam-ni, where I learned that the British had supplied us with a fighting force. Before that, we laughed at the words "UN Forces" because we had not seen troops of any other nation, except the Chinese. I was delighted to meet the British. When they came around you could stop looking for a fight, because they would be right in the middle of it and none wore a helmet, just a green beret. I have never been to your country, but if I ever come to England, I'd like to say thank you to every man in 41 Commando and then look up the man who sent 41 Commando to the 1st Marine Division, and thank him too.'

10

Cyprus and Suez, 1955–56

Our business, like any other, is to be
learned only by constant practise and
experience; and our experience is to
be had in war, not at reviews.

General Sir John Moore, 1801

After leaving Malaya, in June 1952, the 3 Commando
Brigade returned to the Mediterranean, and made its
home in Malta, which, with frequent excursions to other
Mediterranean countries, would be its principal base for
the next nine years.

The Brigade's stay in Malta was significantly marked in
November 1952, when HRH The Duke of Edinburgh,
who was later to become Captain-General of the Royal
Marines in 1953, arrived in Malta to present Colours to
the three fighting units of the Brigade, in a colourful
ceremony on the parade ground at Floriana, where the
Brigade paraded under the command of Brigadier J. L.
Moulton, CB DSO, OBE, sometime CO of 48 Royal
Marines Commando.

There was an element of politics in this ceremony, for
the future of the Royal Marines, and especially of the
Brigade, was, yet again, coming up for review at the
Admiralty. 'The truth of the matter was,' says General
Moulton, looking back, 'that if the Board had the choice
between a new ship or a Commando, they would go for
the ship every time.' There is something faintly
anachronistic about the Brigade in the 1950s. It was a

strange little force, a relic of World War II, that had somehow lived on into another era, transported about the world in a small flotilla of ageing ships, but somehow managing to retain its fighting edge, and its sense of humour.

In May 1953 the Brigade, still commanded by Brigadier J. L. Moulton, was widely dispersed, with 45 and the Brigade HQ in Malta, 42 field-firing near Tarhouna in Libya, and 40 taking part in a Combined Operations exercise in Cyprus from *HMS Striker* and *HMS Reggio*, when the bugle blew again.

The Brigade was hastily summoned back to Malta and sailed for the then British-garrisoned Suez Canal Zone. This Zone or strip of land ran down the Canal and was then owned and occupied by the British under the terms of a long-standing treaty with Egypt, which recognized the fact that the canal itself was owned and operated by the British and French owned Suez Canal Company. Talks between the British and Egyptians with the aim of handing over the Canal Zone to Egypt had broken down and violence threatened. 3 Commando Brigade were sent to reinforce the garrison and stayed in the Canal Zone for the next fifteen months.

Lt Michael Marchant was there with 42: 'I joined 42 in Malta, where they were commanded by Peter Norcock, and went with them to the Canal Zone. It wasn't much of a campaign, mainly IS (Internal Security) work, stopping the 'Klefti-wallahs' digging up the communications cable, and cutting off large sections.' Lt Marchant was a sniper-trained officer, who went on to win the Service Rifle Championship at Bisley in 1956.

The Brigade's return to Malta in August 1954 was signalled by the departure of 42 Commando to Britain, and a memorable two-night street brawl between the Marines and the Maltese police . . . 'one of several that have occured during 3 Commando Brigade's time here,' as *The Times* put it. In fact, such incidents are only notable because they are rare, for Royal Marines usually get on very well with the local people, and rarely fight among themselves. However, clashes with the Maltese police, or with the crews of visiting ships, were certainly not unknown.

'I remember the CO getting us on parade one morning at St Andrew's Barracks,' said Terry Brown of 42 Commando, 'and telling us about 45's latest battle honour, St Paul's Bay – that was the time your lot threw a piano off a roof, and the street below was full of black and white keys.'

Terry Brown also recalls a memorable night on shore patrol. 'I was sent out with an old three-badge Marine, who had served in Malta before, and had no intention of poncing about the town telling other Marines to put their berets on straight. He led me straight to the Klondyke Bar in Floriana, where we removed our RP armbands and white gear and settled down to booze the night away. We had collected an impressive array of Anchor beer bottles, when we were joined at the table by a large drunken sailor from the American Sixth Fleet, who wanted to know where we'd been. "Korea and Malaya," said the three-badger briefly. "That's nothing," said the Yank loudly. "I've been to twenty countries . . . I've been to Spain, 'n Italy, 'n France, 'n Greece," emphasising each place by poking my companion in the chest. After about ten countries, the old Marine got up and punched him in the mouth. The whole place then errupted into the sort of brawl that any film director would have paid good money for, while the Shore Patrol, him and me, beat a hasty retreat out the back door . . . it was a fitting introduction to the rather dull delights of Malta.'

The conclusion of the 1954 brawl, which raged up and down the 'Gut' and King Street in the Valleta, was that the Brigade was confined to Barracks, while 45 Commando were ordered to Troop their Colours, 'in full blues and white gear', after which, with 42 now in England, 40, 45 and Brigade HQ departed for exercises in the Libyan desert, at Tarhouna well south of Tripoli, where they remained until Christmas.

1955 began with the depleted Brigade back in Malta, and continued with various exercises, notably a visit to Arzew in Algeria, before another emergency arose in Britain's now rapidly shrinking Empire, this time in the Crown Colony of Cyprus.

Cyprus is a long, beautiful, mountainous island. From the top of the Troodos mountains in the centre of the island it is possible to make out the shores of southern Turkey, only fifty miles away to the north. In the Middle Ages, Cyprus belonged to the Venetians, but the Turks captured it in the sixteenth century and held it until the nineteenth, when it came into the possession of the British. Although it has never belonged to Greece, it still contains a large Greek population, and with the British withdrawing from all their colonial possessions, the Greeks on Cyprus made a bid, not simply for independence but for *Enosis*, or union with Greece, This, needless to say, did not please either the large Turkish minority on the island, nor yet the government of Turkey itself, just to the north. The seeds were there for yet another bitter colonial struggle, which broke out with the usual rash of riots, ambushes and shootings, in August 1955.

RSM F. C. Townsend recalls his first journey to Cyprus: 'I can't remember now whether it was *HMS Triumph* or *HMS Ocean*, which transported 3 Commando Bde HQ from Malta to Cyprus to deal with the EOKA troubles, but I remember the LAD (Light Aid Detachment), of which I was then OC landing at

Famagusta and motoring through to Limassol, where we made temporary camp in one of the villas just off the beach.

'We hadn't been in Cyprus very long before we moved up to Polhemedia Camp on the outskirts of Limassol, where 40 Commando had their lines. It was a tented camp and facilities, such as galleys, wash-places and showers, were pretty scanty and in poor condition. As always in these circumstances, it fell to the LAD and the unit tradesmen to try and improve conditions. At the time we had as Engineer Support a tremendous character by the name of Reg Orton, a WO2 QMSI RE. Reg was a hard-drinking, hard-swearing, down-to-earth chap, who approached everything with a laugh. As an engineer he needed some beating, but as a scrounger he was un-equalled. Reg reckoned he knew the Civil Engineer in charge of the Camp from way back and so he set about talking him into letting us have the pipe, timber and corrugated sheeting that we needed. At the same time, and to ensure that we finished up with enough of every-thing, he planned it so that on the first run he would keep the CE talking whilst we raided the dump and got away with a buckshee load. It worked a charm and with what we got we were able to set the camp up with decent showers and wash-places and improve the galleys. There was only one problem out there, with the pipes all laid above ground – it was very difficult to ever get a cold shower.

'We ran a very lively Sergeants' Mess there. One par-ticular evening we were celebrating the award of two 'Blues' (LS and GC medals), and the RSM of 40 Com-mando, Percy Bream, and one or two others, came across from the adjoining camp to join in the fun. QMS 'Dodger' Long, the LAD electrician, one of the re-cipients of a 'Blue' finished the evening up a tree echoing Tarzan, while Percy was wheeled back to his own lines in a wheelbarrow – or at least, he thought they were his own lines. Having arrived at what he said was his own tent, he was duly tipped in, only to find that it belonged to the Brigade Major. With much beery apology he stumbled out, realigned his compass and staggered off into the night.'

The Brigade, now consisting of 40, 45 and Bde HQ and now commanded by Brigadier Rex Madoc, received the order to move to Cyprus on 6 September. The main body embarked on ships of the Amphibious Warfare Squadron, and *HMS Birmingham* later that day, and four days later the first troops of 45 Commando were deployed and on patrol in the Kyrenia mountains.

'The Troop Sergeant-Major grabbed me as I got out of the transport at Aghirda and told me to take my section up the mountain and stand guard that night, while the unit – mostly "S" Troop – pitched camp far below. We trailed up there and were out all night . . . it was quite uneventful for a while. Then an Army Kinema Company van arrived, and showed the unit *Seven Brides for Seven Brothers*. We could hear the music clearly and fought each other for the use of my binoculars to see the screen. Half-way through the show the unit had to rush off after some terrorists who had escaped from Kyrenia castle; it was over twenty years before I finally saw that Howard Keel movie.'

Sgt Eric Blyth was in Cyprus with 40 Commando. 'My boss was P. R. Thomas, OC of "S" Troop, and we operated up to and around the monastery at Kykko, out of Paphos. One day, we slid into the monastery dressed as tourists, and stayed in overnight for a look round . . . found a lot of compo rations but not much else.'

Priests were frequent supporters of the terrorists, but their clerical garb did not always ensure them undisturbed passage, as when a carload of monks arrived at a 45 Commando roadblock set up by Sgt Tom Powell of 'B' Troop.

'Out!' said Tom, 'and quick about it.'

'His Beatitude does not like this,' protested the driver.

'I don't like his B-attitude either,' said Tom, 'now hop out quick, the lot of you, and let me search this car.'

The Brigade were widely deployed, with 45 in the Kyrenia mountains in the north-eastern corner of the island, and 40 Commando and Brigade HQ in Limassol. Both units were involved in the usual weary round of Internal Security duties, guards, day and night patrols, road blocks, cordon and search operations, and controlling riots, of which 40 Commando, based in the large town of Limassol had more than their fair share. The terrorists, who had laid low when the Brigade first arrived, soon began to strike at the Commando units. In November 1955, a National Service NCO, L-Corp Maghee, gained a well-deserved Queen's Commendation for Brave Conduct, when the lorry in which he was travelling was ambushed in the Troodos. The truck was loaded with explosives for the local asbestos mines, and in spite of continuous enemy fire, Maghee climbed back into the cab and drove the truck out of the ambush zone, even though a bullet had knocked a large section out of the steering wheel. Maghee had been in the Corps just over a year and had been in the middle of his Junior NCO's course when the Brigade moved to Cyprus.

The main terrorist offensive against the British was organized and spearheaded by EOKA, the Greek Cypriot terrorist organization, led by a Colonel Grivas. EOKA enjoyed considerable support from the local people, and its members had moved at will among the mountain villages around Kyrenia and the Troodos, until 45 came on the scene. Three months of constant patrolling, or on 'cordons and search' operations, with troops or sections of marines based in all the villages in the Kyrenia range soon reduced EOKA's effectiveness in this area, and so in November, 45 moved south to the centre of the island, into the main Cyprus range, the Troodos mountains, which rise to over 6000 feet are under snow for much of the winter.

Operations continued up here throughout the winter,

during which parts of 'X' Troop of 45 were transferred on the 'from here to the left' principle, into ski-troops, and supplied with skis found in a store at the winter sports centre at Platres. After two days' ski instruction from a young cavalry Cornet from the Blues, 'X' Troop took up ski patrolling with enthusiasm, and were given the task of delivering explosives and detonators to the asbestos mines at Amiandos, which the Commando had taken over in case this material was used to manufacture bombs.

'They would ring up from the mine and say how much blasting they intended to do, and the Assault Engineer Officer would check the calculations on explosives needed, and then we would take it down. I have never been much of a skier, but I still don't fall much. When you have learned to ski while carrying a rucksack full of fulminate of mercury detonators, you tend to stay on your feet.'

Patrolling in the deep snow and bitter cold of winter in the Troodos was hard work. Two men died of exposure in February 1957, when their truck broke down, as RSM (T) Townsend remembers. 'The LAD didn't appreciate being stuck in Polhemedia Camp and I kept angling for a move to a more active sector. The opportunity came when 45 Commando moved into the Troodos and took over the Platres region. We took over a small garage and forecourt at the lower end of Platres and were kept very busy, as much with recovery as with straightforward repair work. The terrain was typically mountainous; well wooded with narrow winding roads, containing many steep sections and quite a few hairpin bends. It required only a slight loss of concentration for a driver to find his vehicle off the road and in trouble and recovery was always "exciting". In this area there were villages thought to be friendly and other known to be distinctly hostile, where you could be pretty sure of getting a few stones chucked at you on the way through if not something more substantial. We invariably went out as a two vehicle team for mutual support. One particular job landed us deep in the Paphos Forest, where a three-tonner had broken down. We were stoned on the way out, but without damage. On finding the truck it was clear that we would have a hell of a job towing it out, because it would mean pulling it up a very narrow logging track cut into the side of the hill with an untold number of sharp slopes and bends to negotiate. Examination of the truck revealed a blown head gasket, repairable if we could get the spares. Unfortunately, we had no signals communication, so we had to despatch the Landrover back to camp to get what we needed, running the gauntlet both ways. By the time it returned we were running out of light, so we completed the repair but I decided it was too risky to attempt the run home in the dark and so we set up defensive positions and settled down for the night.

'The journey back up the logging track next morning was hair-raising. The steering lock on the old Austin Recovery was notoriously poor and there were times when it was necessary to back and fill on the corners with the outer wheel dangerously close to the crumbling edge of the track. The driver of the Recovery vehicle was a Marine named Lloyd, a most untypical Marine; always scruffy, excused boots, large glasses, a beret several sizes too large, the last person in the world you would want to go to war with, or so it seemed.

'On return to camp I reviewed the orders for teams going out on recovery and made arrangements for a signaller always to be included to ensure communication with camp. Not many weeks later, I was on my way back to Malta aboard *HMS Chaplet*. There I would rejoin my wife and daughter and fly back to England to be commissioned. As I came down the gangway my wife rushed up to me with tears in her eyes and told me that Alf Wheeler, the RSM (T) I had just turned the LAD over to in Platres, and a friend of very long standing, was dead; frozen to death in the snow on the Troodos. It was some fourteen years later, when I was serving on the staff of CGRM that I came across the full story. One call for help had already been received that day and answered, and then came a call for recovery somewhere up the Troodos road. Out went the Austin K6 with Marine Lloyd driving, accompanied by the RSM (T) Marine Blakeway, and three others, but no signaller. They were clad only in their normal working clothes and light overalls, suitable for work in Platres but totally unsuited for the Troodos at that time of year; we had already had a foretaste of snow in December and now it was early February. Some miles from Platres they ran into heavy snow and were finally forced to stop by the drifts. Why they didn't settle down to weather it out or make for the village only a short distance up the road ahead was never answered. The wrecker was always well stocked with provisions and the means of brewing-up but for some reason the decision was taken to abandon the vehicle and strike back to camp.

'They had not got very far when it became clear that the RSM and Marine Blakeway were slowing the party right down, so Lloyd took on the task of bringing them on while the others went ahead to fetch help. Before long things were desperate, the RSM could go no further, and so Lloyd settled the pair of them down under the slight cover of a bush with instructions to try and stay awake while he went on. It was Lloyd, the scruffy, excused boots Marine who was one of the two who finally made camp and raised the alarm. The search party found RSM (T) Wheeler and Marine Blakeway dead from exposure but happily the remaining two were discovered in time, sheltering in a hut, still alive but very weak.'

Eric Blyth remembered the fires that swept the

Troodos in the hot summer of 1957. 'Frightening . . . I never saw anything like it, and a lot of men got caught in them and died. I said to myself when I was caught, that if you don't panic, you'd get out – those who panicked didn't.'

When Summer came, nineteen men were lost when a forest fire broke out during a combined Marine/Army cordon and search operations. But trouble was brewing elsewhere in 1956, and in the summer the Brigade returned to Malta and began intense amphibious training for a serious operation of war.

Under the terms of the Anglo-French-Egyptian Treaty, British troops finally withdrew from the Suez Canal Zone in May, 1956. Eight weeks later, breaking the Treaty, President Nasser of Egypt seized the Canal and nationalized the Suez Canal Company. This was 'twisting the lion's tail' with a vengeance, and plans were swiftly made to mount a military assault against Port Said and repossess the Canal. As the months wore on, while this course of action was deliberated and forces gathered, two further strategic and political events began to obscure the Suez issue. The Hungarian people rose up against the Russians in September 1956, and were ruthlessly suppressed in Budapest by the Red Army. At the same time, the second Arab-Israeli War broke out, with Israeli units soon advancing rapidly across the Sinai, towards the Canal. Rumours abounded, and still abound, that the Anglo-French attack on Suez was made in collusion with the Israeli pre-emptive strike against the Egyptians. In addition, the Anglo-French expedition against Suez was both unpopular, at home and abroad, and widely condemned, particularly by the Americans. In the middle of all this, training in Malta for the task to come, was 3 Commando Brigade, joined for the operation – code-named *Musketeer* – by 42 Commando. The Suez landing was originally code-named Operation Hamilcar, which explains the rather baffling fact that all vehicles bound for the landings bore a large white 'H' painted on their sides.

Lt Marchant went out with 42: 'I had just got back from my honeymoon when I received a telegram instructing me to report to Stonehouse Barracks in Plymouth and take charge of a draft. This I did, and we embarked with 42 Commando for Malta. I fetched up with 45 Commando and I carried the Regimental Colours when 45 Trooped their Colour just before we sailed for Suez. My wife arrived in Malta on 29 October, and I was given the weekend off the settle into our little flat in St Pauls Bay, just down the road from Ghain Tuffeiha. We had done a lot of training, with 6 RTR and the anti-tank platoon of the Duke of Wellingtons, while I took charge of the unit snipers . . . anyway, I settled my wife in and on Monday morning I was standing outside the flat waiting for the bus, when Major Ian D'eath came along in his Volkswagen, and stopped.

"What are you doing here?" he asked sharply.

"Trying to get to camp, sir," said I.

"Don't you know that the Brigade are embarking, and about to sail?" I didn't. There was some frantic packing before I joined the unit, embarked with helicopters on *HMS Theseus*.'

Michael Jones was a National Service Marine in 40 Commando. 'I was in "Y" Troop, with Captain Morgan as OC. We formed up at St Andrews and went onto LSTs, living on the tank deck with the vehicles. We tested weapons, but spent most of our time queuing for meals, which took hours. We had practice firing on the Oerlikon anti-aircraft guns, bloody noise, like being inside a biscuit tin, and as we sailed along, more and more ships arrived, including carriers and a French battleship, the *Jean Bart*'. An instruction had been issued that, in the event of hostilities, no guns larger than 6-inches were to be used by the Anglo-French forces – an instruction that banned the *Jean Bart's* main armament.

It was now eleven years since the end of World War II and there was little left of the vast amphibious forces that had largely won that conflict. The naval force that moved against Suez still had plenty of ships, including carriers and the *Jean Bart*, but the landing ships were all of World War II vintage and showing their years, while amphibious techniques were not always efficient.

'I doubt if the ships were properly combat loaded, and that did cause some confusion on landing. I remember one officer looking at the tanks crammed on with the troops in an LST and saying, "Well, we've got them on, now it's up to some other bugger to get them off."'

The Amphibious Warfare Squadron now numbered some twenty ships, and was led by the frigate, *HMS Meon*. Apart from the old faithful LSTs *Striker* and *Reggio*, there were LCTs, motor launches and a troop of fifteen armoured amphibious vehicles, or Buffaloes, from the Royal Armoured Corps, which would take the Marines ashore.

There were eventually seven carriers, *HMS Eagle, Albion, Bulwark, Theseus* and *Ocean* these last two with 45 Commando and the French *Arromanches* and *Layfayette*, carrying a total of 215 aircraft. The total British forces for Suez totalled 45,000 men, with 12,000 vehicles, 300 aircraft and 100 warships. The French added 34,000 men, 9000 vehicles, 200 aircraft and 30 warships. 3 Commando Brigade totalled 2800 men.

The Egyptians had an army of eighteen brigades, and sent several to Port Said, including some artillery units armed with British 25-pounders and Soviet 122mm cannon. They had a good airforce, with over 200 combat aircraft, including MIG 15s and 17s, as well as seventy bombers.

'Telescope', a last-minute variation to the original 'Musketeer' plan called for the 3rd Bn, The Parachute Regiment, to land on Gamel airfield, 5000 yards west of Port Said on D – 1. At H-Hour on D-Day 6 November, 40 and 42 Commandos, with tank support, would land in amphibious vehicles on the beach just north of Port Said, with 42 Commando turning west once off the beach, and advancing to meet 3 Para at Gamel. Meanwhile, 45 Commando would be at sea as floating reserve, and if committed, would come in by helicopter to an LZ (Landing Zone) close to the De Lesseps statue at the head of the Canal. This helicopter landing of 45, would be the first helicopter assault in military history. While the British troops were assaulting Port Said, French forces, including parachute units of the Foreign Legion, would be landing at Port Fouad, on the eastern bank of the Canal.

The days before the landing, as the invasion fleet moved east from Malta, were full of uncertainties, as order and counter-order came from Whitehall, the Russian massacred the Hungarians in the streets of Budapest, the Israelis thrashed the Egyptian Army in Sinai, and resolutions and condemnations of the Anglo-French attack poured out of the United Nations. Among limitations reaching the invasion force was a refusal of air support, and a ban on all naval gunfire in support of the landings from naval guns larger than a 4.5-inch calibre. In fact, it was only one hour before the landing that, after persistent pleas, Brigadier Madoc, commanding 3 Commando Brigade, obtained a promise of fire support at all.

As the invasion fleet sailed east, the men of 45 got down to learning about helicopters, under the guidance of Lt Marchant.

'I was appointed the Unit Emplaning Officer, and my first task was to work out the "sticks" or loads, to get the various Troops ashore in the proper order – it seemed terribly dull. On *Ocean* we had Whirlwind helicopters of 845 Squadron, while *Theseus* had the Joint Experimental Helicopter Unit (JEHU) aircraft, a mixture of Whirlwinds and Sycamores... and JEHU had a different configuration from the Fleet Arm types; the Fleet Air Arm types took seven, the JEHU five, and the Sycamores only three, but we got it all worked out in the end. I don't recall seeing any helicopters in Malta, so I am sure that for most of the unit their flight ashore into action at Port Said was their first-ever flight in a helicopter. I remember three things about the voyage: playing pontoon in the Gun Room – we lieutenants were not allowed in the Wardroom – putting all the clocks onto GMT the night before the landing, and getting a signal which said that the *JEHU* was now the Joint Helicopter Unit and no longer "Experimental". Plans changed every hour, and we got very little sleep.

'One unexpected diversion was the appearance of units of the American Sixth Fleet, which signalled *HMS Ocean*, "What ship? Where Bound?" – to receive the reply from *Ocean*, "What Fleet?" *HMS Meon* then signalled "Why don't you join us?" "No thanks, we'll hold your coat" came back the reply, and the Sixth Fleet ships altered course and sailed away.'

Frigates, supported by air strikes, bombarded the landing beaches from 06.00. As 42 and 40's landing craft inched their way in at H-Hour (06.45) the bathing huts at the back of the beach were well alight and a tall, spreading pillar of smoke from blazing oil tanks, spread a useful smoke screen over the shore. Fortunately, the beach defences were unmanned, and the defenders put up little resistance, enabling both the Commandos to get ashore intact. At 07.00 their tank support came ashore in LCTs, and once these had formed up, at H + 90, 40 Commando moved off. 'P' Troop led 40 out from the beach-head, with 'Y' Troop in support and, in spite of growing volume of small arms fire from the tenement buildings and side streets, the advance went well, all the way down the canal side to the Suez Canal Company offices.

Mike Jones went along with 'Y' Troop. 'We went ashore in LCAs. There was a bit of fire on the way in, but not very accurate . . . down ramp, out troops . . . we went through the beach huts, and spread out going to ground along the road, taking a few practice shots at the large street lights. There was very little enemy at this stage. We went on, keeping the Canal on our left, with more fire from the side roads, so we edged over to the Canal. We were pinned down by fire from a tall building across the main road, and took cover behind a wall, which blocked our advance until we breached it with a brace of Energa anti-tank grenades. Then we had our first casualty, the No 2 on the Bren, shot through the head, as we tried to get along on the pontoons. I suddenly realized that the funny plopping sound was bullets hitting the water. I got the hell back to the Troop, which called up a tank, and the tank fired to cover our advance to the Suez Canal Co's offices. There was some opposition here from men in blue battledress. The Stengun is not very effective – it took most of a magazine at 20 feet to stop one man. I saw another picked off by a Bren burst. We got into the Canal offices – we cleared one ground floor room of occupants with a 36 grenade, then we got the Egyptian flag down by shooting the rope and toggles away.'

Sergeant Eric Blyth, late of 41 (Independent) Commando, and the campaign in Malaya, was now Mortar Troop Sergeant in 'S' Troop of 42. Sergeant Blyth had a particular interest in supporting the unit's fighting troops for his brother Bert had now joined the Corps, and was somewhere up ahead, with 'P' Troop. 'We came ashore from LCAs off *HMS Striker*, and I bedded in the mortars in the beach, and then went to join up with Bert and "P" Troop as MFC (Mobile Fire Controller). I stayed with them most of the day, but I remember being up on the roof of the police station, spotting with the binoculars, when a man with a rifle said, "Make room", and I looked round to see the Commandant-General of the Corps, General Campbell Hardy, up there with the lads. When I went back to bring the 3-inch mortars forward from the beach that morning, I saw 45 coming ashore in their helicopters . . . Lofty Impett, a mate of mine, got shot in the guts and was lifted out to the carriers by helicopter. Poor old Lofty, he got hit everywhere he went.'

'B' Troop now took the lead, while the rest of the Commando got down to street fighting, winkling out snipers and grenade throwers from the buildings; two officers of 'Y' Troop, 40 Commando, Lts McCarthy and Ufton were killed and two Marines wounded in the fighting around the Canal Company offices, but in the mid-afternoon 'X' Troop 40 Commando put in an attack with tank support and overran the Post Office buildings in Navy House Quay, killing most of the defenders.

42 Commando, packed into Buffalo amphibious vehicles, moved out of the beach-head at 09.30, led by a tank, with 'B' Troop's leading driver anxiously asking his Troop Commander, Captain Derek Oakley, if he should stop at red lights and drive on the left. A sergeant of 45 Commando recalls clearing a house of snipers, and bumping into one of his Marines, who complained that the people in the flat below wouldn't answer the doorbell. 'Not only that, but when I stormed down to smash the door in myself, I found it was made of glass! I slammed my rifle butt through it, kicked the frame in and told the Marine not to be so bloody wet . . . we took our two Egyptians from there, each armed with a rifle and a box of grenades.'

'B' Troop's tank ran past the agreed rendezvous, and had to be chased down the road by the Troop's amphibious vehicles, but otherwise the 42 advance went well; 'X' Troop of 42 captured a power station, while 'A' Troop became involved in a very noisy battle with some Egyptian troops in the central market.

45 Commando, waiting on the carriers *HMS Ocean* and *Theseus* were ordered ashore at H-Hour + 55, just before seven o'clock in the morning.

'It was a beautiful day as we came up on the lift onto the flight deck. A big cloud of smoke hung over the town on the skyline, one or two ships were banging away close by, and the choppers were lined up along the deck, rotors whirling, all ready to go.'

The emplaning officer, Lt Marchant, watched his unit fly away with increasing gloom. 'Fortunately, a Sycamore took off, hovered, then crashed back onto the deck . . . the Marines crawled out unhurt, but I had to get busy and re-allocate the sticks. So I didn't feel entirely useless. Then another helicopter just fell out of the sky a few hundred yards off the deck – not hit, just running out of petrol – they all got out all right as well. We had wounded coming back within forty-five minutes, in fact one Marine got ashore, got wounded and came back in the helicopter all within fifteen minutes or less; we sent him to surgery down the bomb lift. Anyway, after the Unit had gone, I jumped into a helicopter and it put me ashore by the fish market. There was a tall building there with two bloody great shell holes in it, below which a Maltese family were distributing cups of coffee, so the first thing I did on landing at Port Said was to have a cup.

'What else do I remember? Lt Peter Thompson – we called him "Gin" because he loved the stuff – and I had nothing much to do so we mooched about a bit. Peter Montgomery was seen driving about Port Said during the battle in an Italian Fiat – the MPs ran him in for it. Two other officers found a rather splendid oil painting of a nude, which they smuggled back onto *Theseus*, and presented to the gun room. I remember that the "Cease Fire" came at about midnight and how desperately disappointed we all were.

'Until we withdrew, 45 HQ was in a school. We did the usual IS work, patrols and guards, but it was getting increasingly nasty, with ugly crowds forming very quickly. A young Army Officer, Lt Moorhouse, was kidnapped and murdered after the ceasefire. We sailed back to Malta on the trooper *Devonshire*, an excellent passage, and got there towards the end of November. Then we went back to Cyprus and formed the 45 Heliforce.'

45's CO, Lt-Col Norman Tailyour, made an eventful recce of the proposed landing ground in a football stadium, to find it obscured with smoke, cluttered with telephone and power wires, and under heavy rifle fire from the stands and buildings round about. The Colonel's recce party scrambled hurriedly back into their helicopter, and found another landing zone by the statue of de Lesseps, the builder of the Suez Canal, where the first wave of 45 landed at 08.15. This change in plan caused consternation in at least one helicopter, when the pilot came up on the radio after the take-off to ask the Marines he was carrying ashore where they wanted to go, but in just over an hour the Whirlwinds and Sycamores had put 415 men ashore with all their equipment. This force included the dauntless General Campbell Hardy, now Commandant General of the Royal Marines, who had come from England to join his men in action and landed from an LCA. Three helicopters were hit by ground fire, but once ashore 45 were quickly in action, although their first casualties were due to an accident when their advancing column was strafed by a Fleet Air

Arm Wyvern fighter, which injured eighteen men, including Lt-Col Tailyour.

Lt Marchant arrived at the HQ immediately after this accident: 'I then went to find Commando HQ, and I actually saw the Wyvern coming in, which zapped 45's Tac HQ, arriving there just after it happened; the scene was one of shock and confusion. The CO had been hit and Dick Crombie, the Second-in-Command, took over. A number of signallers were hit and a lot of chaps were lying around with nasty injuries. I don't recall having any first-aid training, but we did what we could, and evacuated the wounded. John Weston, the Intelligence Officer, had been hit, so I became IO next day.

45 Commando moved west, into the centre of Port Said, clearing a tall, seven-storey building as they went, using the gunfire of their supporting tanks to smash in steel doors and shutters. A fire broke out in the Shanty Town to the west of Port Said, but 42 broke through to join up with the 3 Para early in the afternoon, leaving over 150 Egyptian soldiers dead in the streets behind. The Navy House, which had been strongly defended, fell to 40 Commando, and by 19.30 the bulk of the fighting in Port Said was over.

Marine Mike Jones again: 'After we took the Canal company offices, we took over the bonded warehouse as our base, where some liberation of the duty-frees became popular. There were airstrikes going on now, some of them pretty inaccurate. That night, the firing went on for a while, with Vickers MGs on fixed lines firing into the flats. On Day 2, the Paras came into the town in comandeered vehicles, plus engineers from the ships who shuffled along in plimsoles and started on repair work. The French didn't like the "gyppos" one bit – we could tell that from the way they drove trucks right through crowds of them.

'On Day Six or thereabouts, we gathered at the docks,

for the return to Malta, much and varied was the loot carried by all, but just outside Grand Harbour there were rumours of the police and SIB, so much ditching of valuables over the side, money, guns, jewellery, goodies of all descriptions, but definitely cars came back, plus – it is thought – a yacht.'

The Commando Brigade, with the Paras and other infantry units, including the Royal Scots, stayed in Port Said for the next week, searching for arms and enduring sniper fire, but the political will to continue the advance down the canal to Suez had gone. The Anglo-French forces withdrew, handing over to multi-national UN Forces around D + 8, when 40 and 45 withdrew to Malta, followed later by 42 which then returned to England, as the other two units returned to spend the winter in Cyprus where the Brigade would be engaged on operations on and off for the next three years. 3 Commando Brigade lost 9 killed and sixty wounded during that violent day in Port Said, about fifty per cent of total Anglo-French losses.

When 40 and 45 returned to Cyprus, winter had set in, but the skirmishing with EOKA continued. 'Like all such campaigns,' writes one 45 Commando NCO, 'it was a Corporal's War, of guards, and patrols and road blocks, and bloody hard work. Some bright spark had introduced the idea of "repat troops", where all those coming out at about the same time went into one Troop, on the theory that they would already know each other. This meant that we had one Troop pig-ignorant, one Troop half strength since the others had gone home, a shortage of NCOs and a lot of work. That and the weather was killing. I slept under seven blankets at Platres and I was still cold.'

Mick Jones again: 'My section were sent up Mount Olympus to guard the radar station; there was plenty of snow on the ground and the huts were thick with it. We managed to nick enough skis to form a ski patrol . . . the RAF were very nervous at stand-to I remember, the only light relief was a trip to the local village for a night on the Keo brandy or the visit of the whores bus, which wasn't allowed in the gates . . . very chilly. There wasn't much light relief, for the deaths continued, by ambush or accident.'

Lt Marchant: 'We got the hang of helicopters at Port Said, so on our return to Cyprus we formed 45 Heliforce, with our area of operations in East Cyprus and our base on the airfield near Nicosia. It was said that the Whirlwind could not operate at altitude, so our first task was to fly up and land one on top of Mount Olympus, over 6000 feet.

'In many ways though, it was a terrible time. We learned by mistakes. I remember one tricky operation in the Panhandle, when sending troops to form a cordon round a supposed terrorist group. The map reading has to be spot on, and we were jubilant when we got the report, "Contact opening fire", then sounds of doubt . . . it turned out that one "stick" had been landed in the wrong place. There were no terrorists but the cordon shot up and killed Snowy Baldwin, a super Sergeant, and another Marine, while a couple of others were wounded.

'Our CO, Colonel Jack Richards, was badly injured when his helicopter lifted off just as he was roping down to the ground. He fell and severly injured his feet and ankles . . . then I got ambushed. I was at Troodos and was given command of the company – we were re-mustered in companies by then I think – while the OC was on leave. My first thought was to go out to Agros and meet the boys, so I went in my Champ with a quarter-tonner behind as escort vehicle, with a Marine as passenger, riding shotgun. As we went through a village, a lorry appeared in front of us and shot off at speed, rather surprisingly, so we went after it, getting further and further away from the escorting quarter-tonner. Finally, before we caught it, the lorry shot off down a side road, so we slowed for the escort which hurled up, lights flashing, horn going, and said we had driven through an ambush. I suddenly realized the Marine was sagging in his seat, shot, and in a very bad way . . . he was dead when we got him to hospital. We went back to the ambush position and found a ten-pound explosives charge and two grenades lying in the road, none of which had gone off.'

Cyprus kept the Brigade occupied during the last years of the 1950s, but the following decade was to see many changes in the stucture of the Corps, and fresh fields for the fighting units.

11

Aden and Borneo, 1960–67

The old order changeth, yielding place to new . . .
Lest one good custom should corrupt the world.

Tennyson: *Idylls of the King*

The 1960s were eventful years in the ever-eventful life of
3 Commando Brigade. Their period of duty in Cyprus
ended in April 1959, and the formation entered the new
decade with 42 Commando back in UK, and the rest of
the Brigade in Malta. The Suez operations and the work
of 45 Heliforce in Cyprus had put new thoughts into the
minds of Britain's amphibious warfare specialists and, as
early as 1957, a few months after Suez, the Admiralty
designated *HMS Bulwark* as a Commando ship. The
work of conversion began at once and 42 Commando
embarked for a commission in the Far East in March
1960. Next year, a second Commando ship, *HMS
Albion*, was put into commission, and the expansion of 3
Commando Brigade into a small-scale replica of its
mighty cousin, the United States Marine Corps, began in
earnest. An Air Troop was added to each unit, flying
small helicopters; in 1962, 29 Regiment Royal Artillery,
became a Commando unit, armed with 105mm pack
howitzers, followed later by the 95th Commando Light
Regiment, Royal Artillery. In addition to these artillery
units, two fresh Commandos were raised by the Corps,
reactivating the honourable names of 41 Commando,
reformed in 1960, and 43 Commando, raised again in
1961. The units expanded in size, changing from the

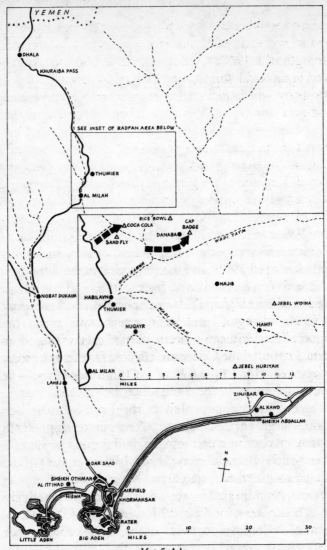

Map 5 Aden

old troops into a company formation, although the word 'troop' was retained to describe a platoon, with the total strength of a 1960s Commando set at 680 men, organized in three rifle companies, each of 109 men, a support company which included a reconnaissance and assault engineer troop, an anti-tank troop as well as heavy weapons troops and an HQ Company. Future developments include the creation in 1972 of the Commando Logistic Regiment, the 'Loggies', and two squadrons of Royal Engineers, all having passed the Commando course and wearing the green beret. Command structures also changed, with HQ Commando Forces, being established first at Stonehouse Barracks Plymouth, then at Hamoaze House, Mount Wise where it still remains. As a final landmark, 1964 saw the Tercentenary celebrations of the Corps, marked by a representative parade in the garden of Buckingham Palace, among many other events.

These changes, and this expansion, were not accomplished without a certain number of teething problems. On board the Commando ships, for example, some doubt existed as to the role of the Commando, and who was in charge of it, the Colonel or the Captain.

'This arose,' says one officer, who prefers to remain anonymous, 'because certain naval captains regarded the Commando as the ship's armament, like guns, or aircraft, over which he, the Captain, had ultimate control – and one can see a certain similarity. A number of COs were certainly disconcerted by receiving an order to parade the unit so that he – the Captain – could inspect "his Commando". The snag was that a Naval captain with sufficient seniority to command a capital ship, usually outranked a Lt-Col of Marines – quite apart from the fact that they thought they were God anyway. Wherever possible, we tried to embark our Brigadier, and that usually did the trick.'

Introducing Royal Marine pilots to the Commando

Air Troop could also be eventful, as Major Ian Uzzell recalls. 'My aviation service began in 1965, and I was in the penultimate week of my pilot's course when the crash happened. We were asked to do a night cross-country flight, first of all with an instructor and then, later on, solo. It was a three-legged course, of which the middle leg was along a ridge 600 feet high. The dual trip caused no problems at the height to be flown, 1800 feet. On the first leg of my solo flight, I went into a cloud at 1500 feet and as the Sioux is without blind flying instruments, I rapidly descended out of the cloud and levelled out at 1200 feet. I reported this on my radio and was instructed to continue. I reached the first check point without further incident and set course for my second leg along the ridgeline (near Wilton in Hampshire). As this was 600 feet high, it gave me only 600 feet clearance above the ground. On this leg I ran into a heavy rain shower and lost outside reference points. I was asked my weather situation on the radio and reported bad visibility. It was just after that, that the helicopter hit the ground, cartwheeled and disintegrated, leaving me strapped in the seat. I lost consciousness for a short time. When I came round I unstrapped myself and got out of the helicopter. I was in some pain due to mainly internal injuries and debated with myself whether to remain with the helicopter until help came or go and find help. It was very dark and I was in the middle of a ploughed field. The predominant thought was that I should stay as I had signed for the helicopter and it was therefore on my chit (Royal Marines are *very* stores-conscious). But then I felt that no one would find me there and started out for some lights I could see. If I had continued on that course I would be dead now. I stopped after 50 yards and turned to look at the wreckage. I saw car lights on a track the other side of it, so decided to try and head it off. It was about 100 yards to the track and through a barbed wire fence. I decided to lay across the rutted track to stop the vehicle – which fortunately did stop. I asked to be taken to hospital but was told that the car was full – but they would go along the track and see if they could locate any help. Luckily we had a Landrover along the track looking for me and they took me straight to Salisbury Hospital, where two large cuts on my hand were sewn up and I was operated on for a ruptured spleen. They pumped four and a half pints of blood into me – so if it had not been for the car on the the track, I would not be alive now.

'In February 1966, I was proclaimed fit to fly and was allowed to complete my course, qualifying for my flying badge on 2 March 1966.'

Expansion, re-organization and accidents apart, there were still wars and rumours of wars to keep the Royal Marines Commandos busy. In June 1961, the Ruler of Kuwait, in the Persian Gulf, requested British help urgently to deter a threatened invasion from nearby Iraq.

This request arrived on 30 June, and the follow-up gives some idea of the speed with which Commandos can move. On 1 July the first Marines arrived by helicopter from *HMS Bulwark*, followed by ships of the Amphibious Warfare Squadron, which disembarked tanks of the Carabiniers. On 2 July, the Marines from *HMS Loch Alvie* came ashore to join 42, while on 3 July, 45 Commando completed its arrival by air from Aden. By the 7th, a sizeable British force was deployed in the desert to protect Kuwait, and the Iraqi invasion threat collapsed.

In January 1964, another alarm flared up in East Africa, when President Nyerere of Tanzania reported increasing unrest in his Army, and made a request for British help. 45 Commando, then in Aden, were hurriedly embarked on the carrier *HMS Centaur*, and by 24 January were lying just below the horizon, off the coast of Zanzibar. The Commando was told to act at midnight and went ashore in Wessex helicopters at first light, surprising a mutinous battalion at the Colito barracks near Dar-es-Salaam, and supressing the mutiny at the cost of two mutineers killed. On the same day, another battalion was disarmed at Tabora, three hundred miles inland, and the whole mutiny brought under control by the evening of the 27th, to the great satisfaction of President Nyerere.

During this time, two other and far more serious struggles were in progress – in Aden and the Radfan, where 45 Commando were engaged; and in Borneo, where 40 and 42 Commandos with many Army units, fought out an undeclared jungle war with the armed forces of Indonesia.

Aden, in the days of Empire, fell into two main parts, the Aden Colony, and the Aden Protectorate. The Colony was a Crown Colony, about seventy square miles in area, on the eastern shores of the Red Sea south of Saudi Arabia, and had been a coaling and oil station for the British Royal and Merchant Navies for over a century. The Protectorate was much larger, ran inland for about a hundred miles, and covered an area the size of England, which was crossed by one major road which led to Dhala on the frontier with Yemen, about ninety miles from the coast.

The problems that initiated the troubles in Aden were, as was usual in the declining or post-Colonial period, complicated by local divisions, tribal, ethnic and religious. In this case, while the British clearly intended to withdraw, the problem was who would take power when they had gone? The existing treaties in the Protectorate were with autocratic, often feudal sheikhs, who were under strong pressure from nationalist elements among their own people. In addition, the British had created trade unions in Aden, which were now clearly left-wing inspired, and eager to see both the British leave and scores settled with the local sultans. Into this simmering brew stepped the long-suffering British Army and our particular concern, 45 Commando, Royal Marines.

45 arrived in Aden in April 1960, to relieve an army battalion guarding the important oil refinery complex at Little Aden, with two Troops detached to Dhala, up on the frontier, to guard against insurgents crossing into the Protectorate from the Yemen.

The uneasy situation in Aden finally exploded in violence in December 1963 with a bomb attack on the British High Commissioner. Rioting and grenade attacks became common in Aden and Little Aden, but the bulk of the action initially took place up on the frontier east of the Dhala road or in the stark mountain country of the Radfan, six thousand feet above sea level, where dissident tribesmen could assemble to raid the road and shoot up the convoys that passed along it.

These Radfan tribesmen were, according to one 45 officer, 'a xenophobic lot ... every man had been equipped from boyhood with a rifle in his hands, knowing how to use it, and frequently doing so if any argument had to be settled. The arrival of the British Army in the area was seen as another chance for some target practice.'

These tribesmen had once earned a useful living extracting tolls and tribute from caravans on the Dhala road and, with Yemini help and knowing every inch of the ground, mining the road and ambushing convoys, they soon had Dahal cut off and the garrison on the defensive.

Robin McGarel Groves, who served long tours in Aden first as Second-in-Command, and then as Commanding Officer of 45, gives a description of a journey up the Dhala road.

'Ever since 45 Commando had been in Little Aden, one troop had been stationed at Dhala, some ninety miles north of Aden and only a few miles from the border with Yemen. Having sorted out most of the administrative problems concerning a new Second-in-Command in Little Aden, it seemed time to visit Dhala; so I arranged to join the next convoy.

'It was about 4 a.m. when the 45 Commando part of the convoy formed up. It consisted of three 3-tonners and my Landrover. It was not yet light but in Little Aden the flame from the refinery never let it get really dark. We moved off from the sleeping camp, past the refinery and the few shops in Little Aden and onto the 20-mile tarmac road leading to big Aden. It was cool enough to wear a denison smock, yet the air was fresh and as we drove along the various smells associated with the area were quite distinct. The oily smell of the refinery was replaced by what is best described as 'night-soil', as we passed various small villages. As we passed the largest of these at Hiswa, there were quite a few signs of early morning activity, but no attention was paid to our passage and we went on our way to Lake Lines, an Arab barracks, outside of which the convoy was being marshalled.

'The bulk on the convoy consisted of Aden Protectorate Levy (APL) vehicles, as HQ APL were changing over their battalion at Dhala. In addition there were a number of Scout cars from the APL Armoured Car Sqaudron. We did have one distinguished visitor from the War Office, complete with brass hat and he was put in the centre of the convoy for maximum protection. He had come out to see how the British Officers seconded to the APL were getting on and to learn at first hand of their problems. Bringing up the rear of the convoy was a vehicle full of likely vehicle spare parts and a Scammell Recovery Vehicle.

'At about 6 a.m. the order was given to start up and then to move off. We passed through Sheikh Othman, the furthest point reached by the invading Turks during the Great War, through Dar Saad, best known for its licenced arms dealers, and the border village between Aden Colony and the Western Aden Protectorate. Beyond there we were into the desert. There were still traces of the tarmac road built by British troops for the Great War advance on Lahej, 20 miles North of Aden; but it had become badly potholed, so we ran parallel to it, throwing up great clouds of dust. The convoy got steadily more spread out as drivers tried to avoid the dust of the vehicle in front. The desert was relatively featureless except for the odd well near the road, with mounds near it from a long disused caravanserie, usually sprinkled lavishly with pot shards. Apparently, it is almost impossible to get on or off a camel without breaking something.

'As we approached Lahej there were signs of cultivation and greenery from the dried-up Wadi Tiban, which when in spate finally reaches the sea at Hiswa. The rains up-country had ceased, but the dried-up wadi bed was still moist enough for crop growing. Lahej looked like an Arab town ought to. Near the gateway was the Sultan's Palace, built four-square of stone, with crenellations on top and narrow slits for windows, outlined in whitewash to draw in the light. Most of the houses looked as though they had been built with an eye for their defence, for they had the same thick stone walls and narrow windows. There were also lesser buildings built of mud brick, colour washed in ochre and pink and sometimes decorated with designs in black. During the Great War advancing British troops occupied Lahej after the Turks had withdrawn. In the confusion, following the great privations suffered by British troops from the heat and lack of water during the advance from Aden, the Sultan of Lahej, who was our ally, was shot by a British soldier during one of the less glorious episodes of British history in Aden.

'The streets of Lahej were narrow and only just wide enough for our vehicles to pass. Beyond was more cultivation with a very dusty track winding through fields separated by high banks to catch and retain the water when the wadi flooded. Soon we were once more out in the desert and approaching the foothills. At Nowbat Dukaym were further relics of British encampments from just after the Great War. Only the surrounding barbed wire, protective walls and shells of huts remained of what must have been a distinctly dreary duty. At Nowbat the track divided. To the left was the road to Taiz in the Yemen. To the right was our road to Dhala.

'After Nowbat Dukaym the track followed a wadi bed, which still had the odd pool of stagnant water, where birds and frogs abounded. This track washes away regularly every time it rains. The Turks must have experienced the same problem for on our left were the remains of the road they built to supply their troops attacking Aden over 45 years ago. Although built on higher ground, sections had been eroded so as to make it impassable. The wadi bed was a brilliant yellow, contrasting with the dark rust red of the surrounding country. Soon we started to climb and the first of several breakdowns occured. Some were punctures and easily fixed. Others were more serious, such as broken springs, but the recovery team at the back of the convoy had been this way before and nothing seemed too much for them. The convoy had, however, got very strung out.

'At Al Milah was a small Army camp and a Police post set in a pleasantly green cultivated area in the Wadi al Milah. From now on there were pickets visible on the hilltops for the basic rule in this country was that to hold the high ground was vital. At Thumair, about the half-way mark, the convoy halted to top up with petrol and water, to allow time to eat a bag ration and to let stragglers catch up. Our VIP was complaining bitterly about the dust. Thumair is the centre of the Qataibi tribal area, with a bad reputation for molesting travellers. This was the cause of several British punitive expeditions earlier this century. Just beyond Thumair we saw a dead donkey off to the right of the road, literally covered with vultures. On our approach, gorged with meat, they ran across the plain, trying to gain airspeed, reminding one of a heavily-laden Walrus amphibian struggling across the water, trying to get airborne.

'The track became progressively more bumpy as the hills closed in around us. Many more pickets were visible. We passed several small villages perched on hills, well sited both for defence and surface drainage. As we approached the foot of the Khuraiba pass, one could see that the pickets were wearing green berets, presumably men from our Dhala troop. The Khuraiba Pass is a fascinating piece of engineering. The track is cut into the side of the mountain with a sheer drop on one side. It also contained a number of hairpin bends, some so sharp that for a 3-tonner to get round involved making what was in effect a three point turn; but instead of a curb to stop you when reversing, there is only the sheer drop, with one or two burned-out vehicles below to encourage you to be particularly careful. One young marine literally froze at the controls, the engine revving and the clutch slipping. With some trepidation, someone had to climb in alongside him, ease him out of the driving position, and with his assistance outside, negotiate the vehicle around that hairpin and hand it back to him.

'We had a short wait at the bottom to allow two Arab vehicles to complete their descent and for a camel caravan to get clear. There was much greenery at the bottom of the pass and fascinating weaver bird nests hanging from many of the thorn trees. Frogs were croaking in the stagnant pools and there was a general smell of rotting vegetation. At the top of the pass we did not wait for stragglers, but proceeded independently to the Royal Marine Camp at Dhala. The rest of the convoy went to the APL camp.

'Our camp was situated on a low mound, flattened at the top. The accommodation was in tents, with sandbags at their sides as protection against the tiresome local habit of peppering the camp occasionally at night. The galley and showers were of corrugated iron. Old hands always enjoyed watching young Marines at Dhala for the first time, go to the galley to collect their meal, only to find it snatched from their plate by one of the many kites flying around overhead. The camp was at about 4500 feet, the air was marvellously fresh and clean after Little Aden. On another flat mound about a mile away, was the APL Camp, laid out similarly to our own. About half a mile from each camp was the town of Dhala, with the Emir's Palace and those of his family on another low ridge, with the rest of the town on the lower slopes. All the houses were solid square stone-built towers. Defence in this area was vital for survival, as the many bullet pock marks provided ample evidence. In those days there was a small colony of Jewish silversmiths, famed for their intricate filigree work. One wondered from which lost tribe they came. Most people spending any time at Dhala came back with some filigree work for wives or girl-friends and I was no exception. Dominating the Dhala plateau and towering above it was the Jebel Jihaf. From the Officers' quarters in the morning, the view was breathtaking. The morning light gave the mountains a blue-grey colour. The central feature was a great outcrop standing out and above from the main feature, like the tower of some great cathedral. On one side was what we knew as the Shute, which was the approved way up and down and was a good fitness test for newcomers. About a mile from the camp was a gravel airstrip, where every day a Twin Pioneer aircraft landed to bring up fresh provisions, mail, and those who did not have the time or inclination to come by road.

'Captain Lionel Edwards was commanding the Dhala troop and made me most welcome. He gave me a good look around the area, including the picket positions by the Khuraiba pass. I was fascinated to see a herd of baboons, which he said was quite a common sight in that area. In this environment it was easy to keep fit as everyone took so much exercise, patrolling by day and by night, and if that was not enough, playing volley ball until it became too dark to see.

'The time passed all too quickly, and in two days it was time for the return convoy to leave. Once again we had an early start, forming up at the top of the Khuraiba pass. Our VIP had prevailed upon the Convoy Commander to allow his Landrover to follow immediately behind the leading APL scout car so as to avoid the dust thrown up by the 3-tonners. I did what I was told and took my place in the middle of the convoy, which was just as well as it turned out. When the convoy was just short of Thumair the whole convoy stopped and there were sounds of rifle fire, followed by bursts of machine-gun fire, presumably the latter from the escorting scout cars. There were only two casualties on our side, the War Office Brigadier and his driver. Fortunately neither of them was seriously hurt and both were evacuated by a Twin Pioneer aircraft, called up by radio to the emergency landing strip at Thumair. The Brigadier had a flesh wound on his ample midriff and presumably would dine out on this story for many months to come, on his encounter with the Qataibi and the problems of British officers seconded to the APL.

'The rest of the journey, being all downhill, was relatively uneventful, but still very dusty. The bottom of the welcome shower after arrival in Little Aden indicated just how much of the Dhala road each of us had brought back with us. Nine hours was about par for the trip in either direction.'

George Newman first went to Dhala as a Marine. 'I was drafted to Aden, 45 Commando in November 1963. It should be remembered that Marines are drafted as individual people and not as a regiment like the Army. I found it terribly difficult leaving my wife who was by then expecting our first child. I remember stepping off the plane mid-day in Aden; the heat was terrific, even though I had known what to expect from my visit on *Bulwark* – I was still surprised that I could be so hot in November. We were met by a 3-ton truck and driven out to our barracks, some 20 miles out across the causeway from Little Aden. Our camp was lines of prefabricated huts with four-man rooms, air-conditioned. It was next to a large BP Works where a 100-foot pylon burned off gases twenty-four hours a day. I was to find out that it was our only source of lighting at night, and very effective. In fact, when the Arab dissidents were to start launching the odd attack on us at the barracks, we would have preferred to extinguish the damned thing.

'When we arrived, the Company we were to join was "Y" Company at Dhala. For a week or two we acclimatized, getting used to the extreme heat, swimming at our nearby beach (we had a choice of two – one was widely used and a smaller one was available if we wanted to swim nude, the aptly named "Bare Arsed Bay").

'When the next convoy went up to Dhala four of us went with it. Again, I was happy to be teamed up with my brother-in-law, Marine Peter Kelly. He and I were fortunate enough to travel up on a truck full of mattresses, lying on top of them with loaded weapons. The 3-ton trucks had no canopies, the heat would have been too intense inside them. Then again, they may have protected us from the traditional stoning when we passed through Arab villages. The trip to Dhala was some 90 miles, most of it rough, bumpy road. When we reached the Khuraiba Pass, which was the start of the very mountainous Jebels region, vigilance was necessary. It was an ideal place for an ambush, or for the narrow, extremely rough road to be mined. It was a long, hard climb to the top of the pass and we were always aware of the havoc an ambush could create.

'Once at the top and aboard the trucks, we found the climate more agreeable. It was slightly more fertile and cooler. This was the norm for Dhala, and a favourite posting, as each Company took its turn, six weeks each. My first sight of Dhala was the impression of a temporary encampment on a long hill. On my next tour of duty I was to see a dramatic difference, literally a fortress, impregnable by an army attacking on foot. It should be remembered that during 1964 the situation got worse and worse, and the sandbagged walls of Dhala went higher and higher, as the dissidents attacked with first rifles, building up to mortars. The lifestyle was different, still a disciplined force, but a relaxed approach. Dhala rig was khaki floppy hat, sides generally sewn up cowboy style, no shirt, khaki shorts, boots with grey socks rolled down over them. Patrol rig was the same, with the addition of a shirt. All webbing, pouches, packs, straps, belts etc., were drawn from stores on a G1098 chit. It was always referred to throughout the Corps as G10 gear. On my arrival at Dhala I was placed in a section (10 men) and the Corporal in charge promptly left for England. As the longest serving Marine in the section with good conduct, I was promoted to L/Cpl. At that time we had Bren-guns in each section (magazine fed). The GPMG (belt fed) came in mid '64.

'That first tour of duty in Dhala was an experience. We patrolled to show the flag, got shot at only once, and kept fit by playing hours of volley-ball under Dhala rules, which meant virtually anything went, fists through the nets etc. Local Arabs visited the camp selling their wares, the Emir gave us a cow (live) for Christmas dinner. It was promptly painted red, white and blue and became such a fixture that local Arabs had to kill it for us as we hadn't the heart. We had a pack of dogs, fairly big Labrador types, which although they were Arabian, hated all Arabs. They had found that the white men treated them with love, which they could never find with the Arabs, who were actually very cruel to them.

'For a period I was at barracks; another Company had gone up to Dhala. We trained every day – weapon handling, tactics, and maintained a high standard of fitness. We had a scramble course over the Jebels leading down to the beach. We used it on many occasions to relieve boredom. Our NAAFI was basically open-air – a roof over it, with a low wickerwork-type windbreak. The windbreak had large holes in it where many a man had been punched through it. Many millions of cans of lager were drunk, the object was for each table to pile up empty cans until they reached the roof. We had an open-air camp cinema which was well used; basically, besides drinking, it was our main source of recreation. Tombola was played in the galley once a week – it had a particular fascination for the Arabs who filled the hall.

'While I was in Singapore, 45 Commando were sent up to the Radfan, where the dissidents had been roaming in bands of 100-200. They had killed some SAS men who had been living rough, keeping an eye on the situation. I was flown up to my Company and naturally was pleased to join them again. The Radfan area had been cleared of its population. It was our job to try to catch the rebels. It was a vast, inhospitable place, very craggy, rough terrain, little, if any, vegetation. We generally lived in Arab houses, from which we launched patrols twenty-four hours a day virtually. Really, we policed the area. Eventually the large marauding bands of Red

Marines of 42 Commando patrol the backstreets (Aden, 1967).

Personal search of civilians in Aden by a patrol of 42 Commando, 1967.

45 Commando patrol on the jabel near Dhala, Aden.

Jungle patrol of 40 Commando.

'Hearts and minds' in Borneo (2nd Division, Sarawak, 1966, with 40 Commando Air Troop).

A strong point in Borneo.

Lieutenant Uzzell in a 41 Commando OP, Divis Street Flats, Belfast, October 1969.

Street patrol, Belfast, 1969. Lieutenant Uzzell took these photographs to brief his Troop before their tour, hence the annotations.

BUTLER ST

CHATHAM STREET

→ N

BROOKFIELD ST

BUTLER ST

BUTLER ST

CRUMLIN ST

'For putting out burning Marines', Belfast, 1969.

Royal Marines Commandos embark for the South Atlantic.

Keeping fit and ready for action on the way: Falklands-bound Marines on SS *Canberra*. (*Photo P&O*)

Royal Marines Commandos yomp into Stanley, 1982.

Briefing for battle: Commando 'O' Group on the Falklands.

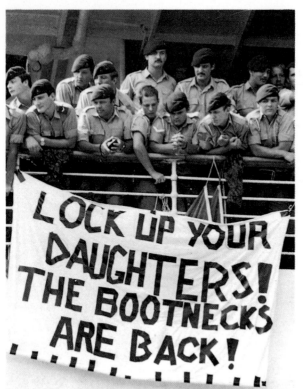

'You have been warned'. 3 Commando Brigade on SS *Canberra* returning from the Falklands.

Wolves were broken down into little groups. They preferred to snipe at us from long range, their .303 rifles (bundocks) had extended rear ladder sights for long range shooting. They were good shots, but we were better. We were supported by artillery, Saracen tanks and scout cars. Air support was provided by the RAF Hunters (Jet fighters), helicopters and small army Scout helicopters. Indeed, at one time we had one of our sections fired on by our tanks by mistake. Luckily no one was killed, but there were a couple of serious injuries and concussions. We moved generally at night. I took my turn taking my section out to some specified area. We would lie out for a few days, either in a deserted village, or we would simply build a sangar (a low, wide wall and a shallow dugout) suitably camouflaged. The idea was to ambush the ambushers, to turn the tables. There was one famous incident when we hid out in a large house for a few hours at night. We saw what appeared to be an Arab approaching and shot him to bits . . . it turned out to be a white-fronted cow.

'We learned the hard way that should we move by day, it was essential that we took the high ground. As we moved along wadi bottoms, our troops would move with us on the high ground on either side. The Arabs used a very heavy explosive bullet at times and we weren't keen to stop one of them. We were once fired on by a large group from hilltops ahead. We called up RAF Hunters to support. They flew over our heads, firing their cannons at the dissidents. Unfortunately their ejected empty brass cases rained down, hurting our troops.

'At that time we looked more like guerrillas; we couldn't wear our green berets. The Arabs feared us so much that if they suspected 45 Commando was in the region they wouldn't come near us. Our big problem when sleeping rough was to find a place to sleep comfortably, due to the rough lava rock. I've seen men having a violent row over who had claim to a flat piece of rock. We never concerned ourselves about the scorpions, camel spiders, or poisonous centipedes. It only rained once while I was there, extremely heavily for about half an hour. The Arabs relied on deep wells for their water. We relied on our rear echelons for water. When deep in the Radfan, loads of water were dropped in by parachute. We found a thin-skinned silver square container named a "flimsy" better than jerry cans. Besides, if a parachute overshot and got lost, flimsies were cheap to lose, but jerry cans were expensive.

'We regularly carried out a sweep on villages, searching in case dissidents were hiding up. We were very tough if we suspected a deserted village was being used. We didn't hesitate to wreck or burn; on occasions we called in air support and they used their rockets to good effect.

'The overall picture was of 45 Commando companies scattered in the Radfan, sending out sections to enforce curfews and to try to capture dissidents. I think we had reasonable success in keeping the Radfan cleared and peaceful. The dissidents had no chance against our weapon superiority and skilled troops. But they were brave enough to try, albeit generally by long range sniping.

'It was a hard life for us, extreme heat by day, freezing at nights. We were often thirsty and hungry but I can say that we were never bored. We walked every part of the Radfan, every day brought something different, but morale was never low. We lost very few men, but took our toll on the dissidents.

'"Y" Company then faced another tour of duty at Dhala. This time the situation had changed. We faced hostility wherever we went. One particular village en-route to Dhala always attacked our convoy viciously with stones. We turned the tables by stowing piles of rocks under our seats, and as soon as the crowds massed to stone us, we bombarded them. We found that they liked to dish it out, but couldn't take it. The Dhala road was more perilous all round than months before. We had to approach it tactically, especially the Khuraiba pass.

'When we reached the camp, we were amazed at the difference. It had always been secure, but was now a fortress, surrounded by an 8-foot thick wall of sandbags. There was only one way in. It was heavily guarded by a machine-gun post. When the other troops had left and we had settled in we took stock. Things had changed, there was now a 24-hour guard on Temple Hill over-looking the camp, and a guard on a small ridge to the side of the camp. These guards meant extra duties to be covered, along with sentry positions around the camp. We were now in the position of having a dusk until dawn curfew to enforce, attacks on the camp were to become more frequent. By this time I was a full Corporal, which meant more responsibilities, like guard commander, patrol leader, etc.

'We had with us teams from our Support Company, MMGs, 3-inch mortars, and Mobats (firing anti-tank or personnel rounds). The mortars were invaluable at night, they were ranged in on targets which normally gave the dissidents cover. They could fire HE or White Phosphorous, the latter giving instant smoke but also burning everything around.

'We used to link up with the FRA (Federal Republican Army), or the FNG (Federal National Guard) to escort them and support them in their operations. We toured outlying forts, boosting their morale, teaching them to lay out grenade necklaces and generally showing the flag.

'Our day started by mine-sweeping the road to the airstrip about a mile or so away. A team relieved the picket on Temple Hill and the low ridge; they had been up there all night freezing. The sniper in the front trench stood down. Troops would go about their duties, wherever or whatever. Night-time was our patrol time and ambush time. The Arabs named us the *fedayeens* (nightfighters). We were generally led by a young Lieutenant, with a Corporal at the rear, our faithful dogs always went with us. Their hatred of Arabs was an asset; we were warned by them if an Arab came within a mile. We would select a village and lie up to watch for curfew breakers – they were fired on. If we suspected dissident movement, we would lay an ambush that would last all night. In that case, we froze for hour after hour, but had to lie still on the rocks.

'We were generally fired on every night. They graduated to bringing up their own mortars. Luckily for us, they weren't very accurate, but they were gradually improving. The Emir's large fortress above Dhala village was a favourite target; its white walls were pock-marked with bullet holes. Our Assault Engineers built up a large bomb for us to lay on the edge of the low ridge on a blind side to our standing picket. The bomb was a large steel ammo box, filled with pounds of high explosive; Phosphorous hand grenades, pieces of metal and ball bearings. It was permanently sited, but made safe every morning and primed every night by the standing picket. They could detonate it by battery on command from the Company Commander. Its code-name was "Steptoe". The hope was that dissidents would lie near it and we could destroy them by blowing "Steptoe". I never had cause to ignite it.

'In the guardroom we had a master switch for the generator supplying our lighting. One of the guards had to sit next to the switch at all times; his orders, first shot, switch off. Sentries had to be very alert and again our faithful dogs helped. They lay alongside them, growling at the slightest noise. Obviously night time was tense, but we were well defended by barbed wire and mines. Patrols were going and coming most of the night; the dogs never growled at our approach.

'One day we carried out an area search. We found

nothing. The FRA were with us, our trucks met us to bring us back to camp. We drove off along the road followed by the same size trucks of the FRA. We went along the track all right, but the first FRA truck behind us hit a terrorist mine with its rear wheel, literally blowing apart a couple of men above the wheels. We had been very fortunate, it could have been us.

'We ate well generally, the food was cooked in a shed made up of corrugated metal sheeting. We had it dished onto our plates in there, then had to carry it across a clearing to the dining tent. That was the problem, large, buzzard-type birds hovered constantly, dive-bombing the unwary and taking the food off our plates. Very few people escaped these "Shite hawks" – we never managed to outwit them.

'My time was running out in Aden; my year was almost up. It had been a long, hard, arduous year. I had a daughter born while I was away and I was longing to see her, and my wife. We returned down country and had a couple of weeks general duties, then flew home to Gatwick, but I was sad to leave an excellent fighting unit.'

45 Commando, with three battalions of the Federal Army, some tanks, field guns, air support for Hunter ground-attack fighters and Wessex helicopters from *HMS Centaur* were first deployed against the Radfan tribesmen in January 1964. By the end of the month they had driven them off, re-opened the Dhala road, and built another road up into the Radfan itself. This effort could not be maintained, and when the force withdrew, the tribesmen came back, claiming that they had in fact beaten the British and the Federal Army. In March, the Federation Sheikhs called for more British help to suppress the Radfan tribesmen, as they were entitled to do under the Treaty, and the task was given to 45 Commando.

The CO of 45, Lt-Col T. M. P. (Paddy) Stevens, had anticipated just such a situation and drawn up plans for a strike deep into the tribesmen's stronghold in the Radfan, to demonstrate that even their houses were not safe if they continued to harass the Dhala road. Lt-Col Stevens' plan called for 45 to secure a hill feature, code-named 'Cap Badge', which lay in the centre of the Radfan, and overlooked the main tribal village, Danaba. To completely dominate the area, other fit and well-trained troops were required, and Lt-Col Stevens' force eventually contained 45 Commando; 'B' Coy, 3 Para; 'A' Squadron, 22 SAS Regt, plus Federal units, Royal Engineers, guns from 'J' Battery, Royal Horse Artillery, and helicopters.

Considerable reconnaissance was necessary before this infiltration was implemented, and 'X' Coy of 45 spent several weeks patrolling south of Dhala, while the rest of 45 returned to the coast and trained on the *jebels* around Aden. Colonel Stevens' plan of attack called for the SAS to infiltrate the Radfan and prepare a DZ (drop-zone) for the company of 3 Para. The Paras were to land near 'Cap Badge' and occupy it, while 45 made a fast, night-march into the Radfan to occupy a hill north of it, code-named 'Rice Bowl', while one company seized a firm base in the hills, code-named 'Sand Fly', three miles east of the Dhala road – thus dominating the heights, a necessary manoeuvre before any operation in the Radfan.

Paddy Stevens remembers the Cap Badge operation. 'It could only have been carried out by very fit troops. Luckily we had a low hill right behind Litte Aden, with a track over the top, covering a distance of about one and a half miles. I went out and set the check time which everyone had to better. Some of the very fit men put up astonishing times, though with a daily run or two over the top, in that heat and humidity, we all got a lot fitter. When the operation was first proposed, doubts were expressed as to whether we could move our entire Commando through that country in single file at night, but the SAS did it with small parties and I remembered how my Brigade had moved out of Normandy in '44, so that's how we did it. Once we had Cap Badge, we controlled the entire country, and thanks to Mike Banks, we got up on "Coca-Cola" and so on. It always takes longer than you think but the men were terrific, a keen, cheerful, fit, very professional crowd. The original idea was to use helicopters, but there never were enough helicopters, and in that heat and humidity, plus the thin air up at Dhala, their lift is restricted, so I said, "OK we'll walk it" – the first yomp maybe.'

Another Aden hand was Sgt Eric Blyth, still serving with the Mortars. 'I joined 45 after they got back from Tanzania, when Paddy Stevens was the CO. We went on the long march to Cap Badge with "B" Company of 3 Para attached. Up country, Aden is a rugged place to soldier in, you had to be fit. I didn't like the fact that you could be seen for miles and their snipers were excellent. The Paras once got hit badly in the Radfan, because the enemy were waiting for them. They had six killed and we fired over 300 smoke bombs to cover their position. When I was with 'X' Troop, 45, on Battery Ridge in the Radfan, we had to go down into the valley, but the heights had not been properly picketed. You *had* to control the heights but, as it was, we got pounced on by their snipers. The Area Commander, Farrar-Hockley, arrived by helicopter and landed right in front of us, so we had to go forward, and various people got hit. We usually got on well with the Paras but there was always a friendly rivalry . . .'

The SAS patrol infiltrated towards Cap Badge, but were quickly discovered by a shepherd, then surrounded by tribesmen, who came swarming up from Danaba. Pinned down and under heavy fire the SAS lost their

Commander and their radio operator, and the patrol was only saved from complete annihilation by calling RAF Hunters to strafe their position. Since the DZ could not be secured, the parachute drop was called off, but 45 began their march into the Radfan, at last light on 29 April.

In spite of the going, which was rough, and their loads, which were heavy, 45 made good time. Radio communication is always difficult in the mountains but by midnight the leading section of 'X' Coy were near the hill feature code-named Coca-Cola, west of Danaba. This feature had to be scaled and Col Stevens held a hasty conference with Maj Mike Banks, OC 'X' Coy, after seeing that the route up would be difficult, especially for the Heavy Weapons Troop. The Commandos no longer carried toggle ropes, but Maj Banks was a Himalayan climber of considerable experience, and there were other trained climbers in 45, some fortunately equipped with ropes. Major Banks assembled his climbing team, established a route to the top of Coca-Cola, and laid out a 'rather tatty' length of line up which the ladened men of 45 hauled and panted their way to the top. By first light the Commando were on top and in position overlooking the Danaba basin, much to the consternation of the tribesmen, who had been busy harrying the SAS.

Cap Badge mountain, the Commando's ultimate objective, lay away to the east, rearing up 4000 feet above the sea, and after five days on Coca Cola, probing out into Danaba, 45 moved to take it, having been joined meanwhile by 'B' Coy 3 Para. The Commando descended into the Danaba valley, skirted the village and with 'X' Coy again leading the way up the rock faces, were established on Cap Badge by first light. 'B' Coy 3 Para captured the village of El Naquil, losing six men wounded and two killed, and they had to be reinforced by 'Z' Coy of 45, before the Marines and paratroopers were tasked to consolidate their positions on the mountains. 45 stayed on for three days, patrolling the Radfan, entering all the tribal villages in the area, before they returned to Dhala, but although this quelled the tribesmen's activities for a while, 45 would be kept busy in the Radfan on and off for the next two years, during which time 45's Recce Troop were particularly active on patrol, and the tribesmen relentlessly hostile.

Major Ian Uzzell again: 'Aden was more interesting than Malaya, for we flew continuous operations right up to the end. I was shot at three times that I know of. The first was south of Habilayn, where an engineer convoy had been ambushed, losing two dead and ten wounded. The convoy commander called for air support, and I was tasked as airborne FAC (Forward Air Controller), to control air strikes. I couldn't find the target until four Arabs started shooting at me from a cave 300 feet below. One round hit the aircraft, causing considerable damage, but I brought the Hunters in to strafe with cannon and rocket, killing two dissidents while the other two had the misfortune to run into Lt Terry Knott, RM.'

Terry Knott commanded the Recce Troop of 45, and the citation for his Military Cross takes up his story. The Troop arrived at the ambush site in a Wessex, but . . .

'As the Wessex came in to hover, it was plain that the LZ was in the middle of the enemy. The pilot was unable to land due to heavy rifle and MG fire, so Lt Knott deplaned by leading his troop out, ten to twelve feet off the ground, where they immediately came under fire from the Jebel Lahmahr. The Troop killed one dissident on landing, then moved into a steep gulley, where another dissident emerged from a cave and fired with an automatic rifle at Lt Knott at point blank range. Lt Knott and one of his troop fired back, hitting the dissident who withdrew to a sangar in the cave. An M62 grenade, thrown into the cave, was thrown out again, after which

Lt Knott, regardless of his own safety, went into the cave and shot the dissident dead.'

George Newman recalls: 'I didn't take part in the original push for Cap Badge, although my section and I moved onto it to hold it. It was after the Cap Badge battle that the Red Wolves started to break up. All we had to do was continually hound and harass them. At Dhala the dissidents fired on us from predictable areas like Commando Ridge, Turkish Road, or a village below the top end of our camp. We had fixed lines on those with MMGs, mortars and Mobats – a round of HESH (High Explosive Squash Head) from the Mobat was a great deterrent.

'A dramatic incident was caused by an "S" Troop member manning a machine-gun post (GPMG) overlooking Dhala village. He was bored, trained the gun on an FRA soldier in the distance and pressed the trigger. He hadn't realized that the gun was cocked and shot the legs from under one of our allies. The FRA decided that they would wipe us out so we took to our trenches ready to fight back. But fortunately, political manoeuvres worked and the FRA backed down. Our "S" Troop member received 28 days inside.'

In June 1967, 45 handed over their bases in the mountains to the South Arabian Army and withdrew to Aden for the final phase of the British presence in the Gulf. Since 1964, terrorist incidents in Aden itself had continued to mount, with the emergence of two rival groups, the NLF (National Liberation Front), which was supported by the tribesmen and was opposed to Federation, and FLOSY (Front for the Liberation of Occupied South Yemen), which was a largely Yemeni organization, largely Communist inspired and backed by the Adeni trades unions. Both hoped to control Aden after the British left, and fought each other in what time they could spare from attacking the British. Strikes by

FLOSY paralysed the port, and the British eventually elected to hand over to the NLF and withdraw.

By September 1967, all service families had been evacuated, and 45 Commando moved into a defensive perimeter along the so-called Pennine Chain, where they were reinforced by 42 Commando on 11 October.

During this period, 45 was under the command of Lt-Col John Owen. 'When I arrived in 1967 we still had two troops in the Radfan and were running the Dhala convoys, but our problem during the withdrawal phase was in Aden itself, at Ma'Lah. It was the usual "Corporal's War" of patrols, road blocks, bomb-throwing, sniping . . . the troops were wonderful as usual, full of good humour. I remember an order coming down from HQ saying that the Arabs were no longer to be called "Wogs" and within hours the troops to a man were calling them the "Gollies". We were fighting with one hand tied behind our backs, denied hot pursuit. We eventually withdrew to what was referred to, for a while, as the Owen Line, on the outer rim of Crater from where we withdrew into the airfield itself at Khormaksar. As we handed over equipment and buildings to the South Arabian Army, we could see them flogging anything that wasn't tied down – fridges, Land-Rovers, anything – it was most galling, especially as we knew the administrative trauma that Freddie Townsend, our quartermaster, was going through. We all vied to be the last out. 45 were the last of the garrison, 42 from the commando ship *Albion* were disappointingly, but wisely, the last troops to fly out – but by helicopter. However, the last five into the last Hercules were myself, the Brigadier, the RAF station commander, the Brigadier (General Staff) and the Senior Air Staff Officer, in that order. I sometimes wonder whether, had we been under fire, the order would have been reversed!'

The end in Aden is also remembered by Capt F. C.

Townsend, then QM of 45. 'At the time I was the Quartermaster, the one who had "volunteered" for the job, well knowing that it meant closing the place down. After a couple of weeks acclimatization and sorting things out down in Little Aden, I flew up to Habilayn to join the main body of the unit and look at things there. About 6 or 7 June, I flew on to Dhala, my first visit, to liaise with the QM of the newly-formed South Arabian Army unit, perched on the neighbouring hill, and to sort out one or two ledger problems. We were due to transfer all camp stores and a quantity of ammunition to the SAA on withdrawal from Dhala, which was expected to happen about a fortnight later.

'On Sunday morning, 11 June, the CO unexpectedly called an "O" group in Habilayn Camp, at which he disclosed the plan for an immediate withdrawal of "X" Company from Dhala. It was arranged that the Adjutant (Capt Terry Wills) and I should fly up to join the company that afternoon to help with the arrangements. It was not unusual for the occasional officer to swan up there, so our visit didn't cause any undue speculation, especially as we brought up some extra beer and goodies for the men.

'Nothing was done to alert the company about the evacuation until early evening. There wasn't a great deal of packing to do because the place was virtually under seige and things were kept ready. There was a bit of a celebration; the Officers' Mess brought out some bottles of champagne, obviously saved for the occasion (I still have a cork as a memento). By the time the light began to fade, activity in the camp was already dying down. At "Stand To" I parked myself outside the heavily sandbagged fortress of the Officers' Mess with the Command Post perched on top – a bit like the Alamo. The lights of Dhala town across the valley began to twinkle and gradually many more lights began flickering away beyond and all round the hills. Overhead droned a Shackleton aircraft, periodically dropping parachute flares which hung in the night sky for what seemed an age, flooding the ground with light and dancing shadows and then blackness as they extinguished. Away in the distance occasional streaks of tracer roared skywards. It wasn't long before I realized that they were flying our way and I retreated inside the mess. With no part to play in the defence, I settled down with Terry to listen to reports coming over the intercom.

'It wasn't long before a rocket or mortar shell exploded alongside the Officers' showers and started a fire which was soon lighting up the whole of the top end of the camp. Terry and I immediately turned firemen and went out to see what we could do to put it out. The large two-wheeled foam extinguisher was soon used up and we carried on with smaller extinguishers which we grabbed from wherever we could. By this time I was down on my belly, working in towards the seat of the fire, which was dangerously near what I thought to be empty 40-gallon AVCAT drums, some of which I discovered afterwards to be not to empty. Suddenly, I was spluttering like a landed fish, half-drowned by a bucket of water, not aimed at the fire, but deliberately thrown over me by Terry. "I thought you were getting too hot," he said with a big grin on his face. The fire was eventually put out and the camp returned to normal, with me soaking wet, trying to get some sleep on the floor under the Company Commander's bed.

'It wasn't over then, because about an hour later the duty officer called the Company Commander to report movement at the wire below No 1 Sangar and sought permission to open fire. I remember Major Donald Brewster MC, saying "OK, but just give them one burst and only the one sangar. I don't want the whole camp disturbed again." Next morning that post had the satisfaction of reporting seeing a body being carried away.

The camp was awake very early. As the Civil Labour came in to begin work, so they were detained. Next came the arrival of a convoy from Habilayn, usually routine, but this time empty, onto which were quickly loaded all G1098 heavy stores and equipment and personal baggage. At this point I motored quickly over to the SAA Camp to grab a much surprised Arab quartermaster, half-dressed and in the middle of his ablutions. I needed him to take over the stores and give me the signature to clear my ledgers. He wasn't particularly happy with the speed of turnover. We'd reached the point of transferring some stocks of ammunition, including mortar shells which we swore were raining down on us later in Aden, when the convoy began to wind up and head down the slope out of camp. By this time of course, the main body of troops had marched blithely down to the tiny airstrip to be met by an incoming Beverley and away. No one seemed interested in a QM's troubles. I was told that if I didn't get on a truck I'd be left behind. With the ink still wet I had to run virtually alongside the last vehicle and mount it, like the hero in a western movie, leaping into the saddle and galloping from the scene.

The ride back to Habilayn was not without its moments of humour. Some of the loading had been very hasty indeed, and as we ran down the pass and across the desert beyond the one-ton trailer being towed behind, a three-tonner in front of us kept spewing out kitbags and cases. Every time it bounced over an outcrop of lava rock, something came flying out, but on the driver went, in blissful ignorance. Soon he was out of sight, as we stopped alongside each piece of baggage and took it on board. One of the local buses came groaning towards us, loaded to the gunwhales with men and stores, and just to be sure they hadn't purloined any of the jettisoned baggage in front of us, the bus was stopped and searched, much to the annoyance of its passengers.

'Closing the Dhala ledger was probably the least of my worries in the frog-hopping withdrawal to Khormaksar and home. It was a simple matter to transfer queries to the Habilayn ledger to give time to sort them out. Habilayn was a different story. For years the camp had seen units come and go, with quartermasters content to muster just the important stores and accept the run-of-the-mill camp stores as OK. I was at the end of a very long chain. Everything on those ledgers now had to be accounted for, one way or another. Either they had to be handed over to the South Arabian Army on signature, or returned to Ordnance and a receipt obtained to reduce ledger holdings to zero, or perhaps put in for survey and write-off with write-off powers being fairly limited. There were many headaches, especially with more personal items like camp beds (1600 of them!) but somehow or other my RQMS and his small staff worked the miracle and a few weeks later, back in BP Camp, Little Aden, we were able to present the books for audit.

'The handover at Habilayn was almost leisurely. Each day we were able to draw in unwanted stores as people moved out of our own camp, and the Engineer Camp up the road, which was also our responsibility. The Arab QM had set up a compound on the other side of the airstrip and we were able to dump many things on him; unwanted refrigerators particularly. On the day we departed, I wasn't too concerned about the steady stream of 'ants' creeping into the bottom of the camp and staggering away back to the Souk under the weight of a mattress or bed. I'd already got my signature.

'Back in Little Aden the QM's warriors were faced with three major tasks. There was the overall planning for the return to UK; heavy baggage and stores by sea, to be followed by an air lift of lighter stores as we thinned down and then the final evacuation, with particular worry about how personal weapons and important items of G1098 would be handled. At the same time, we had to prepare operational bases along and around the Ma'ala straight with galley and store facilities ready for the withdrawal into Aden, and then close down BP Camp. By now, the QM's compound had taken on the appearance of a Pickford's Repository, hundreds of boxes piled row on row. The paperwork was enormous; a contents list in quintuplicate for every box, manifestos in quintuplicate for every consignment. When the road convoys by way of Al Mansoura and the Causeway began to be sniped at, we resorted to moving the vast bulk of our boxes by Z lighter across the harbour. Having got them to the docks, we were baulked by a dock strike, so that troops had to be diverted to do the loading. It was essential to get as much as possible away by sea because the air-lift allocation was constantly changing, usually downwards, depending on aircraft availability. We were determined to leave nothing behind and that included the CO's desk, a splendid piece of furniture which strictly didn't belong to the unit but which exemplifies the strong character of 45 Commando. It was carefully taken to pieces by the unit carpenter, just as carefully wrapped and crated and delivered to Khormaksar, where it was air-freighted to UK to serve successive COs of 45 Commando – I believe it is there to this day, up at Arbroath.

'It wasn't all work. The last few days in BP Camp were relatively quiet with the camp cut off from Big Aden except by means of armed convoy, usually once a day each way. We even managed a farewell party in the messes with outlying guests having to stop the night and return next day by the morning convoy. BP Camp was duly handed back to the Refinery Company, which had no wish to have the SAA there, and so the last elements of the unit departed to join the force already established in Ma'ala and the Khormaksar. The leapfrogging continued. The main QM's party moved into Khormaksar to prepare individual company stores cages and set up accommodation for each of the companies and HQ. Back in Ma'ala looting of the flats along the straight became a problem. As if the QM hadn't enough to do, he was vested with responsibility for the security of the 1000 or so flats there, most of them still full of furniture, just as the families had left them. The unit carpenter and a small team spent a lot of time fitting hefty padlocks to the outer doors, but it took more than that to deter an Arab thief. Gradually the furniture was sold off to the local entrepreneurs and the flats returned to their Arab owners. One particular block, half way along the straight, gave the unit a lot of trouble. An OP had been set up on the roof and the men manning it occupied just the top flat, but somewhere along the line, before we got there, most of the funiture from the remaining flats in the block had been thrown down to the bottom of the stairwell and was good only for matchsticks. The place was a real shambles. The Arab owner, being a sharp businessman, thought he could screw the unit for a goodly sum. He pressed his claim right back to the UK and caused the CO a couple of journeys from Plymouth to London to fight the case. Happily he got nothing.

'A few weeks before the end, it was decreed that I should return to UK to prepare for the arrival of the unit in Stonehouse Barracks, leaving RQMS Goring and the AQM, Lt J. Barrie, to watch over the final withdrawal of stores. It was no simple task for them to collect in all the arms and pieces of eqipment, as men filtered in through Khormaksar and to freight them out through Bahrain. The bulk movement of weapons is a serious business at any time – here it was doubly difficult. Back home in Plymouth, it was equally hectic. We began a round of hunt-the-boxes, which lasted right through to the end of January. I became a mine of information about shipping movements and airfreight schedules. We ran convoys the length and breadth of England; Tilbury, Avonmouth, Liverpool, Brize Norton, not just once but time after time, tracking down and collecting nearly 1000 crates.'

Outside the British perimter, Aden had been abandoned to the conflicting groups of FLN and FLOSY supporters, who then fought it out in the streets. 45 flew out of Aden on 28 November with 42 leaving the next day, in helicopter lifts back to *HMS Albion*. Gunfire could be heard from the colony as the Commando sailed away, not too sorry to be out of a situation where 'steadfast patience had been tested and found to hold firm on thousands of unrewarded, forgotten occasions.'

45 Commando served in Aden from April 1960 until November 1967. In the middle of this period, from December 1962 until August 1966, the Royal Marine Commandos of 40 and 42 were fighting another and very different kind of war, in the jungles of Borneo, during the so-called 'Confrontation' between Indonesia and the federated states of Borneo.

After Malaya became independent, in 1957, it was still necessary to provide military aid to the fledgling nation, and help to hunt down the two or three thousand Communist terrorists who still roamed in the jungle. This task was complicated and compounded by the fact that two years after independence the Federation of Malaya fell apart. Singapore became independent from Malaya in 1959, and it was not until 1963 that both nations joined up once again, combining to form the Federation of Malaysia. These states are now independent once again, but their brief federation was viewed with instant hostility by the government of the nearby Republic of Indonesia, which itself laid claim to the states of Borneo, notably Brunei and Sarawak, and what is now Sabah, which was then British North Borneo.

The states of Sarawak, Brunei and Sabah, occupy the

smaller, northern half of the island of Borneo, which is otherwise occupied by Indonesia. To the north-west lies the southern tip of Malaya, with Sumatra beyond; to the south lies Java, and to the north-east, the Phillipines. The main areas of conflict were along the southern frontiers of Sarawak and Sabah, but the affair began in December 1962, when the Kendayan people of Brunei, who are of Indonesian stock, rebelled against the more numerous local Malays, and the Sultan's plans to set up an independent state. By 11 December these rebels had occupied Brunei town and the river port of Limbang, just across the border of Sarawak and a number of other centres. They had also taken a number of hostages, among them the Resident of the 5th division of Sarawak and his wife.

42 Commando were then in Singapore, and on 10 December 'L' Company flew to Brunei, under the command of Captain Jeremy Moore MC. 'L' Company stayed at the airport overnight, while Gurkhas retook the town, and Captain Moore set about looking for craft which could carry his company up the river to Limbang. Eventually two open, car-carrying lighters or Z-craft, were found, and after crews arrived to man them from the mine-sweepers *HMS Fiskerton* and *Chawton*, Captain Moore embarked his men and sailed for Limbang on the night of 11 December. The rebel strength was estimated at around 150 men, armed with an assortment of weapons. Captain Moore had only his under-strength company and a section of Vickers MMGs.

'I joined 42 in Singapore in 1962, when Robin Bridges was the CO. I wrote to him first asking for command of a rifle troop and he replied saying, "OK, when I can, but you will still have to be my adjutant for a bit." I joined them on *HMS Bulwark*, off Muscat, then we went to Aden and up to Dhala for a while, then we went on a visit to Hong-Kong and it was there that the Commando changed from Troops to Companies – a

Commando troop today is like an Army platoon – the idea was that we left Singapore in Troops, and returned in Companies, using the voyage to Hong-Kong and back to sort everything out and iron out any snags, which we did. The unit's Second-in-Command was Johnny Taplin and my QMS – Company Sergeant-Major now – was Cyril Scoins, a fine man.

'So, Brunei . . . The 9 December was a Sunday and that morning I was in my room at Simbang, doing my Christmas cards, when a Marine came in and said the Colonel would like to see me. I went to his room and he asked me "How quickly can you move the company?" I then had 'L' Company. His 'O' Group was amusing, as all the other Company Commanders were either out on picnics, or water-skiing, and messengers were scurrying everwhere, trying to get them back.

'We got to Brunei airport in the evening of the 10th. 'L' Company were about 87 strong, and we were joined later by a section of Vickers MMGs (two guns). There was a lot of confusion but the Gurkhas had already retaken Brunei town from the rebels. When I telephoned for orders I was told to take my rifle company and guard the British Resident's Residence . . . at which I exploded. "I've got one of the best trained rifle companies you are ever likely to see," I told the caller, "and we're not here to do a policeman's job!" Next day, Pat Patterson, commanding the 99th Gurkha Brigade, arrived and said to me, "I want you to think about Limbang and prepare for the arrival of the rest of the Commando – and find some transport – that's three tasks."

'We did all that, but there was not much information about Limbang. I knew it was a town in Sarawak, that there were half-a-dozen or so hostages and an unknown number of rebels. A police launch went up there – most movement in Borneo is by river – and got fired on. I got an air photograph of Limbang, not a good one but enough to identify the main buildings, the police station, the hospital and so on. Then our CO arrived, so I handed the task over to him, but later that day he told me to take "L" Company and do the job.

'I went down to the waterfront and met the Senior Naval officer, Lt-Com Jeremy Black, who had two minesweepers under command. We had also found some sampans and a couple of great flat craft called Z-Lighters. We decided to go through the 'leads' up to Limbang in the Z-Lighters . . . one of them had two yellow bulldozers on board, which came with us; we didn't have time to get them off. Jeremy Black came too with the local Captain of Marine of Brunei Town, a man called Mouton came to help us find the way. Now we knew there were quite a few rebels there, and a few hostages, so I didn't want to make a slow, grinding advance through the town which could put the hostages at risk, and I decided to go directly for the police station, which I thought might well be the rebel HQ, and contain some, at least, of the hostages. We had my Recce group, company HQ and a troop of Marines in my craft in front and the main company HQ, the MMGs and another troop and a half on the rear craft. We made good time up the leads into the Limbang river and lay up for a sleep before setting off again aiming to arrive at first light. We came to the town quite suddenly when we rounded a bend in the river . . . all the lights were on but they all went out abruptly, so we thought we had been spotted – in fact they were putting out the lights because dawn was breaking.

'When they finally did see us the place exploded; it was exactly like an ant-heap, with people running everywhere. Our "I" Sergeant then hailed the town through a loudhailer, and told them the rebellion had failed, to lay down their arms, and so on. This news was greeted with a hail of shot.

'We drove our landing craft straight at the bank, opposite the police station, with the second craft with the Vickers in support . . . the enemy had light machine guns, lots of rifles and shotguns, so the fire was heavy and a number of people were hit, including the helmsman of the leading craft – lots of bullets were coming aboard and splinters were flying about – something hit me in the middle of the back, hard enough to knock me down, and I thought, "Good grief, Moore, you seem to have been hit!" but I put my hand up to feel my back, and there was no blood, so I thought, "Get up, man – there's a battle to be fought." My Second-in-Command was hit on the other craft, so Cyril Scoins took over and asked the naval officer on board, "Move the craft over, please Sir, so I can give fire support." The naval officer shook his head and said, "Sergeant-Major, Nelson would have xxxxx loved you," but he moved the craft over and we got good support.

'The two sections ashore were doing everything perfectly – observing, firing, checking magazines, moving position – all the things we had practised so many times – it's very exciting to see the blokes doing it just right – you could pick the moment when the Corporal said "Go!" One of them told me later, that he hated my guts in training when I had them doing these drills day after day, ". . . but I understand what it was all for in about two-thirds of a second as soon as we came under fire".

'Then I realized that my craft had drifted off the bank – the helmsman had been hit and the Naval Officer in charge was busy firing a rifle. I wanted to put my third section ashore, so the officer took the helm and put us back again, but we were now about a hundred yards further upstream. Sergeant Macfarlane took his men over the bow to clear the shoreline down from there to the Police Station, accompanied by the "I" Sergeant.

'We then found that we couldn't get the craft off again, so I went ashore. The main deck was by now pretty chaotic, with lots of packs and cartridge cases littered about, and a couple of bodies. I went up the road past the hospital where Dick Morris, the Resident, and his wife were held hostage. Dick had worked out that the relief would come either from Marines or Paras and to stop us chucking a grenade in, had made up a doggerel verse to let us know they were there. This, to the tune of "She'll be coming round the Mountain" went:

> They'll be wearing bright green bonnets,
> But they won't be singing sonnets,
> They'll be wearing bright green bonnets,
> When they come . . . etc.

'He was only half right, because in fact, I had a book of Shakespeare sonnets in my pocket. Sergeant MacFarlane and two of his Marines were killed here, at very close range. Dick Morris told us there were about three hundred rebels in the town and where the furthest hostages were kept . . . they included a young American from the Peace Corps. We had some resistance from the bazaar, and after Cyril Scoins landed the other two troops, we set out to do a bit of street clearing. The two troop subalterns hadn't done this, so we taught them on the job – a real live firing exercise. One colossal marine fell through the roof of one house and plummeted all the way down through various floors to the ground floor, landing in a heap beside a bath containing an entire Chinese family, all of them peering at him worriedly over the rim . . . The Company performed extremely well and I was very proud of them.'

For his successful assault on Limbang, Jeremy Moore received his second Military Cross.

Two Commandos, 40 and 42 were commited to the Confrontation, and over the next three years returned to Borneo again and again, first for three months and later for five month tours of duty up on the jungle frontier. This was an undeclared war, and a vicious one, for the Indonesian troops that came across the frontier to fight it were well equipped and trained and often in considerable strength, while in the jungle the Marines had to cope with the usual extreme tropical conditions and (an added horror) vast numbers of rats, which infested their camps. Transport in the jungle was always a problem, so the Marines got about by helicopter, by river craft or, more often than not, on foot.

Captain Townsend, who was to figure in the evacuation of Aden, was here to organize the arrival of 40 and 42. 'HQ 3 Commando Brigade was away in Aden towards the end of 1962, combining with 45 Commando and, I believe, 40 Commando, in Exercise Long March. It was a time of changeover between the carriers *Albion* and *Bulwark*, so that there was a great gathering of the clans at Little Aden with one or two big parties. The main body flew back to Singapore at the end of November, while all the heavy stores made a leisurely run back in *Albion*. The order came for the Brigade to move to Borneo for action against the Indonesian infiltrators, and "L"Company, 42 Commando, had already been in action in Brunei. We embarked the majority of our stores and transport in *Albion* leaving only a small rear party and sailed about 13 December direct for the mouth of the Sarawak River, the capital Kuching being some miles up the river. We were met there by a couple of rather ancient river boats, which fussed around us and after a brief discussion, we proceeded to air-land 40 Commando by helicopter on to the racetrack at Kuching. It meant much stripping of Landrovers to get them down to weight but it all went pretty smoothly, and having got rid of the

Commando we turned and headed up the coast towards Labuan, an island at the northern end of Brunei Bay. Here we set about landing the Headquarters. It was quite a long job with all the vehicles having to be lowered over the side and ferried ashore by lighter and LCAs. As Brigade MTO I had the task of seeing everything off, so that by the time we came to the end I was pretty tired and not a little bit fed up. The ship's main crane had a habit of packing up and much of the time we were restricted to a mobile jumbo. By early evening, *Albion* was under orders to move again. She was steaming very slowly towards the anchorage entrance with the last Landrover suspended half way down, an LCA waiting underneath to catch it, and the crane gone wonky. I really did think that this time I was going to be left behind but, as always, we made it. The crane jerked into life, the Landrover was lowered into the LCA, and I was ferried ashore. As soon as I reached land I was required to report to the CO. It seemed that having got everything ashore in Labuan, the whole HQ was now to be flown down to Kuching and as I was the unit Air Loading Officer, it was up to me to prepare the loading plan.

'We were initially allocated a couple of Beverleys and three Hastings aircraft with more to follow as they became available. The first aircraft would be leaving about 6 a.m. next morning. I hadn't expected anything like this. I could have done with some sleep. Instead, I set-to to permutate the various sub-unit loads against the aircraft and priorities. I can't remember when I finished but it must have been all right, because when I awoke I was informed that the first flight had got away on time and I was just left to keep loading them up and winging them on their way as the aircraft returned empty. We had a couple of good air-loading teams and I had the Asst Brigade Sigs Officer, Lt Jim Oatley RM working with me. He and I had served together before and we could read each other's minds. Loading Hastings aircraft with Landrovers and trailers was not easy. You side-loaded at an angle up a fairly steep pair of ramps and it entailed a lot of heaving and swearing. At the same time you had to be careful not to damage the aircraft. Inevitably, once the bulk of the unit was gone, the local staff on the airport lost interest and aircraft seemed to find other more important people to fly to more exciting places, like Singapore.

'We were left to kick our heels on the airport perimeter, brewing up and sleeping, with the occasional saunter over to the Station office for another row with the controller. It was next day before we finally got under their skins so much that they found an aircraft to get us away. We landed at Kuching airport, I think it was 18 December, and this time I didn't have to report to the CO, he reported to me. At least he was at the airport, and I think he was waiting for me. He wanted to be the first to tell me that the unit needed an Imprest Officer and that he thought that I was the best chap for the job. (The CO at the time was Major John Owen OBE.) The Corps Paymaster back in UK had already been given my name and there were a couple of Bank Drafts for so many thousand Malaysian Dollars waiting for me to cash at the local bank. I had no safe and I didn't ask for one. I paid out what was needed and kept the rest on my person, sleeping on it at night. The Corps Paymaster nearly had a baby when he eventually learned of my unorthodox methods. However, I had a splendid Imprest SNCO and we never had any difficulty in balancing the books each day.

'One interesting little cameo on the Imprest side was a request from an ad-hoc patrol far out in the jungle for their food drop to be replaced by a money drop. The going was so tough that they prefered to buy food from the natives they encountered rather than carry the extra weight. We worked out a rate for so many days rations and made up a package of dollars. It was expected to pass through about four pairs of hands before the final drop and the Brigade DAQMG was insistent that each one would have to get a signature for the money, so we had to make a series of receipts. I got mine from the first pilot, flying from Kuching, but the whole thing broke down because the last one couldn't get his chit signed. The money eventually got back to Imprest and the patrol survived without it.

'For the first few nights in Kuching, Jim Oatley and I were billetted in a small Chinese hotel, about five minutes from the HQ. It was a pretty sleazy place, and had a reputation for being a brothel. The first night there, I had just turned in when there was a discreet tapping on the door. I thought, "Ah ha, this is it – Room Service." I cautiously unlocked the door to let her in, but it was the "boy" wanting to know if I had any dirty washing!

'It was a memorable Christmas. I was among half-a-dozen officers and SNCOs who were invited to have Christmas lunch with the Governor and his lady in the Istawa. Clad in our best jungle greens we were met at the landing stage by the State Barge, a magnificent canopied affair, and rowed over the river to the Istawa, where we were greeted by the Governor. A walk up through the beautifully laid-out gardens and we were in the cool of the palace, sitting down to a splended meal, with His Nibs doing the honours, carving the turkey at the head of the table. Plum pudding aflame and lashings of real brandy butter, washed down with Tiger beer with liqueurs and cigars for ballast – it was enough to have even the best of us burbling by the time we came to leave. I enjoyed Kuching, but that tour didn't last long. By the end of January, we were on our way back to Singapore, only to return to Kuching again at Easter. This time the tour lasted right through to beyond Christmas again, with a short break for me half way through, when I took over as Married Families Liaison Officer at Rowcroft Lines. That second tour in Borneo was quite enjoyable. There was plenty going on, on the military side, but there was also plenty of time for seeing something of the country and its people. I caught up with a wedding in long house, spent one or two weekends cruising up the river in one of those ancient river boats which really were very comfortable, umpired a lot of hockey for the local hockey teams, particularly the Borneo Company and the Post & Telegraph, I learned to play golf in a fashion on the local golf course, did a regular run with the Hash-Hound Harriers, which was always fun, and did one or two things which still raise a smile, like fining a couple of Marines, I think about £10 each, for drinking beer out of a glass in the local market, at a time when there was a cholera scare and drinking out of glasses was not advisable.

Major Uzzell, then a Second Lieutenant, was in Borneo with 40 Commando: 'I joined 40 Commando as a 2nd Lieutenant in November 1962 at Aden, where they were involved in the changeover of *HMS Bulwark* and *HMS Albion* – the 2nd Commando ship. In that month we had 3 Commandos in Aden at the same time; 45 Commando, resident in Little Aden, 40 Commando from Singapore, and 43 Commando (I believe) from UK, who travelled out with *HMS Albion*.

'40 embarked on *Albion*, and as we left harbour we pulled over and sunk one of the tug boats helping us. "A" Company, who were lining the port quarter of the flight deck, had full view of the happenings, and gave a great cheer as the tug crew abandoned ship as it turned over. Unfortunately two did not get out and were drowned.

'En-route to Singapore we heard of the trouble in Brunei and that 42 Commando had landed at Limbang with the loss of five men. We increased speed and we all knew we were heading in the direction of Borneo. We were not allowed to know our destination until after we had paused at Singapore to collect stores etc. The wives of the married men had already been told and, of course, informed their husbands during the four hours they were allowed ashore. It was Kuching, in the First Division of Borneo.

'We were using the Wessex helicopter for the first time on this tour and on exercises had only used fighting order. When we went ashore at Kuching, we had to take our full marching order. Being unfamiliar with the new helicopter, my Troop loaded all the weighty stores at the back. This caused the pilot nearly to have a heart attack when the front of the helicopter rose but not the back! A hasty landing and re-sorting of stores, and then we were safely taking off for Kuching Racecourse. Not knowing what to expect on our arrival, I had briefed my troop of 33 men to form an all-round defensive position. Control was lost on landing, when it was noticed that a number of ice-cream vendors were plying their trade around the Commando.

'My company were sent to Serian and I went to a border outpost called Tebedu, to patrol the border. After a week or so, we were withdrawn and flown north to Tawau in North Borneo and carried out river and coastal patrols. We returned to Singapore in January 1963.

'At Easter, Tebedu was attacked by Indonesian forces and 40 Commando were recalled from weekend leave to return to Borneo. Once again, "C" Company were based at Serian, and this time I was sent up river to a village called Muara Mongkos. Here we carried out patrolling, and an intensive "hearts and minds" campaign. Rifle Troops worked very much on their own with radio contact to Company Headquarters, 20 miles away. Resupply was usually by air-drop (parachutes) or by helicopter.'

David Lee was a Marine in 42 Commando: 'Having arrived at Sembawang Barracks in late November, after a long flight from England, I wondered how many familiar faces I might see on my first day. I was assigned to 5 Troop, "L" Company, and was soon greeted with a few cheers by the crowd that usually gathers to welcome new arrivals at the accommodation block.

'It didn't take long to settle into life with a Commando unit. When you're a long way from home, people seem to find a closeness, uncommon to civilian life, and lasting friendships develop. Everything is shared, and typical of this was Reg Chapple (our section Cpl) who shared his family and his dinner with us on Christmas Day. It was a generous gesture and one which was much appreciated.

'Training was accelerated following the announcement of our move to Sarawak in late January, and it was with certain apprehension that we relieved 40 Commando at Lundu. The journey was made by boat, truck, and finally, helicopter. That same night we were out on patrol as word had reached Headquarters that Indonesian border raiders were heading into our district. Was it always going to be this hectic?

'After three days of patrolling and three nights of ambushes, there was still no sign of the enemy, and we were recalled for a rest at HQ. It was luxury to have a shave and a cold shower, and even canned beer tasted good. So went the routine – a three or four-day patrol, and a rest.

'The local villagers were very friendly, and with a big wide smile, might offer to shin up a tree to cut down a coconut or pick a pineapple from their plot of land.

Their simple, but peaceful way of life seemed worth preserving to me.

'All the time in the jungle, the weather was very humid and you clothes were soaking with sweat, even if you weren't exerting yourself. The monsoon season was the worst, with heavy rain, which sometimes lasted for several days. This, of course, made the going very rough underfoot, and there was no escaping the mud. Jungle boots were all right for keeping out the leeches, but were certainly not waterproof and so your feet were constantly wet. It was only when you stopped for the night, that it was worth changing your socks and giving the shrivelled-up flesh a respite. Leeches were a constant menace and a stab with a cigarette end seemed the best solution. After crossing a river, a good search of the body would reveal several of them. When the sun came out, life was a bit more bearable, but your clothes dried on your body and only time will tell if this has any drawbacks in later life. Some patrols were easier than others, not on your nerves or the way you went about it, but if it was near the coast the tracks were easier and the jungle not so dense. Mind you, the mangrove swamps threw up a different problem when being searched. They had to be patrolled at low tide and they were the perfect place for the enemy to hide their boats. Here you learnt to try to keep your feet on the tree roots; if not, it was mud up to your knees. Swarms of mosquitoes made it even worse, the repellant you had only having a limited effect.

'Early evening was the time to make up your mind where to camp for the night. Chosen carefully, it could bring a little relaxation and a steaming hot stew. Cooking with the solid fuel tablets was easy and a hot cup of tea to finish brought thoughts of home. I was 24, and this was my second commision, as it was for Reg Chapple, Jock Balderstone and Jim Gooding. For the rest, straight from England, Scouse Gardiner, Oggie Howes, L-Corp Davis and Jock Findley, it must have seemed a million miles away. Nevertheless, we were all in it together and learning all the time about how to survive the rigours of jungle life.

'A combined operation where the whole troop of roughly 20 Marines would be sent out would bring the added thoughts of "safety in numbers". Here we would have local tribesmen employed as trackers and lead scouts. They certainly made the patrol easier with their knowledge of the local area. We were able to cover the ground faster and if we were in full pursuit of the enemy so much the better – we had them on the run.

'There were times when our numbers were rather restricted, then the section would be divided into two small units. Three men would be sent out in the morning, then the remaining four or five in the afternoon or evening. So it was, that on 20 February, the section was split, and L- Corp Davis, Jim Gooding, and myself found ourselves on a routine patrol to search random "bashas". We came across one in particular which the owner (a Chinese) did not appear keen for us to investigate. With an uneasy feeling, Jim and Davis inspected it while I kept watch with the Bren gun. I had a prickly sensation down the back of my neck, and unlatched the safety catch, just in case. The three big sacks of rice and two outboard engines in the "basha" just didn't add up, so we withdrew. We reported our find to Second Lieutenant Christie Miller at HQ, and he despatched the remainder of the section under the command of Cpl Chapple to make further investigations during the evening. Under the command of Reg Chapple they set off on the early evening, to give them time to reach the "basha" before dusk, and the rest of us settled down to relax after the day patrol.

'About 10.30 we heard what we thought was gunfire

in the distance, because sound travels for miles, but bamboo cracking has a similar sound, so we couldn't make our minds up at first. Then came a couple of deep explosions and we put this down to hand grenades. Confirmation of this came from the villagers themselves, when they put the shutters over their windows, which were normally open . . . they knew something was up.

'Questions were going over in our minds; was it our lads caught in ambush, had they set one themselves, and above all, were they all right? All went quiet for about an hour, then our answer came in the form of Oggie Howes, who had come back with the news that they had been caught in a fight and that Cpl Chapple had been killed and the rest seriously wounded at the same Chinese "basha". Oggie himself was wounded, with several bullets in his arms, which were taken out by the Medic. A radio message was relayed to Company HQ and it was decided to send a helicopter to the village at once, even though this entailed flying in the dark, and it duly arrived with torches being uses as landing lights. The plan was to try and bring the wounded back to the village and so get them to hospital quicker. Things did not work out this way though, as it was up to the rest of us to effect a rescue and decide what to do when we got there. The rescue party consisted of 2-Lt Christie Miller, L-Corp Davis, Jim Gooding, myself and Oggie Howes, who insisted on going back. Well, anyone who has been in the jungle at night would know how pitch black it is, and so as not to get separated we decided to tie a length of rope onto the back of our belts, which was held fairly taut by the man behind; this enabled us to keep some distance between ourselves, but keep in contact at the same time. There was the added danger of coming under fire from the enemy if they decided to ambush us on the main track while effecting the rescue.

'After what seemed like hours, we finally reached the

"basha" about 01.30 and saw for ourselves the fight the lads had put up. They had the Chinese owner whom we had spoken to earlier in the day as a prisoner. The place was an absolute wreck, bullet-holes were evident all over and the back-room walls had gaping holes in them, no doubt from the hand grenades. Jim started to attend to the wounded, Scouse's legs were bleeding badly, Jock Balderstone had arm wounds but seemed in good spirits and morphine was given to them both to ease the pain. Not so for Jock Findley though, as he had several bullets in his chest and was coughing blood so could not be given it. Reg Chapple was in a small room and nothing else could be done until the morning when the helicopter could land and evacuate the wounded. The rest of the night passed without incident, but looking round, each man had his own thoughts and not many words were exchanged. The Section mourned the loss of Reg, as indeed did the whole Commando.

'The enemy had retreated and the only sign we could see were blood-stains leading into the jungle, so they had at least some wounded. We had radioed our position to the rest of the company, and at first light came the helicopter and both the Troops' other sections on foot led by Cpls Bell and Mick Fulton, with some Iban tribesmen who quickly set off in pursuit of the enemy. The helicopter left within minutes of landing and quiet returned again.

'A police patrol arrived on foot with some more Iban tribesmen and started to interrogate the Chinese, and after searching his out-buildings found the rest of his family. It turned out that he was harbouring twenty Indonesians and admitted that the three Marines who had first searched his place in the day were being watched by them all the time. He was led away and we returned to Sekembal once more for some rest.

'Sleep doesn't come easily after an experience like that. Your mind keeps repeating the events over and over again, and changes your whole outlook. On reflection, the hit and run tactics of the Indonesians made you more aware of the need to be constantly on the alert when on patrol, the jungle being an inhospitable place, with so many localities ideal for ambush. With this in mind, the mental, as well as the physical strain takes its toll.'

In 1963 40 Commando found themselves with a patrol area in Sabah which extended over seven thousand square miles. The Marines and Gurkhas kept this area under control by constant patrolling, enduring the heat and humidity, the wildlife and the rats, and continued to do so until the Confrontation ended in August 1966.

The Commando ships proved their worth, transporting the Brigade about the Far East and the Indian Ocean, enabling it to put in a surprise appearance when needed, or tackle any sudden emergency with the Corps' characteristic speed, but in 1968 it was decided that the Royal Marines must be reduced in size and restricted to Europe. This meant the disbandment first of 43 Commando, and eventually the loss of the Commando ships, though *HMS Hermes* came into Commando service for a while to replace *HMS Albion*.

By the early 1970s the situation of the Royal Marines Commandos was roughly as follows: 45 Commando was Artic trained and assigned to the NATO Northern flank. 42 Commando were Arctic trained much later, in 1978, and 40 Commando were kept for *blackshod*, mountain work and the more traditional Commando roles. When they were in the UK, 45 Commando were at Arbroath, 40 Commando at Seaton Barracks, Plymouth, and 42 at the old Commando

School at Bickleigh. 41 Commando exercised abroad in Commando ships and went to Malta, before being disbanded once again, and all Commando Units took their turn in Northern Ireland.

12

Ulster and the Falklands War, 1968 – 82

They never go into battel other than in the defense of
their country or to drive out of their friends' lands
enemies that are comen in.

Sir Thomas More

The war in Ulster goes on. It has bad moments, and
more hopeful times, but no end to the troubles is really in
sight. They have been going on, on and off, for centuries,
and when the present phase began in 1968, the Royal
Marines were soon on the scene.

The first unit to be deployed was the recently-
reformed 41 Commando, who were serving their turn as
'Spearhead Battalion' of the Strategic Reserve when they
were ordered to Belfast in September 1969. The British
Army had only moved into the streets a month before, in
an attempt to assist the police in controlling an ever-
growing series of riots between Civil Rights marchers
and extremist elements from the Protestant community.
41 spent six weeks in Belfast, mainly in the Divis Street
area. Lt Uzzell was then Second-in-Command of 'F' Coy,
41 Commando.

'We were taking our turn as Spearhead Battalion, and
it was the unit's practice to parade one company fully
equipped and ready to move, every morning. This latest
round of trouble occurred on a Saturday night, and on
Sunday morning the company was told that it was not

going home, but to Belfast – there were many unhappy wives that morning.

'The first time I came under fire in Belfast was during 1969, in the Divis Street flats area. At that time 41 were based in a Catholic area and well accepted, with the main trouble coming from Protestants in the Shankhill. My troop were responsible for a street on the Peace Line, and one Saturday night a major riot took place in the Shankill – we could hear the noise from some distance away.

'When we came under fire, the order was passed that we could only fire back if a fire control order was given to a specific target. Shortly after that, my sentry position at the end of the street came under fire and I heard my Troop Sergeant's clear, concise fire order – "For xxxx sake . . . shoot back!" Fortunately they missed us and we missed them.

'To make ourselves less conspicuous, some of the troops were detailed to put out the street lights, and it was a bit disconcerting, when dodging along the street from door to door, to have a door open and a hand come out with a cup of tea and a sticky bun. We kept up to date with the situation by the residents passing on information from their TV sets – which was often more effective than our own radio network.

'What else? Well, in those early days, the Catholics were friendly; our accommodation was quite spartan, camping out between patrols in old cotton mills and we could only take a shower two or three times a week in the back of a specially converted three-tonner.'

In June 1970, 45 Commando arrived in Belfast and became responsible for the Crumlin Road area, which has the Catholic Ardoyne at one end and the Protestant areas as the other. The next clash between these two communities came on 26 June, when eight Protestant Orange Lodges, each with its marching band, set out for the Ardoyne, followed by a crowd of supporters estimated at over 2,000. This group soon became the target for stone-throwing crowds of Catholic youths, and the two communities were only kept apart by the presence of 45, the 1st King's Own Scottish Borderers (KOSB) and the 1st Royal Scots, who soon became the focus for the crowd's sectarian fury. The troops were pelted with catapulted rivets, iron pipes, bricks and glass bottles, until nearly every man was injured. One Royal Marine, a second lieutenant, was hit, full in the mouth, by a brick, flung directly and deliberately into his face from five yards' range. That night the Royal Ulster Constabulary and 400 Marines held apart two mobs: one of 2,000 Catholics, the other of some 3,000 Protestants. The mobs did not disperse until dawn, by which time all the troops and police were weary and many were bloody.

On the following day a sniper from the Ardoyne shot a man dead in the street while he was talking to a 'Y' Company patrol. One of 45's Naval medics, PO MacLaughlin, was fired on as he gave First Aid to a riot victim, and hit in the side as he helped the casualty into an ambulance clearly marked with the Red Cross. PO MacLaughlin was later awarded the George Medal for his courage during this incident. 45 then deployed five rifle companies across the Ardoyne, and subdued the rioters for a while, but another riot began that evening when a sniper opened up on the Marine patrol, and the mob set about burning shops and looting; 20 Marines from 45 suddenly found themselves surrounded by a shrieking mob of about 300 people. It took days for the area to calm down, with all ranks of the unit working hard to restore relations with the local communities, taking on 'hearts and minds' projects, offering entertainment, repairing buildings and playgrounds, and as always, taking part in a relentless round of guards and patrols. Since that first violent spell, the Commando units of the Royal Marines have returned regularly to

Ulster, operating in the cities or more often in the so-called 'bandit country' of South Armagh.

In July 1972, both 40 and 42 Commando took part in Operation Motorman, when the Army re-entered the 'No-go' areas of Londonderry and Belfast, but most of the Service operations in Ulster are out at section or sub-section level. More than most campaigns, this is a 'Corporal's War', where the lives of the men depend on the skill, training and patience of the Junior NCOs, who put up with conditions that would dismay a self-respecting vagrant, and endure, apart from the constant threat of attack, a steady level of abuse and insults from the local people.

Col Michael Marchant was with 42 Commando during Operation Motorman: 'I was Second-in-Command to Jeremy Moore, though we were both half-Colonels. 40 Commando were on the street and 42 were to provide assistance as required. We were based in Belfast and billeted in an old mill. Jeremy Moore is so professional, it was a pleasure to work under him and see how a unit can be handled. A typical day might consist of putting a company or two on the streets by 06.00, or maybe before dawn, patrolling, at a firm base, or just sitting in vehicles, waiting. There was little time for leisure, just patrol, eat, sleep, patrol . . . and not much sleep either. So much depended on the Corporal or Lance Corporal on the street. He had to get to know his patch and the people in it like the bobby on the beat, and react in whatever way was right when the need arose. The training of Royal Marine junior NCOs is so good, they were able to handle it, and the experience trains them in judgement, leadership, observation, so many things. The biggest single snag in Ulster is that you are not fighting a soldier's war; you are not allowed to take the initiative. It's a sad story, so engrained is the hatred. I remember driving down one street and one of the

Sergeants said to me, "You know, sir, I was born in this street and I remember going down the end as a child and chucking bricks at the Catholics." The men have to put up with a lot of stick, take a lot of physical and verbal abuse, but they put up with it wonderfully. I don't know when or how it will end – there is no military solution . . . it must come from the people themselves.'

Eric Blyth sees service in Northern Ireland through the eyes of a long-serving professional NCO 'I always found, in any riot, that it was foolish to rush straight in – better wait a bit until they get tired of it. Frankly, I think if the problem had been left to professional soldiers, it would have been cleared up years ago. The daily routine? Well, let's take a police station at, say, Rosslea; we had to man four posts in the town to cover, plus foot patrols, plus intelligence. You noted everything going on in the streets, sixteen to eighteen hours a day. It was nothing for a patrol to go out at 6 am, return at 4 pm and go out again at 10 pm until 4 am or later; it depended on the situation. In that area you needed to clear every road, every culvert every time . . . when you see a pal go up with a hundred pounder, well. . . . The lads were wonderful, they didn't mind what they did, as long as they did a decent job. Foot patrols were nauseating, with the abuse and name-calling you get, especially in the city, but in the rural areas it was better.'

Andrew Tubb went to Northern Ireland with 45 Commando in 1981, only a year after joining the Corps, and was promoted to Lance-Corporal. 'I thought that was a bit much frankly. Luckily I had young lads in my "brick" – a brick is four men including the Lance-Corporal – and our section corporal, Corp Baines, was a very experienced bloke. We had been well trained in a special training area back in England, which duplicated every situation we were likely to find. They even bring in WRENS to act, as housewives on the streets in riots, and you do a four-day cycle in a kind of fort, to go through the whole Ulster routine.

'When we arrived, we went to a Catholic area, Turf Lodge. You get any amount of tasking, job after job, and not much sleep. That goes on for four or five months. Later, we took over from the Royal Welsh Fusiliers at Fort White Rock. To give cover the way out is down a long, thin funnel. We used to send a 'brick' out to give cover, but one day they got engaged straight away by an automatic weapon, a semi, and some single shot. The rest of us went straight out and found the firing point within one and a half minutes! I'll never forget that – the firing, no hesitation, everyone went straight at them.'

Captain Ian Gardiner has so far done two tours in Northern Ireland. 'What is it like? Patrol after patrol after patrol . . . and when you are in, you're asleep. It's not a rewarding task and in spite of what you may hear, I don't think the basic problem is religious. I think it's economic. Anyway, it is also boring, and being bored can be dangerous when you are liable to be shot at, and it's depressing when you look at a lovely city like Armagh, with this . . . cancer . . . in its midst. I find the people themselves quite easy to get on with. Motorman was enjoyable. It was a joy to take some positive action and very well planned, taking the IRA completely by surprise, and I think it was essential to move in and restore at least the charade of law and order; before Motorman we didn't even have that.'

The Commando units have gained useful experience in Ulster, but they have paid the price in casualties. In 1972, 40 Commando had three Marines killed and seventeen injured, but they killed or captured over fifty terrorists. During the 1973 tours, they caught ninety-one terrorists without loss to themselves, but in 1976, six Marines were injured during a mortar attack on the police station at Crossmaglen. In 1981, just before the last phase of this story opens, the IRA struck at the highest echelons of the Corps, and much close to home, when a bomb exploded under the car of Lt-Gen Sir Steuart Pringle, Commandant Commandant General of The Royal Marines, as he started it up outside his London home, inflicting severe injuries . . . and so it goes on. The Commandos return regularly to Northern Ireland, fitting in Ulster tours with their normal round of training and, sadly, look likely to go on doing so for many years to come.

In 1982, their established round was interrupted in a most dramatic fashion by a full-scale war in the South Atlantic. The Argentine claim to the Falkland Islands is based on two factors, one historic, one emotional. The historic claim rests on the fact that when the vast Spanish overseas empire dissolved in the early years of the nineteenth century, its various component parts fell into the hands of the various Latin American republics. In 1810, Argentina claimed all the Spanish possessions in their area, and these certainly included the offshore islands known as the Malvinas. However, the validity of the Spanish claim to the islands was debatable, and although the Spanish garrison on the Malvinas withdrew in 1811, there was no Argentine settlement on the islands until 1826. This garrison was evicted in 1831 by the US warship *Lexington*, because the Argentine troops had interfered with American sealers cruising among the islands.

The Argentines appointed a new governor to the islands in 1832, but his men soon mutinied and he was murdered. His successor, a Commander Pinedo, was attempting to quell this mutiny when a British warship, *HMS Clio*, arrived in 1833, evicted the Argentines yet again, and established British sovereignty. The British settlement of Port Stanley began in that year, and British rule has continued ever since.

The British claim to sovereignty in the Falklands actually pre-dates the end of the Spanish Empire in Latin America. During the seventeenth and eighteenth centuries, these islands were visited fairly frequently by French and English sailors, and it was a Captain John Strong of Plymouth who named them the Falklands in 1690, after Viscount Falkland, then the Treasurer of the Royal Navy. The French arrived a little later, in 1698, hunting seals, and a Breton named them 'Les Isles Malouines', after his home port of St Malo in Brittany, the inhabitants of which are the *Malouines*. The Argentine name, Las Malvinas, is simply a Spanish corruption of this name. The French had, in fact, established a settlement on the islands in 1764, which is still called Port Louis, but a British expedition arrived a year later, raised the Union flag and claimed the Falkland Islands for King George III.

In 1767, the Spanish learned of the French settlement of Port Louis, (but not of the British landing), and after some argument, the French agreed to withdraw and hand over their settlement. A Spanish governor was appointed to Port Louis, which was renamed Puerto Soledad, and the islands then became the Malvinas. It was not until two years later that the Spaniards discovered the British settlement at Port Egmont. They then sent an expedition which forced the British to abandon the settlement in 1770, but in 1771 the British were allowed to return with Spanish permission, although the Spaniards were careful to state that their permission 'did not affect their (the Spaniards) *prior right of sovereignty* to the Malvinas, also called the Falklands'.

In 1774, the British withdrew, but left plaques behind claiming British sovereignty over the Falklands, but these plaques were later removed by the Spanish, who remained in occupation of the islands from 1774 to 1811, when the Spanish garrison withdrew and the Argentine claim begins.

Clearly, therefore, there have always been two claimants to the Malvinas or Falklands – sometimes three. The current argument rests mainly on the emotional claim of the Argentine government and people that they have a *right* to the 'Malvinas'. It is hard to think of any issue on which the British people could feel as strongly except this: that a friendly nation should not invade the territory of another with armed force and without warning, after that friendly nation had been in peaceful (if not undisputed) occupation of the said territory for a hundred and fifty years, – and while negotiations about its future status were actually in (albeit slow) progress.

The British say that if the Argentines want the Malvinas, they must negotiate for them. The Argentines point out that they have been attempting to negotiate for generations but without success; the British point out in turn that the Argentines' idea of negotiation is that Argentina will obtain the islands and agree to arbitration provided only that the arbitrators find in their favour. Meanwhile, the Falkland Islands are the home for 1,800 British people, who simply wish to remain British. In short, in 1982, the Argentines were fighting for the Malvinas, and the British were fighting for a principle; the soldiers, sailors, airmen and marines were fighting because they are professionals and that is what they are paid to do.

I should add that I have shown this brief history of the Falklands/Malvinas to an Argentine friend of mine, and he disagrees with it in every point, returning the draft with the word 'Falklands' heavily scored out every time it appears. It is hard to negotiate with people like that, and after some weeks of sparring, in early 1982, Argentina's patience finally ran out. A landing force was gathered together and sent to seize the 'Malvinas', hoping to put an end to this matter once and for all. It didn't turn out like that.

The Argentines sent a considerable force against the

Falklands and South Georgia. It consisted of a task force, No 40, embarked in two destroyers and two frigates, and the submarine *Santa Fé*, escorting two troopships, the *Isla de los Estados*, and the tank landing ship *Cabo San Antonio* carrying nineteen American amphibious landing craft, while more warships covered this landing force from the north, grouped around the aircraft carrier *Veintecino de Mayo*.

The landing force that would be sent against the Royal Marines garrison of Naval Party 8901 in the Falklands consisted of the 2nd Marine Infantry, a battalion of 600 or so regular troops, and a company of the *Buzo-Táctico* a force of some sixty Argentine Marines trained in Commando tactics. The Royal Marines of 8901 were therefore outnumbered by ten to one.

When the Argentine Navy began landing troops on the Falklands Islands and South Georgia, the Royal Marines garrison stood at the unusually large total of eighty men because the normal garrison of thirty or so men was being changed over and both detachments, the old one under Maj Noote, and the new one under Maj Norman, were ready for action, with Maj Norman in overall command. The eighty was made up of three officers and sixty-six men of the garrison, Naval Party 8901, and two officers and nine men from *HMS Endurance*. To these could be added twenty-three members of the local defence force who had little training and few weapons, and a Canadian, Bill Curtis, who offered to join in the fight. The weapons of the local defence force were taken from them to arm the Royal Marines who had arrived with Major Noote. Finally, to prove once and for all that there is really no such thing as an ex-Marine, there was Jim Fairfield, formally a corporal in the Corps, who had left the Royal Marines and married a local girl two years before. Jim Fairfield was given a 7.62 rifle and sent to join the garrison at Government House. Then the

Royal Marines, the people of the Falklands, and most of the world settled down to wait. Firing broke out at 06.30 on the morning of 2 April 1982.

The *Buzo-Táctico* attacked both the Royal Marine Barracks at Moody Brook and the garrison at Government House, Stanley, hoping to overwhelm the Marines and capture the Governor. The Royal Marines had actually withdrawn from their barracks, but the *Buzo Táctico* assaulted it anyway, clearing room after room with fragmentation and phosphorous grenades, spraying it with machine-gun fire and doing considerable damage to the interior. Meeting with no resistance, they then hurried off to join in the attack on Government House, where the Royal Marines were already in action.

The first Argentine attack on Government House took place at about 06.15, when a snatch squad entered the grounds, hoping to seize the Governor. These were shot down by the Royal Marines, and three more were captured later by Maj Noote. Firing between the Royal Marine defenders and the attacking Argentine troops went on around Stanley for over half an hour before Argentine reinforcements arrived in armoured Amtracs, bringing men of the 2nd Marines landed from the *Cabo San Antonio*. These were swiftly engaged on the outskirts of the town by a Royal Marine picket of eight men, commanded by Lt Bill Trollope. Marine Brown scored a direct hit on one Amtrac with a 66 mm rocket, and when an 84 mm Carl Gustav round hit it again, the Argentine advance stopped. The Royal Marines engaged the Amtrac survivors with rifle and machine-gun fire, before withdrawing without loss into the town.

Such fire-fights were taking place all over Stanley between small groups of Royal Marines and the advancing Argentine forces. Even after the town had been overrun, the Royal Marines fought on. One detachment, Corporal Stefan York and five Marines, hit an Argentine landing craft with a Carl Gustav round as it entered the harbour, and clearly the Royal Marines were putting up a good fight everywhere, but it couldn't last. More and more Argentine troops were coming ashore, their cordon began to tighten around Government House and, as it got light, Argentine aircraft began to land more infantry at Stanley Airport.

At 08.30 Maj. Norman told Rex Hunt, the Governor, that his house would soon be under fire from heavy weapons, to which the Royal Marines had no response, and suggested that the time had come to break out into the hills. There were negotiations with the Argentines, and the Governor finally ordered the Royal Marines to cease fire at 09.25. Meanwhile, other Argentine forces were meeting the Royal Marines on South Georgia and getting a warm reception.

The Royal Marines garrison at Grytviken on South Georgia consisted of twenty-two marines commanded by Lt Keith Mills. Their heaviest weapon was the 82 mm Carl Gustav anti-tank rocket, but when a frigate of the Argentine Navy, the *Guerrico*, arrived offshore and summoned them to surrender, the Royal Marines promptly opened fire. A Puma helicopter from the landing ship *Bahia Paraiso*, unwisely overflew the Marine positions and was shot down by machine-gun fire, while a round from the Carl Gustav and a 66 mm rocket scored hits on the *Guerrico*. The *Guerrico* hastily withdrew out of range and began to shell the British positions with her 100 mm gun. The Royal Marines had no means of replying to this weapon, so Lt Mills wisely decided to surrender. The Royal Marines on South Georgia suffered one casualty, Cpl Nigel Peters, hit by two rounds while firing a 66 mm rocket into the *Guerrico*.

The Royal Marine garrisons of the Falklands and South Georgia were repatriated to England by the Argentine forces, and were sent to join 42, where Naval

Party 8901 became 'J' Company of 42 Commando. Estimations vary as to the losses and casualties they caused to the invaders, but a fair calculation would be one landing craft and one Puma helicopter destroyed, one frigate damaged and, assuming that the Amtrac hit outside Stanley was fully loaded with troops, about 50 Argentine soldiers killed or wounded. As far as the rest of the Corps were concerned, waiting anxiously in England for news, the important thing was that the Royal Marines in the South Atlantic had put up a fight, and given the Argentine forces a small taste of what they could expect in the not too distant future.

'Bye for now,' the Marines of Naval Party 8901 told their captors as they were marched aboard the transport, 'but don't get too comfy . . . we'll be back.'

Britain's ability to retake the Falklands would particularly depend on two arms of the Service, the Royal Navy, which must convey the troops to the landing beaches while fighting off any opposition *en route* from enemy ships and aircraft, and 3 Commando Brigade, Royal Marines, the one British formation fully trained in amphibious warfare.

By 1982, 3 Commando Brigade, Royal Marines, was much more than a simple brigade of highly trained in-fantry. It was a little army, an independent, highly mobile Brigade Group. The cutting edge, as always, was the three Commando Units, 40, 42 and 45, totalling some 3,000 men. 42 and 45 Commandos were specially trained in Mountain and Arctic warfare, and all three units had seen recent active service in Northern Ireland. Their artillery was provided by 29 Commando Regiment, Royal Artillery, their sappers were from 59 Commando Squadron, Royal Engineers, and the Brigade also had under command a Logistic Regiment, which was to prove vital, an Air Squadron equipped with Gazelle and

Scout helicopters, an Air Defence Troop, equipped with Blowpipe missiles, the 1st Raiding Squadron, equipped with assault craft, also manned by Royal Marines and the Mountain and Arctic Warfare Cadre of the Royal Marines. It also usually contains, and works closely with, amphibious units of the Royal Netherlands Marine Corps. This Brigade was selected as the core of the Task Force, but in view of the strong enemy forces now established on the Falklands, it was decided to increase 3 Commando Brigade's strength by adding another infantry battalion, the 3rd Bn, the Parachute Regiment (3 Para), two troops of light tanks from the Blues and Royals, and a battery of the Air Defence Regiment, Royal Artillery, equipped with Rapier anti-aircraft missiles. Various other units were added to this force including two Squadrons and the RHQ from the 22 Special Air Service Regiment, and some SBS men. It was decided later that this force was still not sufficient, and so yet another battalion from the Parachute Regiment, 2 Para, was added to the Task Force, along with various support and logistic units. 2 Para joined the force at Ascension. This entire force was placed under the command of a Royal Marine brigadier, Julian Thompson, commanding 3 Commando Brigade, with Maj-Gen Jeremy Moore, Major-General Commando Forces, Royal Marines, as Land Force Commander once 3 Commando Brigade and 5th Infantry Brigade were ashore. This operation, to retake the Falklands, also acquired a code-name. They called it Operation Corporate. By 26 April, the units had sailed or flown for the South Atlantic and, as the Task Force gathered strength and sailed south, the world settled down to wait.

Maj-Gen Jeremy Moore: 'I suppose my involvement began on 17 October 1981, when the IRA exploded that bomb under Robin Pringle's car. As the next senior General, I took on part of his work while he recovered from his injuries, but I was actually due to retire in May 1982. Robin Pringle took over command of the Corps again on 31 March, and we had a General Officers' Meeting on 1 April, at which we discussed the alarums and excursions in the Falklands and what to do about Naval Party 8901. We considered various options; first stand by to send a troop, or a company, or a Commando out by air; then stand by to send the Air Defence Troop: The snag was that lacking a major runway, we would have to fly in via Argentina – so, picture the Air Defence Troop arriving in Buenos Aires to trans-ship to the Falklands, all thinly disguised as civilian double-bass players! On 1 April I was at Commando Forces then at work in my study until midnight. The phone rang at about 3 am on the 2nd and Michael Wilkins said, "You had better get up again," so I got up and we got on with it.'

Brigadier Julian Thompson was also in bed. His phone rang at 03.15 on 2 April, and Gen Moore said briefly, 'You know those people down South – they're about to be invaded. Your Brigade is to come to seventy-two hours notice to move with effect from now.'

Brig Julian Thompson: 'I joined the Royal Marines to be a Commando. I took a Heavy Weapons qualification for the same reason, because Heavy Weapons ratings never went to sea, and as a result I spent a lot of my service in the Brigade, notably in 40 Commando. I was first a Lieutenant in the MMG platoon, then the troop commander of 'S' Troop, the Adjutant of 40 – you could say I'm a child of 40 Commando. That's where I was brought up. I finally became the Commanding Officer of 40 and took the Unit on tours to South Armagh.

'3 Commando Brigade is always at seven days notice to move, but the invasion came at a difficult time. Many of my Brigade Staff were in Denmark, planning an exercise. 45 Commando were about to go on Easter leave, and one company was jungle training in Brunei; 42 were already on leave after an exercise in Norway, but 40 Commando, at least, were intact and had just finished a range course.'

Marine Andrew Tubb: 'Having done a sniper course, I was then with the Recce Troop of 45. Our OC was Lt-Fox, who got the MC in the Falklands. Lance-Corporal Pete McKay, who was killed at Ajax Bay, came into our room about 5 am and shook everyone awake. "Leave is off," he said.'

Colonel Andrew Whitehead, CO of 45, was abroad. 'I didn't get a phone call. I was in Denmark, planning the Brigade exercise, and someone came thumping on my door at 5 am. I flew back and got up to Arbroath in one of the Air Troop Gazelles. The unit was about to go on leave but "Y" Coy were in Hong Kong, after a jungle exercise. I actually got the whole Commando together for the first time on Ascension.'

Captain Ian Gardiner, also of 45, was in bed when his call came at 04.00. 'Where else would a good man be at that hour of night? I was at home in Newbiggin when Maureen on the manual telephone exchange called me up. I think my reaction was quite usual. "Pull the other one, 1 April was yesterday." I got up, ferreted about in the garden shed for my kit and was in barracks by 06.00. We had an "O" Group at 06.30 when, as I recall, our orders were: "3 Cdo Bde is called to readiness for amphibious operations in the South Atlantic." The bulk of the unit were off within four days, but "X" and "Y" Companies were left behind to fly out to Ascension on the 13 April.'

The period between that initial call and the departure of the Task Force was packed with activity.

'It was pretty chaotic,' recalls Andrew Tubb. 'We spent most of our time packing and unpacking trailers. I phoned my family and told them I wouldn't be home for leave.'

Jeremy Moore: '3 Commando Brigade had ... has ... one great, but little-known asset, that of the Commando Logistic Regiment, to maintain us in the field. We had a logistical system that worked because we had exercised it, and gone to the trouble to see that it worked. It was a major factor in all we were about to do, namely move eight thousand miles rather quickly, then land and win a battle. Without good logistic support you just grind to a halt. Did I believe we would have to fight? Well, I hope I gave that impression ... but no, I didn't really believe it would come to fighting, not until the loss of *HMS Sheffield*.'

Col Whitehead: 'The Brigade is always on seven days notice to move, and we were brought to 72 hours notice – when we actually did move, one of our problems was to load about 4,500 *tons* of stores and ammunition, over the weekend. Did I think we would have to land? Yes, I did. I knew the Argentines, being the way they are, would not lose face and pull out, and so either the British Government would fold or we would go ashore; and I knew Maggie Thatcher wouldn't fold, so ...'

Lance-Corporal Andrew Spiers was with Commando Brigade HQ. 'It was exciting – crowds in the street, Pressmen about, people taking photographs ... Half of me thought we would go all the way, half of me thought not – we didn't get a lot of news before we sailed on *Fearless*.'

Andrew Tubb remembers leaving harbour. 'We sailed on the *Stromness*, a Fleet Auxiliary, all on one deck ... the largest mess-deck in Naval history. We lined ship for leaving harbour – it was raining but there were crowds of people to see us go. The dockyard maties – the dockies – had a whip round to buy us videos! Can you imagine that? The rest of the unit either flew out or were on the *Tristram* – or was it the *Galahad*? On the way south we ran a full training programme, fitness, first-aid, aircraft recognition, weapon training.'

Captain Gardiner: 'Everyone wanted to go. I had men in

my office in tears – literally – because they couldn't come with us, and men who had finished their time in the Corps, twelve years, begging to be allowed to stay on and come to the South Atlantic. I didn't think it would be easy. I knew we could have casualties, wounds, deaths. I told the men so and I asked them to think about it . . . but never let it be thought that the Royal Marines didn't want to fight – everyone was mad keen to go. I was never in any doubt that we had chosen and trained the right kind of people and I was proud of them. If I don't mention that again, you can assume it. I loved them.'

And so they sailed.

It is not the purpose of this book to detail the diplomatic moves, the subtle manoeuvres, the UN resolutions and the pleas and counter-pleas that flooded the airwaves of the world while the Task Force ploughed south towards the Falklands. A more interesting personal view comes from my Argentine friend, Juan-Carlos Garcia.

'We never thought you would do it – not for a moment. These are not the gunboat days of the Empire and why would you, a European nation, send a whole army, ships and men, all that way to help a few hundred people and a lot of sheep? And yet it happened! I think – we all thought – that somehow there would be no fighting, that it was all a bluff, that the Americans or the UN would make you stop. Anyway, if you did try, you did not have the aircraft there. Then you sank the *Belgrano*, and the Malvinas war was not so glorious for us any more.'

A fleet was on the sea. Sixty-five ships sailed south, liners, cargo ships, destroyers, frigates, aircraft carriers, landing ships, transports, submarines, carrying 7,000 men of 3 Commando Brigade to the assault. Initially all these ships were heading for Ascension Island, 3,000 miles north of the Falklands, where the hurriedly loaded ships could sort out their stores and the men could go ashore to fire and test their weapons, while fresh supplies and reinforcements arrived by air from England. The first ships of the Task Force arrived at Ascension Island on 10 April, but the last did not come in until 10 May. At sea, the troops took a renewed interest in first aid, practised weapon drills endlessly, and ran around the ships' decks trying hard to stay in trim and fighting fit.

Ascension did give some of the men a chance to get ashore and stretch their legs, while stores and men were transferred or 'cross-decked', most of the Brigade 'cross-decking' to the liner *Canberra*.

'The Brigadier was with us,' recalls Lance-Corp Spiers. 'He was always very highly spoken of by everyone, a real soldier's soldier. He'd come up for a chat with no barriers at all. We spent a lot of time waiting for our SOPs (Standard Operating Procedures) to come out from England from Commando Forces. These had to be collected from the airfield – the first day only a couple of us went, bimbling about; we found the Yank PX and had a few beers . . . it was great . . . eventually *everyone* went to get the mail every day.'

Col Whitehead: 'Ascension was a bit limited for training, but we did what we could. There was no doubt that we would fight, and the Navy kept us at very short notice to sail. When we did sail, on a still, hot night, just after sunset, I thought to myself: this is the beginning of the last phase.'

Andrew Tubb recalls his 'S' Coy scrounging ammunition to zero their rifles, and filling sandbags to build sangars on the *Canberra*, while 'X' and 'Y' Coys of 45, who had arrived earlier, had tucked themselves away at the end of the island and, according to Ian Gardiner, 'got down to some of the best tactical training I have ever seen.'

On 12 April the British Government established a Maritime Exclusion Zone around the Falkland Islands. On the same day a force of three ships, the destroyers *HMS Antrim* and *HMS Plymouth* accompanied by the tanker *Tidespring*, sailed from Ascension. On board were 'M' Company 42 Commando, and 'D' Squadron 22 SAS, with men from 2 Section SBS and 29 Commando Regiment, Royal Artillery. Their task, Operation Paraquat, was the liberation of South Georgia.

On 14 April this small Task Force met *HMS Endurance*, which had been cruising the South Atlantic since the Argentine landings. On 19 April the submarine *HMS Conqueror* put a reconnaissance party of Marines from the Special Boat Squadron ashore on South Georgia. A landing force of Marines, SBS and SAS men went ashore by helicopter at Grytviken, under cover of shellfire from *HMS Antrim* and *Plymouth*, and at 17.00 on 25 April, the Argentine garrison surrendered, without the invading force firing a shot, although the SAS lost two precious helicopters in crashes. 'M' Company of 42 Commando were particularly put out at this swift success, because while the others were ashore 'enjoying themselves', 'M' Company were still 150 miles out at sea on the *Tidespring*, and the pleasure of recapturing South Georgia went to other Marines and the SAS. It was a useful prelude to the campaign. The South Georgia task force had also sunk an Argentine submarine, the *Santa Fé*, and captured 150 Argentine troops, including one Capt Alfredo Astiz, a particularly unpleasant character who was wanted by several countries on charges of torture and murder. Most important of all, they had retaken South Georgia only twenty-two days after the Argentine forces had attacked Lt Mills' small party – and done so at no cost in lives. 'M' Company of 42 were obliged to remain as the garrison of South Georgia until the war was over, much to their disgust.

On 2 May, the submarine *HMS Conqueror* sank the Argentine cruiser *Belgrano*, one of the most controversial acts of the Falklands War. Whatever anyone may say, hostilities were in progress, the *Belgrano* was an enemy warship, and an Argentine Admiral has since publicly admitted that, had he been in command of the British forces, he would have done exactly the same thing. Sinking the *Belgrano* had the beneficial effect of alerting the Argentine Navy to the probability of attack by British submarines, and from then on their Navy took no part in the war, which is particularly important, because aircraft flown from the carrier *Veintecinco de Mayo*, could have severely hampered the Task Force which had few aircraft and was particularly vulnerable to air attack. Meanwhile, the Fleet sailed South.

The main Task Force sailed from Ascension Island in various groups between 30 April and 8 May. Andrew Tubb again: '"S" Company in a Commando consists of five Troops; Recce, Mortar, Anti-Tank, Assault Engineers, and Surveillance. I was in Recce, but the whole Company cross-decked to *Intrepid*, where we were briefed for the landing at San Carlos. The sailors put us on their mess-decks, looking after their own, while the Paras just had to doss down where they could, in the companionways and stairwells. When we ammo'd up, we had all manner of ammo, it was coming out of our ears.'

While they were at sea the Commanders were still debating the best place to land, and the final decision, to land at San Carlos on East Falkland, was not taken until 12 May. As always, the decision was a compromise, for San Carlos was not ideal. On the one hand it had sheltered anchorage for the ships and two good landing beaches, but it was close to the Argentine garrison at Goose Green, and within range of air attack, both by Pucara ground-attack fighters based on the Falklands and other aircraft sent from the mainland; nor was it ideal for the deployment of air-to-ground missiles. Worst of all, it lay fifty miles from Port Stanley.

The first task was to eliminate an Argentine artillery and mortar post on Fanning Head, which overlooked the entry to San Carlos Water. This was carried out by an SBS force equipped with GPMGs, and accompanied by Captain Rod Bell, a Spanish-speaking Royal Marine officer, equipped with a loud-hailer. 'We gave them plenty of chances to surrender, but they wouldn't . . . it was a duck shoot.' The landing forces could see the tracer arcing about Fanning Head, as they embarked in the assault craft.

The initial main landings on 21 May were made by 40 Commando and 2 Para, who landed under the Verde and Sussex Mountains by San Carlos settlement, and went ashore in darkness at 04.40 local time, an hour late. Delays continued to accumulate as the landing craft returned to the troop ships waiting off San Carlos Water to bring 45 Commando and 3 para ashore, 45 Commando landing at Ajax Bay, 3 Para a mile west of Port San Carlos. Dawn had now broken, and helicopters hurried to bring in the Brigades' Rapier air-defence missile launchers, and the 105 mm guns of 29 Commando Regiment RA, while the Marines and Paras around the beach-head began to dig in. The first action of the day began when Argentine small arms fire from Port San Carlos shot down two Gazelle helicopters and damaged another. 3 Para continued to advance and finally cleared the Argentines out of the Port San Carlos, and with the landing area now secured, the troop and supply ships came through the narrows into the San Carlos anchorage and the work of ferrying men and stores ashore got under way in earnest, with the vast white bulk of the cruise liner *Canberra* looming over the smaller ships. An Argentine Pucara aircraft attacked the ships with cannon two hours after dawn, but veered away when faced with a

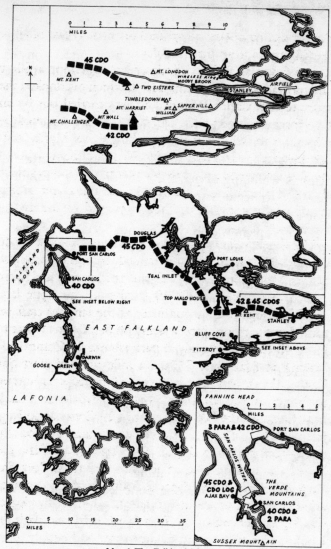

Map 6 The Falkland Islands

wall of fire from the ships and the troops around the shores of the bay. Other more serious air attacks on the landing strips by mainland-based Skyhawk and Mirage aircraft began at 10.30, and went on at intervals throughout the day, doing some damage to the ships.

L-Corp Andrew Spiers: 'The first wave got away in the dark, but by the time the second wave went off, it was broad daylight. It looked like a bloody regatta . . . Geminis whipping about . . . a bit of fire on Fanning Head . . . to begin with it was like an exercise . . . there wasn't even a sheep on the shore to meet us.'

L-Corp Spiers was in the Defence Section of Brigade HQ but, like many of his mates, he had been sent to man the defences on the liner *Canberra*, now discharging troops in the middle of San Carlos Water. 'We had built sandbag sangars round the decks, each with a GPMG and a two-man crew, about thirty guns in all, I should think. From up there I could see the troops digging in up on the hill and then three Mirages whistled overhead. The Captain of the *Canberra* was very good, getting on the loudspeaker to tell everyone below deck what was going on. I clattered away at everything in range – it was frightening at first, but then it was fun. The jets came screaming down the valley, firing cannon, dropping bombs on the ships . . . everyone was firing at them with machine guns, rifles – everything.'

Andrew Tubb: 'Everyone came leaping out of their trenches and opened up at the aircraft. It was like a party . . . we got hits too . . . a lot of aircraft had smoke coming out as they went away.'

Andrew Spiers: 'The only snag was, we got a bit over-enthusiastic. Our fire from the port side was falling on 45 Commando, and off the starboard side it was landing around 40 Commando – equally their "overs" were coming onto the ships . . . they didn't seem to hurt anyone though.'

Corporal Colin Gillingham was ashore at Julian Thompson's command post: 'I was busy digging a nice deep trench, when the aircraft started making passes. The sky was full of tracer, and the Blowpipe missiles got going – one took out a Pucara.'

Eventually the air attacks ceased and the rest of the Brigade came ashore. L-Corp Spiers: 'We came off *Canberra* in the afternoon. They landed us on the wrong beach (of course), and we hung about there for a bit until a Gemini took us over to Brigade HQ at San Carlos, where all the "Odds & Sods" were formed into a defence section.'

Four Argentine fighters were shot down in the morning, with Sea Harriers adding six more later in the afternoon, although the Argentines then succeeded in hitting the frigate *HMS Ardent*, which had to be abandoned on fire and later sank. In fact, the Argentine Air Force hit every ship in the anchorage, as Julian Thompson remembers: 'I could hear the Naval net, and captain after captain was reporting to Mike Clapp, "I can steam and fight but not steer", or, "I can fight but I can't steam". I remember that *HMS Argonaut* had to be towed by three LCUs commanded by Euan Southeby Tailyour.'

Over the next few days San Carlos Water became known as Bomb Alley, as wave after wave of Argentine fighter bombers came in at low level to attack the shipping, hitting the frigate *HMS Antelope* on 23 May and the landing ships *Sir Galahad* and *Sir Lancelot* the next day. *HMS Antelope* sank later. Most of these attacks were against the ships and it was not until 27 May that the Argentine airforce turned its attention to the troops on shore. By 27 May though, the landing area was secure, and enough supplies had been landed for the force ashore to advance.

Corp Colin Gillingham: 'After a day or so they reckoned that Brigade HQ had been compromised, so we moved. I met my brother, who was a Marine in Support Company of 40 Commando. They used to go through our lines to go out and patrol and I saw him pass . . . I hadn't seen him for a year until then.'

3 Commando Brigade had been waiting for the arrival of 5 Brigade, but as the Navy were suffering considerable losses at sea, with *HMS Ardent* sunk on 21 May and *HMS Antelope* sunk on 23 May, with *HMS Argonaut* and *Antrim* damaged on 21 May, and the destroyer *Coventry* bombed and sunk on 25 May, in addition to the loss of *HMS Sheffield* on 4 May, it was decided that 3 Commando Brigade should move out from the beach-head and proceed to invest the defence of Stanley, leaving 40 Commando to defend the beach-head. 2 Para then advanced on Goose Green while 3 Para and 45 Commando began to march – or yomp – across East Falkland towards Stanley, followed later by 42 Commando, lifted forward in helicopters. This phase began on 27 May.

Julian Thompson: 'Helicopters were the key, and when we lost a number of them when the *Atlantic Conveyor* was hit, that was a real blow – but even helicopters have their limitations. For example, it took eighty-five Sea King helicopter lifts to move just one battery of 105 mm guns forward to Mount Kent, and so to move the battery forward out of the beach-head to cover our assaults on Two Sisters and so on, a round trip of over an hour, would take *three days* – to move one battery!

'We had planned to raid Goose Green before 5 Brigade arrived – a battalion raid by 2 Para, with gunfire support, wellie-in, duff-up the garrison and bugger off, that's all . . . but I couldn't move the guns because we were short of helicopters, so I called the raid off. Then people back in the UK started getting impatient, and asked me what I was doing.

'I replied, "Recce-ing Mount Kent, and I can't move the guns to support 2 Para, so the raid on Goose Green is cancelled."

'They said – quote, "You don't *need* recces for Mount Kent, and you don't *need* guns to assault Goose Green."

'Well, two comments. First, you don't send men forward unless you can support them – and war uses up ammo very fast – and ammo weighs one hell of a lot . . . it's not *easy*.

'Secondly, the purpose of infantry is to take and hold ground. You can perform both parts more effectively if you know all about that ground and who is on it . . . and that means recce. Infantry warfare is a creepy-crawlie business, and with my available helicopters I could either move to occupy Mount Kent, which was the key to the next phase, or assault Goose Green, but not both – and the real aim was to take Stanley.

'I was given a direct order to attack Goose Green, so I sent 2 Para against it. But they got their gunfire support, and they needed it.'

The battle fought at Goose Green on 28 May must be told by the Parachute Regiment, who fought it, for our story follows 45 and 42 on their famous yomp to Stanley, leaving a highly disgruntled 40 Commando sitting in their wet trenches above San Carlos, where most of them remained for the rest of the war.

Julian Thompson: 'If I'd known that 40 were to be kept back at the beach-head, I'd have moved them out before the order arrived. Quite apart from any other consideration, I had Malcolm Hunt in mind as Deputy Brigade Commander – he'd have made a bloody good Brigade Commander. As his HQ was close to Brigade HQ, I saw more of him than I did of the other COs, so there was a practical element in it, apart from the fact that 40 was my old Unit, and a damned fine one.

'One thing you must point out about 2 Para and

Goose Green,' says Captain Ian Gardiner of 45 Commando. 'That battle set the tone for the whole war. 2 Para showed them – and us – that we could beat the Argentines, whatever the odds. They scored the first goal and gave us moral ascendancy. After that we never looked back.'

Jeremy Moore: 'I went ashore just after Goose Green, arriving in time for the burial service of Lt-Col 'H' Jones and his men of 2 Para, a very moving experience on that muddy, bloody ground. We were based first at Ajax Bay, where there were still two unexploded bombs on the roof of the hospital. All in all, I arrived at a good moment, 3 Commando Brigade were moving out, 5 Brigade were about to come ashore, and 2 Para's action at Goose Green was a great boost. One of the things I have learned from history is that the side which establishes moral ascendancy has gone a long way towards winning the fight. I can't think of a better bunch of men to go to war with than the Paras, and 2 Para were a fine fighting unit. . . . Look, when a battalion wins a bloody battle, they give the CO the DSO, because the CO *is* the unit – the unit fights the way the CO wants it to – it takes on his attitude and spirit.'

45 led the advance from the beach-head, first crossing Ajax Bay to Port San Carlos in landing craft, passing through the 3 Para positions and covering fourteen miles across the boggy, tussocky ground before nightfall. The march went on all day and night until the following morning, when, after a wet night in the open, 45 marched into Douglas Settlement and then on to Teal Inlet, where they found that 3 Para had already arrived by a more direct route.

Col Whitehead: 'Each marine was carrying about 120lbs with all his kit and ammunition. We yomped to Douglas Settlement via New House, over murderous ground. On the first day we stopped an hour before dark and cooked a meal, then marched across country on a compass bearing until 2 am. 45 marched every step of the way from the beach-head to Stanley – about fifty miles, and we took Two Sisters on the way.'

Ahead lay the first major obstacle, the snugly defended Argentine positions on the 1500-foot high slopes of Mount Kent only twelve miles west of Stanley. The task of taking this position was given to 42 Commando on the night of 29 May.

Three Sea Kings collected 'K' Company of 42 from San Carlos and tried to fly them forward the 40 miles to Mount Kent, but were forced to turn back by blizzards. On the following night they tried again, taking the 'K' Company, Commando TAC-HQ, and the Mortar Troop. 'K' Company advanced on Mount Kent and found it deserted, and so on the following night, more of 42 arrived, accompanied by artillery, and dug in on Mount Kent, where they waited for more stores, ammunition and men to join them before the next phase of the advance, on Mount Harriet and Two Sisters. Reconnaissance teams and patrols went out to observe the ground for this advance, to harass the enemy, and to eliminate one possible obstacle, when twenty men of the Royal Marines Arctic and Mountain Warfare Cadre were lifted forward to eliminate a party of Argentine troops at Top Malo House, south of Teal Inlet, killing five and taking twelve prisoners, including their commander, an Anglo-Argentine officer, Lt Luis Albert Brown, who received four wounds but survived. With this obstacle removed, 3 Para, 42 and 45 Commando continued to ease up on Stanley, until they were right up against the Argentine defences, with Brigadier Thompson's HQ now established at Teal Inlet. General Moore established his TAC-HQ at Fitzroy on 10 June. All this was complete only one week after they had left the beach-head at San Carlos.

Andrew Tubb of 45's Recce Troop was on these patrols,

penetrating the Argentine positions on Two Sisters: 'The Falklands terrain? Like a harsh Dartmoor or the Highlands, no trees, lots of long stone runs, all covered with moss, very slippery . . . the weather was sunny to start with, crisp autumn-like, but always a wind, it never stopped blowing.

'We didn't go on the yomp to Teal and then Douglas Settlement, we got lifted by helicopter . . . that made Recce Troop *very* popular. Then we were tasked for a 26-man patrol to the Stanley side of Two Sisters . . . saw five Argentines and called in artillery fire. We were actually inside the Argentine positions, so we ended up shelling ourselves. We did a lot of patrols up to Two Sisters . . . that time we pepper-potted for about 400 metres to get out, through the Argy lines, firing 66 rockets to fight through and regroup. We got the artillery again to smoke us out. It took us well over an hour to get away and it seemed like a few minutes. We killed seventeen of them, and all we had was one bloke with a flesh wound. Then we had a 17 kilometre march back to our lines.

'Next night we were tasked again to go out with a fighting patrol of 'X' Coy. We took the same route into the rocks. We knew that way pretty well, but of course, when the attack went in, we went with the main body, not with 'X'. Col Whitehead said he got a lot of information out of these recces and patrols. He would always listen to what the Marines had to say and alter his plans accordingly and when the attack went in the Colonel was right up there, just behind the leading company.'

Col Whitehead: 'The best instrument for a Commander to use before an attack is the Mark I eyball. We sent out a lot of recce patrols to Two Sisters, and followed them up with fighting patrols.

'Our orders were to take Two Sisters by a two-phase, two-pronged attack with a silent approach. In other words, we had artillery support but they didn't fire until I said – they altered the range, kept to a fire plan, did everything in fact but pull the lever that fires the shell, while we worked our way up and got as close as we could.'

The Argentine forces defending the hills around Stanley numbered between 8,000 and 9,000 men, of whom about 5,000 were infantry. These forces were well armed but not altogether well trained, many of them being conscripted and reluctant soldiers, now know in the Argentine as '*los chicos de la guerra*', the 'young lads of the war'. However, they had had plenty of time to dig in, were well supplied with mines, and made good use of an abundance of heavy machine guns. Their supply arrangements were poor, with very few rations getting forward to the troops in the trenches, but they were on the defensive and still ready to fight.

Maj-Gen Jeremy Moore, commanding the land forces ashore in the Falklands, had four front-line units ready for the Port Stanley battle, and three others close behind. To the south, in front of Bluff Cove, were the 2nd Bn Scots Guards, of 5 Brigade, while to the north lay three units of 3 Commando Brigade. Here on the right flank, facing Mount Wall and Mount Harriet was 42 Commando. In the centre, 45 faced Two Sisters, and finally, on the left flank, 3 Para faced Mount Longdon. In addition to this were 1/7th Gurkhas; 2 Para, cock-a-hoop after Goose Green; and 1st Bn the Welsh Guards, which had two companies of 40 Commando attached to make up the losses sustained on the *Sir Galahad*. The Argentine positions lay across a long strip of 'No Man's Land' which varied in width from five miles in the north to two miles in the south. British patrols went out across No Man's Land every night, and the British forces suffered many casualties from mines in this probing reconnaissance phase.

General Moore's final plan for the assualt on the

defences of Stanley called for a two-phase attack with 3 Commando Brigade attacking Harriet, Longdon and Two Sisters on the first night, 11/12 June; and both 3 and 5 Brigade attacking again and together on the next night, 12/13, on Tumbledown, Wireless Ridge and Mount William. If the Argentines continued to fight, Sapper Hill (only a mile south of Stanley) would be attacked on that night, but on the other hand, if 3 Commando Brigade achieved early success with their initial attacks, they were given leave to press on, supported throughout by artillery and naval gunfire. The assault began with 3 Para moving out to attack and take Mount Longdon, which they took, losing eighteen men, including Sergeant Ian McKay, who won a posthumous VC for his gallantry during the action.

45 Commando moved against their objective, Two Sisters, south-west of Mount Longdon, at 23.00 local time. This attack was delayed because 'X' Coy, which had to attack the southern peak of the Two Sisters, was seriously delayed by the rough going to their start line and the weight of their equipment. Lt-Col Whitehead took advantage of this delay to order the two companies detailed for the northern summit, 'Y' and 'Z', to work their way forward. They had advanced to within three hundred metres of the Argentine position before they were spotted and came under fire. A fierce fight then broke out which found the forward Troops of 'Z' Company pinned down out in the open, under heavy fire and taking casualties.

Lt Dytor's 8 Troop of 'Z' Company then charged the Argentine positions, and the rest of 'Z' followed up close behind, with 'Y' Company swinging in to take the southern edge of the northern feature, while 'X' Company leap-frogged up the steep southern one. 45 took Two Sisters with the loss of four men killed and eight injured, capturing a number of Argentine soldiers.

Captain Gardiner: 'Two Sisters . . . yes . . . but first let me tell you a little about the Brigade. Julian Thompson's officers were his friends, and the Brigade *worked*; we had our own engineers, our own artillery, and amphibious operations were – are – our bread and butter, *plus*, don't forget, we had attached to us two of the most able infantry units in the British Army, 2 Para and 3 Para, who took Longdon. Now 5 Brigade had lost 2 and 3 Paras and were given two Guards battalions without recent field experience. They had no logistics unit then – they have one now – and were briefed for a garrison role in the Falklands.'

General Moore disagrees with this last point: 'I always intended to use 5 Brigade in the fight. Tony Wilson of 5 Brigade clearly wanted a piece of the action for his Brigade and we discussed this frequently during our five days on the *QE2*. The snag was that his Brigade lacked logistical support, and the battalions were short of field training. Of course, 40 Commando wanted to go forward. Their CO, Malcolm Hunt, came to see me with the request that his unit should march out of San Carlos and I was entirely sympathetic, but . . . I did my best for them . . . two companies went to reinforce the Welsh Guards after they lost men at Port Pleasant – *please* don't call it Bluff Cove – and their Milan Troop went to Two Sisters with 45.'

Captain Gardiner again: 'I was given my objectives quite early on, and the recce or fighting patrols brought back lots of information on the enemy and the ground. I went forward to Mount Kent, and saw the lie of the land, saw people wandering about on the saddle between the two peaks – it's only about a thousand feet high, but it is littered with large, bungalow-sized rocks. It was like fighting in a ruined city, set on a steep slope. We managed a rehearsal and 'Z' Company did the same. I talked the company through each phase, man by man – what are you going to do? Think! Think!

'What went wrong? We got lost, that was one problem – then the men were carrying 80lbs each at least, and some had Milan rockets as well – we had 40's Anti-Tank Troop along. Eventually I broke radio silence and told the Colonel, who was marvellous about it. He said, "Get in position, sort yourselves out, and then we'll go", and that's what we did.

'Our attack – 'X' Coy – was to take three successive ridges on the south peak. I put the Troops in one after the other to leapfrog up the hill; 1 Troop first, then 3, then 2. I stayed with my HQ just behind the lead Troop. I'll talk you through it . . . No 1 Troop . . . Go!

'Lt James Kelly's 1 Troop took the first objective unopposed – not a shot, so in went 3 Troop, Lt Stewart, who also took his objective unopposed – as he thought. In fact he had only taken two-thirds of it – it was an easy mistake to make in the dark on that broken ground. He came on the radio and said, "I've got the position unopposed, shall I press on?" . . . and then he ran into fire.

'2 Troop were held up, so I said "Right, we'll withdraw you fifty yards and call in some artillery," but no Arty. We could see a real ding-dong going on on Harriet, and the other 45 companies were engaged, so there wasn't enough artillery to go round so, right . . . mortars. I called for mortars. The mortars got off half-a-dozen rounds and on that boggy ground their baseplates and barrels sunk half-way into the ground. So, no mortars . . . think . . . Milans – right! . . . Called up Lt Steve Hughes with 40's Anti-Tank Troop. "Can you see where I am?" He was 2,000 yards away – and I also flashed a torch. They fired four or five rounds over our heads, wire guided, remember. They went off with a hell of a bang, and then 2 Troop went up the hill, like banshees out of hell . . . the front was very narrow, only 3–4 men wide, no room to deploy, so the weight was on the Corporals and Marines, not on me. 2 Troop cleared 3

Troop's objective and then their own – we had one man wounded – we killed seven of the enemy and the rest legged it. I went up the hill and found 2 Troop eating Argy rations and rooting around in their stores. When I looked back down that long, steep ridge, a massive objective over 1,000 yards long, I could hardly believe it. We stayed up there for the next 24 to 36 hours and watched the Scots Guards take Tumbledown – they took a hell of a long time about it.'

Col Whitehead: 'I can't believe that Ian got lost – but let me say that it takes someone of great experience, initiative and character to break radio silence at such a time. I was very worried and bloody glad to hear from him.

'Although I *knew* Ian was going in there was still no firing, because, as I realized later, over the four previous nights our fighting patrols had driven the enemy back from the first two positions we thought we would have to take – so time ticked on and when I could stand it no longer, at 03.50 hrs. I got onto Gerry Akhurst of our Commando Artillery and said, "Switch to Noisy . . ." and the two rifle companies to my front opened up, at which moment Ian's lead troop bumped the enemy on the other feature – and so all of 45 attacked together . . . a lot of tracer, plenty of flares. "Z" and "Y" poured it in and then got up and began to advance. When we got up to the feature, I found myself talking to Lt Clive Dytor, commanding 8 Troop. He took his troop round the back of the rocks and into the enemy position . . . he also won the Military Cross. I estimate that some 200 Argentines held the position. We found twenty bodies and the rest had legged it. We had four killed and ten wounded.

'I remember 45 as a band of brothers. We were the "can-do" Commando, whatever it was we had to do, we could hack it.

'What else? We went on to Sapper Hill,' says Ian

Gardiner. 'We had stretched ourselves but we could have gone on. In fact the longer we stayed out, the more we adapted and the easier it was. It was bloody cold that night though, – 5°C or thereabouts. I slept in a shellhole, cuddled up to my company clerk, or I got up and trudged around the Company – it was a real bugger of a night.'

While 3 Para and 45 were tackling Longdon and Two Sisters, 42 Commando were attacking the Brigade's final objective for that night, Mount Harriet, which was considered the most difficult of the three, not least because it was heavily protected by minefields. The CO of 42, Lt-Col Nick Vaux, had sent out several patrols to reconnoitre Mount Harriet, and they had finally found a relatively mine-free route on the southern side of the mountain. Lt-Col Vaux therefore decided to attack the Argentine positions from the flank and rear, sending his rifle companies on a four-mile approach march through the minefields, hoping their advance would not be detected. To achive this, they would need to swing south into 5 Brigade's area, and it was therefore agreed that their Start Line for the attack should be secured by the Welsh Guards. While 42 were marching south, artillery fire would provide a diversion by falling on the western slopes of Mount Harriet. When 42 arrived at their Start Line, they were less than amused to find the Welsh Guards Recce Platoon not deployed along the position, but sitting behind a fence, chatting and smoking. Hard words were said and then the attack went in.

2 and 3 Troops of 'K' Company, 42 Commando, led the attack up the south-eastern side of Harriet and were already among the Argentines before they were detected. Firing broke out everywhere and in all directions as 'K' Company went ahead clearing enemy trenches and mortar pits, pushing their way up the mountain to the first dip or saddle, working their way forward in small groups, using Milan anti-tank missiles against heavy

machine-gun posts. The forward troops of 'K' crossed the saddle and took the forward slopes of the far ridge before 'L' Company came up to carry on the assault up the eastern slope, where they met with considerable opposition from snipers and heavy machine-gun posts. One particularly persistent sniper was finally silenced by a direct hit from a Milan rocket, and after one last skirmish on the top of the feature, the Argentine resistance ended. 42 took Mount Harriet after an eight-hour battle, at a cost of only one man killed and twenty wounded. Twenty-five Argentine soldiers died in the assault on Harriet and 42 took over 300 prisoners.

Julian Thompson: '42's battle for Harriet was a real Commando battle; they infiltrated the Argentine positions and just rolled them up. 42 took more prisoners than they mustered in the assault companies, for the loss of one man killed and 20 wounded . . . a real crafty, cunning attack, with all the Commando elements – quite brilliant.'

3 Commando Brigade had now pushed a hole in the defences surrounding Stanley. The Marines and Paras were able to spend the following day removing Argentine casualties and consolidating their positions on the three features, because the follow-up attack, on the night of 12/13 June, had to be postponed as the Scots Guards and Gurkhas had insufficient time to recce their tasks. On the following night (13/14), the Scots Guards attacked Tumbledown Mountain and took it after a fierce fight with the Argentine 5th Marines, which lasted almost until dawn. This delayed the Gurkhas' assault on Mount William, but 2 Para, again part of 3 Commando Brigade, attacked Wireless Ridge with Naval gunfire and artillery support and took it for the loss of only one man killed and a handful wounded.

The time had now arrived for a general assault on Stanley, but after three nights under attack, the

Argentine forces were finally disintegrating, abandoning their positions and weapons, and running back towards the town. 2 Para were ordered to speed this up by taking the road into Stanley, while 45 Commando went forward to Sapper Hill. They arrived at the bottom only to find the Welsh Guards landing by helicopter on the top, having been ordered forward by 5 Brigade. 'Thank God it was daylight,' says Andrew Whitehead, 'or our two units might have fired on each other.'

Andrew Tubb: 'When we had taken Two Sisters, we went to Sapper Hill and caught a young Argy up there, a young lad, and we also caught Galtieri's Gallops. From Sapper Hill you could hear the Argy 155s firing in the streets of Stanley, then the shells came whistling in – we'd been out about three weeks then and were really getting settled into the environment. We had no trouble with our feet at all – and then they surrendered and it just stopped . . . a bit of a let-down, because the adrenalin stopped flowing and we missed it. I wasn't scared – only of not doing a good job, or the fear of letting your oppo down – not otherwise.'

The Argentine Commander in Stanley, General Menendez, had already received surrender proposals from the British Commander, and he accepted these at 20.59 on 14 June, by which time many of the Argentine soldiers had already laid down their arms.

Jeremy Moore: 'On the morning after the Scots Guards took Tumbledown, I went up onto Goat Ridge, between Harriet and Two Sisters, where I met the two Brigadiers to see what had happened, and decide what to do next. I told Julian to move his Brigade along the south of Stanley, but to stay out of the town. If we went in there was too great a risk of civilian casualties. We looked out to the south and saw some Argentines moving about one of their positions, and shelled them.

'I had hoped that when the Commando Brigades'

attacks all succeeded, that would convince them that they had to surrender, but no – so the Scots Guards went in and took Tumbledown. Still nothing – I went back to my TAC-HQ and thought about how we might get Menendez to call it off. I must say Rod Bell was invaluable; he had lived in South America, spoke the language, understood the mentality and he explained how we must handle them. We had been in communication with an Argentine Staff Officer in Stanley for some time. We established a short wave link quite early on, because there could be situations, even during the battle, when we needed to talk – about evacuating civilians, or wounded, so contact existed. Rod explained that these people regard themselves as honourable soldiers, and their honour is very important to them – no one will surrender until they feel they have done their best. Our job is to persuade them they can do no more and therefore, to save lives, surrender is the honourable course.

'So I was back at Fitzroy, kicking my heels against tufts of grass, thinking, "Why doesn't this man see he's beaten", when someone called out from the tent that white flags were appearing in Stanley, and then *Fearless* came on and said "They want to talk". I went outside again and jumped about like a two-year-old – and quickly called off an airstrike.

'I sent Michael Rose and Roddie Bell into Stanley to discuss terms. The Government wanted the phrase "unconditional surrender" in the document, but I saw no point in that. If we had won, we'd won, and that was an end of it – but the Government insisted, so I told Michael and Roddie to put it in, but added that if Menendez jibs, take it out – and he *did* jib, so I crossed it out. I didn't want the war starting up again over a phrase, and we didn't want to seem to be glorying in their defeat – that's why we kept the cameramen out of the signing – and that was that.'

Julian Thompson: 'I remember the finish; a cold grey

day with just a snowflake or two. Their 155s were still malleting our positions, firing DF tasks – I didn't see any of the white flags some people claimed to see, but when it was over, my main emotion was no more of these young men are going to die – and great relief about that. The young men were . . . remarkable. It did my morale good every time I saw them – you come to love them, with their cheerful dirty faces.'

Julian Thompson had already ordered his Brigade into Stanley, and the final advance began, led by 2 Para and the light tanks of the Blues and Royals, with 3 Para close behind and 45 yomping yet again for Sapper Hill, where they started to dig in and spent the next two days since Julian Thompson had no intention of letting his guard drop at the last moment. 42 Commando, which had been helicoptered forward to Tumbledown, came forward marching on Stanley, and were to be billeted in an old hangar on the western side of the town, which the Argentines had used as a dressing station. Several limbs and pools of blood lay on the frozen floor, and a dead Argentine soldier lying in a wheelbarrow was gently wheeled outside. In these rather grisly surroundings, the Commando settled down to rest and clean up. 45 Commando left Sapper Hill to the Welsh Guards and the two rifle companies of 40 Commando, and came on into the town, arriving just as 2 Para were marching off to a Church parade.

'Stanley was a mess,' recalls Andrew Tubb. 'Telephone wires down, drains overflowing, a lot of Argentines floating about. We went up to the Town Hall, and spent a few days organizing working parties of prisoners to get the place cleaned up before they were repatriated and we came home again.'

Coming home! From Brigade Commander to Recce Troop Marine, no-one in 3 Commando Brigade will ever forget their welcome.

Andrew Tubb again: 'We'd heard a bit about it, but we had no idea really. We came home on *Canberra* – they took the Paras off, and it was just Marines and the Army Commandos – we didn't do a lot on the voyage back, just turned to in the morning, did 12 laps of the promendade deck, that's three miles, and that was it for the day. On the morning of the day we docked, we had steak for breakfast and I went out onto the after-deck and I couldn't believe it – it was only 8am and there was this great flotilla of ships out there, all cheering – it was – it's difficult to describe – like a Carnival – we had a big banner hanging over the side – "*Lock up your daughters – the Bootnecks are back*". When we got ashore we had to go through Customs, only one bloke there, then into coaches. Someone said "Your parents are over there", and I was really surprised, because my dad hates crowds, but there they were. They found it overwhelming, and when we got to Arbroath my grandparents were there.'

Lance-Corporal Spiers and Cpl Gillingham have similar memories: 'I've never seen anything like it. The Brigadier, Julian Thompson, had his people in for drinks in his cabin – then, when we were coming up the Channel the night before, we could see the cars ashore, all flashing their lights. In the morning we had a steak breakfast. The band "Beat Retreat" on the deck, I remember . . . and scores of boats coming out to meet us . . . it was a misty morning. But it was really too much to take in – overwhelming. The coach trip back to Plymouth down the A303–38 was amazing. People were on all the bridges, waving, stopping the coaches to put crates of beer on board . . . it took our convoy an hour or more to get up Union Street to Stonehouse. All Plymouth was out there cheering.'

General Moore agrees: 'That drive back from Southampton to the West Country was memorable. Large hairy marines were reduced to tears as every village came out to cheer, and rightly so, the men deserved it.'

And so 3 Commando Brigade came home again, dispersed for six weeks leave, and then got back to business.

'Did I enjoy the Falklands?' asks L-Corp Andrew Tubb. 'Yes, I did. I don't want to talk about it much, because all people outside the Corps ask you is . . . did you kill anyone? Which makes it difficult. They simply don't understand that we were there to do a job. It was good to use everything I'd been taught, from basic training through the Sniper's Course, Recce Troop, all that, and put it into practice in my chosen profession. We were all volunteers, all Marines, and freeing the Falklands was secondary. They could give them to Argentina tomorrow and it wouldn't worry me. I've no regrets either way, because I did my job and I was in the Royal Marines.

The story of the Royal Marines Commandos goes on. 'There have been changes,' says Maj-Gen John Owen, 'and in a number of ways the Corps is more tightly knit, more professional than it ever was. Commando training has improved the Corps in many ways, in fitness, in better leadership and man-management at all levels, in the encouragement given to all ranks to use their initiative within the overall framework of the plan or their orders – I think that today the Corps is better at "soldiering" than ever. A number of the old problems have gone – there are more command opportunities for senior officers – not enough, but more than before, and the training and expertise of the more junior ranks, those corporals and sergeants on whom so much depends, is second to none. We still have some problems – the almost perpetual state of Defence Reviews, the dead hand of bureaucracy always stifles initiative and we need more money for amphibious equipment, especially ships – but all in all, the Corps is in good shape.'

This account has followed the Royal Marines

Commandos from the beaches of Dieppe to the wind-tugged moorland of the Falklands, over mountains and *jebel* and jungle-clad hills, through a thousand little fights and many thankless tasks, through great wars and bitter, long-forgotten campaigns . . . It should all add up to something, if only to point out how little has really changed among the men who serve in a fighting Corps. The Royal Marines remain much as they were forty years ago, cheerful, professional, loyal to each other and their Corps. May fortune smile upon them in the future and should their future ever again be in doubt, may our leaders recall what Napoleon said about them long ago: '*One could do much with ten thousand soldiers such as these.*'

Glossary of Service and Royal Marine Jargon

The Andrew	The Royal Navy
Bandwagon	The Volvo BV 202E oversnow vehicle. Not to be confused with its predecessor, the Snowtrac.
Banjo	(a) A sandwich
	(b) Broken or broken down (Banjoed).
Basha	Originally a temporary jungle shelter, now generally applied to any temporary shelter in the field.
Beating Retreat	Band ceremonial performed in conjunction with the Naval 'Sunset' ceremony to mark the end of the day.
Belay	To cease an action.
Bimble	To walk casually; to wander; i.e. 'thumb up bum, mind in neutral'.
Bite	To be drawn into an argument or to accept an untruth.
Bivvy	A bivouac – temporary field shelter, constructed with a waterproof poncho.
Blues	The ceremonial blue uniform of the Royal Marines.
Bootie	RM and RN abbreviation of the term used for a Royal Marine (see *Bootneck*).
Bootneck	A Royal Marine. Believed to be derived from the leather uniform stock worn during the Nelsonian era (USMC term 'leatherneck' may have the same derivation). However, the term only appeared to gain common usage post World War II, therefore this explanation is open to doubt.
Boss	Respectful but casual means of referring to the officer in command.
Bren	A light machine-gun (303/7.65 cal) or LMG.

Brothel creepers	Suede casual shoes, or desert boots, worn with denim uniform on board ship.
Buzz	A rumour, or a generic term used for a description of the situation.
Charlie-G	The 84 mm Carl Gustav anti-tank weapon.
Chopper	A helicopter.
Chippie	A carpenter.
Chit/chittie	A small piece of paper.
Clear lower deck	When personnel of a unit are called together for an address by the Commanding Officer; a 100 per cent turnout.
Corps-pissed	To be intoxicated with the Royal Marines.
CTC	Abbreviation for: Commando Training Centre Royal Marines – now at Lympstone, Devon.
Dhobi	To wash or launder.
Dig-out (blind)	To make an all-out effort.
Dig-out/dip	To come off worse in any situation.
Ditch	To throw away or discard.
Dog watch	Two short watch periods that equalize the watch roster. 'Been in a dog watch' – one who has little experience.
DRORM	Abbreviation for: Drafting and Records Office Royal Marines – part of *HMS Centurion* at Gosport.
Fall over backwards	To go to great lengths over something.
Flakers	Exhausted.
Four Five	45 Commando RM; also Four Two, Four Three etc., but always Forty for 40 Commando.
Galley	The kitchen and/or dining hall.
Gemini	A small inflatable rubber raiding craft powered by an outboard motor.
Gen	Genuine, the truth.
Globe and Buster	The Corps Crest or Badge (the Globe and Laurel) or the Royal Marines magazine.
Green	Naive.
Grey Funnel Line	The Royal Navy.
Guz	Plymouth (believed to originate from the World War I radio identification letters for the Port – GUZ).

Hand	A member of an organization/crew. Commonly used to refer to an individual of good repute.
Heads	The lavatories on board ship.
Horse Box	The Sergeants' Mess.
Jack	A member of the Royal Navy.
Jack-up	To arrange or organize something.
Jenny	A member of the Womens Royal Naval Service (WRNS).
Jimpy	Phonetic abbreviation of: General Purpose Machine-Gun.
Jolly	An easy job, or organized recreation.
Jollies	Original nickname for a citizen soldier of the Trained Bands of London in 1664, from whose ranks Marines were first formed. Later became RN slang for a marine, hence Kipling's 'HM Jollies'.
Kit muster	A check, in which an individual's complete equipment is laid out to ensure all is accounted for. The term is also sometimes used to describe the act of vomiting.
Lash-up	To treat
Lovats	The No 2 Service Dress uniform of the Royal Marines; lovat green in colour.
LCM	Abbreviation for: Landing Craft Mechanised (now: Landing Craft Utility). Also LCA (Landing Craft Assault); LCF (Landing Craft Flac); LCG (Landing Craft Gun); LST (Landing Ship Tank) etc.
Make and mend	A period allocated to the maintenance of an individual's equipment, or personal administration; time off.
Mankey	Filthy.
Matelot	A sailor.
MOA	Abbreviation of: Marine Officer's Attendant – the equivalent of a batman.
Muscle bo'sun	One who prides himself on the strength of his body.
Neaters	Undiluted spirits.
NP8901	The Royal Marines Garrison on the Falkland Islands.

Nutty	Confectionery.
OD	An abbreviation indicating 'Other Denomination' as a person's religious conviction. Commonly used as a derogatory term for someone who should know better.
'O' Group	A meeting whereby orders for an operation are given to subordinate commanders, or subordinates.
Oolu (also Ulu)	Originally the term applied to jungle. Now sometimes given to any area of rough country or heavy vegetation.
Oppo	A close friend. The 'opposite number' of a two-man team; a system used to ensure maximum effectiveness in military activities.
Picturise	To be put in the picture; to receive an explanation.
Pipe	To broadcast a message, usually via the public address system on board ship or barracks.
Piso	Careful with money.
Pompey	Portsmouth.
Pongo	A soldier; derived from the common Naval belief that soldiers seldom wash.
Pussers	Apertaining to the Service; stores and equipment issued from Service sources, or the source of such issues. Anything done unimaginatively or 'by the book' is done in a 'pussers' manner.
Rabbits	Gifts or souvenirs obtained by going on a 'rabbit run'.
Raider	Abbreviation of: Rigid Raiding Craft. A small glass-fibre craft powered by outboard motor.
Recommend	Formalized approval or praise, as in 'take a recommend'.
Rigid-inflatable	A small raiding craft with a combination rigid and inflatable construction.
RMR	Royal Marines Reserve (formerly RMFVR)

Rock ape	A member of the Mountain Leader branch. Also used to describe a member of the RAF Regiment.
Run ashore	To leave ship or barracks for recreation or relaxation. Even in the desert a visit to the local oasis would be a 'Run ashore'.
Sad-on	To be unhappy. (Got a sad-on).
SB	Abbreviation of: Special Boat Squadron. One who has joined the SBS is said have gone SB.
Scran	Food.
Scran bag	A bag on a mess deck in which spare or damaged clothing and rags are collected. When one is untidily dressed one is said to 'look like a scran bag'.
Sea Daddy	An experienced marine or sailor who looks after a recruit to show him the ropes.
Secure	To finish and tidy away after a job or watch.
Sin Bo'sun	A Naval Padre.
Sippers	A liquid measure, a sip offered from one's own drink.
Snowtrac	The predecessor to the Bandwagon.
Sods opera	A show produced by a ship's company or unit to entertain themselves.
Stag	Sentry duty.
Stand easy	An official break in the work schedule; equates with a tea/coffee/NAAFI break.
Sweating neaters	To be worried.
Teenies	Abbreviation of TWA (Teeny Weeny Airways) – the small utility helicopters flown by the Royal Marines Air Squadron.
The Corps	RM and RN generic terms for the Royal Marines: also 'The Mob'.
Three Badger	A marine or sailor of low rank but great experience. Derived from the good conduct badges (chevrons) worn to denote years of service; three badges being the maximum.
TRF	Abbreviation for: Training and Reserve Forces Royal Marines.

Troop bible	A book containing all the relevant details of the individuals in a Troop, or any sub-unit.
VP	Abbreviation of the initials for: Landing Craft (Vehicle) and (Personnel).
Wallah	The operator of a small shop or stand, usually un-official (e.g. 'Goffer Wallah').
Winger/wings	A comrade or close friend (see also 'oppo').
Work your ticket	To arrange to leave the Service.
Yaffle	To eat hurriedly.
Yomp	To force march with a heavy load.
Zap	To shoot or be shot.

Bibliography

The Royal Marines by Major General J.L.Moulton, CB, DSO, OBE, RM (Royal Marines Museum 1981)

The Unquiet Peace by Maurice Tugwell (Allan Wingate 1957)

The Green Beret (The Story of The Commandos) by Hilary St George Saunders (Michael Joseph 1949)

Assault from the Sea by Rear-Admiral L.E.H.Maund CBE (Methuen 1949)

Dieppe – The Dawn of Decision by Jacques Mordal (Souvenir Press 1962)

48 (Royal Marine) Commando 1944-46 (Privately Published 1946)

The War in Korea by Major R.C.W. Thomas OBE (Gale & Polden 1954)

The Eighty Five Days (Walcheren) by R.W. Thompson (Hutchinson 1957)

The Battle Coast (D-Day) by Brown & Hunter (Spur Books 1973)

The Battle for Antwerp by Major-General J.L.Moulton, CB, DSO, OBE, RM (Ian Allan 1978)

Storm from the Sea by Peter Young (William Kimber 1958)

Dawn of D-Day by David Howarth (Collins 1950)

The Battle for the Falklands by Max Hastings and Simon Jenkins (Michael Joseph 1983)

Last Post: Aden 1964-67 by J.Paget (Faber & Faber 1969)

Green Beret, Red Star: The Royal Marine Commandos in Malaya by Anthony Crockett: (Eyre and Spottiswoode 1954)

D-Day by Warren Tute, John Costello (Pan Books 1974)

No Picnic: 3 Commando Brigade in the Falkland War by Julian Thompson (Fontana 1985)

The Marines were There by Bruce Lockhart (Putnam 1950)

Operation Corporate: The Story of the Falklands War by Martin Middlebrook (Viking 1985)

Haste to the Battle (48 Commando) by Major-General J.L.Moulton CB, DSO, OBE, RM (Cassell 1963)

The Royal Marines 1919-1980 by James Ladd (Jane's 1980)

War in the Falklands by Sunday Express Magazine Team (Weidenfeld & Nicholson 1982)

The Story of 46 (Royal Marine) Commando by Captain P.K.W.Johnson RM (Gale & Polden 1946)

Four-Five: The Story of 45 Commando, Royal Marines by David Young (Leo Cooper 1972)

Overlord: D-Day and Normandy 1944 by Max Hastings (Michael Joseph 1984)

Raiders of the Arakan by C.E. Lucas Phillips (Heinemann 1971)

Cassino: Portrait of a Battle by Fred Najdalany (Longmans 1957)

Prelude to the Monsoon by C.F. Jacobs (Purnell (SA) 1966)

Norway. The Commandos: Dieppe by Christopher Buckley (HMSO 1957)

A Short History of The Royal Marines by Col G.W.M. Grover OBE, RM (Gale & Polden 1959)

Index